No. 16. Lands ceded to the
No. 17. Western half of Creek domain ceded to the United States by
No. 18. Lands ceded to Seminoles by United States treaty of 1866, and those purchased by act of 1882.
No. 19. Lands occupied by the Sac and Fox Indians.
No. 20. Lands occupied by Citizen band of Pottawatomies and Absentee Shawnees.
No. 21. Lands occupied by the Kickapoos.
No. 22. Lands occupied by the Iowa Indians.
No. 23. That part of Creek cession lying within Cheyenne and Arapahoe Reservation, created by Executive Order of August 10, 1869.
No. 23½. Creek ceded lands covered by the treaty of 1867, with the Cheyennes and Arapahoes.
No. 24. Oklahoma.
No. 25. Lands originally ceded to the Choctaws.
No. 26. The Chickasaw District.
No. 27. Choctaw and Chickasaw leased district, ceded by treaty of 1866.
No. 28. Lands occupied by Kiowa, Comanche, and Apache Indians.
No. 29. That part of Choctaw and Chickasaw cession embraced in Cheyenne and Arapahoe reservation. Executive Order of August 10, 1869.
No. 30. Lands occupied by Wichita, etc., Indians. Unratified agreement of 1872.
No. 31. Part of Choctaw and Chickasaw cession of 1866, claimed by the State of Texas.
OSAGES
PAWNEES
CHEROKEES
Treaty Feb. 14. 1833.
Vol. 7, p. 414
Treaty Dec. 29, 1835. Vol. 7, p. 478.
Treaty July 19. 1866.
Vol. 14, p. 799.
CREEK COUNTRY
Treaty Feb. 14. 1833. Vol. 7, p. 417.
Treaty June. 14. 1866. Vol. 14, p. 285
15.
CHOCTAW NATION
Treaty June 22. 1855.
Vol. 11, p. 611.
25.
ARKANSAS
MISSOURI
TEXAS
RED RIVER
ARKANSAS RIVER
COFFEYVILLE
TULSA
MUSKOGEE
TAHLEQUAH
VAN BUREN
FT. SMITH
DENISON
Ft. Gibson Mil. Res.
Bartlesville
Osage Agency
Coody's Bluff
Vinita
Chelsea
Maysville
Evansville
Webbers Falls
Eufaula
McAlister
Krebs
Savannah
Limestone Gap
Stringtown
Atoka
Boggy Depot
Caddo
Doaksville
Ft. Towson
Wheelock
Goodland
Ultima Thule
Rocky Comfort
The Seven Devils
Sans Bois Mts.
Poteau Mt.
Rich Mt.
Kulli-Inla
Greenwich
Washington
REFERENCES
Townships Subdivided
Capitals of Nations
Towns, Villages
Military Reservations
Boundary of Indian Reservations
Roads and Trails
Railroads constructed
" proposed

Praise for *The Oklahomans: The Story of Oklahoma and Its People, Ancient through Statehood*

John J. Dwyer's book *The Oklahomans: Ancient through Statehood* is a splendid first volume of a proposed two volume set of Oklahoma from earliest exploration to statehood and the Haskell Administration. It is as fine a treatment of the subject and period as we are likely to witness in our lifetime because of the precise detail presented in a sinewy prose which is augmented by beautiful paintings, illustrations, maps, and photographs.

The work is almost as much an encyclopedia as a work of history because it recounts the contributions of the usual principal characters as well as colorful secondary figures who are often overlooked or minimized. It also features the most comprehensive coverage of the Indians of any Oklahoma history book I have ever read.

A significant achievement of the book is that the author, without being burdensome, has included the roles that ministers, institutions, and precepts of the Christian religion have played in the development of the area and its people.

—**James Caster**, Professor Emeritus of Political Science
University of Central Oklahoma

This attractively designed history of the Sooner state is sure to provide even the most serious scholar information not previously known. Drawing on primary and secondary sources, Dwyer demonstrates his love for the people and the land throughout as he tells the state's story from earliest inhabitants down to the present. With classic artwork he illustrates the key events which have shaped the place and culture loved by so many. For solid content and pure enjoyment of reading on Oklahoma, I could not recommend it more highly.

—**Loren Gresham**, President
Southern Nazarene University

I am most impressed by the format, color, ample photographs, documents, art, and maps that illustrate Volume One of *The Oklahomans*. This is engaging reading and new imagery I've not seen before. I especially like the timelines at the beginning of each chapter. Very well done. I am enthralled with what Dwyer has accomplished.

—**William D. Welge**, Director
Office of American Indian Culture and Preservation
Oklahoma Historical Society

And I thought Texas had cornered the market on rowdy, hard-ridin' history! By John Dwyer's attestation, our neighbors in Oklahoma hold their own nicely, rousingly, sometimes a little fiercely. This is a wonderful read—clearly written, copiously illustrated, objective in research and presentation—that should do the Sooner state proud for some time to come. We've got triumphs and tragedies here of a very Southwestern— yes, a very American—kind: for everyday enjoyment and, a Texan has to add, for honest admiration.

—**William Murchison**, nationally syndicated columnist and former senior editor
Dallas Morning News

Read a history book for fun? Not for most people. *The Oklahomans* will inform, entertain, and provide topics of conversation for years to come. Reaching deep into the rough and rugged history of the great state of Oklahoma, John J. Dwyer makes it clear what has produced a people that are so resilient and independent. Okies can read this book with pride as we discover our heritage, others will be amazed that this simple state on the southern plains has such a colorful and rich history.

—**Mark Braisher**, Executive Vice President and Academic Dean
Randall University

The reader will be pleased to find early in his read and throughout the book an incredible trove of maps and drawings and visuals of all kinds, vivid and colorful, to explain what the author is saying. John Dwyer has written a wonderful story. It is the story of the crash and conflict of peoples, ideas, ambitions, and technologies.

—**Frank Keating**, former Governor of Oklahoma
from the Foreword

Also by John J. Dwyer

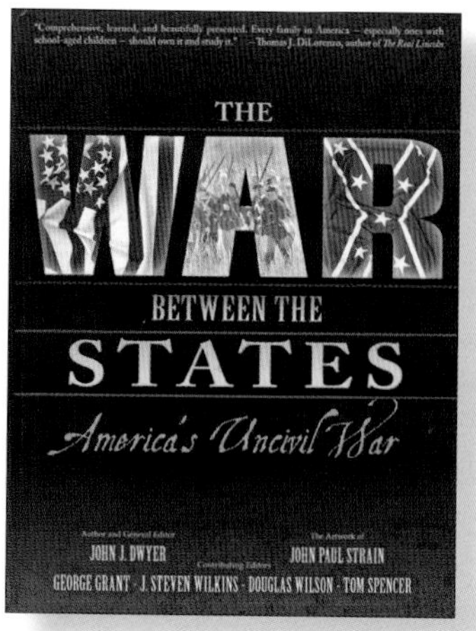

"Every family in America—especially ones with school-aged children—should own it and study it."

—Thomas J. DiLorenzo, professor of economics, Loyola College

"The best textbook for the high school, preparatory academy, or junior college I've ever read."

—Roger D. McGrath, professor of history, UCLA

"A magisterial account of a tragic story that most Americans have yet to confront."

—Donald W. Livingstone, professor of philosophy, Emory University

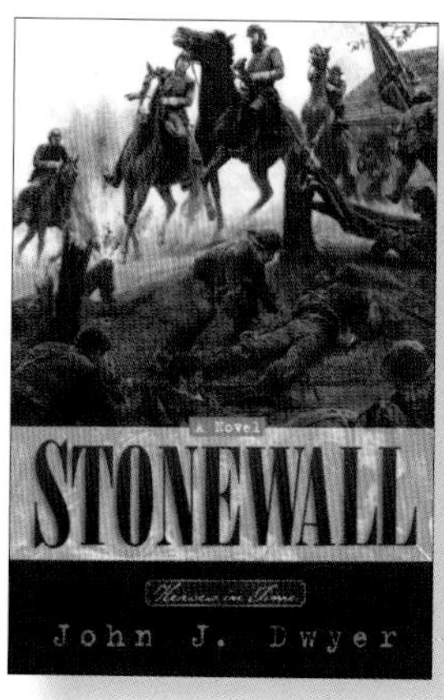

"John J. Dwyer makes one of the great heroes of American history accessible to modern readers."

—*The Oklahoman*

"I still savor with pleasure reading *Lee.* So much good and truth so well told."

—Clyde Wilson, professor of history, University of South Carolina

"A must-read for Christian families."

—*Norman Transcript*

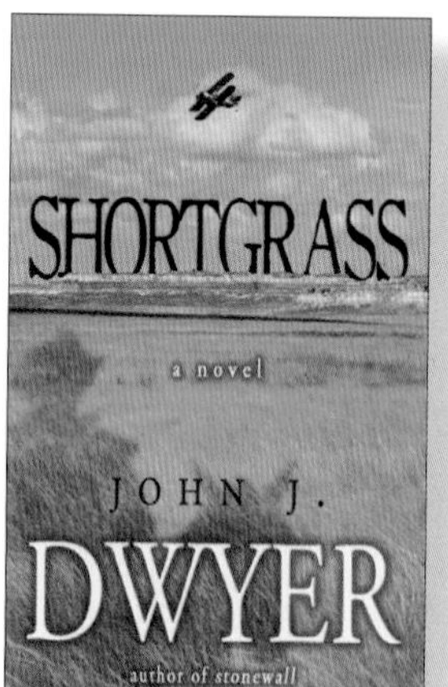

Coming in April 2017, the first of John's two-novel set depicting the epic saga of a Dust Bowl-era Mennonite Oklahoma farm boy whose beliefs are sorely challenged as he rises to college football and World War II aviation glory.

www.johnjdwyer.com

THE OKLAHOMANS

THE OKLAHOMANS

The Story of Oklahoma and Its People

Volume One: Ancient–Statehood

Author and General Editor

JOHN J. DWYER

Foreword

FRANK KEATING

Consulting Editor

STEVE BYAS

The Artwork of

Wayne Cooper, John Paul Strain, G. N. Taylor, Andy Thomas, Charles Banks Wilson, Mike Wimmer, and others

RED RIVER

Norman, Oklahoma

Published in the United States of America
by Red River Press in association with the Burbridge Foundation

For information about our other books and products or for permission to use material from this text, please contact us:
e-mail: redriverdwyer@gmail.com
Mail: P.O. Box 721664, Norman, Oklahoma 73070
Phone: (405) 496-6460
Website: www.johnjdwyer.com

Printed in China

Page design and composition: Scott Suckling for MetroVoice Publishing Service
www.metrovoice.org

Cover design: Casey Cowan for Oghma Creative Media
https://oghmacreative.com

Front cover image by G. N. Taylor:
A Run for All Reasons
www.gntayloroklaart.com

Back cover image by G. N. Taylor:
Choctaw Chief George Hudson
www.gntayloroklaart.com

Back cover image by Don Stivers:
The Promise
www.framery.com

Front end page image:
1889 Map of Indian Territory. Courtesy Library of Congress.

Back end page image and page 301:
Map of the State of Oklahoma. The Kenyon Company, Des Moines, Iowa. 1907. Courtesy Edmon Low Library, Oklahoma State University. Oklahoma Digital Maps Collection. (http://www.library.okstate.edu/collections/digital-collections/oklahoma-digital-maps-collection/)

ISBN: 978-0-9853470-2-4 (Hardcover)
978-0-9853470-3-1 (ebook)
978-0-9853470-4-8 (Audible)

This volume is dedicated to Garman O. Kimmell—beloved husband, father, grandfather, great-grandfather, engineer, inventor, leader, founder of Kimray, Inc., Oklahoman, and above all, a Christian man.

Contents

The cloud icons below indicate sidebar features which begin in this book on the indicated pages, then "jump" to our new web-based cloud repository that you will be able to access through an electronic *Oklahomans* mobile app. This pioneering and ongoing process will allow us to add more and more post-publication material for you as we produce it in the months and years ahead.

4 The Trail of Tears (1830s) 59

5 The Cross of Christ (1840–1850s) 89

About the Contributors

Author and General Editor

John J. Dwyer is an adjunct professor of history and ethics at Southern Nazarene University. He is the former History Chair at Coram Deo Academy, near Dallas, Texas. He is the author of the *The War Between the States: America's Uncivil War*, the historical novels *Stonewall* and *Robert E. Lee* and the upcoming *Shortgrass* and *Mustang*, and the novel *When Bluebonnets Come*. He is the former editor and publisher of the *Dallas/Fort Worth Heritage* newspaper. Dwyer's grandfather Jay J. Dwyer arrived in Oklahoma at age twenty-one, two years after statehood in 1909, and twice served as president of the Oklahoma City Metropolitan Association of Realtors, after his own father immigrated to America by himself from Ireland at age seventeen. Dwyers have lived in Oklahoma in the more than one century since.

Consulting Editor

Steve Byas is a professor of history at Randall University in Moore, Oklahoma, editor of the *Oklahoma Constitution* newspaper, and a regular contributor to *New American* magazine. He has authored a high school government textbook, as well as *History's Greatest Libels*, and two mystery novels. His work has appeared in the *Tennessee Historical Quarterly.* Byas' great grandfather, Jonah Byas, homesteaded near Tecumseh in 1894, thirteen years before Oklahoma statehood.

Maps

Foreword

Governor Frank Keating

The story of Oklahoma is a centuries old story of mankind's extraordinary capacity to tame the wild, create life out of conflict and agony, and to take full advantage of nature and God's goodness. A land blessed with a varied landscape, navigable rivers, prairies and plains of different capacities for farming and grazing and ranching. A vastness filled with deer and antelope and buffalo and a staggering variety of wildlife of many kinds. Before man first touched the place, it offered plants and shrubs and trees of many types to entice wildlife and human life to pause and make this wet and warm and dry and cool spot in America's middle a place to call home.

John J. Dwyer assembles all of this for a centuries old look back at how it happened. He tells the story of the arrival of the first native peoples. Oklahoma is, after all, the Choctaw word for "Red People." He writes of the arrival of the Europeans and the clash of empire between the explorers of the French and the Spanish.

The United States between 1800 and 1820 finds the creation of the trading families following the Louisiana Purchase and the absorption of our land into the growing American continent. Years before, Three Forks became the first trading post (1795–96).

The Chouteaus made trade the first part of a new economy in the early nineteenth century. That family and others that followed brought countless men of toughness and skill to their new prairie home.

The story of the early explorers, particularly Stephen Harrison Long, tells of the exploits of an incredible and courageous man who discovered the headwaters of the Arkansas and Red Rivers. The early Oklahoman, Nathaniel Pryor, diplomat, soldier, trader, merchant, explorer, Indian agent, is an added example of the grit and vision needed to survive in a wild and hostile place.

The reader will be pleased to find early in his read and throughout the book an incredible trove of maps and drawings and visuals of all kinds, vivid and colorful, to explain what the author is saying. The writing is complemented by these myriad historical sources and aids.

A searing part of Dwyer's tale is the story of Indian removal. The "Trail of Tears and Death," as immortalized by a Choctaw chief, witnessed for that tribe alone some twenty-five hundred deaths as they traveled from their ancient homes to their new home in Indian Territory. "It was a journey calculated to embitter the human heart." The Cherokees alone reportedly lost twenty per cent of their tribal family. That tribe's chronicler wrote: "It was the place where we cried." The Seminoles, Creeks, and Chickasaws all experienced disruption and sadness on their journeys west.

The 1840s and 1850s witnessed the creation of schools across tribal lands as well as the invasion of the railroads. The insatiable appetite for land, and the incessant pressure of white migration, even into a land promised solely to the native peoples, is another piece of the story. The arrival of Christian missionaries. The growth and health of the Indian republics. The swirling tales of the mid-century cowboys, Indians, outlaws, and traders are all essentials to understand the emerging Oklahoma.

The Civil War (1861–1865) and Reconstruction (1865–1870) and the tribes roles throughout are told in detail. Tribal support for the Confederacy sprung from the Union's termination of tribal annuity payments, the North's hint that tribal lands should be cleared for white settlement, Indian ownership of slaves, and early Confederate victories. But it would prove to be a bad bargain. A fifth of the Five Civilized Tribes died in the conflict. The railroads, cattle drives, further white migration, and resulting conflict, all suggested that it was surely better to be on the side of the blue than on the side of the grey. Those tribes that were Union supporters, however, were eventually absorbed into the amalgam that would be a white dominated land. It is interesting to note, however, that the last Confederate general to surrender and the only Native general on either side was Stand Watie. He is given an appropriate nod in the text.

Dwyer describes the late nineteenth century as a "New Invasion." Indian Territory contained some 100,000 people, mostly Natives, residing on 70,000 square miles. Shortly, that land became the scene of an "armed migration" of whites. The Civil War emptied out many places, both North and South. Many came to the promised land of the fledgling pre-state place of Oklahoma. They came as cattlemen, miners, farmers, hustlers, thieves, and honest folk in desperate search for a new life and new opportunity.

Congress passed the Dawes Act, which became the beginning of the end of Indian Territory and exclusive Indian ownership of land. David Payne and the Boomers appeared on the scene. The Run of 1889 opened up a chunk of Oklahoma Territory to settlement. It was a time of larger than life personalities: the Boomer Pawnee Bill and the fiddler, express mail carrier, and future symbol of OSU athletic excellence, Frank "Pistol Pete" Eaton.

And more land runs: Sac and Fox 1891, Cheyenne and Arapaho 1892, Cherokee Outlet 1893, Kickapoo 1895. The migration became a flood. In the decade that followed, the population of pre-statehood Oklahoma exploded. Oklahoma and Indian Territories together contained 1.6 million people.

The breakup of Indian ownership and control gave opportunity to the newly emancipated black slaves. In 1910, African Americans owned 1.5 million acres of land. There were twenty-seven all-black towns. But it would not last.

When statehood came in 1907, political leadership was in the hands of anti-out of state corporatist progressives, union leaders, miners, working men of all stripes. They were largely white and largely Democrats. The constitutional convention drafted "the longest constitution yet written by human hand," at fifty thousand words. The drafters included the initiative, referendum, restraints on railroads and large out-of-state corporations, schools for all, and an eight hour work day for miners. They aimed to create a new state and also to create "a new kind of state." But not for blacks. They paused a bit so that Republican President Theodore Roosevelt would not block statehood, but when they were in the Union, segregation and Jim Crow would become the law of the land. Oklahoma Senate Bill One enshrined Jim Crow into law and was the first bill passed by the Democrat legislature. It would be generations before things changed.

John Dwyer has written a wonderful story. It is the story of the crash and conflict of peoples, ideas, ambitions, and technologies (oil would become the state's dominant export). Few places personify the symbol of an egalitarian, no classes society better than Oklahoma.

It is little wonder that, unlike other places, it is not uncommon for those who have lived here to believably say, "I really do love Oklahoma."

—**Frank Keating**
Governor of Oklahoma
1995–2003

Introduction

Over a decade ago, Oklahoma Historical Society Executive Director Bob Blackburn, having previously read my historical works, encouraged me to write a new, comprehensive history of Oklahoma. He hoped for a work of quality descriptive narrative that featured a straightforward sequential structure and chronicled the remarkably diverse composition of the state's people and history. In addition, he hoped to see proper attention devoted to Oklahoma's accomplishments in the business and entrepreneurial realm, as well as the state's momentous recent history.

He also cited the importance of not just including but exploring "hard-hitting parts" such as the Trails of Tears, the War Between the States in Indian Territory, the Tulsa Race Riots, the Dust Bowl and "Okie" migration, and the 1980s oil boom and bust. He urged me to write about these and other such events in such a way that would both encourage the process of recovery and learning, and demonstrate the resilience of human history in general and Oklahoma history in particular.

Bob and I were both keenly aware of the widespread lack of knowledge or even interest in our state's history by its people. Beyond elementary school, only one brief semester of Oklahoma History was required for school children—and even that one was temporarily eliminated! Yet we both believed that the story of *The Oklahomans* was one of such epic sweep, drama, tragedy, and valor that if presented properly, it could and should grip the imagination of our people and perhaps those beyond the Sooner State.

In undertaking this daunting task, I have attempted to craft a flowing narrative rich in facts and surprises, deep in researched perspective and analysis, aglow with an incomparable gallery of illustrations, and filled with memorable, often complex drama that is not always easily condensed or explained. For instance, can John Ross and Stand Watie—larger-than-life Cherokees who held different visions for their tribe's destiny and clashed many times in many ways—both be accounted as great men who loved that tribe and mightily contributed to the building of Oklahoma? I would answer yes!

And can we remember indomitable Oklahoma founding fathers such as Charles Colcord and William "Alfalfa Bill" Murray—as well as the tiny, lionhearted Irish-American spitfire Kate Barnard with whom they bitterly contested—with gratitude, even awe, for the contributions they all made, though they often opposed one another? Yes!

This volume and the next one aim to weave throughout the narrative the history, deeds, and varied opinions of minority groups such as African-Americans and Native Americans in the integrated way they should be, not just as add-ons or sidebars. Also, the large and vigorous throng of white Texans who settled so much of Oklahoma and provided so much of its early leadership and lasting character. Because this is a general work, I have not interrupted the flow with footnotes. A significant, if not exhaustive bibliography, broken out by chapters, appears following the narrative.

Underlying all is a Christian worldview once common to such histories. Yet in *The Oklahomans* it is both surpassingly critical of the failures of that faith and its adherents, and more cognizant of and hopeful for their singular accomplishments and deeds. This work aspires to draw from a framework of "moral philosophy," to use a somewhat archaic term, without which I dare suggest that a consistent understanding of history and its lessons is impossible.

The Oklahomans aims to enhance the interest and learning experience with a multi-media approach presented in sequential decade or semi-decade chapter packages wherein you will always know where you are on the timeline. I spent over a year just compiling Volume 1's aforementioned gallery of illustrations, including dozens of the greatest works of art ever produced about Oklahoma and its people, the most compelling photographs, and an armada of maps, posters, and other images.

As with my historical narrative of the American Civil War, *The War Between the States: America's Uncivil War*, scores of biographical features spice up and enrich the narrative. This time, in order to deliver more information to you about people, events, and themes that grab your interest, the beginning of these sidebars appear in this volume. Then the bulk of their content "jumps" to our web-based cloud repository, which you will be able to access through our new electronic *Oklahomans* mobile app.

This particular ongoing project will involve an enormous amount of additional material that is nowhere near complete. It will eventually equal hundreds of additional pages of reading. We will also provide you with a growing collection of complementary web-based audio and video presentations.

In the decade I have labored on *The Oklahomans*, traveling the state to conduct scores of interviews and consult primary and secondary source documents of countless sorts, I have learned more about Oklahoma, its people, and its history than I would have dreamed possible. For one thing, I learned that an Oklahoma history work aiming to be interesting, accurate, and thoughtful is a difficult if not impossible task to accomplish in one volume, at least for this author. Thus, this book begins with the ancient history of present-day Oklahoma and concludes just after statehood. Volume 2, already well underway, will pick up from there, around 1910, and chronicle the state's history up to the present.

The title, *The Oklahomans: The Story of Oklahoma and Its People,* was not arrived at casually. The history does center around a particular geographic area. It is also true that the land and its singular complex of elements itself rises up as a character in the immense drama unfolding on the pages that follow. Yet the *story* is about the people who came to that land, every one of them descendants of ancestors from other places, a diverse people, simple in some ways and complex in others, sometimes at odds with one another and many times in many ways throughout history unshakably united as a block of granite.

Authoring any significant work of history is a humbling experience for a self-examining scribe. You realize that most of the true heroes will not appear in your books because you will never even know they lived. They rarely gain fame because they won't compromise themselves or deprive those who depend on them in order to attain it. Yet conversely, inscrutably, and inexorably, they are the sort of people upon whom communities, nations, and the kingdom of God are quietly built and sustained. Thus, I dare to present *The Oklahomans* to you, regretfully cognizant that though I was unable to learn about most of the folks by whom we could have benefited best, I've shared with you what I have learned about those I could find.

Writing history is also humbling because one realizes after doing enough of it that the work he or she presents to you and hopes that you will read, learn from, and be inspired by—especially a work of this enormity and complexity—contains unintentional errors. Despite thousands of hours of work, multiple sets of scrutinizing eyes, and every possible human exertion to ferret them out, as well as extreme effort not to repeat mistakes found in previous works on or even original documents from Oklahoma history, some will remain for you to (hopefully) catch. Fortunately, we now have the technology to acknowledge and/or correct them more swiftly and comprehensively than in the past.

I close this introduction with words written at the outset of this project a decade ago:

> *The Oklahomans* will present the history of Oklahoma and its people as they should be presented—as a rough and challenging chunk of Americana, where a determined and tenacious people of diverse backgrounds and cultures struggles against setbacks and disappointments, suffering and loss and heartbreak, in order to establish a special place for themselves and their children.

This book, and the volume to follow, will demonstrate how much Oklahoma is a land of hope and the second chance—sometimes the last chance—a land of sorrow and laughter, folly and bravery, violence and kindness, scheming and honor. It will also explore how the state has, late and stealthily with the passage of time, become a singular *place*, a place beyond a location on a map, *sui generis*. How it is, in the final reckoning, a heroic land and people—black and white, red and yellow and brown, rich and poor, Northerner and Southerner, liberal and conservative—who have fought against all the odds and who stand unique in themselves, even as they exemplify all that it is to be American, in the best and sometimes worst sense of that word.

May *The Oklahomans* be not only the story of that people, but a challenge and a charge to us to become what we might yet be, in the same way that Scott wrote both of and to the Scots, and Yeats the Irish.

—John J. Dwyer
Norman

Acknowledgments

Properly acknowledging all those who have helped one in a gargantuan ten-year project is a daunting but important task.

Consulting Editor Steve Byas, my friend since our adventurous days in "Ms. O's" Duncan High School journalism classes, brought the vast knowledge that comes from teaching Oklahoma History classes for thirty-five years, as well as his journalist's acumen to the manuscript. Fran Lowe, an accomplished author in her own right, provided her typically brutal (for me the author) and masterful (for you the reader) proofreading and copy editing job on *The Oklahomans.*

Scott Suckling and his MetroVoice Publishing Services (www.metrovoice.org) have now applied his brilliant design and production talents to the newspaper that my wife Grace and I published for nearly a decade and to three of my books. It should be obvious as you traverse this one why Scott must now sandwich us in between jobs for the largest educational publishers in America.

Bill Welge, longtime Oklahoma Historical Society (OHS) archivist, research director, and director of the American Indian Culture & Preservation Office, provided guidance on many facets of Oklahoma history, not least the OHS's magnificent twelve million-plus image archives. He also granted us permission to use many of those images, including their treasure trove of Kiowa ledger art, never before seen in a book. Consummate OHS researcher and archivist Jon May, meanwhile, spent many hours locating hundreds of those images, which reach back to the earliest days of American photography.

Delilah Joiner, Heather Clemmer, Cathy Hutchings-Wedel, Bob and Sue Anne Lively, and Southern Nazarene University have allowed me the privilege to teach history and ethics classes at that school for the past decade, design an original Oklahoma History course, and learn with and from a vast and precious legion of learners. Former Oklahoma City Community College President Paul Secrist provided me the golden connection to SNU.

Two-term Oklahoma Governor Frank Keating, who didn't know me from the man in the moon, took time from his busy schedule to read this entire book, then write its compelling Foreword, with no remuneration nor benefit to himself. He has subsequently encouraged and helped me in multiple ways.

How exciting that most of the greatest Oklahoma historical art has been produced in the past generation, much of it in the past few years! The unparalleled company of contemporary artists whose work beautifies this book, integrates with and complements the narrative, and helps tell the story itself have in most cases not asked for one penny for the right to share the beauty of their creative genius with you. These artists include, in alphabetical order: Katherine Roche Buchanan, Wayne Cooper, Harold Holden, Wilson Hurley, Mike Larsen, Christopher Nick, Dennis Parker, Linda Tuma Robertson, Gordon Snidow, Max Standley, Don Stivers, John Paul Strain, G. N. (Neal) Taylor, Sonya Terpenning, Andy Thomas, Timothy Tyler, Jackson Walker, Charles Banks Wilson, Mike

Wimmer, and Xiang Zhang. Many of their paintings adorn the walls of our State Capitol, where the final night of my Southern Nazarene Oklahoma History class always convenes. Please run, don't walk to that great old building to see them if you have not been there lately.

In addition to the artists themselves, Amber Sharples, Clint Stone, Scott Cowan, and the Oklahoma Arts Council played crucial roles in making possible the appearance in this book of the many beautiful paintings of Oklahoma history from the Oklahoma State Capitol Art Collections that the Arts Council manages.

Blake Wade, who served as executive director of the Oklahoma Centennial Commission, endorsed this work and embraced it as an official Centennial Commission non-profit project, which aided our effort in many ways. Bruce Fisher of the OHS granted me many hours of valuable interviews on Oklahoma history in general and the state's African-American history in particular. Doug Miller, longtime Oklahoma State Representative and my friend going back to the days of our Norman vs. Duncan high school basketball rivalry, helped connect me with various key individuals and initial financial contributors that launched this project.

Others who provided significant assistance, with no recompense for themselves, include Richard Drass, Lee Bement, and the Oklahoma Archaeological Survey at the University of Oklahoma, photographer David G. Fitzgerald, Holly Hasenfratz and the Donald C. & Elizabeth M. Dickinson Research Center at the National Cowboy & Western Heritage Museum, Beverly Kinzie and the Alva Mural Society, Saundra Mackey, Augusta Slagle, and the Stephens County Genealogical Society, Ian Swart and the Tulsa Historical Society, Brock Wiggins and Digital Media Warehouse, and Cova Williams and the Stephens County Historical Museum. Also, the Bizzell Memorial Library, Western History Collections, and Carl Albert Center, all at the University of Oklahoma.

Expert photographers Lori Hansen Lane, Rhys Martin, and Susan Thweatt provided beautiful original images for this book, as did artist Michelle Noah.

Those whom I overlooked, please forgive me and my poor old memory!

The historians who preceded me in crafting Oklahoma histories, at whose feet time and sometimes death have not prevented me from sitting at and learning from these many years include W. David Baird, Edward Everett Dale, Angie Debo, Odie Faulk, Grant Foreman, Arrell Gibson, Danney Goble, Marvin E. Kroeker, Gaston Litton, W. F. Morrison, Joseph Thoburn, and the afore-mentioned Bill Welge.

My mom, Helen Miller Dwyer (1925–2005) kindled a passion for history and heroes in our Oklahoma home as my brother Paul and I grew up. My alma mater the University of Oklahoma and such professors as Gordon Drummond, V. Stanley Vardys, David Levy, Chuck House, and Wayne Powers helped develop my writing, speaking, and interviewing abilities and kindled my love for history and historiography. OU also provided me a lifetime of associations and opportunities that I have been far too late in appreciating. My writing mentor and professor Reg Grant, who refused to let me quit writing during my frustrating early days, Howard Hendricks, John Hannah, Ken Sarles, other professors, and Dallas Theological Seminary helped craft my worldview, discipline of thought, and research skills.

Three men perhaps loom highest in their belief in this project. Way back in 2001, Bob Blackburn, Executive Director of the Oklahoma Historical Society, encouraged me to write a book for the now-long ago Oklahoma Centennial. That did not happen, but this book did, and for the past decade, Dr. Bob has assisted, encouraged, and mentored me regarding Oklahoma, its people, its history, and its future. He is the one person most qualified to have written this book. I have done my best to provide a work approaching the content and power of what he would most assuredly have done better.

Tom Hill has long been known near and far not only as a consummate businessman, but a great hearted giver and encourager of noble causes great and small. As usual, his motivation in helping and encouraging me, someone he had never met, to write *The Oklahomans*, was the good of someone else. "John," he told me, "I want my grandchildren to be able to read an Oklahoma History book that I can trust." It is a long time ago now that he said that to me, but I am fairly certain that if not for Tom's help in many ways, you would not be holding this book in your hands and reading it.

My old buddy Wes Lane, former Oklahoma County District Attorney and now President and CEO of Salt and Light Leadership Training (SALLT), has aided me in too many ways to count. He held me accountable to a daily writing regimen during the long difficult years when it seemed impossible that a book would ever come of my lonely efforts. He encouraged me to keep going and not give up, that God would not leave me alone in a task to which he and I both believed He had called me. He introduced me to folks with the material wherewithal to help finance this enterprise. And he stepped in and took it on as a non-profit project with his own family's foundation, then devoted some of that foundation's own resources to the effort.

Finally, the town and people of Duncan tolerated this scribe as a foolish, fatherless, sometimes reckless boy, never gave up on me no matter my mistakes and embarrassments, and helped prepare me for the world outside. I see now the wisdom of the saying that, "When a young man leaves a small town to go and face whatever world awaits him, he brings a little of that town with him."

Benefactors

The author wishes to express profound gratitude to the following individuals and organizations who contributed their valuable dollars to make possible a project that wound up taking an entire decade just to complete the first of two volumes.

James and Katrina Almond, Oak Point, Texas
Mo and Richard Anderson, Oklahoma City, Oklahoma
Doug Auld, McAlester, Oklahoma
Joe and Cindy Baehl, Kingwood, Texas
Stan Ballew, Guthrie, Oklahoma
Robert Berry, Tulsa, Oklahoma
John Bode, Washington, DC
The Burbridge Foundation, Oklahoma City, Oklahoma
Bob Carter, Edmond, Oklahoma
Chesapeake Energy, Oklahoma City, Oklahoma
Clark and Janis Curry, Edmond, Oklahoma
Ed and Jenny Dakil, Norman, Oklahoma
Brent and Peggie Gibson, Edmond, Oklahoma
Tom and Kay Hill and Kimray Inc., Oklahoma City, Oklahoma
The Pauline Dwyer Macklanburg & Robert A. Macklanburg, Jr. Foundation, Columbia, Missouri
Jay and Sue Jimerson, Norman, Oklahoma
Kelly Loy, Plano, Texas
William H. Mattoon, Norman, Oklahoma
Thomas H. McCasland, Jr. Dallas, Texas
Ron McCord and **First Mortgage Company**, Oklahoma City, Oklahoma
Rick McNabb, Mendota Heights, Minnesota
Doug Miller, Norman, Oklahoma
Terry and Michelle Noah, Dallas, Texas

Dick Pryor, Norman, Oklahoma

Thomas L. Russell, Norman, Oklahoma

Tiffany Sewell-Howard, Charles Machine Works, and **Ditch Witch**, Perry, Oklahoma

Steve Smith, Muskogee, Oklahoma

Kent Sullivan, Duncan, Oklahoma

Lee Symcox, Norman, Oklahoma

Tim and Angie Vaughan, Dallas, Texas

Mark Verity, Edmond, Oklahoma

Lew Ward and **Ward Petroleum**, Enid, Oklahoma

Greg Womack, Edmond, Oklahoma

You have to leave home to find home.

—Ralph Ellison

1

Ancient–1800

Land and First People

Famed Kiowa artist Monroe Tsatoke's mural of an Osage warrior appears in the Wiley Post Historical Building in Oklahoma City. (Courtesy William D. Welge and Oklahoma Historical Society)

???? BC	Asiatic-descended Paleo Indians
c. 500 AD	Mound Builders
900–1450 AD	Golden age of pre-historic period
1350 AD	Drought scatters settlements
1540–1542	Coronado and Spaniards' trek
Late 1600s	Osages arrive from Missouri
Early 1700s	Comanches arrive from West
c. 1718	French traders, explorers arrive

Any state of the American Union deserves to be known and understood. But Oklahoma is more than just another state. It is a lens in which the long rays of time are focused into the brightest of light. In its magnifying clarity, dim facets of the American character stand more clearly revealed. For in Oklahoma all the experiences that went into the making of the nation have been speeded up. Here all the American traits have been intensified. The one who can interpret Oklahoma can grasp the meaning of America in the modern world.

—Angie Debo

Before the Trails of Tears, before the War Between the States, before the land runs and statehood and Dust Bowl, before world wars and oil booms and busts and the OKC Bombing and Moore tornadoes, there were others who came to present-day Oklahoma. It seems the Sooner State has always been the land of the second—or third or last—chance for people from other places.

The skeletal head of an ancient buffalo that roamed present day Oklahoma. Larger than its modern American bison counterparts, the animal's remnants were found near Fort Supply in present day Woodward County. According to Richard Drass of the Oklahoma Archaeological Survey, the head is more than 5,000 years old. (Courtesy Oklahoma Archaeological Survey, University of Oklahoma)

Asiatic immigrants who became Native American Indians trekked from the Far East, which was to the west. Then European explorers, missionaries, and adventurers came from the seats of Western civilization, which was to the east.

Together, though often through conflict, they sowed the seeds for what would become a vibrant American state known across the world for its triumphs and tragedies, its heroes and villains and legends. Through time, a stubborn and defiant spirit was born of sorrow and loss. One of its fathers was a powerful, permanent presence that contributed to, contested with, and crowned with glory the people of Oklahoma—the land.

Land of Oklahoma

Oklahoma, the forty-sixth state to join the American Union, in 1907, spreads across 69,903 square miles, 1,224 of it water, in the geographic south central United States. Although it features four discernible annual seasons and a climate generally considered

Price Falls, near the Falls Creek Baptist Conference Center south of Davis, in Murray County. The well-known Turner Falls waterfall is thirteen miles west. (Photo by David G. Fitzgerald)

mild, especially by many of its immigrants from northern states, few regions anywhere rival it for its rugged, capricious, even devastating extremes. The confluence—sometimes violent—of three climatic regions (the humid, subhumid, and semiarid) causes these drastic weather swings.

Oklahoma communities have experienced temperature variations upwards of seventy degrees in the same day. The statewide average temperature for July of 2011 was the hottest recorded for any state or month in American history. The most ferocious tornado ever recorded—with winds gusting to 318 miles per hour—tore a historic swath through central Oklahoma in May of 1999. Another wreaked havoc over the largest area of land ever recorded damaged by a tornado in May 2013. Both centered on the same town: Moore. It comes as no surprise that the state, which has averaged 53 tornadoes per year since 1950, sits at the heart of "Tornado Alley," the most destructive zone of tornadoes on the planet.

The dry, wind-swept, foliage-challenged Southern Great Plains dominate the western half of the state, which is sometimes referred to as "short-grass country." Areas of the Panhandle average only seventeen inches of rain per year. The northwestern-most seven counties of this region that helped comprise the infamous 1930s Dust Bowl to be explored in Volume 2 of this work suffered the full wrath of that historic cataclysm. The aptly named Great Salt Plains and Little Sahara areas lie alongside.

The semi-forested Cross Timbers intersects the state from north to south in a five to thirty-mile-wide belt. Continuing eastward across the state—the direction the major rivers flow—the land grows hillier, rainier, and more verdant, and even (modestly)

The Great Salt Plains, north of Jet in Alfalfa County. A coating of salt covers the full 20-plus square miles of this eye-popping geological phenomenon. Scientists believe that an ancient sea with its water level rising originally left the salt, which a saline groundwater current below the surface replenishes. When the water evaporates, a layer of salt remains on the surface. This process also helps form unique selenite crystals. (Photo by David G. Fitzgerald)

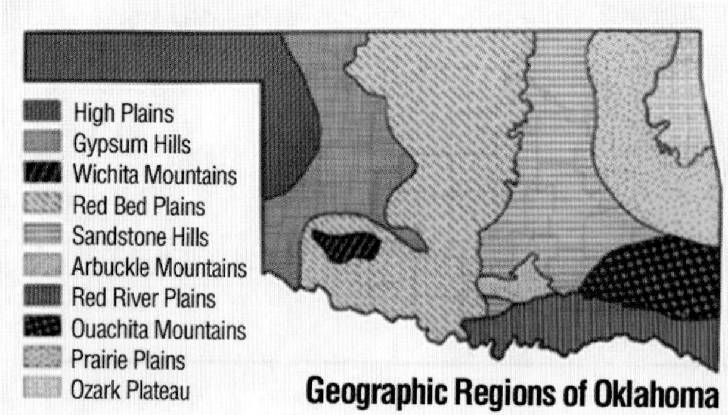

mountainous proceeding across its southeast region. The latter area averages up to fifty-six inches of rain annually. Tallgrass prairies sweep across Osage and other northern counties, transitioning into the lake-festooned northeastern "Green Country."

Geographically and climatically, the western part of Oklahoma fits into the American West; the eastern part, the South. New Mexico and mostly Texas bound the state on the west, Colorado and mostly Kansas on the north, Missouri and mostly Arkansas on the east, and Texas on the south.

Early Immigrants

Archaeologists and anthropologists have established that human life existed in Oklahoma thousands of years ago. Those early Western Hemisphere inhabitants apparently migrated during an ice age on a land bridge from northern Asia by way of modern-day Alaska. So did various animals,

Land of Contrasts

Some years ago, Odie B. Faulk, former chairman of the Oklahoma State University History Department, and William D. Welge, director of the American Indian Culture and Preservation Office for the Oklahoma Historical Society, authored *Oklahoma: A Rich Heritage*. The book remains one of the finest, if not the finest, historical narrative of the state ever written. It also includes one of the premier galleries of illustrations of any such work. The authors have kindly permitted the use of the following excerpt regarding the geography of Oklahoma from their book.

> *The plains country is a windy region, with winds that freeze in winter, parch in summer, and bring seasonal rains in spring and fall that turn it into a vast marsh on occasion. The area has a "continental weather pattern" (according to modern meteorologists); it gets the extremes of weather conditions known on the North American continent. The storms of spring bring tornadoes, hail, and rain, while the "northers" of winter bring sleet and blinding snowstorms. In the summer winds blow from the south into the nearby Rocky Mountains to melt the snow cover and bring silt-laden water rushing down to form yet another layer on the plains.*

A sea of southwestern Oklahoma wheat, west of Quartz Mountain in Greer County. The state consistently ranks at or near the top for winter wheat production and in the top 10 of U.S. states for overall wheat production. (Photo by David G. Fitzgerald)

The Panhandle of Oklahoma is situated almost exactly between the Arkansas and the Red rivers, the two major rivers that drain the state. Because the Panhandle is the highest part of the state, sloping downward to the southeast from almost 5,000 feet to approximately 300 feet above sea level, these two rivers run in that direction. Since the western two-thirds of the state's land is soft and sandy, the rivers do not cut deep and jagged banks, but rather meander in snake-like fashion as they flow toward the Mississippi. On their way across the state they are fed by other rivers: the Arkansas receives the flow of the Verdigris, the Grand (also known as the Neosho), the Illinois, the Cimarron, the Canadian, and, at the border of Arkansas, the Poteau. The Red is joined and increased in size from the north by the Washita, the Blue, and the Kiamichi and from the northwest and northeast by the Elm Fork and North Fork, the Prairie Dog Town Fork, and the Salt Fork.

As these rivers approach the eastern portion of Oklahoma, their channels become narrower and better defined, for the land is more resistant to erosion. This portion of Oklahoma consists of rolling hills and minor outcroppings of sandstone. Once the treeless plains give way to prairie and hills, the rivers flow through the Cross Timbers (running north and south almost through the middle of the state). This is an area of blackjack and post oak intermingled with mesquite and smaller shrubbery, while along the rivers' banks cottonwoods give way to long-leaf pine, giant live and white oaks, and finally to stately cypress and pecan groves.

In extreme eastern Oklahoma, where the rainfall is heavy, Spanish moss occasionally hangs from the branches of these tall trees. Open patches of ground are covered with Indian paintbrushes, sunflowers, and honeysuckle. Wood bison, a smaller cousin of the great beasts of the big plains, graze these areas along with white-tailed deer, while squirrels chatter and fuss at them from the branches of the trees. Frogs, field mice, and lizards keep a wary watch for hawks and owls.

The breathtaking Ouachita Mountains, rolling across southeastern Oklahoma and the old Choctaw country, comprises the Kiamichis, Winding Stair, and other ranges. The Oklahoma Ouachitas demonstrate the varied nature of Sooner State geography.

Grand Lake o' the Cherokees, one of the state's most beautiful waterways, is emblematic of verdant northeast Oklahoma, known as "Green Country."

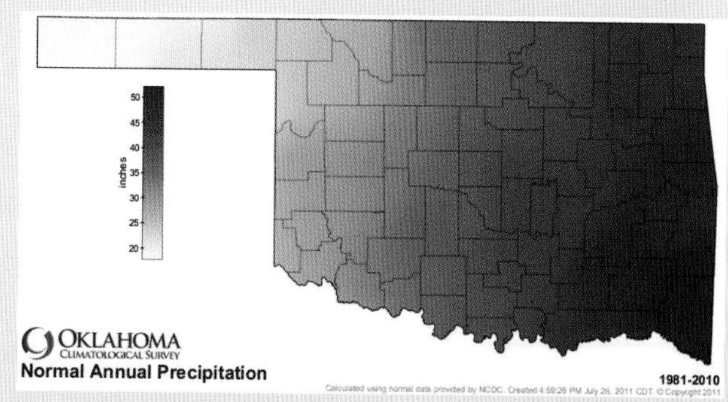

Mount Scott, second tallest peak in the Wichita Mountains Wildlife Refuge of southwest Oklahoma. Located several miles north of Lawton, it can be seen on a clear day in Duncan, over thirty miles away.

Contrasting with the plains to the west are the mountains of southern and eastern Oklahoma. The mightiest chain, known to geographers as the Interior Highlands, is a western extension of the Ozarks and consists of the Boston Mountains, the Cookson Hills, and the Ouachita Mountains; the Ouachitas contain several curving ridges known as the Kiamichi, Winding Stair, Poteau, and San Bois Mountains.

In the south-central part of the state are the Arbuckles, while to their west are the Wichitas. The Wichita Mountains rise 3,000 feet from the plains and are rich in minerals; for centuries water eroded the earth of these hills, carrying mineral deposits to the Red River and coloring its waters a rusty tint (from which the river received its name). The highest point in Oklahoma, however, is located in the Panhandle. Known as Black Mesa, it is not a mountain, but rather was formed by a lava flow thousands of years ago and juts 4,978 feet above sea level. The lowest point, 289 feet above sea level, lies on the Little River in south central Oklahoma.

Sand dunes, possessing little vegetation and ceaselessly reshaped and repositioned by High Plains winds, southeast of the Little Sahara Recreation Area in Woods County, northwest Oklahoma. (Photo by David G. Fitzgerald)

including buffalo like the one whose skeletal head appears on page 2.

The human companies traveled while bundled in the furs and skins of the game the hunters of their community killed. They traversed long and difficult distances in search of better sustenance and shelter, due to the ice age in which they lived. This arduous period stymied life and growth alike and drove people away from the frigid reaches of Siberia and elsewhere in eastern and northern Asia. The road to their new land, however, was no doubt consecrated by the deaths of many of their comrades.

A later age, one of a series through history of global warming, melted much of the ice, flooded the land bridge, and birthed the Bering Strait of modern times. Meanwhile, the "Paleo-Indians," mentioned in the preceding paragraphs, migrated east and south and down through the Americas. Those who reached Oklahoma were among the earliest of any people in the modern United States, according to historian Arrell M. Gibson. The area's moderate climate, abundance of natural shelters, and accessibility to water in some areas likely contributed to this immigration.

The group(s) reaching Oklahoma are known as Big-Game Hunters. Nomadic, or non-settling, they traveled across wide ranges of land to pursue the migratory animals that sustained them. As the generations passed, their descendants continued hunting, but over decreasing spaces of land.

Arrowheads from a 2014 dig near Atoka, Atoka County, by Oklahoman Caitlin Trubey. They comprised the heads of spears used by ancestors of Caddoan or Wichita tribes. They are larger than later arrowheads that formed the leading edges of arrows shot by bows. According to Richard Drass of the Oklahoma Archaeological Survey, these arrowheads are between 2,000 and 3,000 years old and when detached from their shafts or poles were used as tools for digging and other purposes. (Courtesy Caitlin Trubey)

First Settlers

Extant remains multiply during the Mound Builders Epoch, which covered the period roughly from AD 500 to 1350. Manmade mounds across the eastern portion of the state mark this period. Descendants of the Caddoan-language family of tribes who likely emigrated west from the Mississippi River Valley area constructed them after settling in the area. These non-nomadic early Oklahomans used them for a variety of purposes, including religious temples, burial shelters, and homes—the latter designed for protection against flooding.

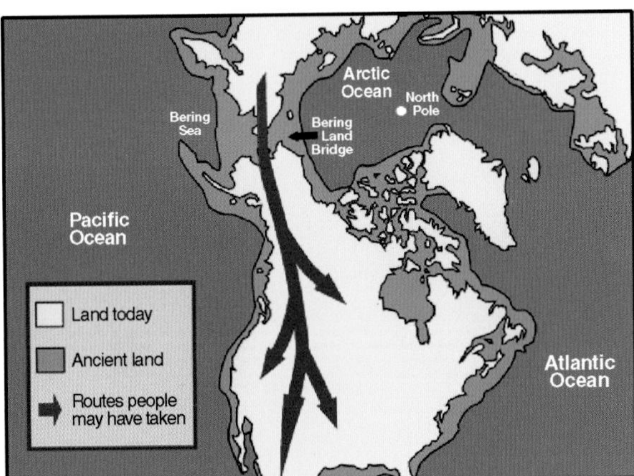

Bering Strait land bridge. (Courtesy State Historical Society of North Dakota)

The Spiro Age, roughly AD 900 to 1450, was the "Golden Age" of the state's pre-recorded history period. Leading Oklahoma historian Bob Blackburn says that though Spiro never had a population of more than five thousand people and was not an economic power, it was the spiritual/religious center of the ancient Southern Mississippian Empire. A manmade hill designed as a burial temple and discovered in the 1930s near the Poteau River valley town of the same name in eastern Oklahoma provides rich insight into the Oklahomans of this period. Featuring a rot-resistant cedar structure and millions of tons of moved earth, the artifacts contained in the Spiro Mound reveal the history of its people, which included artisan and priestly classes.

A devastating fourteenth-century drought, likely combined with warfare against early Plains Indians tribes from western Oklahoma, evidently worked in some combination to break up much of

Reconstruction of a circa-AD 1200 thatched Caddoan hut, as found in the Spiro area of eastern Oklahoma. (Courtesy Smallchief, Wikipedia)

the established Mound Builder presence during the century or two leading up to the arrival of European explorers.

During the same general time frame, other Indians, known as the Plains Village Farmers, built their own early settlements in western Oklahoma, including along the Washita River. These settlers demonstrated acumen in both hunting and farming, and built at least a couple hundred communities before the same drought that plagued the Mound Builders drove the Plains Village Farmers into a nomadic lifestyle of buffalo hunters and evidence of their organized efforts vanished.

The "First People"

Before European explorers, trappers, and soldiers arrived in the sixteenth century, two confederations of Caddoan-language Indians populated Oklahoma—the Caddoans in the far southeast, and the Wichitas along the rivers of the west. Tribes related to the latter were scattered through the Great Plains all the way to modern-day Canada. The Wichitas and Caddoans gained the sobriquet of Oklahoma's "First People" from both themselves and the first Europeans, who met them later in the 1500s.

These two tribes, along with the Caddoan-speaking Pawnees, hunted and farmed and lived in permanent villages. A friendly and expressive people, the Wichitas also demonstrated prowess as traders, first with other tribes and later with Europeans such as the French. Their later troubles with more warlike tribes were perhaps highlighted by these words of the early eighteenth-century French explorer Jean-

Southeastern Native traders parley with Spiro-area Caddoan leaders about trade. (Courtesy Donald R. Johnson and William D. Welge)

Baptiste Bénard Sieur de la Harpe, who described them as "people of good sense, cleverer than the nations of the Mississippi (River), but the fertility of the country makes them lazy. They are always sitting around their chief and usually they think only of eating, smoking and playing."

The warlike Lipan Apaches migrated into Oklahoma from the west sometime in the 1500s. They preferred raiding and plundering other Indians' villages, torturing, scalping, and killing their

This replica of an effigy pipe provides one example of the artistic prowess of early-Oklahoma Caddoan Indians in the Spiro area. These artisans created elaborate ceramics and engraved animal bones for trade and ornamentation for their leaders. Archaeologists have excavated many such works at the Spiro Mounds Archaeological State Park. (Courtesy William D. Welge, photo Jim Argo)

men, and kidnapping their women and children, to such mundane tasks as tending mulberries and growing beans. Tribes like these Apaches help dispel the notion of the ancient North American continent hosting a serene Native American utopia later spoiled by the violent white man. At least two other distinctives marked the buffalo-hunting Lipans for this time period in Oklahoma. While encamped, they employed portable tepees formed with dried, stretched animal skins for shelter. When on the hunt or otherwise moving, they took down the teepees, loaded their possessions on them, then used dogs to pull the whole lot with tepee poles. They also better utilized horses for mobility than other tribes.

No doubt the Wichitas held no great regard for these innovations because the Lipans ranged into their hunting grounds and then attacked them. Gradually, this fierce Plains tribe drove many of the Wichitas east and north, into Arkansas River enclaves as far north as southern Kansas and north central Oklahoma and east to present-day Tulsa County.

The Spaniards

The first three centuries of Western civilization contact with Oklahoma came in the historical context of the mercantilist rivalry between the world's great powers, at that time all European. Predicated on the assumption of a limited amount of resources in the world, represented by a nation's stock of bullion (gold and silver), mercantilist powers such as England, Spain, France, and the Netherlands believed that to obtain a larger slice of this finite "pie," one nation must wrest it from another. This could be accomplished by favorable trading activities—exporting a greater amount than one imports—or by success in war and the subsequent treaties, which could deliver additional resources from one country to another. Thus unfolded a crucial plank of mercantilist thought—possessing as many colonies as possible in order to mine the raw materials from them, ship those to the mother country, produce finished products from the imports, and then ship those back to the colony and other countries for sale.

Mercantilism stands at variance with the American founders' consensus economic notions of *laissez faire*, or free trade. The famed Scotsman Adam Smith systematized the latter philosophy in his landmark 1776 work *The Wealth of Nations. Laissez faire*, in contrast to mercantilism, argues against restrictive tariffs toward other nations, the always selective governmental subsidization of industry with citizens' tax revenues, and the federal financing of internal improvements (infrastructure) to any extent beyond what is necessary.

Laissez faire also supports limited government involvement in every area of life, particularly economic matters; low tariffs to stimulate trade between cities, states, and countries; and the notion of an ever-expanding economic pie, rather than a static one. It anticipates vigorous economic competition taking place alongside mutually beneficial results with no specter of serious international tension due to the "win–win" rather than the mercantilist "dog-eat-dog" process between individuals, companies, and nations alike.

Discovery and Exploration 1541–1820, the first of Miami, Oklahoma artist Charles Banks Wilson's epic cycle of four 13 × 27 foot murals that adorn the Oklahoma State Capitol. It depicts famed Spanish explorer Francisco Vasquez de Coronado atop his armored horse in the present-day Oklahoma Panhandle, amidst the Catholic missionaries who accompanied him, Wichita Indians, buffalo, and the Antelope Hills, a key landmark for travelers. (Courtesy Charles Banks Wilson and the Oklahoma State Senate Historical Preservation Fund, Inc., Photo John Jernigan)

Into an admixture of mercantilism and a desire to spread the gospel of Jesus Christ to the non-Christian peoples living throughout the non-European continents of the world came Francisco Vasquez de Coronado. This winsome, fair-haired governor of the New Spain (present-day Mexico) province of New Galicia led his fellow Spanish conquistadors as they rode through wind, sun, barren plain, and Indian Country in search of the fabled Cale, Gran Quivera, and Seven Cities of Cibola. Indians had told the Spaniards that kingdoms of unimaginable wealth larger than Seville, the greatest city in Spain, lay north of Mexico.

Coronado's Conquistadors

Coronado led 336 conquistadors—rugged Spanish adventurers, explorers, and warriors—and a few hundred Indian allies across the American Southwest. Displaying the cool vision and leadership that motivated wealthy men to financially back his expedition and other men to follow him through danger, suffering, and battle, he constantly assessed the unfamiliar terrain of present-day northern Mexico and the southwestern U.S., deploying groups of men at strategic points for communication, reconnaissance, and mutual protection, based on their individual capabilities. He staggered their movements, waiting to advance one company until the natural resources consumed by the previous one had time to replenish themselves.

The conquistadors defeated the Zuni and Pueblo Indians in bloody battles, during one of which Coronado fell wounded and nearly perished. They endured broiling desert temperatures, freezing mountains, dangerous animals, hunger, and thirst. While other maps depicting Coronado's journey

Coronado's Expedition through Northwest Oklahoma, by G. N. Taylor. Coronado's expedition of conquistadors included several hundred Indians and a captured Native guide called "The Turk." The ever-present Catholic priest accompanies Coronado in his search for the Seven Cities of Cibola. (www.gntayloroklaart.com)

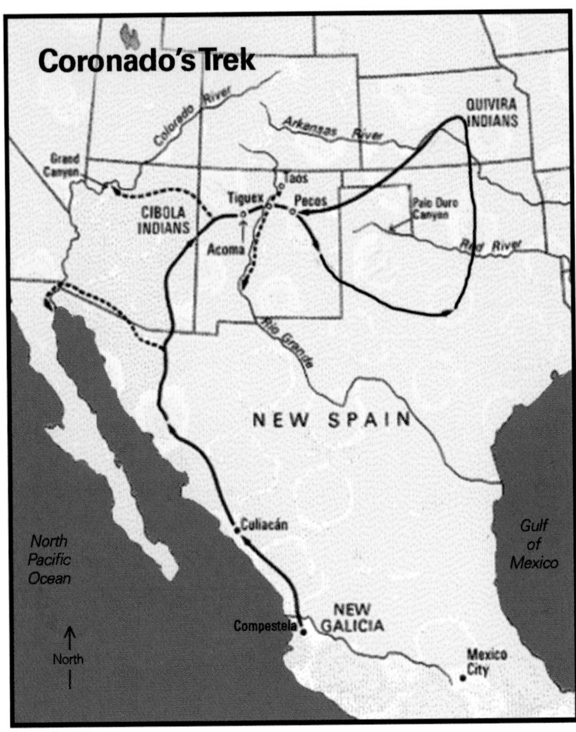

differ, the one above is probably the most accurate. It places key sections of the conquistadors' trek in present-day Oklahoma. According to historians Herbert Belton and Edwin C. McReynolds, they traveled up the future 98th Meridian/Chisholm Trail/U.S. Highway 81 the length of the state near modern-day Duncan, Chickasha, El Reno, Kingfisher, and Enid. A 1907 Temple newspaper reported the unearthing in that area of an apparent Spanish headstone that dated back to 1542.

They later rode across the Panhandle and northwest section of present-day Oklahoma near the modern communities of Tyrone, Optima, Hooker, Guymon, Goodwell, and Texhoma.

They traveled amongst mesquite, cactus, and other bushes in present-day Oklahoma. Turkeys, prairie dogs, jackrabbits, antelope, deer, and wild hogs roamed the land, over the blue grass and buffalo grass that covers the Southern American Great Plains because taller grasses and their greater root system cannot endure those scalding parched climes.

The intrepid Coronado indeed found "Quivera"—such as it was. He considered it the best land he found in the present-day Southwest U.S.: "well settled . . . The land itself being very fat and black and being very well watered by the rivulets and springs and rivers . . . I found prunes like those of Spain, and nuts and very good sweet grapes and mulberries." Its residents "were large people of good build," many towering over the Spaniards at over six feet tall, and scarcely clothed.

Alas, only villages of straw huts and fields of corn, beans, and squash comprised Quivira, and Coronado finally conceded that no glittering cities existed where the people ate from golden forks and spoons and the women poured their men drinks from golden pitchers, atop streets of silver, and amidst the tinkling of bells that hung from tree branches and blew in the wind. Still, his journey through the American Southwest accomplished much that he did not plan. To grasp the magnitude of Coronado's exploits, one should realize they occurred nearly a century before the English landed at Jamestown, Virginia, and a full century before the Pilgrims landed at Plymouth Rock. He and his men wrote and spoke their observations of the Indians, land, and creatures they found, and thus began the recorded history of Oklahoma. And they brought the banner of Spain

Mercantilism
A nationalistic system established on the premise that economic policies benefiting certain groups are good for the nation, and which fosters a structure of imperial state power (at the expense of other nations), as well as special subsidy and monopolistic privileges to individuals and groups favored by the state.

Francisco Vasquez de Coronado (1510–1554)

Already respected and well known at twenty-seven years of age when he launched his fabled trek across Mexico and the American Southwest, this peerless Spanish conquistador introduced modern-day Oklahoma and Western civilization to one another a century before the Pilgrims landed on Plymouth Rock.

Famed artist of the American West Frederic Remington's *Coronado Sets Out to the North,* portraying the journey that compassed present-day Oklahoma.

and Western civilization—and, by extension, Christ and His Church—to Oklahoma.

Further Spanish travels into Oklahoma through the sixteenth and seventeenth centuries were infrequent. Why? The Spanish Empire's fortunes crested with its epochal and devastating naval defeat at the hands of Sir Francis Drake, his whipcord-tough "Sea Dogs," and the British navy in the 1588 Battle of the Spanish Armada. This colossal loss of manhood, treasure, and control of oceanic sea lanes, coupled with a less productive and vigorous work ethic than some of its European mercantilistic competitors—particularly, the British—the vast remoteness of the present-day United States, and the martial dangers of the native Indian tribes, rendered the area untenable for the Spanish.

The French

Meanwhile, by the late 1600s, France rivaled Spain in the mercantilist sweepstakes. Voyages down the Mississippi River from French bases in Canada by explorers such as Joliet, Marquette, and La Salle, and subsequent French claims to the vast lands drained from the west by the Mississippi—which they dubbed Louisiana (and which included all of present-day Oklahoma except the Panhandle) in honor of their dictatorial monarch, Louis XIV—helped establish this enhanced French power. From the 1718 founding of New Orleans at the mouth of the Mississippi into the Gulf of Mexico, French traders and explorers flocked northwest through Oklahoma rivers in search of furs.

The French posed a grave threat to Spanish hegemony over present-day Oklahoma and, indeed, the entire western Mississippi River Valley. Their men proved to be active and vigorous travelers along rivers such as the Arkansas, Red, Canadian, Grand, and Verdigris. They formed alliances with influential Indian tribes such as the Comanches in the Southern Plains and the Wichitas in eastern Oklahoma, and in fact did not hesitate to intermarry with Indian girls. They also traded a galaxy of items to the Indians, including clothing, tools, and trinkets, and—unlike the Spanish—weapons, ammunition, and whiskey.

Gradually, the French parlayed these practices into a loose control over most of present-day Oklahoma and the western Mississippi watershed. This ended, temporarily, in 1763, as England defeated the combined forces of Spain and France in the sprawling mercantilist Seven Years War, whose North American theater gained the name of the French and Indian War. That vast conflict exhausted all of its participants, including the English, who demanded the ceding of Florida by Spain. In compensation for this loss and their costly support of the

> *There is not in the whole colony of Louisiana an establishment more useful to make than on the branch of this (Canadian) river not only because of the mild climate, the fertility of the land, the richness of the minerals, but also because of the possibility of trade that one might introduce with Spain and New Mexico.*
>
> —French explorer Bénard de la Harpe, 1719, regarding eastern Oklahoma

French explorer Bénard de la Harpe explores the Arkansas River in 1722.

French, the Spanish sought to acquire Louisiana. The French gave the territory over to them, largely to keep it out of English hands. Such were the stakes and machinations of European imperialism.

Although Spain's four-decade latter rule of present-day Oklahoma passed without great fanfare, one development illustrated its growing strategic geographic importance despite its spartan population and lack of industrial development. Under Spanish rule, commercial travel developed through the area between French-ruled New Orleans and its environs, and Spanish-ruled New Mexico on the other side of present-day Oklahoma and the sprawling Spanish province of Texas. Ironically, though sponsored and enabled by the Spaniards, the Frenchman Bénard de la Harpe had the vision and French-descended traders and trappers from Louisiana—offspring of the French Acadians brutally and ethnically cleansed from Canada by the British—established the routes, primarily through the Arkansas and Red rivers.

In 1800, powerful French Emperor Napoleon Bonaparte pressured a weak Spanish king into returning the vast territory of Louisiana to France through the secretive Treaty of San Ildefonso. Another war with Britain, coupled with a disease- and massacre-laden slave revolt in Haiti, however, doomed the French to again give up Louisiana—this time to the Americans, and after only two and a half years of ownership.

By the end of the eighteenth century, the French controlled the land again, by virtue of their Napoleonic juggernaut. But they held it barely longer than it took the cash-desperate emperor, immersed in yet another war with England, to sell the colossal tract to the newly independent American republic. Defying opposition in Congress, overcoming his own philosophical bent against such an aggressive, extra-constitutional action, and aiming to provide sufficient land for the sturdy yeoman farmers he envisioned as the bedrock of a good and great nation, the famed Thomas Jefferson—Founding Father, agrarian, and third President of the united States of America—paid $15 million for Louisiana.

In doing so, Jefferson removed the French forever from America, shouldered the British out of the path of westward American expansion, and more than doubled the land size of the fledgling American Union. The visionary Virginian, chief author of the Declaration of Independence, had pulled off perhaps the greatest land deal in the history of the world. Present-day Oklahoma, except for its still Spanish-held Panhandle, was now part of America.

French Leave Oklahoma

Europe's bloody imperial competition had torn the continent—and other lands ruled by its military-political titans—apart during the Seven Years War of 1756–1763. This first true "World War" stretched across half the continents of the globe and nearly every ocean. A crucial fact usually missed when history books recount wars is the future consequences they spawn. Many of these are not at first apparent, nor their contribution to future events.

Consider the archprotagonists of the Seven Years War. The winner—Great Britain—had so exhausted itself in victory that it tightened its chokehold on its American colonies and determined to rebuild its financial fortunes largely on their shoulders. This damaged relations between the Old Country and its New World colonies, through reduced economic autonomy for the colonies, increased taxes, and finally another sanguinary war—the American Revolution—that lost the

Napoleon Crossing the Alps, one of Jacques-Louis David's famous paintings of French Emperor Napoleon Bonaparte leading his forces across the Alps into Italy on their breathtaking ambush of Austrian forces challenging his authority there.

British much of the same North American continent they had fought so long and hard to win in the Seven Years'/French and Indian War, including the colonies that soon formed the American republic.

Meanwhile, the losers—France—had similarly faced near financial ruin. Now greatly reduced in colonial possessions, they laid the burden primarily on their own people. Coupled with a historic drought and economic depression in 1789, the lower and even the middle economic classes rose up in a bloody early-day Communist revolution. They slaughtered thousands of people, primarily from the country's upper classes, including King Louis XVI and his queen, Marie Antoinette. They established tyrannical central government control over every facet of the country. And they outlawed the Catholic church and Christian religion, attempting to replace them with official state atheism. This horrendous solution eventually turned on its own leaders, including Robespierre, and lasted only a few blood-drenched years before giving way to one of history's most daring and grim dictators, Napoleon Bonaparte. Once again, however, as one theologian has said, "You don't break God's commandments—they break you."

The collective sins committed by the French government and people in the late 1700s had brought more revolution—this time terror from the Caribbean colony of Haiti—more social and economic calamity, and more war against old and new enemies alike. Forced to raise cash to bankroll ever costlier and more destructive campaigns against most of the rest of Europe, Napoleon unloaded France's vast North American "Louisiana" to the Americans for a fraction of the land's worth. Barely a decade later, he lost his war and his empire anyway.

Intertribal Wars

The Osages and Quapaws, a Siouan-language confederation of Indians, meanwhile, migrated into present-day Oklahoma later than the Wichitas and other Caddoan tribes. The larger and more powerful of the Siouan, the Osages trekked around the late 1500s from the Ohio Valley into southern Missouri. A tall and physically imposing tribe, they were tough enough that even the ruthless and nomadic Lipan Apaches who roamed south into Texas from western and central present-day

> *The tribes in the west fought one another and they all fought against the Osages, who in turn fought the southeastern tribes. The whites were indeed invaders and conquerors, but only the latest in a long line.*

This Wichita Indian village of 1850s central Oklahoma mirrored those visited over three centuries before by Coronado. (Courtesy William D. Welge and Oklahoma Historical Society)

Oklahoma along the Arkansas River eventually learned grudging respect for them.

The Osages did not at first seem to imperil the Wichitas and their expansive northeastern Oklahoma land holdings. But once the Osages began to buy horses from the Spanish in the late 1600s, they started ranging farther down into northern and eastern present-day Oklahoma. The Wichitas bought horses from the Spaniards even earlier than the Osages, and those Wichita horses, among other human and material possessions, became targets for both their status and their value to Osage warriors.

As the Osages advanced into present-day Oklahoma from the north, the greatest and most brutal of all Indian warrior tribes thundered into the western shortgrass country in the early 1700s. The entry of the legendary Comanches permanently reshaped the history of the state, and indeed America. These "lords of the plains," as historian Odie Faulk called them, earlier roamed the present-day western United States, migrating from the Great Basin over the Rocky Mountains and also through New Mexico. Fierce and nomadic, they evinced no desire to settle down or build permanent communities.

Previously described as scorned, "skulking pariahs" in the eyes of other Western tribes by one of their biographers, once the Comanches migrated to the Southern Plains and got hold of Spanish mustangs—whom they mastered as did no other people—and French guns and ammunition in the late 1600s, they stood virtually invincible against the Spaniards, Mexicans, other Indian tribes, and, for nearly two centuries, white settlers and armies in the Plains country of present-day western Oklahoma and Texas. The Texans had to field a separate army, comprising Texas Rangers and others, to guard their western frontier against the Comanches during the War Between the States, as the rest of the state's men fought Federal soldiers to the north, east, and south.

The Comanches' entrance from the west brought terror to the Wichitas from that direction as the Osages did from the north. Fortunately, the canny "First People" produced and purchased items important to the Comanches, and were able to persuade the latter of that. The Wichitas supplied the Comanches with food from their farms and guns obtained from the French in return for the spoils of the hunter, including horses, buffalo hides, and captives the French would purchase—as well as friendship and peace, at least on their western flank.

The Lipan Apaches, by now the prevailing power on the Southern Plains, including present-day

Renowned American artist George Catlin's painting of prominent young Osage men. The tribe revered physical size, power, and prowess, especially in battle, and highly rewarded such men who exhibited it, including marriage to the most desirable young maidens—and rights to their sisters.

Blending Peoples

"The European quest for the control of North America also changed the skin complexion and tribal power structure of the southeastern Indians. Most of the European traders took Indian wives and fathered large mixed-blood families. These included the Hicks, Ross, Vann, Rogers, and Martin families among the Cherokees; the LeFlore, McCurtain, Pitchlynn, Folsom, and Harkins families among the Choctaws; the McIntosh, Grayson, Stidham, Porter, and Barnett families among the Creeks; and the Colbert, Pickens, Love, Harris, and Cheadle familes among the Chickasaws. The intermarried white men usually chose a European lifestyle, started plantations, and introduced Negro slaves."

–W. David Baird and Danney Goble
The Story of Oklahoma

Oklahoma, executed no such rapprochement with the Comanches. They took a historic thrashing for not doing so. The Comanches' unparalleled mastery of horsemanship included their developing the skill of mounted combat. This afforded them a tremendous advantage in attacking, fighting, and escaping over everyone else, including the Apaches, who, even with the horse, continued to dismount and fight on foot.

The Comanches not only rode better than anyone else, their unique understanding of and bonding with their horses got them more mileage from the animals. And if his mount died on the trail, the Comanche could not only survive by eating him, but by drinking water from his stomach. The Comanche also surpassed all others in his prowess at navigating by landmarks and traveling at night.

All this meant that the tribe could cover vast distances—up to a thousand miles in any direction—in force. And it meant their battering the Apaches and sweeping them southward down the Great Plains. They chased other Apache bands across west Texas and New Mexico and into the deserts of modern day Arizona.

The climactic showdown on the Southern Plains between the two mortal foes took place in 1724 at what the Spanish called the Great Mountain of Iron, in either southwest Oklahoma or north Texas. These fearsome adversaries apparently threw everything they had into a nine-day bloodbath in which the Comanches crushed the Apaches and vanquished them from the shortgrass country.

It was not by accident that later exploits of Apache bands led by famous chiefs such as Geronimo and Cochise occurred in places like Arizona and northern Mexico rather than Kansas, Oklahoma or Texas.

The news was not as positive for the Wichitas to the north and east as a long, dreary war unfolded between them and the powerful and warlike Osages. The Wichitas engineered a variety of strategies to ward off their murderous nemeses, but the Osages gradually drove them south through present-day Oklahoma. By the end of the 1700s, the Wichitas had fled all the way to the Red River Valley bordering present-day Oklahoma and Texas to escape, for the most part, the sanguinary reach of the Osages.

In the run-up to white European and American military control of Oklahoma, Indian tribes constructed ordered societies, practiced one of the most memorable lifestyles in American history, and fought one another for land, buffalo, horses, and other possessions, revenge, and power. The Comanches, Kiowas, Arapahos, Wichitas, Apaches, and other tribes in the west fought one another, and they all fought against the Osages, who in turn fought the southeastern migrant Cherokees, Creeks, and others. They all came from places other than present-day Oklahoma. The whites, who brought advanced technology, Western education and civil institutions, guns and horses, new diseases, and Christianity to Oklahoma, were indeed invaders and conquerors, but only the latest in a long line.

A redbud, state tree of Oklahoma, blooms into new life in springtime along the Talimena National Scenic Drive, amidst the Ouachitas of southeastern Oklahoma. (Photo Jim Argo)

2

1800–1820
The Americans

Celebrated Norman artist Mike Wimmer's *Ceremonial Transfer of the Louisiana Purchase in New Orleans–1803* depicts the signing of the document transferring the Louisiana Territory and ceremoniously passing the keys of the city from the French to the Americans. On December 20, 1803, French representative Pierre Clément de Laussat (center of the table) met with (to his left) James Wilkinson, commanding general of the United States Army, and (to Wilkinson's left) William Claiborne, former governor of the Mississippi Territory, in the Sala Capitular (Capitol Room) at the Cabildo in New Orleans. Courtesy Oklahoma State Senate Historical Preservation Fund, Inc. and Mike Wimmer.

1803	Louisiana Purchase
1806	American explorations begin
1806	A. P. Chouteau, Osages Develop Three Forks
1808	Treaty of 1808 forces more Osages to Indian Territory
1811	Pushmataha confronts Tecumseh
1813–1814	Creek Civil Wars
1817	Battle of Claremore Mound
1817	Seminole Wars begin in Florida
1819	Adams–Onís Treaty
1819–1820	Stephen Long's second journey

"... of the particular features of the region, it will be perceived to bear a manifest resemblance to the desert of Siberia."

—American explorer Stephen Long

Thomas Jefferson possessed one of the great minds in American history—and one of its most audacious spirits. His grand yet tortured vision for "Louisiana," which more than doubled the land area of the United States, did not end with its purchase from dictator Napoleon Bonaparte and the French (Chapter 1). He wanted the colossal mass surveyed and mapped—especially its borders with Spanish-held Texas to the south and west—and American civilization secured from the Spaniards and any other possible threats. Jefferson advocated accomplishing the latter not through American settlement of the Louisiana Purchase, but by using it as a buffer from foreign powers. He did, however, envision setting aside a portion of Louisiana as a preserve for Indian tribes. He had come to believe they should relocate to their own remote lands west of the Mississippi River, both for their well-being and that of the growing white American populace.

Next to his principal roles in the Declaration of Independence and the Louisiana Purchase, sending fellow Virginians Meriwether Lewis and William Clark across North America to the Pacific Ocean on their legendary 1804 to 1806 journey remains perhaps Jefferson's most famous deed. He launched a series of subsequent expeditions into present-day Oklahoma and the Southwest that later Presidents would continue from 1806 to 1820. These efforts

Thomas Jefferson (1744–1826)

Oklahoma Historical Society Executive Director Bob Blackburn, the dean of twenty-first century Oklahoma historians, rated President Thomas Jefferson's Louisiana Purchase as the most important event in Oklahoma history. He cited how the act annexed into the United States all the land of present-day Oklahoma except the Panhandle, and that Jefferson intended a portion of the land to provide a colonization area for American Indian tribes.

Jefferson Speaks about Louisiana

Thomas Jefferson's July 11, 1803 letter to British-born Revolutionary War Patriot General Horatio Gates brims with excitement over the Louisiana Purchase and with contempt for their (and future President James Monroe's) common political adversaries of the Federalist Party, which included John Adams, Alexander Hamilton, and others.

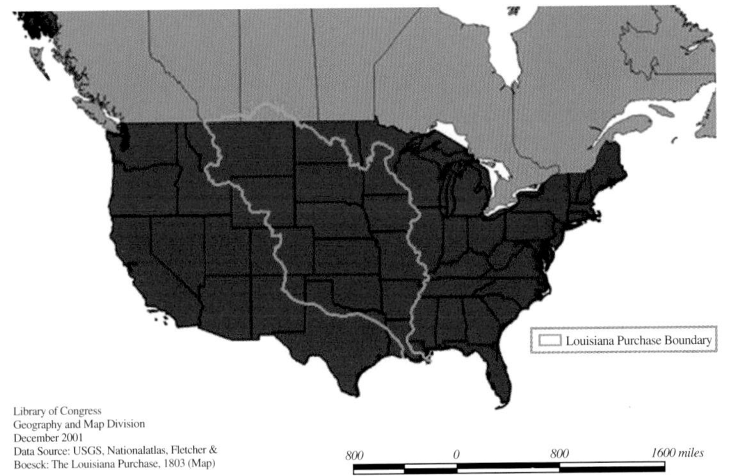

The Louisiana Territory Purchase from Napoleonic France doubled the land size of the existing United States. Courtesy Library of Congress.

> *I accept with pleasure, and with pleasure reciprocate your congratulations on the acquisition of Louisiana; for it is a subject of mutual congratulation, as it interests every man of the nation. The territory acquired, as it includes all the waters of the Missouri and Mississippi, has more than doubled the area of the United States, and the new part is not inferior to the old in soil, climate, productions, and important communications. If our Legislature dispose of it with the wisdom we have a right to expect, they may make it the means of tempting all our Indians on the east side of the Mississippi to remove to the west, and of condensing instead of scattering our population.*

sought to chart the key known waterways through present-day Oklahoma, including the Arkansas and Red Rivers. They began with the dramatic journey of Captain Richard Sparks—the first American official to travel into present-day Oklahoma—partway up Red River in 1806.

French politician François Barbé-Marbois, American Founding Father Robert Livingston, and Secretary of State and future President James Monroe sign the Louisiana Purchase, transferring ownership of present-day Oklahoma from France to America.

The rugged men sent by Presidents Jefferson, James Madison, and James Monroe dared to enter a dangerous and unfamiliar country with scant force, a country hard even for those who had spent their whole lives in it, a country where injury, maiming, sickness, and death were never more than a bullet, an arrow, or a wild beast attack away. Nor were fatigue, loneliness, despair, sorrow, and fear.

Some of these American men fought bedeviling ice floes on the Arkansas; others faced frustrating log jams on the Red; others, unfamiliar and unpredictable Indians; still others, mounted, armed, and hostile Spanish soldiers. They fit no one profile. Soldier and explorer, scientist and trader, they forged on through sufferings and deprivations great and small, and they etched the first dim foundations of the future American state of Oklahoma.

Words of Jefferson

"When the people fear their government, there is tyranny; when the government fears the people, there is liberty."

"Whenever a man has cast a longing eye on offices, a rottenness begins in his conduct."

"I predict future happiness for Americans if they can prevent the government from wasting the labors of the people under the pretense of taking care of them."

The long upstream tangle that jammed the Indian Territory segment of Red River from shipping and economic development in the early-mid-1800s.

American Exploration

Richard Sparks' adventure mirrored the shared triumph and failure born of the early nineteenth-century American odysseys through present-day Oklahoma. Commissioned under Jefferson's Secretary of War Henry Dearborn to follow Red River in present-day Louisiana to its source, Sparks headed up the river from present-day Natchitoches. A seventy-mile tangle of logs and brush called "The Great Raft" bedeviled the journey. Then, near Nacogdoches, Texas, a much-larger and better-armed Spanish force compelled him under threat of imprisonment or death to turn back. Though not accomplishing his mission, Sparks mapped over six hundred miles of Red River, amassed a hefty amount of scientific information about the area, and became the first official American representative who traveled into present-day Oklahoma.

The same year, General James Wilkinson, commander of American forces in the Louisiana Territory, sent Captain Zebulon Pike across the future state of Kansas into the Rocky Mountains to find the source of the Arkansas River and map its course. At the great bend of the river in western Kansas, Pike split his small party. He continued west into the mountains with one group of men. Lieutenant James B. Wilkinson—General Wilkinson's son—had fallen seriously ill and taken the other portion east and south down the river.

Before anyone got back to the States, Pike and his men suffered capture, prolonged transport,

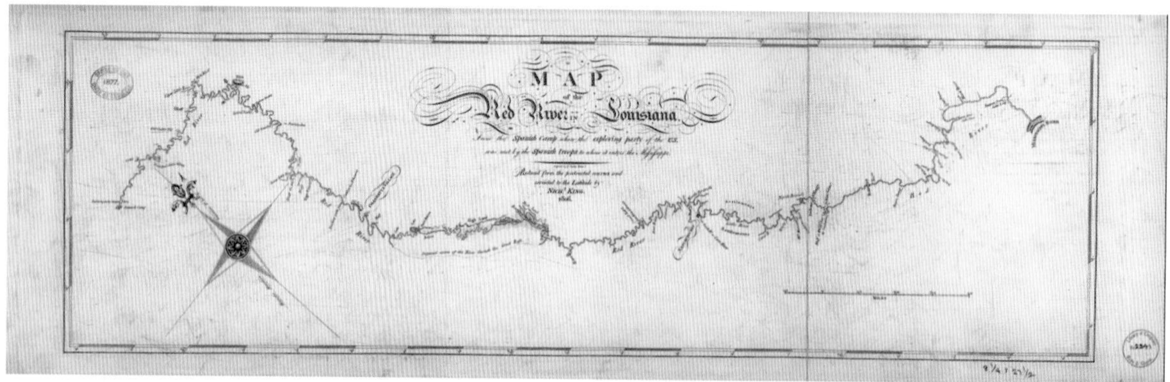

Map of the 1806 Red River Expedition, which sought to determine the remote western source and location of the river's headwaters. Richard Sparks and others contributed the information from which War Department official Nicholas King produced this document.

In 1804 President Thomas Jefferson commissioned his old friend, former personal secretary, and fellow Virginian Meriwether Lewis to lead an expedition to determine the extent of the great Louisiana Territory (which included present-day Oklahoma) he had recently purchased for America from Napoleon. Lewis engaged his own close friend William Clark to help lead the epic trek. Renowned historical artist John Paul Strain (www.johnpaulstrain.com) captured the feat in his painting *Spirit of Discovery*. From right to left are Captain Clark; sixteen-year-old Shoshone guide Sacagawea and her child; Captain Lewis; and Sacagawea's husband, a French trapper named Charbonneau.

and imprisonment at the hands of the Spanish. Meanwhile, young Wilkinson, already in bad physical straits, and his men nearly starved and froze amidst a bitterly cold Kansas winter and canoe capsizings in icy Arkansas River waters. After building a second set of canoes near present-day Wichita, the craft containing most of their food and supplies capsized and sank. So went countless tales of frustration, terror, and heartbreak, most of them lost to history as Christian civilization compassed Oklahoma and the rest of the West.

By the time Lieutenant James B. Wilkinson and his men—hungry, cold, and sick—reached present-day Oklahoma, their prospects for survival traveling back to the Mississippi River looked bleak. Then a group of the feared Osages provided shelter and food for them. While recovering, he returned the favor by helping an ailing Osage chief.

By the time Wilkinson and his men—hungry, cold, and sick—reached present-day Oklahoma, their prospects for survival traveling back to the Mississippi River looked bleak. Then a group of the Osages provided shelter and food for Wilkinson and his men. While recovering, he returned the favor by helping an ailing Osage chief.

In the end, Pike's Peak was scaled and named, and Wilkinson provided the first recorded American account of the future Sooner State. He witnessed Osage villages,

U.S. soldier and explorer Richard Sparks, spearhead of the first serious European or American expedition aimed for present-day Oklahoma.

Choctaw and Cherokee hunting camps, lead mines, and even American trappers. He also chronicled his exploration of the Cimarron and Verdigris Rivers and met Clermont, head chief of the southern band of the Osages. Both the Pike and Wilkinson parties returned safely home. The elder Wilkinson who commissioned the expedition had an aide and United States Military Academy graduate who would gain great renown of his own in Oklahoma history—A. P. Chouteau.

Commercial Pioneers

Its potential as a path from the South and Midwest to the rich Southwestern trading center of Santa Fe in present-day New Mexico made the 1700s-early 1800s Oklahoma country both attractive and dangerous. Santa Fe was part of the vast North American Spanish colonial empire. The Spaniards did not want the Americans, French, or anyone else they viewed as mercantile competitors utilizing Santa Fe, either for profit, to cultivate relationships with the Native tribes of the Southwest, or to establish commercial footholds in the region. Many Americans—businessmen, soldiers, and scientists alike—were turned back from crossing present-day Oklahoma in the early 1800s by Spanish military forces, or even thrown into prisons located in Spain's Mexican provinces.

Historian Stan Hoig's map of early-1800s Three Forks area, from his book *The Chouteaus*, published by University of New Mexico Press.

Entrepreneurs as shrewd as they were tough persisted in their efforts and explorations in present-day Oklahoma. They carved a series of thriving businesses out of the northeastern portion and its rich waterways. The earliest were French traders and trappers. The Americans followed them. As the 1820s ended, however, the area's burgeoning commerce was shifting from the fur trade to farming and mining.

Early commercial efforts among the Europeans and Americans centered on the Three Forks area, where the Verdigris, Grand, and Arkansas Rivers met. Oklahoma historian Bob Blackburn called Three Forks "The cradle of Oklahoma civilization until the twentieth century." The area, located just north of Muskogee in present-day Muskogee, Wagoner, and Cherokee Counties, boasted such attributes as temperate weather and excellent shipping routes, including to the Mississippi River and New Orleans through the Three Forks rivers, which served as the interstate highways of the era. In addition to trade with the Indian tribes in horses, mules, and buffalo skins, the production of wheat, pecans, beeswax, lead, and salt developed into prominent industries.

> *Three Forks was the cradle of Oklahoma civilization until the twentieth century.*
> **—Bob Blackburn**

Men like Lewis and Clark expedition and War of 1812 stalwart Nathaniel Pryor of Kentucky, intrepid French entrepreneur Joseph Bogy, and Cincinnatian Hugh Glenn, who had won and lost a financial fortune, helped build the Three Forks trading hub. They fashioned homes, businesses, warehouses, ferry and shipping enterprises, and entire frontier communities. One family name, however, stands above all the others for its prominence in the commercial history of early Oklahoma—the Chouteaus, from whom the Mayes County town of Chouteau and the creek flowing past it drew their names.

A few log houses on the banks of the river... men in frocked coats made of green blankets... some in sweat-soiled buckskin lounging about on tree stumps or holding rifle matches... stately Osages with blankets about their waists and hair shaved to crests with scalp locks dangling behind... brightly colored Creeks with broad girdles, green or red leggings, beaded moccasins and heads wrapped about with gaudy-print handkerchiefs... a muscular Negro shoeing a horse while a curious little cur watched with head cocked and one ear erect... a veteran trapper spinning tales of past adventures... a pair of half-bloods making iron spoons for melting lead for bullets.

—Washington Irving describing Three Forks, 1832

Madame Marie-Therese Bourgeois Chouteau, courageous matriarch of the legendary Chouteau dynasty that helped build Oklahoma and the West.

Stepbrothers Auguste and Pierre built one of the mightiest commercial empires in early American history. They founded both the great Missouri cities of St. Louis and Kansas City. The Chouteaus earned a fortune in trade through a Spanish-approved monopoly with the Osage tribe in late-1700s Missouri. They lost that bonanza, ironically, when the France of their heritage regained control of the region from Spain.

Demonstrating the resilience that built their fortune and legend, the Chouteaus persuaded the prominent Osage chief Clermont and his tribal band to move south to the Three Forks area, where some Osages already resided. There, the Chouteaus relocated their western operations and resumed business with the 3,000-strong Osages. Now, however, Pierre's son A. P. Chouteau, a West Point graduate appointed by President Jefferson and a soldier-explorer of the West in his own

Indian Department official Thomas McKenney's famous portrait of the Osage woman Mahongo. A. P. Chouteau fathered one of her children, perhaps this one.

Pierre Chouteau's revered status among the Osages spurred Louisiana Territory Governor Meriwether Lewis, of Lewis and Clark fame, to enlist him to persuade them to meet with the U.S. government and agree to the Osages Treaty of 1808, which they did. The pact required the tribe to vacate most of Missouri and Arkansas in return for numerous concessions and annuities.

The Chouteau Empire

Marie-Therese Bourgeois Chouteau—gritty, Catholic convent-reared matriarch of the clan. New Orleans native and mother of Auguste and Pierre Chouteau.

René Chouteau—French-born New Orleans inn and tavern owner who married then abandoned wife Marie and their son Auguste.

Pierre Laclède—Visionary French-born nobleman, planter, and entrepreneur. Either husband or common-law companion of abandoned Marie Chouteau, he faithfully loved her, son Pierre, and adopted stepson Auguste, and launched Chouteau dynasty.

Auguste Chouteau—son of Marie and René. Senior partner in forging Chouteau dynasty.

Pierre Chouteau—son of Marie Chouteau and either René or Pierre Laclède, younger brother or stepbrother of Auguste, with whom he partnered to build Chouteaus' western empire.

A. P. Chouteau—son of Pierre and French-American Pélagie Kiercereau, focused his energies in present-day Oklahoma and the Southwest.

Pierre, Jr./Cadet—younger brother of A. P., focused his efforts on Missouri River region and became the greatest of all Chouteau businessmen.

A. P. Chouteau, explorer and West Point graduate appointed by President Jefferson, was the preeminent American of commerce in 1820s and 1830s Indian Territory. Courtesy Oklahoma Historical Society.

"Col. (A.P.) Chouteau has long been the great friend and counsellor of the Osage Nation, and the unlimited influence the Chouteaus seem to possess over the nation, together with the assurance of a belief that a treaty could be made, induced the Commissioners to intrust the management of the nation principally to them. Indeed, such is their influence that it would be difficult if not impracticable to make a treaty against their opinion."

—U.S. Secretary of War Lewis Cass, after A. P. persuaded the government not to again force the Osage to move to new lands

"As thou (Pierre) hast, since a long time fed our wives and our children, and that has always been good for us, and that thou has always assisted us with thy advice . . ."

—Osage chiefs, upon granting Pierre twenty-five thousand acres

"(A.P. Chouteau is) better acquainted with the situation of Indian tribes, and of Indian manners, habits, and dispositions, than any man west of the Mississippi River."

—Indian Commissioner and former Governor and U.S. Senator Montfort Stokes

1 ***Mississippi River, 1763***—Laclède's and Auguste's epic journey between New Orleans and St. Louis, through wilderness, rushing currents, and dangerous Indian country.

2 ***St. Louis, 1763***—Chosen by Laclède near confluence of Mississippi and Missouri Rivers, cleared from forest by fifteen-year-old Auguste. Grows into great Western gateway and trading center of American West.

3 ***St. Louis, 1780***—Auguste, Pierre, and three hundred area men successfully repel British and Canadian attack on St. Louis. Chouteau home serves as hospital for wounded.

4 ***Fort Carondolet, 1795***—Auguste and Pierre establish first white settlement beyond Mississippi and Missouri Rivers.

5 ***Three Forks, 1795 or 1796***—Pierre founds first resident white trading post in present-day Oklahoma, on Verdigris River.

6 ***West Point, New York, 1802***—President Jefferson appoints Cadet to first class of United States Military Academy; he graduates four years later.

7 ***Three Forks, 1806***—Upon losing Missouri trading rights, Pierre persuades several thousand Osages to join others already in present-day Oklahoma, and re-establishes Chouteau trade operations on Verdigris River with Osages.

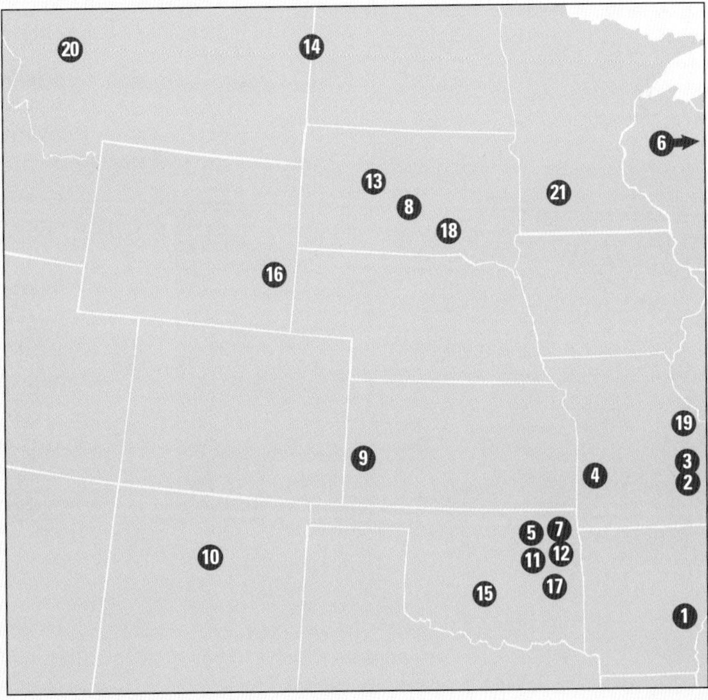

8 ***Great Bend of Missouri River, South Dakota, 1807***—A. P. gun battle with Arikara Indians.

9 ***Chouteau's Island, 1816***—A. P. and fellow hunters battle and defeat large band of attacking Pawnee Indians.

10 ***Santa Fe, 1817***—While trailblazing St. Louis–Santa Fe trade route, A. P. captured, chained in prison for months, nearly executed, and robbed of his fortune by Spanish military officials.

11 ***Three Forks, 1817–1823***—A. P. establishes series of new trading posts, forging cradle of early Oklahoma civilization.

12 ***Grand Saline, 1822***—A. P. builds great log plantation home and becomes first permanent white settler in present-day Oklahoma.

Pennsylvanian George Catlin, one of the foremost American artists of the nineteenth century, gained lasting fame for the eight years he traveled through Indian Territory and the West and painted their epic scenes. Here, he depicts A. P. Chouteau's *Yellowstone* steamboat departing St. Louis on the Missouri River. The *Yellowstone* made history as the first such craft to accomplish the monumental trek up the Missouri to the mouth of the Yellowstone River. Both Chouteau and Catlin rode the *Yellowstone*.

13 ***Pierre, 1832***—Cadet introduces steam travel to Missouri River with his *Yellowstone*, reaches his trading post and his namesake future capital of South Dakota.

14 ***Fort Union, 1833***—*Yellowstone* reaches this frontier post, established in 1828 by Cadet.

15 ***Camp Mason, 1835***—A. P. establishes trading post between present-day Norman and Lexington after serving as U.S. army's interpreter in historic Treaty of Camp Holmes negotiations between southeastern "Civilized" Tribes and Plains Indians.

La Saline, A. P. Chouteau's audacious base of Indian Territory trading operations, forged in the thick of the bloodiest region of the Osage-Cherokee war. It sat beside the Grand River in present-day Mayes County, forty miles north of Three Forks and amidst salt springs. (Sketch by Edward Henderson, *Tulsa World*)

16 ***Fort Laramie, 1836***—Cadet purchases this entrée to fur trading in Rocky Mountain regions of present-day Wyoming and Colorado.

17 ***Fort Gibson, 1837***—A. P. represents U.S. government in important peace treaty between western (Kiowa, Apache, and Tawakoni) and eastern (Creek and Osage) Natives. Treaty assures peace for hunting parties west of Cross Timbers and safety for Santa Fe traders.

18 ***Missouri River, 1830s–1850s***—Chouteaus dominate fur and other trade on America's great northwest waterway.

19 ***Ohio & Mississippi Railroad, 1851***—Cadet co-founds powerful line connecting St. Louis with East.

20 ***Fort Benton, 1859***—Cadet's son Charles pilots steamer *Chippewa* to "innermost port in the world."

21 ***Sioux Indian War, 1862-63***—Charles supplies, supports U.S. Army battling rampaging Sioux Indians.

right, carried forward the family legacy. He towered over all others as the preeminent American of commerce and means in the Indian Territory of the 1820s and 1830s.

Leather-tough, saddle-worn frontiersmen of ingenuity and vision like the Chouteaus, Bogy, and many other early pathfinders and trailblazers of French lineage belied notions held by some modern Americans of inherent weakness in the sons of France. The Chouteaus' feats would have surprised few had they known that Marie-Therese Bourgeois Chouteau, daughter of a French father and Spanish mother and grand matriarch of the entire clan, had overcome abandonment by her husband at age sixteen and raised the children who established the Chouteau dynasty.

The empty, haunting beauty of the Great Salt Plains in which George Sibley made his historic salt discovery. Photo by Ashley Ann Campbell. (www.ashleyannphotography.com)

Commercial Trailblazers

Daring Mississippi businessman Anthony Glass parleyed the favor of the American, Spanish, and Wichita leadership alike to launch a historic trading mission up Red River in 1808. Glass ascended the river farther than had Sparks' armed military expedition. He reached the Twin Villages of the Wichitas, which straddled the Red, one to the north in present-day Jefferson County, Oklahoma, the other across the river in present-day Montague County, Texas.

Glass spent half a year trading horses, hunting for a meteorite of Indian lore, and dealing with the Wichitas and their Comanche allies. When he returned to Natchez, he brought profits and information, too. The latter included Glass's reports of the tyranny imposed on the Wichitas by their longtime enemies, the nearby Osages. That report proved prescient, because within three years, the Osages would drive the Wichitas from their commerce-rich Twin Villages, which they established around 1750.

By 1811 the American government was perceiving the potential natural resource bonanza in what it would soon decree as Indian Territory. This lure, along with peacemaking between the Osages and their tribal opponents from Kansas, prompted the expedition of George Sibley across Missouri, Kansas, Nebraska, and into present-day Oklahoma. A trader and Indian agent rather than a soldier, Sibley led a quest on the Western frontier for salt, coveted commercially as a food preservative. In spectacular fashion, he found it on the Great Salt Plains around present-day Cherokee County, Oklahoma, and the Big Salt Plain around present-day Woods County. "Glistening like a brilliant field of snow in the summer sun," Sibley wrote of the hauntingly beautiful Great Salt Plains expanse.

Intrepid explorer, Indian agent, and college founder George Sibley remains one of the key explorers and statesmen of early nineteenth-century present-day Oklahoma and adjacent territories.

American Explorers of Early Oklahoma

Explorer	Date	Area(s)	Challenges, highlights
James B. Wilkinson	1806	Arkansas, Cimarron, Verdigris Rivers	Freezing cold, illness, ice floes, hunger
Richard Sparks and Thomas Freeman	1806	Red River	Great Raft, Spaniards
Anthony Glass	1808	Red River	Trade with Wichitas
George Sibley	1811	Salt Fork, Cimarron River, Great Salt Plains	Great Salt Plains
Stephen Long	1817	Arkansas, Poteau Rivers	Founded Fort Smith
Thomas Nuttall	1819	Arkansas, Grand, Verdigris, Cimarron, Red, Kiamichi Rivers, Kiamichi Mountains	Wrote earliest scientific book on Oklahoma plants and animals
Stephen Long	1820	Canadian, Arkansas Rivers	Heat, thirst, loss of direction
James Bell	1820	Arkansas River	Thirst, scalding heat, poorly supplied
Thomas James	1821	Arkansas, Cimarron, Verdigris Rivers, Glass Mountains	Comanches, Mexican army, Santa Fe trading
Thomas James	1822	North Canadian River	Keelboat travel, high and low river water, successful trading
William Becknell	1822	Panhandle	Pioneered Santa Fe Trail, thirst, heat, deep mud, hostile Natives

Trouble for Natives

French trappers and traders had traveled the rivers and established commerce with the tribes in present-day Oklahoma from the early 1700s. As the Americans began to compass the area in the early 1800s and root-planting white settlers crosshatched present-day eastern Oklahoma, a separate but converging drama mounted. By the second decade of the nineteenth century, the area appeared destined for statehood, either on its own or as part of the growing Arkansas Territory.

Events back east dictated otherwise. Hundreds of thousands of North American Indians had lived in scattered bands and tribes across the continent as white European Christian civilization began to take root and spread westward from the Atlantic Ocean in the 1600s. In many cases and many places, the Natives existed in peace with white and (usually enslaved) black settlers, often bearing children together and intermarrying. Such was especially the case early in the process of European settlement, when the Puritans, Pilgrims, and others as a whole possessed a keen devotion to the principles and Savior of their Christian faith. This spawned generally superior relations between the settlers and Indians than what occurred as European, then American civilization flooded westward toward the distant Pacific Ocean.

For a jumble of reasons, however, white society—the stronger in force due to greater numbers, superior technology including weapons, and a religion that produced more, better organized, and longer-lasting human life—as a whole gradually determined it would not assimilate the Natives as equal partners. Spurring this rationale were the Americans' and Indians' differing cultures, styles of living, land uses, commercial practices, languages, races, religions, and the tragic dividends of resorting

Chief Clermont of the Osages (?–1828)

This chief of one of the most powerful Native tribes ever to thunder across Oklahoma casts a legacy of enduring fascination and mystery. Gathering at least four wives and thirty-seven children to himself, for many years he engineered sensational coups and military victories over America's most formidable tribes, as well as Spanish, French, and American trappers and hunters who trespassed on Osage lands. It all came at a price, however, as Clermont's Osages suffered many of their own devastating setbacks. They failed to sustain the bursts of prosperity they enjoyed—usually at the expense of other Natives—and wound up with enemy tribes populating their land, economically beholden to the multiplying whites, and in fear and confusion, at last treating away most of that land.

Artist George Catlin was the first non-Native to illustrate American Indians in their home environments. These paintings depict Osage chief Clermont and his wife and child. (www.georgecatlin.org)

to violence to solve problems. For their part, most of the Natives—initially, at least—did not wish assimilation, preferring to be left alone.

War Begets War

The American War of Independence with Britain (1775-1783), wherein most Indians in battleground areas sided with the British, proved to be one enduring issue of conflict between Natives and American settlers. It spawned unprecedented carnage between the two peoples and left enduring bitterness on both sides. That bitterness perpetuated itself amidst the pioneers' westward odyssey like a prairie fire on a scalding dry August day, with the original blaze shooting hot embers forward into other fields, which themselves exploded into new blazes with minimal provocation.

Many Indians in the northern states and territories had fought desperately and bloodily against the Patriots. These tribes lay in the path of the most populous westward white migration. The hatred and violent atrocities generated on both sides by the Revolution contributed to settlers and soldiers combining to muscle these northern tribes west even before most who lived farther south. Most of the northern Indians had retreated toward or across the Mississippi River by the time of the second American conflagration with the British, the War of 1812.

A decades-old agreement between Georgia and the United States triggered growing tension for thousands of Cherokees in that state. The Cherokees were not even a part of the agreement and did not support it. At the time of independence from Britain in 1783, some American states, including Virginia and Georgia, stretched from the Atlantic Ocean westward to the Mississippi River, nearly midway across the North American continent. Within a few years, the American government, pressured by states with more restrictive western boundaries, determined that these sweeping land masses should be split into smaller yet still-sizable states to aid in settlement and efficiency of governance.

In the Compact of 1802, for instance, Georgia agreed to cede the western two-thirds of its lands, which became the states of Mississippi and Alabama. In return, Georgia received $1.25 million from the federal government, as well as the latter's promise to remove the thousands of Cherokees who lived in the state. This foreboding event did not immediately occur, but within two years, Congress followed President Thomas Jefferson's encouragement to pursue the removal of all Native tribes from lands east of the Mississippi River.

"Indian Territory"

Relations between European, then American, civilization and that of the many Indian tribes east of the Mississippi River—north and south—grew tenser as the white (and black) population increased. Despite the continent's vastness, the multiplying numbers of whites increasingly found out that the land they desired was already held, worked, or hunted on by the tribes. Periodic bloodshed between the settlers and the Indians heightened tensions and hatred on both sides.

> *President Jefferson feared the tribes would suffer annihilation unless they could move to their own new lands. He championed present-day Oklahoma as an "Indian Territory" reserved forever for the Natives, and advocated large cash payments to them.*

In the visionary, if controversial, move mentioned a few paragraphs earlier, President Jefferson concluded that the two societies, with their differing cultures, histories, religions, practices, and races, could not co-exist. He feared the Natives would suffer annihilation—through disease, war, and dissipation—rather than assimilation unless they could move to their own new lands. For what Jefferson considered the good of both races in America, he championed the setting aside of present-day Oklahoma as an "Indian Territory" reserved forever for Native settlement and ownership. He also advocated cash payments to the affected tribes for their land, supplies, and travel expenses.

In *A Buffalo Bull Grazing,* George Catlin captures the might, grandeur, and spirit of the West's great native champion. (www.georgecatlin.org)

As the new American nation developed into one of the world's foremost powers in the early 1800s, a gargantuan, well-intentioned, and ultimately tragic effort began to force tribal populations from across the continent—including its western environs—to the new Indian Territory. In turn, the U.S. government ordered the growing white population in the designated enclave to leave and return east to Arkansas or elsewhere.

No-Win Situation

If the Natives' differences with white American culture and history caused problems for them, however, so did their herculean attempts to remedy that problem by acculturating themselves to the swelling United States. Large segments of several prominent southeastern Indian tribes attempted to master the ways of European and American culture, just as early American leaders such as George Washington encouraged them to do.

These five tribes—the Cherokees, Chickasaws, Choctaws, Creeks, and Seminoles—gained the sobriquet of the "Five Civilized Tribes" due to their strong acceptance of most of the key tenets of an American civilization that, by most objective measurements, was succeeding, growing, and thriving far beyond their own. These tenets included its Christian religion, classical Western educational system, social culture, political institutions, and agrarian and other business practices. Famed Oklahoma historian Angie Debo cited the usefulness of the Five Civilized Tribes designation "to distinguish them from their wild neighbors of the plains."

Historian Arrell M. Gibson contrasted the powerful impact of one tribe's mounting mixed-blood population—birthed of enterprising white fathers (Scots, Scots-Irish, Irish, English, French, etc.) and Indian mothers—with full bloods who retained old ways and associations:

> The mixed-bloods (among the tribes), more like their fathers than their mothers, came to adopt an advanced way of living. They developed vast estates, ranches, and businesses in the Cherokee Nation, and became slaveholders. The full bloods continued to live in log cabins, cultivated only a subsistence patch of food crops, raised horses, excelled in the old tribal crafts of hunting, fishing, a life close to nature, and now and then joined a war party for a raid on the encroaching American settlements.

But many of those American settlers, including Georgians furious over the federal government's failure to uphold its end of the Compact of 1802, feared that the Cherokees were growing too "civilized." Why? The Georgians envisioned a large permanent—and sovereign—Indian enclave in the northwest corner of the state. They also worried that Cherokee roads, tolls, and ferries operating beyond the constraints of Georgian laws and regulations would hamper commerce with other states. Also, the tribal chiefs' reluctance to improve the nation's roads angered Georgian leaders. Plus, as earlier mentioned, the federal government had assured

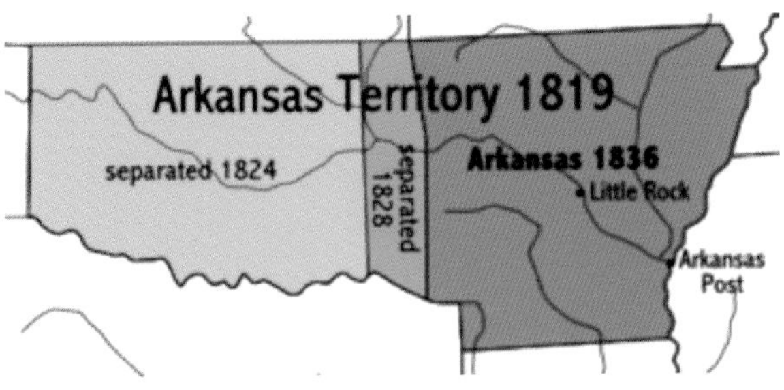

Arkansas Territory in its original form and with two sections split off to form Indian Territory.

the state of the soon departure of the Cherokees. Unfortunately, the tribe itself had no part in that agreement, so they had no intention of fulfilling it.

The Chickasaws, Choctaws, Creeks, and Seminoles faced similar indifference or hostility to their efforts at "civilizing." Whether practicing the old ways or the new, the realization grew among the tribes that they could not win if they remained east of the Mississippi River, no matter what course they pursued.

The Cherokees

The Cherokees stood as one of the largest and probably the most "Americanized" tribe on the continent. A few of their approximately twenty thousand members settled along the Arkansas River in present-day Arkansas as early as 1795. A tough chief named Duwali (or "The Bowl") led this group. Gradually, more migrated into the area. By the end of the first decade of the 1800s, the federal government was actively inducing all Cherokees to move west. It did not, however, specify particular coordinates for the Cherokees' new lands.

At least one additional delegation of Cherokees reconnoitered lands the government offered them in northern and western Arkansas Territory, and more Cherokees agreed to move west. In 1807 American traders in Nachitoches, Louisiana met Cherokees who reported living up Red River to the north, probably in present-day southwest Arkansas. And in 1808 the Osages started complaining about Cherokees hunting on their lands in northern Arkansas and the eastern part of present-day Oklahoma without permission.

Sibley and others had attempted to calm the fierce Osages as they cleared a wide and bloody swath in the wake of their southern migration from Missouri. This tribe of around 4,250 people that included 1,250 warriors raided, plundered, enslaved, and slaughtered their way through one Native group after another in present-day Missouri, Kansas, and Oklahoma. They drove the Caddos, the Wichitas, and others before them (see Chapter 1). Tribes throughout the Southwest feared the Osages.

Soon the Osages did much more than complain about the Cherokees. This time, however, they had

Osage–Cherokee War

The arrival of white-dominated American civilization did not inaugurate encroachment upon and conquest of Indian lands in the American Southwest—or elsewhere on the North American continent. Long before, the tribes themselves threatened, feuded with, stole from, conquered, enslaved, and slaughtered one another. Over a span of centuries, the Osages migrated all the way from the Ohio Valley to present-day Oklahoma, attacking and displacing other tribes as they went. In Oklahoma they violently forced two of the area's earliest inhabitants—the Wichitas and Caddos—south, across Red River.

Claremore Mound, a few miles northwest of present Claremore, where a seven hundred-strong force of Cherokees and their allies decimated the population of an Osage village in the 1817 Battle of Claremore Mound. As so often was the case in the sanguinary Western wars, both between tribes and between Natives and whites, one side attacked when the other's warriors were mostly absent and the women, children, and elderly men present. Far from settling conflicts, such horrors typically sparked reprisals or at least attempted reprisals. Most of the Osage dead and captured at Claremore Mound were women and children. Courtesy Oklahoma Historical Society.

met their equal. The Cherokees who had come west were a smart and rugged lot, and they had no intention of being shoved out of lands for which they had departed their ancient homes and communities and traveled hundreds—in some cases, over a thousand—miles to find. The Cherokees stood their ground and fought back against the Osages, with no less savagery than their opponents.

Plus, these Western Cherokee numbers continued to grow. By 1817 around two thousand lived in Arkansas, a few in present-day eastern Oklahoma. Spurred by federal government treaties that induced the struggling Osages to cede millions of acres of land they controlled in present-day Oklahoma (bounded roughly by the Verdigris River on the west, the present Kansas line on the north, Arkansas Territory on the east, and the Arkansas River on the south) to the U.S., as well as material compensation, the Cherokees' western population swelled to six thousand by 1820.

John Jolly (?–1838)

This shrewd, greathearted man led the Western Cherokees or Old Settlers wing of the tribe through some of their most momentous years. Known in Cherokee as Ahuludegi or Oolooteka, he entered the scroll of history as headman of Cayuga town on Hiwassee Island in present-day southeastern Tennessee upon his older brother Tahlonteeskee's migration west to the Arkansas country in 1809 as a leader of the Old Settlers.

The Creeks

The Cherokees were not the only tribe pressured into moving to the Southwest. To their west and south lay over twenty thousand members of the

Muscogee Confederation of tribes. The powerful Creeks comprised the vast majority of this people, along with smaller numbers of Natchez, Alabamas, Koasatis, and Euchees. Historian Gaston Little recounted the fearsome reputation of the Creeks:

> The Creek men were tall and slender and their women were well-formed and beautiful. Bravery was a characteristic among the Creeks, whose warriors defeated in battle all the surrounding tribes. The Creeks were considered during colonial times to be the most powerful of the southern tribes.

Creeks in a pre-removal Georgia village. Extended families or clans lived in clusters of cabins or teepees.

The Creeks and their related tribes lived across wide expanses of Alabama and southern Georgia. In addition to their martial vigor, they were accomplished farmers and possessed a sophisticated system of governance. On local matters the latter consisted of leaders who each governed a town. A two-house legislative body, meanwhile, governed the nation.

Big trouble loomed, however, both from within and without for the Creeks. Two major factions—the Upper Creeks and Lower Creeks, first so referenced by the English—comprised the Creek Confederation. These names evolved from the brutal Yamasee War of 1715 to 1717 in which the Creeks, Choctaws, and other Southeastern tribes fought a war of extermination with colonial South Carolina, seeking to expel the English from the region. Many of these Indians had earlier conspired with the English in an unholy slave trade involving Indians from weaker tribes. The tainted parties fell out with one another as the colonists grew stronger and wealthier and their Indian collaborators grew increasingly indebted to them. As described by anthropologist Jack M. Schultz, war ensued after English traders also began to enslave their Indian allies and families as payment for their debts.

During the Yamasee War, the Upper Creeks lived mainly to the west of the Chattahoochee River in present-day Alabama and refrained from fighting the Carolinians. The Lower Creeks lived along and to the east of the Chattahoochee and, along with the Yamasees, spearheaded the Indian effort. (Though appearing on maps west and east, respectively, the colonial perspective of the era, with communities narrowly strung along the Atlantic Coast, looked outward to the west from the east. Thus, the more remote western environs then appeared higher, or upper, on maps and the nearer regions lower.)

Creek Civil War

Centered by the 1810s in the Alabama River Valley, the Upper Creeks were led by the determined Opothleyahola. Though not engulfed in the Yamasee War of a century before, they held conservative, traditionalist beliefs with little interest in assimilating into American culture or embracing American institutions. To the east in Georgia along the Chattahoochee, Ocmulgee, and Flint Rivers, lived the Lower Creeks, who had their own strong leader, William McIntosh. Ironically, though desperate foes of the English and proto-Americans in the Yamasee War, they now possessed a more "progressive" philosophy and favored adoption of most American ways, including education, commerce, technology, and the Christian faith.

The philosophical divide between the Upper and Lower Creeks exploded into violent civil war in the Red Stick War (1813–14). Influenced by the great Shawnee chief and war captain Tecumseh, Opothleyahola simultaneously led the Upper Creeks (Red Sticks, for their red war clubs and

"Red Stick" Upper Creeks massacring white settlers, Lower Creeks, and militia in 1813 at Fort Mims, near Mobile, Alabama. Such bloodshed led to the Upper Creeks' crushing defeat by the U. S. and its Indian allies at the Battle of Horseshoe Bend in 1814.

their shamans' supposed magical red sticks) into a disastrous alliance with the British during America's second war with Britain, the War of 1812. The Lower Creeks, meanwhile, sided with the American colonists. This conflict, incited by atrocities such as the Upper Creek massacre of nearly 250 white settlers and Lower Creek men, women, and children at Fort Mims, near Mobile, Alabama, culminated in the Upper Creeks' bloody defeat at the Battle of Horseshoe Bend in 1814. The victorious American forces in that famous fight included General and future President Andrew Jackson, future "Father of Texas" Sam Houston, the Cherokees, the Choctaws, and most of the Lower Creeks.

The 1814 Battle of Horseshoe Bend, the climactic victory of the American military, settlers, and their Creek, Choctaw, and Cherokee allies over defiant "Red Stick" Creeks.

After their landmark pummeling at Horseshoe Bend, the Upper Creeks retreated to a more subtle rejection of American ways. But their anger and bitterness at those—and the Lower Creeks support of them—simmered, to flash into bloodshed again later. The United States government did more than simmer. They forced the Creeks to cede twenty-two million acres of land in Alabama and Georgia and then pressured them to move west.

> *The Creeks voted in a death penalty for any tribesman who attempted to sell Creek land to white settlers.*

All this triggered long-term as well as short-term consequences for the tribe. It turned the majority of Creeks so strongly against further land cessions, including an exchange for lands out west, that they determined to give up no more land to the Americans. They also voted in a death penalty for any tribesman who attempted to sell Creek land to white settlers. Sadly, opinions on the land issue were not unanimous within the tribe.

The Choctaws

Probably the most populous tribe on the entire continent in the nineteenth century, the talented and powerful Choctaws excelled as farmers, hunters, and diplomats alike. Like some other southeastern tribes such as the Cherokees, the Choctaws increasingly adapted the practices and institutions of Western Christendom, partly to forestall their removal from their ancestral homelands. Around twenty-two thousand Choctaws spread from the middle of the Mississippi River Valley southward to the Gulf of

Mexico at the beginning of the 1800s. They traded and conversed effectively with the European powers who frequented the Gulf ports of the area.

The Choctaws organized their country into three regions, each governed by a principal chief, similar to a nation's president. One chief, Pushmataha, gained renown as a statesman, commercial visionary, and warrior. As shrewd and eloquent as he was rugged and brave, he proved to be the match of American leaders such as James Monroe, Andrew Jackson, and John Calhoun, as well as other tribal leaders such as the Shawnee Tecumseh. He sparred with all of them over matters of supreme importance to both the Choctaws and the United States. A national Choctaw council composed of other leaders from throughout the tribe, similar to a Congress, also carried authority.

The Choctaws—notably Pushmataha—demonstrated their hunting prowess and physical vigor with journeys as far west as present-day Oklahoma, hundreds of miles from their Mississippi homeland. Two developments winnowed out the game population of the Gulf States and forced these long and dangerous treks. One was the multiplying American population in the South, the other the burgeoning fur trade with Europe. In present-day Oklahoma, the Choctaw hunters not only slew great hauls of game, they clashed with Osages, Caddos, and other tribes residing in the area, as well as American merchants who traded with them.

Like the other southeastern "civilized" tribes, the Choctaw advances in Western culture failed to prevent growing pressure from the American people and their government for the tribe's removal to the west. To the Natives' surprise, they would face new chapters of oppression even after they made those treks.

The Seminoles

This tribe originated in the early 1700s from Yamasee and Lower Creeks who migrated into northern and central Spanish Florida following their defeat by the South Carolinians in the Yamasee War. Military confrontations with white settlers as well as dwindling game for food perpetuated this exodus throughout the eighteenth century. The emigrants grew increasingly autonomous from the

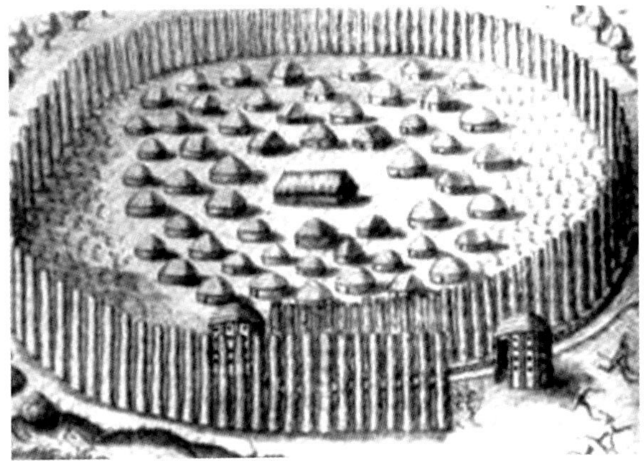

An early 1800s Seminole village in Florida, prior to the tribe's wars with the United States and the exile of most of them to Indian Territory.

Lower Creeks. Gradually, they took on the name "Seminole," meaning "wild," "runaways," or "separatists," which reflected their watershed departure.

Later in the 1700s, the Seminoles welcomed black slaves escaping Spanish masters into their company. Though apparently retaining their servile status, these descendants of Africa lived in communities near the Seminole villages, grew into a significant component of the tribe, and received treatment as virtual equals. Following the American defeat of the Creeks at Horseshoe Bend, more Creeks headed to Florida to join the Seminoles. This time, Upper—not Lower—Creeks, pro-British "Red Stick" veterans of the War of 1812, comprised the majority of the migrants.

The war refugees ballooned the Seminole population from thirty-five hundred to six thousand. By 1815 these disparate companies comprised a formidable though still small nation. Their resistance to removal from their Florida homelands, however, casts a large legacy in American history books. Hunting on lands in that state as well as southern Georgia and Alabama, they centered their communities in Florida and lived as town-dwellers. Unlike the other southeastern tribes, they eschewed farming.

The Seminoles' initial significant conflict as a tribe with the United States occurred in 1817 to 1818 with the first of a series of "Seminole Wars." White Georgian slave owners, whose major (and Constitutionally protected) financial capital in the economic system of the time consisted of their

Mixed-Blood Family Names

Cherokee—Rogers, Adair, Vann, Chisholm, Ross, Downing

Chickasaw—Colbert, Adair, McIntosh, Kemp, James, Cheadle, Sealy, Gunn, McLish, McGee, Allen, Pickens, Bynum, McLaughlin, Love

Choctaw—Juzon, Cravat, LeFlore, Durant, Jones, McCurtain

Creek—Grayson, Stidham, McIntosh, Porter

black slaves, complained to the U.S. government about runaways among these folk living with the Seminoles. General Andrew Jackson, in the latest of a long series of battles (violent as well as non-violent) with Natives, led an American army into Florida to retrieve the escapees, burning down a Seminole town in the process.

As they did in many other places, from the time the United States purchased Florida from Spain in 1819, American settlers began swarming onto the tribe's land, settling it, and then urging the U.S. government to remove the resident tribes. In 1823 the powers in Washington gained the Seminoles' agreement to the Treaty of Tampa, which required the tribe's move south to the swampy inland Everglades region east of Tampa.

Even this did not work, because the Indians accused whites of harassment and the whites accused the Seminoles of theft, property destruction, and violence. The whites demanded the tribe's relocation to Indian Territory. The Seminoles' toughness, geography, history, leadership, and sense of place and other cultural traditions would generate a less than cordial response from them toward federal soldiers' efforts to force them west.

The Chickasaws

The power of this tribe, too, far exceeded its small numbers. The Chickasaws included at most forty-five hundred men, women, and children during the time of their southeastern residence and interaction with Europeans and white and black Americans. Like the Choctaws, Creeks, and Seminoles, the Chickasaws spoke a Muskhogean language. Their homeland included western Kentucky and Tennessee, northern Mississippi, and northwestern Alabama.

The Chickasaws were at least as closely related to the Choctaws as the Seminoles were to the Creeks. The Chickasaws and Choctaws formed a single tribe until sometime prior to Spaniard Hernando DeSoto's 1540 discovery of them. The tribe's very name probably means "they left as a tribe not a very great while ago." But the Chickasaws possessed a much keener commitment to the art of war than the Choctaws, and they were feared by the latter (despite the Choctaws' numerical superiority), other tribes in their region, and even eventually Europe's most powerful nations.

As Britain and France competed for control of North America—and in particular the lower Mississippi River and Valley and the Gulf ports to the south—in the early 1700s, the French cultivated the Choctaws as native allies, and the British did the same with the Chickasaws. So troublesome did the Chickasaws become to French efforts in the region, their governor of Louisiana declared in 1735 that the tribe's "entire destruction . . . becomes every day more necessary to our interests and I am going to exert all diligence to accomplish it."

From 1720 to 1763 several French armies marched into Chickasaw country from southern Louisiana and Mississippi to conquer the tribe. Choctaws, white militia, and black slaves supported the armies. All these efforts failed, and the tribe remained unvanquished when France surrendered its claims on the continent to the victorious British after losing the Seven Years War—including its North American theater, the French and Indian War—to them.

Horatio Cushman in his 1899 chronicle *History of the Choctaw, Chickasaw, and Natchez Indians,* noted how, contrary to the Chickasaws' long conflict with the French European powers, "neither the Choctaws nor Chickasaws ever engaged in war against the American people, but always stood as their faithful allies."

Plains Tribes

Though perhaps not all of it lay in the "Great American Desert" invoked by contemporary

George Catlin's early-1830s depiction of a *Comanche Village, Women Dressing Robes and Drying Meat* as they no doubt would have appeared just a few years before as well, in the 1820s. (http://www.georgecatlin.org)

A series of important American explorations compassed present-day Oklahoma in the late 1810s and early 1820s. Natural and manmade dangers alike lurked in every direction throughout the rough country.

Modern-day place names such as their large namesake city in southern Kansas, the Wichita Mountains near Lawton in southwest Oklahoma, and the city of Wichita Falls across Red River in north Texas indicate the tribes' path.

American explorers and maps, the western half of early eighteenth-century present-day Oklahoma still hosted few people. Most numerous were likely the aforementioned nomadic bands of Comanches and Kiowas who had migrated from the west over the previous few decades. Though their impact on the region would grow through the 1800s, already they occasionally clashed with the Osages, Apaches, and others.

Meanwhile, the Wichitas' long dismal retreat from the Osages southward toward Texas continued.

Exploring Farther

Neither cold nor heat, drought nor flood, dangerous Indians nor hostile Spaniards could stem the surge of American merchants, scientists, adventurers, missionaries, and soldiers who persevered across the rivers, then the lands of present-day Oklahoma. While the imperial powers of Europe drained each other's

Scientist Describes the Cherokees

Among the lasting scientific and historic contributions of famed American botanist Thomas Nuttall during his trip to Oklahoma in 1819 is his description of the sophisticated and advanced Cherokees he met as he traveled the Arkansas River:

> *Both banks of the river, as we proceeded, were lined with the houses and farms of the Cherokee, and though their dress was a mixture of indigenous and European taste, yet in their houses, which are decently furnished, and in their farms, which were well fenced and stocked with cattle, we perceive a happy approach toward civilization. Their numerous families, also, well fed and clothed, argue a propitious progress in their population. Their superior industry either as hunters or farmers proves the value of property among them, and they are no longer strangers to avarice and the distinctions created by wealth. Some of them are possessed of property to the amount of many thousands of dollars, have houses handsomely and conveniently furnished, and their tables spread with our dainties and luxuries.*

Thomas Nuttall

blood and treasure, or sank into non-productive lassitude, the young American nation born of them vibrated with energy and ambition. Indeed, many people would have many ideas for Indian Territory.

Scores of daring American entrepreneurs yearned to reach the bountiful trading hub of Santa Fe to the west of Texas, but well-armed Spanish troops under orders from their distant government prevented that, at the point of the bayonet when necessary. It was no place for the faint of heart or the uncertain of aim. Many of the keenest observations and most notable discoveries by Americans were accomplished by private citizens such as scientists or merchants, rather than those in government service.

One of the most intrepid American explorers of early Oklahoma, though, was U.S. Army Engineer Stephen Long. As the Osage–Cherokee war raged in 1817, the War Department commissioned him to choose a location on the Arkansas River for a fort to help calm that vicious feud, as well as to protect the American settlers beginning to enter the area. Long established Fort Smith, later one of the largest cities in Arkansas.

Then, encouraged by the Adams–Onis Treaty signed between the United States and Spain, a series of important American explorations trekked through present-day Oklahoma in the late 1810s and early 1820s. Natural and manmade dangers alike lurked in every direction throughout the rough country.

Long's Epic Journey

Two years after his first Oklahoma adventure, esteeming his toughness and coolness of mind in dangerous situations, the War Department sent Long west on an even more daunting mission: finding the elusive headwaters of the Arkansas and Red Rivers. Numerous previous American expeditions had failed to do so. Also plagued throughout the expedition by supply shortages due to the financial Panic of 1819, Long trekked across the Great Plains to the Rocky Mountains, then in the summer of 1820 detached Captain John H. Bell and a dozen men to follow the Arkansas back to Fort Smith.

Stephen Harriman Long, early American explorer of present-day Oklahoma.

This group, which included the father of American zoology, Thomas Say, faced its own desperate odyssey, braving thirst and scorching heat before reaching their destination. Say suffered additional heartache as deserting soldiers stole five journals in which he had painstakingly compiled vast amounts of eyewitness data about newly christened Indian Territory's people, plants, animals, geography, and minerals. Forging on from memory and the remnants of his expedition writings, he managed to publish a book chronicling the Bell expedition.

Long, meanwhile, rode south through the Rockies, east through New Mexico, and across the breadth of present-day Oklahoma. Excitement filled

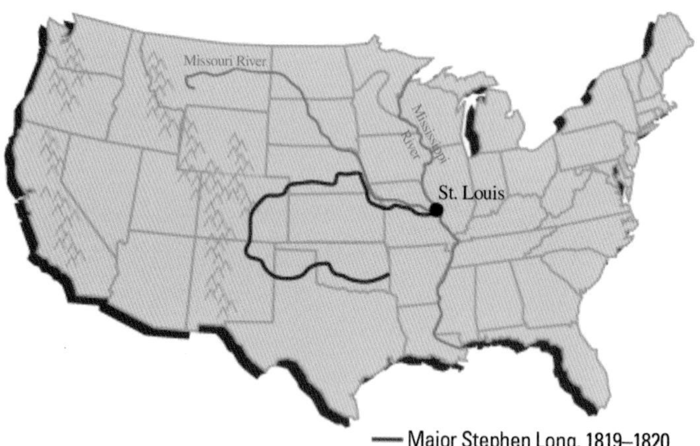

Stephen Long's great 1820 expedition through present-day Oklahoma continued his preceding year's exploration of the Missouri River. The remarkable pathfinder seemed to find a way to answer every one of the many formidable challenges that arose with ingenuity and resourcefulness.

Stephen Long's fabled treks into present-day Oklahoma landed him in such dramatic situations as a Kaw Indian war dance in present-day eastern Kansas (left) and the Rocky Mountain foothills wilderness in present-day eastern Colorado (above). (Courtesy Thomas Gilcrease Institute of American History and Art)

him and his men when they found a wide stream in the Texas Panhandle they believed to be the head of Red River. Only when the part-river, part-creek, part-desert bed he followed across Indian Territory merged with the Arkansas did he realize with shock that he had found the Canadian and not the Red. It was too late in the season to turn back, so he continued on to Fort Smith.

Long accomplished the greatest exploration and chronicling of the future Sooner State of that generation, and next to the Lewis and Clark expedition, the mightiest such feat in American history.

Still, Long accomplished the greatest exploration and chronicling of the future Sooner State of that generation, and next to the Lewis and Clark expedition, the mightiest such feat in American history. Plus, he left vivid comments of what he saw. His views, in fact, are credited for the development of the official proclamation of present-day Oklahoma as the Indian Territory reserve for Native tribes around the continent that very year. He famously declared it "an unfit residence for any but a nomad population," described its "desolate sands," and praised it as "the Providential preventative to the American people spreading across too vast an area." Maps of present-day Oklahoma and the Southern Plains began labeling them as "The Great American Desert."

Noted botanist Edwin James accompanied Long. His journals bring to life the sights, sounds,

Stephen Long and Edwin James Ride the Canadian

A prairie dog digging in a "village" undoubtedly like that seen by botanist and explorer Edwin James.

"We had travelled more than one hundred and fifty miles along the bed of this river, without once having found it to contain running water. We had passed the mouths of many large tributaries, but they, like the river itself were beds of naked sand."

> *[Present-day Oklahoma and the American Southwest] were providentially placed to keep the American people from ruinous diffusion... We have little apprehension of giving too unfavorable an account of this portion of the country. Though the soil is in some places fertile, the want of timber, of navigable streams, and of water for the necessities of life, render it an unfit residence for any but a nomad population. The traveler who shall at any time have traversed its desolate sands, will, we think, join us in the wish that this region may forever remain the unmolested haunt of the native hunter, the bison, and the jackall.*
>
> **—Edwin James, botanist accompanying American explorer Stephen H. Long**

and life of Long's long-ago expedition. With his own eyes James witnessed scenes ranging from bald eagles to pelicans to wild horses to a square-mile-large prairie dog colony. As recounted in W. David Baird and Danny Goble's *The Story of Oklahoma,* he also wrote of the constant bedeviling presence of seed ticks in the lives of Oklahoma explorers:

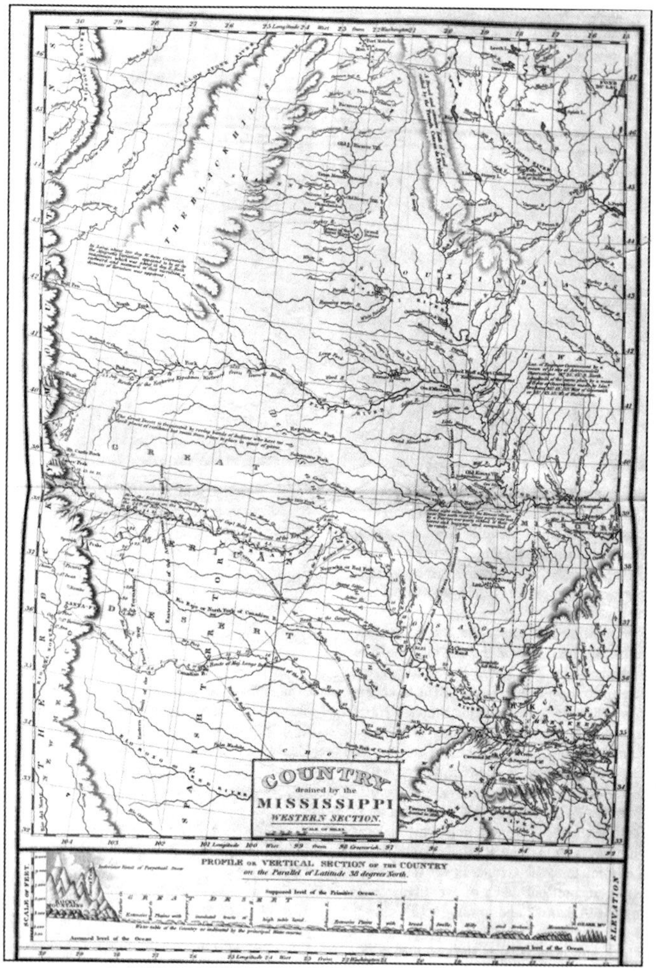

> The bite is not felt until the insect has had time to bury the whole of his beak, and in the case of the minute and most troublesome species, nearly his whole body seems hid under the skin. Where he fastens himself with such tenacity... he will sooner suffer his head and body to be dragged apart than relinquish his hold.

Stephen Long's map of the Great Plains, clearly including his famed "Great American Desert," otherwise known as present-day western Oklahoma. (Courtesy Thomas Gilcrease Institute of American History and Art)

Adams–Onís Treaty

This 1819 agreement, labored over for four years by the United States and Spain, defused serious tensions on several geographic fronts between the expanding new North American country and its European counterpart, whose imperial power was fading. Spain ceded Florida to the U.S., partly to keep it out of French hands, and the U.S. recognized Spanish claims to the land comprising its Texas province and west to California and the Pacific Ocean.

More significant to Oklahoma history, Adams–Onís codified the Sabine River as the eastern boundary of Texas with America's new Louisiana Territory, and Red River as the northern one with Indian Territory drawn from Louisiana. These mandates cleared the way for Americans, whether explorers, military expeditions, scientists, or otherwise, to travel, explore, and even settle in these environs without any threat from Spanish soldiers. They also initiated the official designation in 1820 of "Indian Territory," a large reserve to relocate the Native tribes from back east that Americans grew increasingly determined to have out of their way.

The 1819 Adams–Onís Treaty delivered Spanish Florida to the United States, while recognizing Spain's rule over present-day southwest United States, other than Oklahoma and most of Red River. Only the present-day Panhandle of the state fell outside of the Louisiana Purchase/Missouri Territory and under Spanish rule. Adams–Onís proved pivotal to the subsequent southeastern Indian removals and settling of Indian Territory.

Adams–Onís, deriving its name from U.S. Secretary of State and future President John Quincy Adams and the Spanish Minister to the United States Don Luis de Onís, achieved another important American objective. It gave the U.S. ownership of the Sabine, Red, and Arkansas Rivers in their entirety where they separated American- and Spanish-claimed territory, rather than splitting the rivers as treated boundaries normally did. American eagerness for this stemmed from earlier problems with Spain concerning the previously split Mississippi River. American ownership of Red River would figure in future disputes over oil between not-always-friendly Red River neighbors Oklahoma and Texas.

> *For the southeastern Indians, Adams-Onis meant the United States could move toward removing the tribes from the westward tide of American settlement.*

For the southeastern Indians, Adams–Onís held a different set of portents. Not least, it meant the United States could now proceed unfettered by interference from European powers toward removing the tribes from the westward tide of American settlement.

Secretary of State and future sixth President John Quincy Adams. He spearheaded the Adams–Onís Treaty, pivotal to the subsequent Indian removals and settling of Indian Territory.

3

1820s
Indian Territory

Oklahoma artist Mike Wimmer's *Mahongo at the Court of Charles X in France*, a symbolic and heartrending depiction of the decline of Osage sovereignty in the face of American pioneer migration. A French explorer tricked the Osage Mahongo (Mihanga, Mohongo)—by whom A. P. Chouteau fathered a daughter—and several other tribal members into accompanying him, supposedly to Washington, D.C. Instead, he took them to France, where they were coerced to perform native dances in a Wild West show that traveled across Europe. Their popularity landed them before King Charles X of France. They later suffered abandonment, privation, and several deaths. The intervention of a French Catholic bishop and the American Revolutionary War hero Lafayette finally returned them home. Used with permission from the Oklahoma State Senate Collection and the artist. Courtesy Oklahoma State Senate Historical Preservation Fund, a project of Charles Ford.

1820	U.S. Government establishes Indian Territory
1820	Choctaw Treaty of Doak's Stand
1821	Union Christian Mission established
1821	Sequoyah completes Cherokee syllabary
1822	William Becknell establishes Santa Fe Trail
1825	Creek leader William McIntosh killed
1825	Osage Treaty with U.S.
1826	Lower Creeks move to Indian Territory
1827	Cherokee Constitution completed
1828	*Cherokee Phoenix* begins publication
1828	Cherokees elect John Ross Principal Chief

Halt! Tecumseh, listen to me. You have come here, as you have often gone elsewhere, with a purpose to involve peaceful people in unnecessary trouble with their neighbors.

—Pushamataha

By 1820, multiple historical currents were already in play that would chart the course of present-day Oklahoma for the remainder of the nineteenth century and beyond. American territorial annexation and exploration were setting the stage for the forcible removal of numerous Indian tribes from the southeastern U.S. to the newly designated Indian Territory. Other tribes faced simultaneous loss or reduction of lands they already controlled in the territory. Meanwhile, the southeastern tribes faced mounting internal conflict over how or whether to cooperate with their looming removal.

All the while, remarkable men and women from the various cultures rose up to accomplish great deeds. Defying a withering phalanx of opposition from Spanish, Mexican, and Indian warriors, heat, cold, drought, wind, and the vast prairie itself, lionhearted white explorers carved out historic trading routes across present-day Oklahoma and the Southwest. They also established mutually beneficial trading relationships with and Christian missionary efforts among the Natives of the region.

Indian actions took many forms. Some Natives cooperated with the surging tide of American civilization, even leveraging events to their own advantage. Others hesitated or resisted, defending their culture, heritage, and homeland. Some of these engaged in conflict, sometimes violent, with fellow tribesmen. Still others retreated from American society, with varying degrees of success.

African-Americans, most of them slaves, found themselves caught up in the turbulent fortunes of the dominant white and tribal societies around them. They grew in population and labored for a quality of life and future that would unfold slowly for them in America.

Searching for Santa Fe

With well-known explorers such as A. P. Chouteau and Peter Baum among those thrown in prison by Spain for seeking trade in Santa Fe without the

Depew native and Yuchi Indian Wayne Cooper's *The Santa Fe Trail*, portraying the oldest and longest commercial thoroughfare across the Great Plains. Running nearly eight hundred miles from near Kansas City to Santa Fe, New Mexico, its Cimarron Route, depicted here by Cooper, provided the most direct route. Freight wagon traffic powered by mule and oxen traversed it for a half-century beginning in 1822, crossing the present-day Oklahoma Panhandle's Cimarron County near Wolf Mountain, Flag Springs, Cold Springs, and Camp Nichols. Courtesy Oklahoma State Senate Historical Preservation Fund, Inc. and Wayne Cooper.

permission (and bribery?) of the Spanish government, the dangers of the alluring Southwestern trading hub were well known. The Adams-Onis Treaty, however (Chapter 2), opened the way in 1821 for exploration and travel in present-day Oklahoma without any challenge from the Spanish. The revolution of Spain's North American colony Mexico, begun in 1810, also ended in 1821, with military victory over its European overlords. These events changed everything. The Mexicans immediately adopted a much friendlier attitude than Spain toward both American settlement in Texas and trade in Santa Fe.

Hearing through Baum, who escaped from his Spanish prison, that change might be in the wind, two parties set out for Santa Fe from the Three Forks area in September 1821. One, headed by the Three Forks leaders Nathaniel Pryor of Lewis and Clark Expedition fame and Hugh Glenn, trekked northwest through present-day Kansas and into modern Colorado. So successful was their hunting, trapping, and trading haul, they never reached New Mexico. Instead, the twenty men headed back across the plains to St. Louis to market their haul, before returning to present-day Oklahoma.

Meanwhile, veteran plainsman Thomas James, whose eleven-man party originated in St. Louis, followed the Cimarron River into western Indian Territory. They took a variety of foodstuffs and supplies to trade. As they neared the "Cimarron Country" of the present-day state's northwest and

Panhandle, the journey grew daunting. They sustained life from the bodily components of the country's American bison, better known as buffalo, the term this work shall use for the animal. In danger of dying from thirst, James and his men drank the blood of buffalo. Threatened with starvation, they burned buffalo chips as cooking fuel.

The James party crossed paths with both Comanches and Mexican soldiers, the latter encouraging them on toward Santa Fe. The revolting Mexicans had wrested control of the city from the Spanish and welcomed Americans there for business. James and his men obliged, in the Santa Fe town square, no less. They conducted extensive trade and then returned to Missouri the next spring. The potential of Indian Territory itself impressed James enough that he mounted another expedition the following year, 1822. Traveling by keelboat, horse, and canoe, they generated enough trading business in future Canadian and Blaine Counties that they could not tote it all back to St. Louis with them.

Father of Santa Fe Trail

When the James party hit Santa Fe, they learned that someone else had beaten them there by only a few days: the first successful American trader in the former Spanish-ruled New Mexican settlements along the Rio Grande River. Another Virginian and War of 1812 veteran, Captain William Becknell, had crossed the Great Plains from Missouri and inaugurated his own trading enterprise in Santa Fe.

Becknell, himself a leather-tough plainsman, also launched another Santa Fe expedition in 1822. Mocked and ridiculed across the western frontier, he was also nearly bankrupt. Demonstrating the intrepid audacity in the face of desperate odds that it took to win a continent, he determined this time to ramrod an entire wagon train across the plains, desert, and Indian Country. Becknell rolled out of Arrow Point, Missouri in May with his rough-hewn peers, baptized as the "Caravan of Death"—three large wagons, two dozen oxen, and twenty-one men.

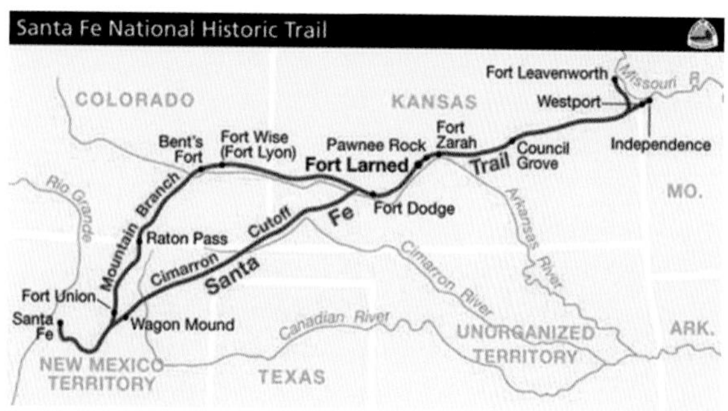

William Becknell blazes the Santa Fe Trail in 1822.

Becknell's epic quest was roundly pronounced a suicide mission, considering the fearsome natural elements, deprivation, Osages, and Comanches that awaited him along the trail. But the shrewd Becknell knew that wondrous opportunity lay in wait in the Southwest. He also realized he could not capitalize on it without sufficient goods to trade, far more than could be loaded onto a few pack horses or mules.

No sooner had the echoes of laughter subsided behind him when Becknell and his wagon train confronted a party that saw no humor at all in his venture—the Osage Indians. Surrounded by as many as a thousand of them, he coolly ordered his men to keep their rifles—for which the Osages had already developed a healthy respect—in view but to hold their fire. Knowing his adversary's ways, he offered items in peaceful trade, which seemed preferable to the Osages to taking more and facing the long guns of the steely-eyed American frontiersmen. The warriors accepted Becknell's deal, and the wagon train proceeded.

Daring Quest

The Osages proved to be far from the worst of the Caravan of Death's challenges. Beginning in western Kansas, bands of armed Comanches—even more feared than the Osages—shadowed it, looming just beyond reach and wearing the Becknell party's nerves to a frazzle. West of present-day Dodge City, Becknell, knowing the land and astutely assessing the most direct route to Santa Fe from the Arkansas River as southwest by way of the Cimarron River, turned his column in that direction. What the Virginian did not know was that therein lay a new challenge—the fabled Jornada, a desert expanse between the rivers that presaged the harrowing terrain just beyond in the present-day Oklahoma and Texas Panhandles.

The Cimarron Cutoff through present-day Cimarron County that William Becknell and his men and other pioneers after them braved. It was not too empty to threaten them with scalding heat, bone-piercing cold, wild animals, thirst, hunger, and hostile Natives. Photo Alvin Rucker. Courtesy Oklahoma Historical Society.

After just two days, the party had consumed its water. They killed their dogs, cut off the ears of their mules to drink their blood, and then did the same with their oxen. Mirages of crystal water appeared across the terrible sands, and some of the men staggered toward them, screaming. Becknell pursued these crazed unfortunates and managed to corral some of them.

> *Gasping with thirst in the scalding sun, Becknell could not rise from the ground. Then he saw a herd of buffalo seeming to rise from the ground, yards away. He managed to shoulder his rifle, fire, and drop a beast with a shot through the heart.*

Finally, near the Oklahoma Panhandle, the day of death seemed to have arrived. Animals and men alike collapsed. Gasping with thirst in the scalding sun, Becknell himself could not rise from the ground. Then he saw what he feared was another mirage—a herd of buffalo seeming to rise up out of the ground maybe sixty feet away. He managed to shoulder his rifle, fire, and drop a beast with a shot through the heart.

Knowing that water must lie somewhere in the vicinity for bison to roam it, he cut open the beast's stomach and found it tanked with water. Becknell drank his fill and made sure his surviving comrades did as well. Then he set out to find the source of the water and soon reached the Cimarron. Delivered from the brink of death by buffalo, as was the Thomas James expedition, Becknell blazed the Cimarron Cutoff, a more direct route to Santa Fe through present-day Cimarron County. He led the remnants of his wagon train into Santa Fe a month later.

Thus was first established the great trail so instrumental in the spreading of the American nation across the continent that would forge it as a mighty people. Long afterwards, one survivor of the wagon train of William Becknell would remember that providential buffalo whom the Father of the Santa Fe Trail dropped on the burning sands of the Jornada: "Nothing ever passed my lips that gave me such exquisite delight as my drink of that filthy water."

American Empire

For many long years now, even centuries, little dispute has existed over the wisdom and benefits of building a great continental American nation. But the concept of "Manifest Destiny" did not always

The dramatic Three Sisters rock formation, near the old Cimarron Cutoff of the Santa Fe Trail in present-day Cimarron County. Photo David G. Fitzgerald

grip the collective mind of the American people as both a right and a responsibility from God to tame, take, and develop an enormous continent, as well as exert a strong—even pervasive—influence upon the affairs of the entire world. Long before that idea gained major support around the 1840s, intense debate raged over how large the American Republic should grow.

At the dawn of America's national history, Thomas Jefferson, James Madison, and other Founding Fathers supported the notion, if not of an empire, at least of a large and diverse republic. Madison, for instance, wrote that small republics faced the risk of powerful local "factions" dominating their communities. Spreading a country's population, he contended, would serve as an antidote to that danger by "extending the sphere" and hampering one faction or cabal from wresting too much power and authority over the government.

Jefferson and others believed America must claim or acquire the sprawling lands stretching forth from its original colonies thousands of miles to the Pacific Ocean. This idea seems to have maintained, if not expanded in, acceptance through most of American history. On the other hand, most of those Founders rejected the notions of seeking other lands to conquer or plunder, as well as centralized economic and political control over their own nation.

In recent years an increasing company of Americans has begun to question the advisability of such a far-flung colossus as the modern United States, divided by increasing and apparently irremediable social, political, and economic differences

Oklahoma artist Mike Wimmer's *Nathaniel Pryor and Sam Houston at Three Forks* presents two larger-than-life builders of early Oklahoma conducting trade at the end of the 1820s or beginning of the 1830s on a flatboat along the Three Forks, where the Grand, Verdigris, and Arkansas Rivers merge. The hub of early Oklahoma civilization and riverboat traffic west of the Mississippi, Three Forks' rivers were important for the export of furs, salt, and tobacco to St. Louis, Arkansas, New Orleans, and beyond. Courtesy Oklahoma State Senate Historical Preservation Fund, Inc. and Mike Wimmer.

and problems. Many of these foes would contend not that wise leaders and good government are integral to the success and prosperity of such a nation, but that history and human nature both teach that no leaders or government are able, in the long view, to happily steer so large a nation's course. They would hearken back at least as far as the great Athenian philosopher Aristotle, who contended for the virtues of small and constitutionally guided republics.

Nathaniel Pryor (c. 1775–1831)

Rugged frontiersman Nathaniel Pryor stands as a giant of early eighteenth-century Oklahoma history. Tall and physically vigorous, sagacious in judgment under duress, and cool and intrepid in countless incidents of combat and other mortal danger, his life and legacy confirm the existence of the early American trailblazer who embodied those attributes. But Pryor was much more—diplomat, soldier, trader, merchant, explorer,

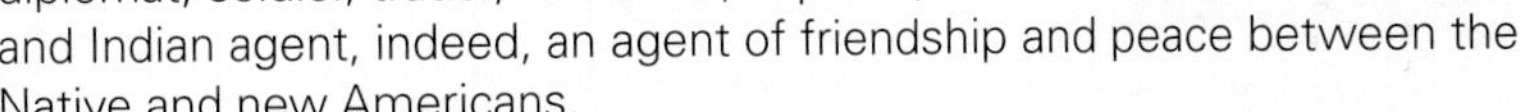

and Indian agent, indeed, an agent of friendship and peace between the Native and new Americans.

They could point as well, more recently, to the beliefs of other American Founding Fathers, including Patrick Henry. Their views were articulated by the arrestingly prophetic words of the pseudonymous American anti-federalist Brutus, who wrote in 1787:

> A free republic cannot succeed over a country of such immense extent, containing such a number of inhabitants . . . as that of the whole United States . . . . In so extensive a republic, the great officers of government would soon become above the control of the people, and abuse their power to the purpose of aggrandizing themselves, and oppressing them . . . .The command of all the troops . . . the appointment of officers, the power of pardoning offences, the collecting of all the public revenues, and the power of expending them, with a number of other powers, must be lodged and exercised . . . in the hands of a few. When these are attended with great honor and emolument, as they always will be in large states, so as . . . to be proper objects for ambitious and designing men, such men will use the power . . . to (gratify) their own interest and ambition, and it is scarcely possible, in a very large republic, to call them to account for their misconduct, or to prevent their abuse of power.

> *(Designing men) will use the power, when they have acquired it, to the purposes of gratifying their own interest and ambition, and it is scarcely possible, in a very large republic, to call them to account for their misconduct, or to prevent their abuse of power.*
>
> **—"Brutus"**

Madison and Brutus both well warned of the challenges and dangers inherent to human government, albeit on different scales. Would it be too harsh to suggest that Madison's concerns of powerful local factions have often played out through the state government of Oklahoma, while Brutus' fears of powerful officials above the control of the people appear almost synonymous with the federal government that has emerged over the United States?

The Providential View

A long and providential view of human history demands a further word, one rarely offered by histories of the country and certainly not supported by most modern Americans, even professing Christians. It presumes a Christ-centered worldview and biblical approach to all earthly matters. It suggests that God has determined to spread the spiritually saving knowledge of and belief in His Son and fellow deity Jesus Christ "to every nation, tribe, tongue, and

The Pilgrims Landing on Plymouth Rock, 1620, by Charles Lucy. The Pilgrims and Puritans who founded Christian civilization in America aimed for nothing less than building a "city set on a hill," spiritually speaking and based on the Holy Scriptures, that would bless its own inhabitants and all the nations of the world. Despite all their enemies, their legacy endures.

people." Just as He ordained or allowed—depending on one's theological perspective—the enslaving and shipping of millions of black Africans to the Western Hemisphere where amidst many sorrows they heard that Christian gospel (literally, "good news" or the "announcing of salvation") they would likely not have heard in Africa, so did He also bring the same message to the American Indians.

Were the individual bearers of that message faultless in their embodiment of their religion and their treatment of the Indians or Africans—or the Mexicans, Chinese, Irish, or Italians—and their descendants? No, and much wrong, bloodshed, and woeful consequence ensued and continues today. Yet does the Christian Bible claim that God has ever used sinless vessels to accomplish His work? Not as evidenced either by His chosen people of old, Israel, or the greatest individual heroes of the Christian faith, whether they were Moses, David, Peter or Paul. But the history of the world evidences that those who oppose the cross of Christ—including those who defy the laws of God while claiming to defend them—are themselves opposed by God, with potentially catastrophic consequences for themselves and those in their charge.

Among the many attributes of God identified by the Bible is impartiality, a refusal to show favoritism to one person or group over another. Thus, persons of any race and ethnicity are imperiled when they ignore and defy God. Those, meanwhile, who claim and abide in Him with humble hearts, whatever their people group, are promised matchless blessing—though often in manners other than mankind would expect—in both this world and the next. Though the Natives, including those who came to present-day Oklahoma, sadly suffered at the hands of many of the "Christ-bearers" whom they encountered, many of them received the wondrous gift of spiritual forgiveness; God's earthly protection, provision, and blessing; and eternal life and joy in His presence by following in the same Christian way as those flawed messengers of life.

Final Days at Home

By 1820 the national government had designated present-day Oklahoma as the hub of America's "Indian Territory," though official Congressional legislation occurred a decade later. Centuries of the Five Civilized Tribes living in their ancestral southeastern homelands were coming to an end.

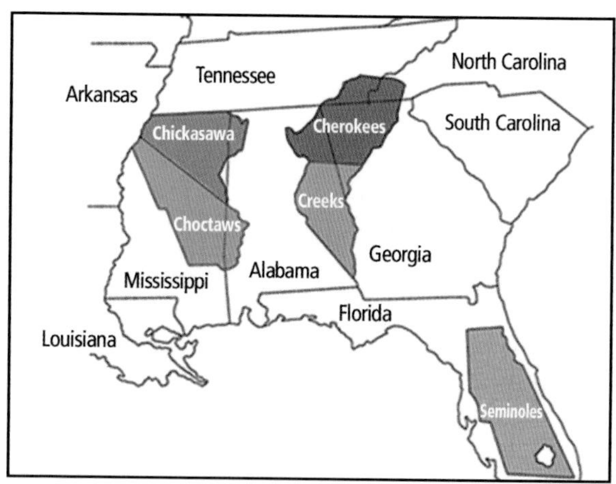

Southeastern homelands of the Five Civilized Tribes, all known for their advanced acceptance and mastery of Western ways, before their removal to Indian Territory. (Adapted from Arkansas Historic Preservation Program)

The southeast, of course, was the original home for none of them, because all had come from other lands. They had lived there for hundreds of years by the time the United States government's policy of encouragement and persuasion evolved into one of pressure and brute force.

In fact, the federal government carried out the wishes of Georgia and other Southern states in particular and the American citizenry in general. Those wishes involved removal of the Indians from the lands where white pioneers wished to settle and from the society that whites did not wish mutated by Native bloodlines or customs. This was accomplished in spite of the aforementioned fact that the southeastern "civilized" tribes in particular vigorously pursued American acculturation.

Pushmataha—Father of the Choctaws (c. 1764–1824)

"A little cloud was once seen in the northern sky. It came before a rushing wind, and covered the Choctaw country with darkness. Out of it flew an angry fire. It struck a large oak, and scattered its limbs and its trunk all along the ground, and from that spot sprung forth a warrior fully armed for war. And that man was Pushmataha."

Katherine Roche Buchanan's magnificent portrait of Pushmataha. (http://portraitartist.com/buchanan/index.asp)

Pushmataha Answers Tecumseh

"Halt! Tecumseh, listen to me. You have come here, as you have often gone elsewhere, with a purpose to involve peaceful people in unnecessary trouble with their neighbors. Our people have no undo friction with the whites. Why? Because we have had no leaders stirring up strife to serve their selfish personal ambitions."

Choctaw Treaty

Choctaw hunting parties had forayed west into Indian Territory for decades. Numerous tribesmen knew the region covering most of modern-day southeast Oklahoma that the U.S. government offered them in exchange for a chunk of their remaining lands in Mississippi. After the Choctaws and the United States had concluded a series of modest treaties over the years, in 1820 Pushmataha and other chiefs were again compelled to negotiate, this time with General and future President Andrew Jackson. And this time the negotiations concerned not hunted-out lands on the periphery of the Choctaw country; instead, they focused on core tribal territory.

In addition, Pushmataha knew white squatters already populated the proposed new Choctaw territory and that these western lands possibly lacked the fertility of those from which his tribe was being forced. Against this tense backdrop, Jackson's steely and immovable tack in the negotiations reportedly brought the two legendary warriors to a famous verbal confrontation, recorded in the following account:

> Gen. Jackson put on all his dignity and thus addressed the chief: 'I wish you to understand that I am Andrew Jackson, and, by the Eternal, you shall sign that treaty as I have prepared it.' The mighty Choctaw Chief was not disconcerted by this haughty address, and springing suddenly to his feet, and imitating the manner of his opponent, replied, 'I know very well who you are,

> but I wish you to understand that I am Pushmataha, head chief of the Choctaws; and, by the Eternal, I will not sign that treaty.'

Indeed, the Treaty of Doak's Stand, which stipulated voluntary migration west by the Choctaws and pledged supplies for all who did, was not signed until Jackson adjusted its provisions to require removal of the white squatters from the land to which the Choctaws were removing. Only about one-fourth of the tribe moved, however, and those who remained suffered pressure, intimidation, and injustice from federal officials and local white settlers alike for an entire decade.

Servants of the Choctaws

Every so often, the true makers of history, those who impact the personal destinies of men, women, and children, find their way into a book that purports to present as representative history the acts of an exclusive company of the most talented, ambitious, strong, and even villainous. Cyrus (1793–1868) and Sophie (1800–1880) Byington, like others after them (Chapters 3, 4, et al.) forsook opportunities that might have brought them fortune, fame, and comfort. Instead, they labored as Christian missionaries in perpetual borderline poverty at rough remote stations serving folk their own society ignored or, literally, removed from their presence. They did so amidst conflict with friends, accusations from friends and enemies alike, and brutal war. And they did not forsake those they served even until death.

Cyrus and Sophie Byington

"These white Americans . . . give us fair exchange, their cloth, their guns, their tools, implements, and other things which the Choctaws need but do not make. . . . So in marked contrast with the experience of the Shawnee, it will be seen that the whites and Indians in this section are living on friendly and mutually beneficial terms."

—**Pushmataha, 1811**

"Where today are the Pequot? Where are the Narragansett, the Mochican, the Pocanet, and other powerful tribes of our people? They have vanished before the avarice and oppression of the white man. . . . Sleep not longer, O Choctaws and Chickasaws. . . . Will not the bones of our dead be plowed up, and their graves turned into plowed fields?"

—**Tecumseh, 1811**

Finally in 1830, years after the death of Pushmataha, the progressive, visionary Greenwood LeFlore and other district chiefs signed a new document, the Treaty of Dancing Rabbit Creek. This time the tribe gave up all lands east of the Mississippi River and promised to clear out for Indian Territory by 1833. The treaty also mandated pensions for twenty old Choctaw warriors among the hundreds who had fought for American independence against the British more than a half-century before. They served under generals such as George Washington, Anthony Wayne, and Daniel Morgan.

The government provided transportation, food, and one year's living support for the entire tribe, also promising never to enfold the Choctaws and their splendid new tribal estates into any U.S. political jurisdiction or legal authority. It would prove to be the first of several such promises to the southeastern tribes.

McIntosh Creeks Leave

As the 1820s unfolded, pressure by the American government, state of Georgia, and white settlers—fueled by bitter memories of the vicious Red Stick

William McIntosh's audacious, controversial exchange at the 1825 Treaty of Indian Springs of southeastern Creek lands for new ones in Indian Territory and other concessions from the U. S. government.

War and the Creek theater of the War of 1812—mounted against the Creeks to remove west. This occurred despite the fact that the Lower Creeks previously fought alongside the Americans.

William McIntosh called a tribal council in 1825 at Indian Springs, Georgia to address the situation. Indian commissioners from the U.S. government attended as well. McIntosh and other progressive Lower Creeks aimed to trade their Georgia lands, beloved though they were, to the United States in exchange for lands out west in Indian Territory.

Opothleyahola led an Upper Creek walkout of the meeting. McIntosh and the Lower Creeks, like the Ridges and other progressive Cherokees a decade later, knew the danger to their very lives because of the controversial death penalty enacted by the tribe several years before. McIntosh himself had voted for it. They nonetheless signed the treaty with the Americans, thus exchanging the Creeks' Georgia lands for new lands in central and eastern Indian Territory.

The Creek council soon met again, this time pronouncing guilt and execution against William McIntosh for breaking

Creek Chief Menawa, bitter opponent of William McIntosh and his removal actions, and leader of the tribal party that murdered him.

William McIntosh (1775–1825)

Like so many others who made great contributions to Oklahoma history, Creek chief William McIntosh left a legacy shrouded in controversy and passionate opinions. Born of a talented Scots father and a mother from the respected Creek Wind Clan, McIntosh, like other mixed-blood leaders of southeastern tribes, moved with confidence and competence in American, British, and Indian culture alike. But not with all Creeks. The Upper and Lower Creek opposition over nearly everything—European and American cultural influence, Christianity, agrarian practices, U.S.–British conflicts—coupled with McIntosh's leadership of the Lower Creeks, marked him for controversy. Upper Creeks "Red Stick" leaders like Mun-ah-we—also of Scots-Creek descent—detested him.

> *This knowledge makes the white man like the leaves; the want of it makes the red man few and weak. Let us learn to make books as the white man does and we shall grow again and become a new nation.*
>
> —William McIntosh

Charles Bird King's majestic portrait of Creek Chief, visionary, and martyr William McIntosh.

An artist's rendering of the nighttime murder of William McIntosh.

tribal law in ceding lands without council sanction. On April 29 over a hundred Creeks surrounded McIntosh's home near Milledgeville, Georgia. After allowing women and children to leave, they set fire to his home. When McIntosh and a male colleague emerged, the attackers brutally killed them.

So horrified at the killings was U.S. President John Quincy Adams, he abrogated the Treaty of Indian Springs and summoned Opothleyhola and other Creek leaders to Washington. There, in 1826, they agreed to the First Treaty of Washington, which accomplished the land trade intended by the commissioners and Lower Creek leaders at Indian Springs. Led by Roley McIntosh, half-brother of the slain William, around twenty-five hundred Lower Creeks soon left Georgia for verdant Indian Territory lands situated between the Arkansas and Canadian Rivers. These early Oklahoma Creeks became known as the McIntosh Creeks, thus codifying the legacy of their leader.

The bulk of the tribe, including the Upper Creeks, refused to migrate and remained in Alabama. But the Creeks' westward trek had begun in earnest, and the tribe avoided another looming civil war, as well as the uncompensated confiscation of much land and property, by allowing the Georgian Lower Creeks to leave.

Western Cherokees

By 1825 Osage fortunes waned. They counted the "civilized" tribes migrating to eastern Indian Territory as well as the Plains tribes to the west as enemies. They had lost hundreds of people to their long war with the Cherokees. Their overall population was declining. They faced mounting debts to other tribes. And they knew that American settlers multiplied just beyond the Cherokees, and those settlers had a fearsome army ready to defend them. Two famed Osage chiefs, Clermont and Pawhuska, consented to renounce all claims to land in present-day Oklahoma to the U.S., thus clearing the way for its conveyance to the Cherokees coming from the southeast and Arkansas, as well as opening the latter to American citizens. The Osages, shoved aside again, received land in Kansas.

Those citizens complicated matters, however, by pouring into the country intended for the Cherokees subsequent to Lovely's Purchase (see Osage–Cherokee War, this chapter). They badgered the Arkansas legislature into declaring the area a county of that state. This stunning chain of events also cost the Cherokees their promised land outlet for buffalo hunting across northern Indian Territory to the west. A delegation of Cherokee leaders, including the famed Sequoyah, traveled to Washington to protest. They did so during what would prove a landmark year in Cherokee history, 1828. Their eloquence and logic prevailed, and the United States ordered whites out of Indian Territory and Cherokees out of Arkansas, to the consternation of many on both sides. Roughly the northeastern

Cephas Washburn and other Presbyterian missionaries planted Dwight Mission in 1820 at Russellville, Arkansas, after the Western Cherokees requested Christian outreach. It was the first organized Protestant effort to educate and evangelize Arkansas Natives and one of the first west of the Mississippi River. The missionaries closed Dwight in 1829 and reopened it at Sallisaw when most of the Arkansas Cherokees moved to Indian Territory. (From *Historic Arkansas*, courtesy Butler Center for Arkansas Studies, Central Arkansas Library System)

In *Sequoyah*, by Charles Banks Wilson, Cherokee legend Sequoyah holds the Cherokee syllabary he created in 1821, which enabled his tribe to read and write in their own language. A measure of the man's greatness is displayed both in the fact he himself could not previously read any script, and that his syllabary remains the only workable writing system ever created by someone from a non-literate people. His fellow Cherokees initially mocked Sequoyah's efforts, but upon adopting the syllabary they rapidly advanced past the literacy rate of nearby white settlers. Used with permission from the Oklahoma State Capitol, courtesy Oklahoma Arts Council.

quadrant of Indian Territory, however, would now host the Cherokee, supported by federal bayonets if necessary.

Sequoyah's legend burgeoned even then, years before his death. The U.S. government chose the occasion of the 1828 treaty to honor the brilliant part-Cherokee, part-Scot's accomplishments in the

Ꭰ a	Ꭱ e	Ꭲ i	Ꭳ o	Ꭴ u	Ꭵ v
Ꭶ ga Ꭷ ka	Ꭸ ge	Ꭹ gi	Ꭺ go	Ꭻ gu	Ꭼ gv
Ꭽ ha	Ꭾ he	Ꭿ hi	Ꮀ ho	Ꮁ hu	Ꮂ hv
Ꮃ la	Ꮄ le	Ꮅ li	Ꮆ lo	Ꮇ lu	Ꮈ lv
Ꮉ ma	Ꮊ me	Ꮋ mi	Ꮌ mo	Ꮍ mu	
Ꮎ na Ꮏ hna	Ꮑ ne	Ꮒ ni	Ꮓ no	Ꮔ nu	Ꮕ nv
Ꮖ qua	Ꮗ que	Ꮘ qui	Ꮙ quo	Ꮚ quu	Ꮛ quv
Ꮜ sa Ꮝ s	Ꮞ se	Ꮟ si	Ꮠ so	Ꮡ su	Ꮢ sv
Ꮣ da Ꮤ ta	Ꮥ de Ꮦ te	Ꮧ di Ꮨ ti	Ꮩ do	Ꮪ dü	Ꮫ dv
Ꮬ dla Ꮭ tla	Ꮮ tle	Ꮯ tli	Ꮰ tlo	Ꮱ tlu	Ꮲ tlv
Ꮳ tsa	Ꮴ tse	Ꮵ tsi	Ꮶ tso	Ꮷ tsu	Ꮸ tsv
Ꮹ wa	Ꮺ we	Ꮻ wi	Ꮼ wo	Ꮽ wu	Ꮾ wv
Ꮿ ya	Ᏸ ye	Ᏹ yi	Ᏺ yo	Ᏻ yu	Ᏼ yv

Cherokee syllabary with a five-hundred dollar stipend—worth tens of thousands of dollars in modern currency—and give the tribe a thousand dollars to purchase a new printing press.

Eastern Cherokees

Despite these happy events of concord, ominous tidings lurked on the horizon of Cherokee destiny back east. More than two-thirds of the tribe remained in the southeast, with no intention to leave no matter what incentives the United States offered. Georgians, meanwhile, having forfeited title to the rich country that became Alabama and Mississippi, grew angrier with each passing year at the federal government's apparent amnesia regarding its *quid pro quo* promise to remove the Cherokees west.

> *We the Cherokee people, constituting one of the sovereign and independent nations of the earth, and having complete jurisdiction over its territory to the exclusion of the authority of every other state, do ordain this Constitution.*

The Eastern Cherokees strived to bridge these apparently irreconcilable positions. In 1827 they wrote their own constitution, patterned after that of the United States. Like that famed document, the Cherokee Constitution featured legislative,

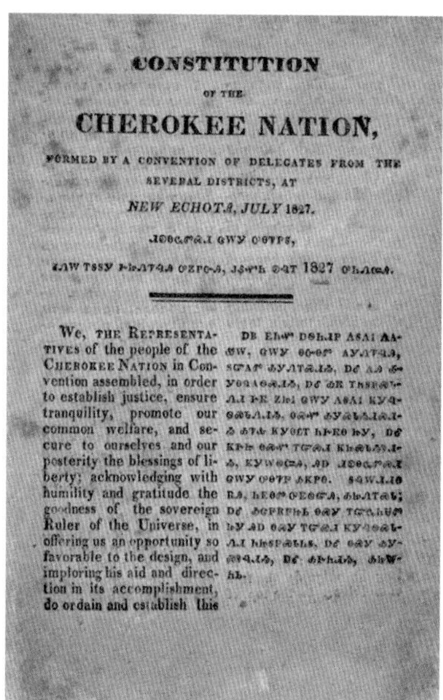

CONSTITUTION

OF THE

CHEROKEE NATION,

FORMED BY A CONVENTION OF DELEGATES FROM THE SEVERAL DISTRICTS, AT

NEW ECHOTA, JULY 1827.

We, THE REPRESENTATIVES of the people of the CHEROKEE NATION in Convention assembled, in order to establish justice, ensure tranquility, promote our common welfare, and secure to ourselves and our posterity the blessings of liberty; acknowledging with humility and gratitude the goodness of the sovereign Ruler of the Universe, in offering us an opportunity so favorable to the design, and imploring his aid and direction in its accomplishment, do ordain and establish this

The landmark 1827 Cherokee Constitution demonstrated the tribe's intellectual heft, understanding of and commitment to republican government with its rule of law, respect for the individual and federalistic separation of powers, and desire to live in concord with the growing American nation around them.

executive, and judicial arms of national government. A two-house body comprised the Cherokee legislature, including representatives selected by the tribe's eight districts. The National Council selected a tribal treasurer. A president-like principal chief with veto power over legislative acts headed the executive branch, which also had an assistant principal chief. The judiciary featured a Supreme Court and circuit court system. Locally, the districts' legislative officials appointed justices of the peace and sheriffs.

The Cherokees and other tribes such as the Chickasaws, Choctaws, and Creeks who also framed U.S.-like constitutions intended to cooperate with the American nation. But they did not intend either to be absorbed by it east of the Mississippi River or remove themselves from it to the west. The opening line of the Cherokee Constitution declared those intentions in clear terms: "We the Cherokee people, constituting one of the sovereign and independent nations of the earth, and having complete jurisdiction over its territory to the exclusion of the authority of every other state, do ordain this Constitution."

As chronicled in Ralph Gabriel's book *Elias Boudinot, Cherokee, and His America*, the leaders and people of Georgia understood the message, but it only accelerated their own agenda. By the end of 1827, their legislature codified the temporary, tenant-like status in which they viewed the Cherokees resident within the boundaries of Georgia. They announced that the state could take possession of Cherokee lands by any means necessary should it choose to do so and then extend its laws over them. Georgia notified the United States Congress that in twelve months it would, in any event, do so.

In 1828, the same year the United States and the Cherokees successfully treated in Washington, the Georgia legislature declared all tribal members within the state subject to its laws. The magistrates also disallowed Indians from testifying against whites in a court of law. This accelerated a practice that had already begun—the physical taking of Cherokee land by whites.

> *This witches' brew of anger, mistrust, cultural differences, and greed bubbled over with the emergence of another element in northern Georgia—a historic gold strike on Cherokee land.*

The following year, this witches' brew of anger, mistrust, cultural differences, and greed would bubble over with the emergence of an additional element in northern Georgia—a historic gold strike on Cherokee land. Now the legislature squeezed its tightening grip on the tribe. It abolished their government, claimed all tribal lands as Georgia property, disallowed Cherokee leadership from meeting other than to discuss moving west, and instituted other harsh restrictions on the Natives.

Ross and Conflict

Amidst these mounting tensions, a pivotal event of tribal history occurred in 1828 as the Cherokees elected John Ross, a successful planter and businessman, as principal chief. Barely qualifying as a mixed blood—he was only 1/8 Cherokee, the rest white—Ross nonetheless towered over the chronicle of his people for the next forty years to become the most powerful Cherokee of the nineteenth century.

John Ross in his late 30s, circa 1828, by Thomas McKenney.

Under the leadership of the eloquent, urbane, and determined Ross, the tribe's course, for better or worse, was charted regarding that century's greatest issues. These ranged from relations with the United States, to Indian removal, to the War Between the States and Reconstruction. One of Oklahoma history's enduring questions is the degree to which Ross guided the views of the full blood/traditionalist Cherokee majority—or reflected them. He initially co-labored with other mixed-bloods in the Progressive wing of the tribe, encouraging cultural assimilation into white American society. For instance, he influenced the transition in 1827 from tribal government to the aforementioned national Cherokee written constitution with federated powers and republican governmental philosophy.

Ross also supported the founding, in the momentous year of 1828, of the Cherokee *Phoenix* newspaper. White Presbyterian missionary Samuel Worcester and three-quarter Cherokee but Progressive Elias Boudinot helmed the publication, which they printed in both English and Cherokee. This devout young pair possessed a sweeping vision for the *Phoenix*: helping teach the tribe to read in two languages, solidifying the loose Cherokee community, establishing and promoting a Cherokee nation, aiding the tribe's success in white-dominated America, and spreading and teaching the Christian gospel.

The well-preserved little Cherokee *Phoenix* structure in New Echota, Georgia.

ᏣᎳᎩ ᏧᎴᎯᏌᏅᎯ.

CHEROKEE PHŒNIX, AND INDIANS' ADVOCATE.

E. BOUDINOTT, Editor. NEW ECHOTA, WEDNESDAY FEBRUARY 11, 1829. VOL. I.—NO. 48.

The cover of an early *Cherokee Phoenix*, the first American Indian newspaper, founded in 1828. Cherokee and eventual Indian Territory immigrant Elias Boudinot edited it and translated the Cherokee text into English, the two versions appearing in alternating columns.

With the onset of the 1830s, however, Ross and the mixed-bloods/Progressives gradually evolved into mortal enemies. Indeed, the fate of all five major southeastern tribes grew uncertain as American opposition to them increased and relocation to Indian Territory increasingly loomed as a consideration. The Chickasaws and Seminoles remained en masse in the southeast as the 1820s concluded, and so did most Cherokees, Choctaws, and Creeks. But the citizens, government, and military of the United States, cognizant of the many past bloodlettings between the two peoples, became even more determined to change that situation. Smaller tribes such as the Quapaws and Caddos, longtime residents of present-day Oklahoma, faced the prospect of losing their own land and property to Natives forced westward by the federal government.

Then, in 1830, the U.S. Congress, exhorted by new President Andrew Jackson in his State of the Union speech and elsewhere, passed the historic Indian Removal Act. This launched the first in a series of federally mandated dictates that would compel tribes east of the Mississippi River to vacate for the West. The 1830s would bring more bloodletting—including a war with one tribe—horror on an epic scale, mass migration, and no small amount of courage and valor.

Sequoyah (c. 1767–c. 1844)

Few people seem less likely to have been the only person in Oklahoma history to create the written form of a language than the great Sequoyah, known also by the English names George Guess, Guest, or Gist. To begin with, his humble Cherokee Indian background is reflected in the fact that neither his birthdate nor place of birth are known. In fact, historians can narrow the former down no closer than to sometime between 1760 and 1776, the latter to the Southern states of Alabama, Georgia, Tennessee, and the Carolinas. His white father apparently abandoned Sequoyah and his mother when he was a young boy. Sequoyah also had a serious physical disability, perhaps from childhood.

Osage Principal Chief Clermont receives the signing pen from U.S. Indian Commissioner William Clark (of Lewis and Clark fame) in artist Mike Wimmer's *Osage Treaty of 1825*. Designed to separate the warring Cherokees and Osages, the treaty stipulated that the latter forfeit most of their Indian Territory lands in return for significant financial and material annuities and land in present-day Kansas. Though not ending the tribal fighting, it reduced it. Among other stipulations, the treaty assured safety for non-Natives traveling the Santa Fe Trail. Observers included Pawhuska and other Osage chiefs, as well as famed frontiersmen/entrepreneurs Pierre Chouteau and his son Pierre "Cadet" Chouteau, Jr., and Illinois governor Edward Coles. Used with permission from the Oklahoma State Senate Collection and the artist. Courtesy Oklahoma State Senate Historical Preservation Fund, a project of Charles Ford.

4

1830s
The Trail of Tears

Choctaw Chief George Hudson carries his mother's body across Arkansas to present-day Oklahoma on the Choctaw Trail of Tears, the first of several tragic journeys forced on the Five Civilized Tribes. As the clouds part, the sun illumines her face and the surrounding snow in G. N. Taylor's heartrending work *Choctaw Chief George Hudson.* (www.gntayloroklaart.com)

1831	Choctaw removal begins
1832	Creeks' Second Treaty of Washington
1832	*Worcester v Georgia*
1834	*Cherokee Phoenix* newspaper stops publishing
1834	Dodge-Leavenworth Expedition
1835	Treaty of New Echota
1836–1837	Creek Trail of Tears
1835–1842	Seminole Wars
1838	Cherokee Trail of Tears
1839	Cherokee Treaty Party leaders assassinated

> *By a combination of bribery, trickery, and intimidation the Federal agents induced all five (Indian republics) during the 1830s to cede the remainder of their Eastern lands to the United States and to agree to migrate beyond the Mississippi. All these removal treaties contained the most solemn guarantees that the Indians' titles to these new lands should be perpetual and that no territorial or state government should ever be erected over them without their consent.*
>
> **—Angie Debo, *And Still the Waters Run***

The nineteenth-century Indian removal, which affected most tribes east of the Mississippi River, confounds and bedevils American history as the years pass. The removal period of the 1820s and 1830s has spawned shelves of books brimming with explanations, viewpoints, and lessons. In the retrospective of nearly two centuries, perhaps the overriding moral principle is best evoked by Scripture: "There is a way that seems right to man, but therein lies death."

In this removal a stronger, more numerous Christian civilization forcibly compelled a weaker people to leave its homelands for a distant and dangerous land, in turn harming and uprooting yet weaker groups already there. For the benefit of an expanding nation—and the protection of the Indians themselves—the government determined that the southeastern Indians had to move to Indian Territory (present-day Oklahoma). Amidst much debate, intra-tribal division, bitterness, and even wars with both themselves and the United States, the Five "Civilized" Tribes signed treaties agreeing to abandon their ancient homelands and remove westward, albeit with financial remuneration for their losses and travel, along with free land at their destination.

The advent of the 1830s found no more than one-fourth of the Choctaws moved or in the process of moving west to the Indian Territory region, as well as about one-third of the Cherokees and at most a quarter of the Creeks. The majority of Cherokees, Choctaws, and Creeks and virtually all the Chickasaws and Seminoles remained in their southeastern homelands, to the growing consternation of white American inhabitants there. In fact, tensions and violence between Natives and whites grew so extreme by the mid-1830s that nearly all of even the Indians most opposed to removal consented to forfeit their lands in the southeast for new ones in Indian Territory, along with various financial and material provisions. How that journey unfolded is an epic saga whose drama was matched only by its horror.

Choctaw Trail of Tears

The *Arkansas Gazette* newspaper quoted a Choctaw chief calling it "a trail of tears and death." Thus was coined one of American history's most memorable and poignant terms. That tribe—which had fought shoulder to shoulder with the Americans against foes ranging from the British to the Creeks—was the first to remove en masse from the southeast to Indian Territory. Led by mixed-blood men who had labored to assimilate their tribe into white American culture, such as devout Christian chief David Folsom and future plantation titan Robert M. Jones, the bulk of the Choctaws—between eleven thousand and fourteen thousand souls—nonetheless headed west in the autumns of 1831 to 1833.

The colossal suffering these treks produced carved the Choctaw migration into the history of America as its first Trail of Tears. Hunger, fatal diseases such as cholera, freezing weather, exposure, and too much water (floods) as well as not enough (thirst) combined to kill as many as twenty-five hundred members of the tribe en route. One group walked for twenty-four hours straight through snow and ice—barefoot. A U.S. army officer supervising one exodus lamented, "Our poor emigrants, many of them quite naked, and without much shelter, must suffer; it is impossible to do otherwise." A grieving Choctaw wrote, "It was a journey calculated to embitter the human heart."

Alfred Boisseau's 1846 painting of the Choctaw Trail of Tears, *Louisiana Indians Walking Along a Bayou.*

> *The disgusting sight of a vessel loaded with human beings under no control or regularity, leaving their evacuations in every direction through the whole range of the Cabins and deck, would create in the mind of any one an additional allowance for the transportation.*
>
> **—U.S. Army Lt. William S. Colquhoun** describing Choctaw steamboat traveling conditions

As eloquently stated by Oklahoma historian Angie Debo in her controversial landmark chronicle of the five Indian republics, *And Still the Waters Run,* the lamentations of the exiles were "matched only by the saturnalia of exploitation to which they were subjected by land speculators who crowded them from their homes before the time fixed for their emigration, and who possessed themselves of their individual allotments by every possible combination of violence and fraud." In other words, the migrating Choctaws often suffered threats, extortion, violence, and removal from their original properties, even though they were already preparing to head west.

A Choctaw Speaks to America

"We go forth sorrowful, knowing that wrong has been done. Will you extend to us your sympathizing regards until all traces of disagreeable oppositions are obliterated, and we again shall have confidence in the professions of our white brethren? Here is the land of our progenitors, and here are their bones; they left them as a sacred deposit, and we have been compelled to venerate its trust; it is dear to us, yet we cannot stay, my people is dear to me, with them I must go. Could I stay and forget them and leave them to struggle alone, unaided, unfriended, and forgotten, by our great father? I should then be unworthy the name of a Choctaw, and be a disgrace to my blood. I must go with them; my destiny is cast among the Choctaw people. If they suffer, so will I; if they prosper, then will I rejoice. Let me again ask you to regard us with feelings of kindness."

George Harkins

David Folsom, the Choctaw Moses (1791–1856)

As the ancient Jewish prophet Moses led his people out of bondage and into the Promised Lands of both this world and the next, so did Mississippi-born, mixed-blood Choctaw David Folsom. Like Moses, Folsom faced enemies within and without, beginning with his rescue as an infant from the hands of legally empowered murderers. In Folsom's case, his birth occurred in 1791, while his white father Nathaniel conducted business away in New Orleans. His brother and sister had just died of pneumonia, and his full-blood mother Ainichihoyo contracted it too. Doubting Ainichihoyo would survive, the Choctaw "doctor" attending her advised the standard full-blood practice of killing a baby whose prospects for proper nurture and care looked bleak.

> *It rests me to look upon (God's) varied lovely scented landscape which is in reality a means of education to the susceptible mind, and which so often has been invested with the charm of poetry and romance.*
>
> —David Folsom

Choctaw men, women, and children struggled through thirty straight miles of waist-deep wintertime cypress swamp water in Arkansas. (Courtesy James E. Thompson Co., Knoxville, TN)

Folsom Calls the Missionaries West

Confirmation that the Choctaw must remove to Indian Territory wilderness perhaps struck the Christians of the tribe hardest of all, due to what one historian called, "the breaking up of the meetings of the churches, the schools and Christian neighborhoods and the separation of the missionaries and teachers." David Folsom responded by imploring the Presbyterian missionaries serving the tribe in Mississippi to accompany it west on what became the original "Trail of Tears."

> Friends and brothers, we can multiply words and say much on many advantages that we have received. When you came among us good many years ago, you found us, no school, no gospel, no songs of praise to Jehovah was heard. Friends and brothers, we will give glory and praise to Jehovah in sending some here to teach us the way of life. It is you our dear friends, whom the Savior of sinners has been pleased in his own goodness to make you an instrument in his hand of what has been done for us.

Yet over five thousand Choctaws still refused to leave. The barbaric treatment they too—the supposedly uncivilized ones—received is best described by one of their own: "We have had our habitations torn down and burned, our fences destroyed, cattle turned into our fields and we ourselves have been scourged, manacled, fettered and otherwise personally abused, until by such treatment some of our best men have died."

Most of this sizable remnant drifted west to join the bulk of the tribe by 1850, even though Choctaws still arrived in Oklahoma from Mississippi into the early twentieth century. Yet over a thousand members of the tribe remained in Mississippi in 1930.

Creek Wars

Most of the Creek nation refused to emigrate west with the McIntosh Creeks in the 1820s. For years afterwards, they suffered the wrath of the white Alabamians among whom they continued to live. Theft, violence, and lack of state or federal protection drove the Creeks to despair—and finally to treat with the United States regarding leaving for present-day Oklahoma.

In 1832, Opothleyahola (Chapter 6), a longtime leading opponent of removal, joined other Creek chiefs in signing the Second Treaty of Washington with U.S. government representatives. In essence, the treaty offered the Creeks, in exchange for giving up title to their southeastern lands, two options. In both, they would receive land allotments in Alabama. They could then choose to sell their allotment and receive assistance in moving to their Indian Territory lands, or they could remain in Alabama on their allotment and become American citizens.

Some Creeks left, but most of them still defiantly refused. That proved calamitous, as it had for the Choctaws who remained. Not only did the Alabama Creeks continue to suffer abuse, but most of them, not understanding the concept of private property ownership, soon lost their land through one means or another to whites.

Rather than peace, the despair spawned by these events resulted in escalating episodes of property theft and destruction, along with violence against persons, both perpetrated by the Creeks against the whites and vice versa. It also propelled the Creek Wars of 1836-37 in Alabama and Georgia, led by eighty-four-year-old Chief Eneah Emathla, and 1836–40 in Florida. Given short shrift in most Oklahoma history books, these conflicts were a vicious war of genocide between civilizations. Many hundreds died on both sides, including scores of both red and white women and children.

President Jackson sent a federal army to quell the Alabama-Georgia rebellion. He also enlisted the assistance of Opothleyahola and two thousand Upper Creeks. Despite the snuffing-out of this uprising, however, the violence shifted to the Florida Panhandle. The Seminoles—cousins of the Creeks—were already fighting U.S. armies there and in other parts of Florida. Here, too, the Natives were gradually ground down, even though sporadic spurts of violence involving them and white Americans flared until the 1850s.

Creek Removal

At the close of the First Creek War, Andrew Jackson's government insisted that all Creek—including those who fought for the United States against their own rebelling people—leave Alabama for Indian Territory. Though the Cherokee Trail of Tears looms as the most famous American Indian exodus, the proportion of Creek suffering during their removal approached that of the Cherokees. Over twenty-five hundred Upper Creeks considered as participants in the rebellion were forced west in chains. Many hundreds of tribespeople perished in transit from disease, malnutrition, or exposure during the frigid winter of 1836–37. They included men, women, and children, young and old. One boat—the small steamer *Monmouth*—sank after a nighttime collision in the Mississippi River with over

Paul Bender's painting of the *Monmouth* going down at night in the Mississippi River after a larger ship cut it in half. Over seven hundred exiled Creeks had packed onto the small steamer, and more than three hundred perished.

seven hundred Creeks crammed on board. More than three hundred perished.

Historian Grant Foreman quotes one Creek Trail of Tears trekker in his landmark book *Indian Removal*:

> When we left our homes the great General Jesup told us that we could get to our country as we wanted to. We wanted to gather our crops, and we wanted to go in peace and friendship. Did we? No! We were drove off like wolves . . . lost our crops . . . and our people's feet were bleeding with long marches. . . . We are men . . . we have women and children and why should we come like wild horses?

Such experiences helped foment a suspicious and sometimes hostile attitude toward even such white American institutions as Christianity on the part of many Creeks. Until 1822 the tribe resisted the mere presence of Christian missionaries in its country. Later, the removal escalated antipathy toward the Church. Many Creeks assigned it partial blame for their forced migration west. Most of this anger faded as the tribe reestablished itself in its new western lands, however, and the Creeks became as Christian a people as most other ethnic American groups.

Leaders of the Creek Loachapoka clan establish their first "town" upon arriving in present-day Oklahoma in Mike Larsen's *Creek Council Oak Tree*. One-fourth of the clan had perished during their mid-1830s Trail of Tears. Loachapoka was a daughter of Tallasi, from whom the name Tulsa is believed to derive. The post oak council tree still stands—between Seventeenth and Eighteenth Streets and Cheyenne and Denver Avenues in Tulsa. Courtesy Oklahoma State Senate Historical Preservation Fund, Inc. and Mike Larsen. (www.larsenstudio.com)

If the tragic saga of the Creek Trail of Tears holds any silver lining, it is that upon the emigrants' arrival in their new land, Roley McIntosh and the McIntosh Creeks, previously considered enemies by many of the newly arriving group, welcomed them with open arms, provided them with food and succor of all sorts, and guided them to fertile lands where they could settle within Creek country. This proved nothing short of deliverance for a people of whom U.S. Army Captain F. W. Armstrong spoke when he said he had "never seen so wretched and poor a body of Indians as this party of Creek; they really have nothing."

Putting hatred, suspicion, and violence—including the killing of William McIntosh—behind them, most of the eighteen thousand or so Creeks who moved to present-day Oklahoma lived in peace with one another until the early 1860s and the onset of a new tragedy, the War Between the States.

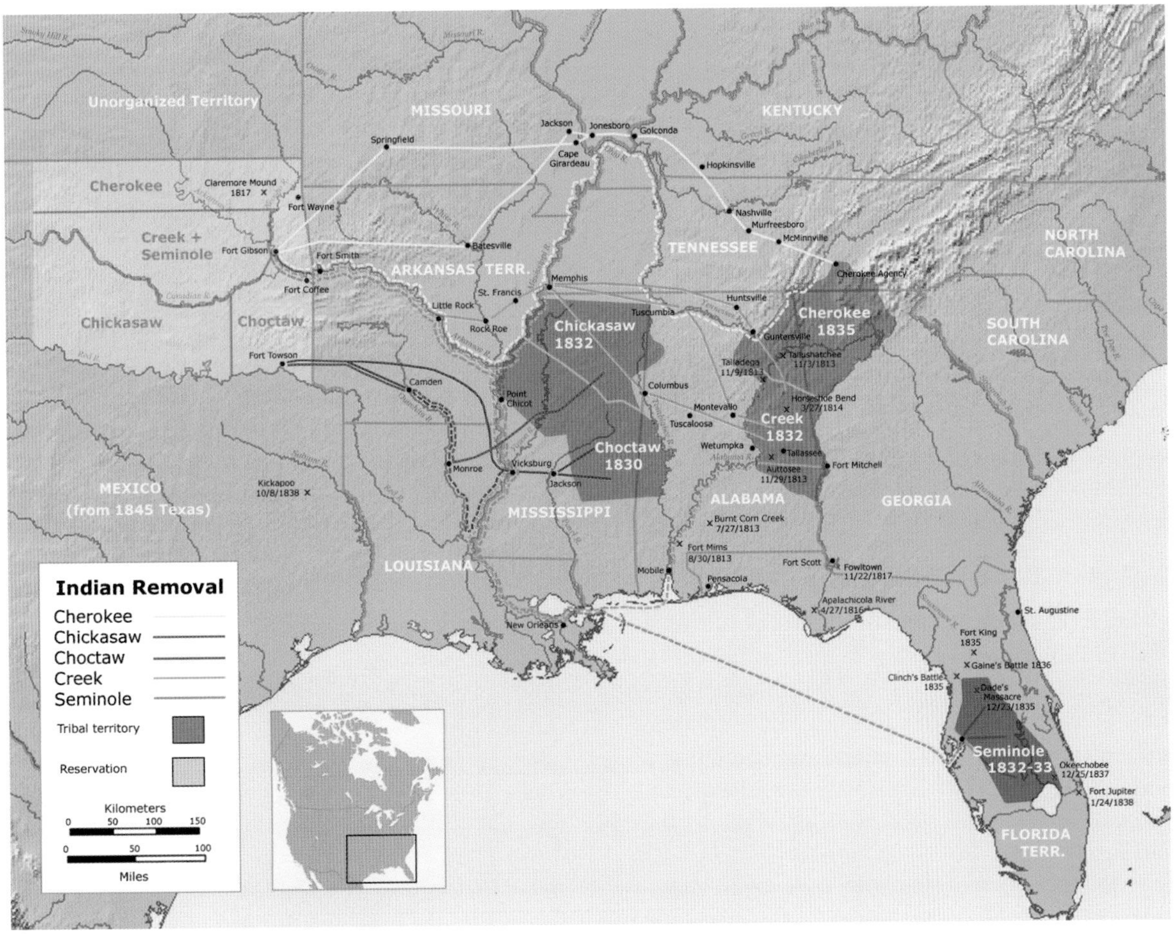

Southeastern homelands, removal dates and routes, and western destinations of the Five Civilized Tribes.

Samuel Worcester, Cherokee Messenger (1798–1859)

If the courts of Oklahoma history were to assemble their own company of founding fathers for the state, surely Samuel A. Worcester would stand in the front ranks. His decades-long dedication to the Cherokees helped lift, strengthen, and grow them in an era when so many influences conspired to shatter them. The Cherokees' actions in turn impacted the whole of Indian Territory and eventually the state of Oklahoma and all of the United States.

> *Observing Worcester and the other beleaguered prisoners suffering for the tribe, the Natives' skepticism melted away. Forever after, the Cherokees would prove fertile spiritual ground for Christian missionaries, and many of their own would rise up in Christian service.*

21st CONGRESS.
1st SESSION.

S. 102.

IN SENATE OF THE UNITED STATES.

FEBRUARY 22, 1830.

Mr. WHITE, from the Committee on Indian Affairs, reported the following bill; which was read, and passed to a second reading:

A BILL

To provide for an exchange of lands with the Indians residing in any of the States or Territories, and for their removal West of the river Mississippi.

Cherokee Persecution Grows

Conflict surged throughout the Cherokee people in the 1830s from within, without, and among. The landmark 1830 Congressional Indian Removal Bill fomented yet greater audacity among the people of Georgia—through their elected officials and armed militia—to seek the removal of the Cherokees from their state, through lawful means or otherwise. Sometimes the lines grew blurry between those means.

The escalation of gold fever (Chapter 3), white settlement, and desire for Indian land spawned new laws against the Cherokees. By early 1831 the Georgia legislature recognized the crucial intellectual, moral, and religious succor being conveyed to the reeling tribe by scores of white Protestant missionaries. The legislature thereupon disallowed whites from living in the Cherokee country unless they were licensed and submitted to a loyalty oath to the state government and its actions. The legislature also created the Georgia Guard, ostensibly a state militia unit, but actually an armed force tasked with ratcheting up the pressure on the Indians to leave Georgia.

That pressure grew to unbearable levels. Mixed-blood John Ridge, son of renowned Cherokee chief and business leader Major Ridge and one of the most brilliant young leaders in the tribe, wrote how his people were being "robbed and whipped by the whites almost every day." Cherokees of grand and mean estate alike were attacked, many of them murdered. Even Principal Chief John Ross (Chapter 3) narrowly avoided assassination.

The Georgia Land Lottery that auctioned off the Cherokee homeland. (Courtesy Georgia Department of Archives and History)

One of America's great gold rushes, in late-1820s to early-1830s north Georgia, helped sweep the Cherokees from their homeland as frenzied white wealth-seekers swarmed the area from all points of the map.

In 1832, the Georgia Guard acted upon the state's laws prohibiting non-"licensed" whites from living on Cherokee land. The Guard took eleven missionaries prisoner, including the widely-respected Presbyterian minister Samuel Worcester. He was the close friend of and laborer on the Cherokee translation of the New Testament with Elias Boudinot, as well as co-founder with him of the tribe's *Cherokee Phoenix* newspaper. This audacious assault on the Church by the state—with the vigorous moral support of President Andrew Jackson—triggered the famed *Worcester v Georgia* case. That landmark legal donnybrook went beyond Worcester's rights to minister to the Cherokees and

White Presbyterian missionary Samuel Worcester lost his home in the Georgia land lottery like the Cherokees to whom he ministered.

came to grips with the general question of Cherokee land rights.

In 1833 Chief Justice John Marshall and the United States Supreme Court handed down a resounding verdict in favor of the Cherokees, rebuking the state of Georgia. President Jackson famously—or infamously—and unconstitutionally refused to enforce the ruling. The executive branch should have done so, despite protestations from its defenders then and since that it had not the constitutional authority to enforce this like other laws of the land. And so the Cherokees could look to the governments in neither Georgia nor Washington for support.

Stalwart female Presbyterian teacher-missionaries such as Ester Smith, left, and Cassandra Sawyer Lockwood, right, served the Cherokees at Dwight Mission after its move to near present-day Sallisaw even before the majority of the tribe was forced west from their southeastern U.S. homelands. Courtesy Oklahoma Historical Society.

Ann Worcester

Spring Place Mission Station, the sacred site where generations of Cherokees—including Elias Boudinot, Stand Watie, and John Ridge—had learned the education and religion of Christendom, was commandeered by the Georgia Guard. Its Moravian missionaries were evicted, and their home was converted to a tavern where the alcoholic spirits so ruinous to Cherokee and white alike were dispensed.

Tribal Opinions Diverge

By now, John Ridge had arrived at a momentous conviction, one shared by his young, talented colleague and cousin Boudinot. They and other Cherokee leaders, particularly among the better educated mixed-blood group, now believed that the Cherokees' very existence as a people lay in jeopardy if they did not remove themselves from the pernicious influences of the whites around them. Evidencing concerns over both the tribe's fortunes if they remained in the southeast and Ross's judgment on the matter, Ridge wrote the Principal Chief:

> I have the right to address you as the chief of the whole Cherokee Nation, upon whom rests, under Heaven the highest responsibility—and well being of the whole people; and I do trust that you will return as I know you are capable of acting the Part of a statesman in this trying Crisis of our affairs . . . .We all know . . . that we can't be a Nation here, I hope we shall attempt to establish it somewhere else! Where, the wisdom of the nation must try to find.

Businessman, soldier, chief, Cherokee Constitution framer, and Treaty Party leader Major Ridge. He declared, "(The whites) are strong and we are weak. We are few, they are many. We cannot remain here in safety and comfort. . . . I know we love the graves of our fathers. . . . We can never forget these homes, I know, but an unbending, iron necessity tells us we must leave them. . . . I would willingly die to preserve them, but any forcible effort to keep them will cost us our lands, our lives and the lives of our children. There is but one path to safety, one road to future existence as a Nation."

As articulate Cherokee voices for migration west multiplied and inter-tribal feuding and even violence escalated over the issue, Ross made repeated trips to lobby American lawmakers in Washington against removing the tribe. He had many allies on the removal debate in Congress and elsewhere in government and among the public, particularly in the North. As with the burgeoning debate over black slavery, however, Northerners stood on shaky moral grounds considering their own disposition of the issue. New Englanders in particular, once they realized the economic unprofitability of slavery in their geographic region, often sold their slaves to Southerners rather than free them. Meanwhile, northern Indian tribes had mostly suffered extermination or brutal expulsion by the time of the southeastern tribes' removals.

The U.S. government, purposing humane treatment of the tribe but increasingly decided for removal, proposed at least two major deals to the Indians. The first, in 1832, as chronicled by Ross biographer Gary Moulton, promised the Cherokees autonomous government in Indian Territory, expenses for and authority over their move, financial provision for all their expenses for a year, a guaranteed annuity after that, payment for their lost land and improvements, the right for some to remain in their southeastern lands as citizens of the United States, and their own western lands "forever without the boundaries of any State or Territory."

John Ridge's shift toward support of removal occurred about the same time as Ross's influential opposition to this deal became known. The Cherokees' conditions worsened until, in 1835, government representatives met again with Ross and his lieutenants. Ross had finally indicated willingness to move, but demanded twenty million dollars as well as other costly considerations for the tribe to do so. The federal officials, nonetheless, secured his promise "to abide (by) the award of the . . . Senate . . . and to recommend the same for the final determination of our nation." The Senate indeed committed to provide the Cherokees multiple financial considerations, including millions of dollars in cash—but five million, not the proposed twenty million.

Ross, though infuriated, promised to take the proposal to the Cherokees and then comply with it as he had promised. Instead, according to Moulton, Ross portrayed it to his tribe as a rejection of his own proposal and an unofficial opinion by the U.S. Senate not confirmed by President Jackson, not binding on the Cherokee, and constituting collusion between the Ridge faction and the Jackson administration.

Treaty of New Echota

Only a small minority of Cherokees considered westward migration palatable, and fewer still wished for it, most of those having already gone. So, through his partisan manner of presentation and selection of the information he conveyed to the tribe,

Treaty Party leaders sign the Treaty of New Echota in the parlor of Elias Boudinot's home. According to historian William Welge, "When it came to signing the Treaty of New Echota, the Ridge-Watie-Boudinot faction saw it as frivolous to hold onto the land when they were being overrun by the federal forces."

Ross succeeded in sustaining their opposition to the removal treaty offered by the U.S. government. After informing the latter of the tribe's rejection of it, he then continued traveling to Washington at tribal expense, determined to negotiate better terms for the Cherokees—in particular, millions of dollars more in cash.

A long and ruinous dispute hatched between Boudinot, the Ridges, and others in what became known as the Treaty Party, and Ross and the majority Ross Party.

Both the American government and the Ridge faction—or Treaty Party as they came to be known, as opposed to the anti-removal majority Ross Party—pleaded with Ross to relent from his continued efforts to thwart the removal treaty, but he refused. Upon arriving in the nation's capital yet again in 1835, he received a less than cordial memorandum from the Commissioner of Indian Affairs, which read in part:

> The delegation of the Cherokee nation . . . which visited this city last winter, was emphatically assured . . . that no delegation would be received here to make a treaty; and, in defiance of that notification, you have come on and presented yourself for that purpose. How could you, under such circumstances, imagine that you would be received by the Department as the duly constituted representatives of the Cherokee people? It is not easy to account for that strange error of opinion.

Yet, the majority of Cherokees continued to back any actions Ross took that might forestall their removal. Thus, he found himself still in Washington on December 21, 1835, when U.S. officials met with Treaty Party leaders in the Cherokee country to sign the controversial Treaty of New Echota. The government, determining it had a deal with the Cherokees, in effect secured the most respectable and credible tribal leaders it could find to craft a written document of removal along the lines of the accord Ross had promised he would support. The fact that those leaders voiced the views of an informed but minority portion of the tribe mattered not to President Jackson nor to most of the government.

The Treaty of New Echota—passed by one vote in the Senate, then signed into law by President Jackson on May 23, 1836—gave the Cherokees two years to remove to Indian Territory. It conferred legal sanction to the conveyance to whites of tribal property and improvements throughout the southeastern states. And according to Cherokee law, crafted partly by Major Ridge, it carried the death

If Christianity is the basis of the laws of nations and the common law of the United States it surely is not out of place, though it should be unnecessary, to remind our lawgivers and judges that one of the great maxims of Christianity for the regulation of intercourse between men is that we should do to others whatever we would desire that they in like circumstances should do to us. Let the people of Georgia and the people of the United States reflect whether they would be willing to receive the same treatment with which the Cherokees are threatened.

—Jeremiah Evarts,
protesting efforts of the federals to persuade the Cherokees to move beyond the Mississippi River

penalty for those Treaty Party leaders—including Ridge, his son John, and his nephews Elias Boudinot and Stand Watie—who conveyed lands to the United States without tribal sanction. They did so despite knowing the mortal peril they now faced, and they neither sought nor received personal gain from the treaty.

Cherokee Tragedy Begins

Around two thousand Cherokees, primarily of the Treaty Party persuasion, traveled west of their own volition in late 1837 and early 1838. These people had settled their affairs in the southeast, prepared for the trip, and traveled in decent conditions with minimal suffering, although their hearts were rent with sorrow at leaving the land of their fathers.

Still, their Christian faith animating them, the Ridges, Elias Boudinot, and others saw the providence of God in their journey and found joy in their new land. John Ridge and his party arrived in present-day Oklahoma a few months after his father, Major, near the end of 1837. The younger Ridge rode throughout the new Cherokee country and found his already settled tribesmen preferring their new land to their old. As recounted by Thurman Wilkins in *Cherokee Tragedy*, he called it,

> the finest region . . . I ever beheld in any part of the United States. The streams of all sizes, from the rivers to the brooks, run swiftly over clean stones and pebbles, and water is clear as crystal, in which

Max Standley's *Forced Move,* depicting the sudden and heartbreaking expulsion of the Cherokees from their southeastern U.S. homelands, from his "Trail of Tears" series. (www.maxdstandley.com)

> excellent fish abound. . . . The soil (ranges) from the best prairie lands to the best bottom lands, in vast tracts. Never did I see a better location for settlements (with) better springs. God has thrown His favors here with a broad cast.

Meanwhile, most of the tribe not only remained in their southeastern homes, but they also took no action toward leaving, looking to John Ross for direction. The Principal Chief remained absent from the Cherokee country much of the next couple of years, still arguing in Washington against the removal and for more tribal money. These events set the stage for the horrific sequence of events inaugurated by the May 1838 arrival in Tennessee and Georgia of U.S. Army Major General Winfield Scott and several thousand federal soldiers. Though ordering kind, merciful, non-profane, and respectful treatment of all the Indians, Scott broadcast throughout the Cherokee nation a declaration that the departure deadline was past and all must leave.

> *It is mournful to see how reluctantly these people go away—even the stoutest hearts melt into tears when they turn their faces toward the setting sun—& I am sure that this land will be bedewed with a Nation's tears—if not with their blood. . . . Major Ridge is . . . said to be in a declining state, & it is doubted whether he will reach Arkansas.*
>
> —**Moravian Missionary H. G. Clauder** at the 1837 departure of Major Ridge and his party

Scott grew encouraged when some of the tribe began to leave. Then word came from Washington that the Ross delegation might soon win a two-year postponement of removal. That news quashed voluntary departures. The Cherokees en masse determined to stay put, and within days the bluecoats swarmed over the tribe, forcibly removing them by the hundreds to stockade concentration camps. No one has better recounted the pitiable chain of events that now unfolded than ethnologist James Mooney, who interviewed both white and Indian participants:

> Squads of troops were sent to search out with rifle and bayonet every small cabin hidden away in the coves or by the sides of mountain streams, to seize and bring in as prisoners all the occupants . . . . Families at dinner were startled by the sudden gleam of bayonets in the doorway and rose up to be driven with blows and oaths along the trail that led to the stockade. Men were seized in their fields or going along the road, women were taken from their wheels and children from their play.
>
> In many cases, on turning for one last look as they crossed the ridge, (the Cherokees) saw their homes in flames, fired by the lawless rabble that followed on the heels of the soldiers to loot and pillage. So keen were these outlaws on the scene that in some instances they were driving off the cattle and other stock of the Indians almost before the soldiers had fairly started the owners in the opposite direction.

Cherokee Trail of Tears

Federal soldiers soon began sending groups of Cherokees west. Historian Odie Faulk chronicled how both federal troops and Georgia militia committed acts of robbery, rape, and murder against those Indians who had not yet been shipped out. When Principal Chief Ross finally returned to the Cherokee country from his latest unsuccessful trip to Washington, his people's suffering had grown so extreme, even he ceased negotiating for better removal terms.

Rising at this point to a station of leadership matched by few American statesmen before or since, Ross secured General Scott's agreement to allow the Cherokees to conduct the remainder of the removal themselves. He separated the Cherokees into traveling parties of around one thousand people each. Then he delegated responsibility for food and other necessary provisions, monumental as those tasks proved to be.

These Cherokee travelers' pilgrimage started by boat, but much of it eventuated on horseback, wagon, or often foot. Many of the Indians, due to their sudden capture from their homes and elsewhere, possessed little more clothing than what they wore,

Robert Lindneux's epic portrait of the Cherokee Trail of Tears, which the tribe called, "The Place Where We Cried." Courtesy Woolaroc Museum.

if any more at all. Drought, exposure, lack of clean water, inadequate food, deadly cholera, measles, dysentery, and other illnesses, along with intense heat, bitter cold, and ice all conspired against the emigrants.

Historians have long claimed that as many as four thousand of them—nearly 20 percent of the entire tribe—perished through capture, captivity, journey, and adjustment to their new life in Indian Territory. Whatever the death toll, what the tribe called "The Place Where We Cried" remains one of the epic tragedies of American history. Examining the actual numbers derived from the various Cherokee groups who traveled west suggests a lesser number than four thousand. Based on the work of Jerry Clark, a Cherokee and archivist for over thirty years with the National Archives and Records Administration, the number of fatalities appears closer to twelve hundred.

Indian pastors like Jesse Bushyhead preached the Christian gospel to their people even on the Trail of Tears. Bushyhead—a Baptist and a Cherokee chief— had already translated parts of the Bible into the tribe's language. He led a Cherokee contingent on the journey west and conducted church services every Sunday. He later served as Chief Justice of the tribal nation.

In his *The Cherokee Indians and Those Who Came After*, historian N. C. Browder wrestled with the death count in his chapter on "Cherokee Arithmetic." He, too, challenged the four thousand figure and argued for a far smaller toll. He concluded, "[T]here is doubt about any Cherokee statistics," and contended that many historians have simply made wild guesses.

How could such an inflated number gain acceptance? Chief John Ross had collected money for the removal from the U.S. government based on a head count of emigrants. The more emigrants, the more money. For whatever reasons, this likely resulted in a higher than actual claim of removed Cherokees. When the number who arrived in Indian Territory proved far fewer than what Ross originally claimed, many were assumed to have died on the long journey. Ross's subsequent determination to be named Principal Chief of the entire tribe, including the previously separate Western Cherokee, gave him control of the national treasury.

The Dwight Mission that served the Cherokees from 1829 until, with some interruptions, 1948. Courtesy Oklahoma Historical Society.

Considering the horrible conditions of the camps into which the U.S. Army herded the Cherokees in the southeastern states to await the forced removal, as many if not more tribal members may have died before the infamous Trail of Tears than during it. The exact number who died remains unknown, but the number of four thousand has no evident grounding in the historical record.

> *Long time we travel on way to new land. People feel bad when they leave Old Nation. Women[s] cry and make sad wails. Children cry and many men cry, and all look sad like when friends die, but they say nothing and just put heads down and keep on go towards West. Many days pass and people die very much.*
>
> **—Cherokee full-blood regarding the "Trail of Tears"**

In a deadly irony—if not providential reciprocity—some of the same area of northern Georgia where the Cherokees suffered was visited one generation later with an even greater horror upon those who had succeeded the tribe in possessing that land. These later victims likely included descendants of the 1830s Georgia militia, and perhaps some of the militia themselves. General William Tecumseh Sherman and his Union armies during the War Between the States wreaked historic havoc on the land, often unwittingly duplicating deeds committed against the Cherokees. One example of how precise an imitation many of these acts were was the digging up and ransacking of the graves of the dead.

Max Standley's heartrending *The Trail of Tears,* from his "Trail of Tears" series. (www.maxdstandley.com)

As the Cherokees poured into present-day Oklahoma from the east, others were forced there from Texas, to the south. By 1839 rage over the violent toll taken on American life by the Comanches and other Plains tribes filled Mirabeau B. Lamar, the Republic's second president and a hero of the Texas War of Independence against Mexico. Lamar ordered the expulsion—or death—of all Indians in Texas. The longtime peaceable Cherokees, among whom famed Texas founding father and first president Sam Houston had lived in Indian Territory only a few years previously, fell under this dictate and rejoined their kinsmen there.

Chickasaw Removal

The Chickasaws, unlike the other Five Civilized Tribes, signed an agreement—the Treaty of Pontotoc with the United States in 1832—that provided for payment to them for their lands east of the Mississippi River. This treaty called for the Chickasaws to secure land in Indian Territory to which they could move. That process proved much more difficult than expected. In fact, five years passed before the Chickasaws, pursuing their land, signed the Treaty of Doaksville in 1837 with the Choctaws. The two tribes shared common blood, history, and traditions.

Most of the Choctaws had already removed to the west, and they sold a large expanse on the western side of their new land to the Chickasaws. The new treaty called for the two tribes to live under a unified government. Many Chickasaws, their tribe only about one-fourth as populous as the Choctaws from whom they had long stood independent, did not like that provision. It spawned trouble between the tribes, so they eventually jettisoned it.

Though the Chickasaw tribe suffered similar mistreatment and pressure to leave their mostly northern Mississippi homeland prior to leaving, they prepared more diligently to do so than other tribes and were thus better equipped to navigate the journey. Also, launching from northwest Mississippi, they had fewer miles to cover than most parties in the other tribes.

By 1840 they had settled en masse along the Washita River in the rolling plains, hills, and forests of south central and southwest Indian Territory. They suffered negligible loss of life and far less suffering than the other tribes during their migration, even though disease took a toll on them after they arrived. Blessed by the diligent leadership of Cyrus Harris, Winchester Colbert, and others, the Chickasaws soon established a productive new homeland.

Pressure on Seminoles

The U.S. government labored through the late 1820s and the 1830s to persuade the Seminoles to move west of their own volition. It offered money, supplies, and transportation. It offered land. It paid for Seminole leaders from the west to travel to Florida and persuade their fellows to migrate, as well as for Seminole leaders from the east to scout the Indian Territory and determine if they found it an acceptable new home. It offered to let the Seminoles conduct their own journey west.

In 1831, however, on the heels of the election of Indian removal zealot Andrew Jackson as President, Congressional passage of the Indian Removal Act, and a drought that devastated the Seminoles' already paltry crops, the federal government got deadly serious about detaching the tribe from its southeastern lands. Long before his election as President, Jackson had played a key role in forging nine of the eleven treaties between 1814 and 1824 that loosed portions of the southeastern tribes from their lands and moved them to new ones in Indian Territory. Now, with Jackson the tip of its figurative spear, the government determined to move the Seminoles—the poorest of the five major southeastern tribes—west and once there, to force its reunification against the tribe's will, with

Seminole leaders who followed different paths toward the United States. Charley Emathla, left, like leaders of other southeastern tribes, was executed for negotiating the sale of tribal homelands in return for Indian Territory lands and other considerations. Osceola, right, fought it out against the Americans, and then died after capture.

White Settlers Massacred by the Seminoles: During the Seminole War of 1835–36 dramatizes atrocities committed by the Seminoles against white American settlers in Florida. From a woodcut in *An Authentic Narrative of the Seminole War, Providence, 1836.*

their Creek cousins. Otherwise, they would receive no financial annuities and would face the bayonet.

Striving for a peaceful resolution, the U.S. first offered provisions to those Seminoles who would leave. When most of the hungry tribe rebuffed the overture, the government orchestrated a reconnaissance trip to Indian Territory by key Seminoles to scout the available land and report back to their people. Through the 1832 Treaty of Payne's Landing and the 1833 Treaty of Fort Gibson, the government maneuvered the Seminole representatives who had traveled west into agreeing to forfeit their southeastern lands and move west.

Indian Removal chronicled the ominous foreshadowing of tragic events among the Cherokees that now unfolded with the Seminoles. The tribe rejected the removal deal, asserting that the traveling delegation had no authority to finalize such an arrangement. They also opposed joining the community and governance of the more numerous Creeks, as well as the jeopardy in which they feared that union might place their ownership of black slaves, a generally looser practice than that of other tribes and American whites.

Even members of the Seminoles' western delegation, led by legendary chief John Jumper, fumed that the United States intended to place the Seminoles in proximity to violent nomadic Southern Plains tribes such as the Comanches and Kiowas. Jumper believed the government had already sized up the Seminoles as a tribe that demonstrated similar proclivities toward theft, violence, and dishonesty. The federals' refusal to allow a tribal council to discuss the matter convinced the Seminoles they were being snookered, so the tribe abandoned plans to leave. When the supposed time of removal arrived, it warned its members not to leave, and tribesmen murdered Charley Emathla, a chief and one of the treaty signers.

The U.S. government warned the Seminoles to prepare for removal. Not only did the tribe ignore that admonition, but one of its most famous chieftains, Osceola, led a series of coordinated attacks that slaughtered scores of American officials, soldiers, and citizens. American troops and citizen militia from the Southern states thundered into Florida. Thus exploded the piteous Seminole Wars (Chapter 5, Wildcat feature). It took seven years, a

Seminole warriors hide from pursuing American soldiers during the Seminole Wars.

couple thousand deaths, tens of millions of dollars in expense, the killing of most of the tribal leadership including Osceola, and the devastation of much of the Seminole nation before the rebellion was put down and its removal west began.

Seminole Removal

The Seminoles began removing west in April 1836 from Tampa Bay, Florida. Numerous parties ranging in size from a few dozen to the eleven hundred-plus Seminole War captives imprisoned in New Orleans rode steamships, keelboats, wagons, and horses, and walked to Indian Territory between 1836 and 1842. One hundred sixty-five Seminoles traveled to the new country as late as June 1858.

The emigrants suffered in many ways. Over and over, rivers such as the Arkansas on which they traveled dried to such shallow drafts—or no drafts at all—that overland travel had to commence. Once on foot, exhaustion, exposure, scalding summer heat, terrifying winter blizzards heretofore unseen by the sub-tropical Floridian Indians, and additional sickness decimated the young, the old, and even some in their prime age of strength. Boats faltered, collided, or sank, and at least one boiler heater exploded, killing more Seminoles.

The terrain of the land across which the migrants traversed posed its own nightmares, not the least of them the dearth of roads or even cleared paths. Medical attention, as one Oklahoma historian referenced it, "provided to the emigrants . . . (was) little more than an impotent gesture in human kindness." Physicians assigned to the travelers proved as rare

Jackson Walker's *Do Your Best!*, an epic portrait of U.S. Major Francis Dade and his hundred-man force who went down fighting against a large force of Seminole and former black slaves. Once the American public learned of the massacre through the reports of a couple of wounded survivors, its fury launched the Second Seminole War that exacted a fearsome toll on both sides. Courtesy Jackson Walker Studios. (http://jacksonwalkerstudio.com/default.html)

Missionaries and Indians Battle Liquor (Part 1)

by Grant Foreman
Chronicles of Oklahoma

Choctaw Indians many years ago said that Neal Dow, the Maine apostle of temperance, was yet a boy when the first "council fire against whisky was kindled" by them. No class of people in this country had more reason to understand and dread the evils of intemperance than the American Indians. Particularly susceptible, they were from an early day the victims of white exploiters armed with this most potent weapon of spoliation. The government, in the administration of what passed for an Indian policy, enacted laws intended to protect the Indians from its devastating influence. As far back as 1802 in what was called the Indian Intercourse Act, the President was empowered in his discretion to prevent the sale of liquor to the Indians. Twenty years later Congress strengthened his hand slightly by the grant of power to search the stocks of traders in the Indian country for ardent spirits.

While outlawing whiskey in the Indian country when introduced by others, the government reserved to itself the use of it in negotiations with the Indians.

as lightning striking, and rarer still their ability to address the galaxy of physical and emotional maladies that beset the fatigued, often terrified, refugees.

White slave owners, some more akin to slave stealers, boarded Seminole-laden vessels, claimed ownership of the Natives' slaves, and took them. Sometimes the blacks were freedmen; sometimes they did belong to Seminoles, some living in much equity and freedom; sometimes they had run away from their Creek owners; and sometimes, indeed, they had run away from the whites who legally sought their return.

Finally, the Seminoles, along with thousands of other emigrants during the removal, suffered from poor government commissary contractor performance. The emigrants experienced inadequate food provisions, food delivered at unhelpful times or to wrong locations, and food that lacked nutrition or was outright rancid.

The U.S. government shipped nearly three thousand members of the tribe—many of them treated as prisoners—west to Indian Territory during the Seminole Trail of Tears between 1836 and 1842. When they arrived at their destinations, they faced bitterness, illness, federally mandated domination by the Creeks from whom they had already separated themselves in the southeast, and attacks from ferocious Plains Indians.

Some, including Wildcat of Seminole War fame and the brilliant black Seminole, John Horse, refused to remain in such a situation and eventually trekked to Mexico. There they took up land offered by the Mexican government in exchange for fighting the Apache Indians who, bludgeoned south by the powerful Comanches, raided Mexico. Others, like Micanopy, died during the process or soon thereafter. Still others, including Chief John Jumper, though rent with grief and bitterness, rose from the ashes of their tribe's ruined fortunes, shook the dust from their boots or moccasins, and set about crafting a better future than the past they had so sorrowfully survived.

Removal in Retrospect

The brutal nature of the Trails of Tears wrought havoc across the pantheon of "civilized" tribes and among every age and socioeconomic group

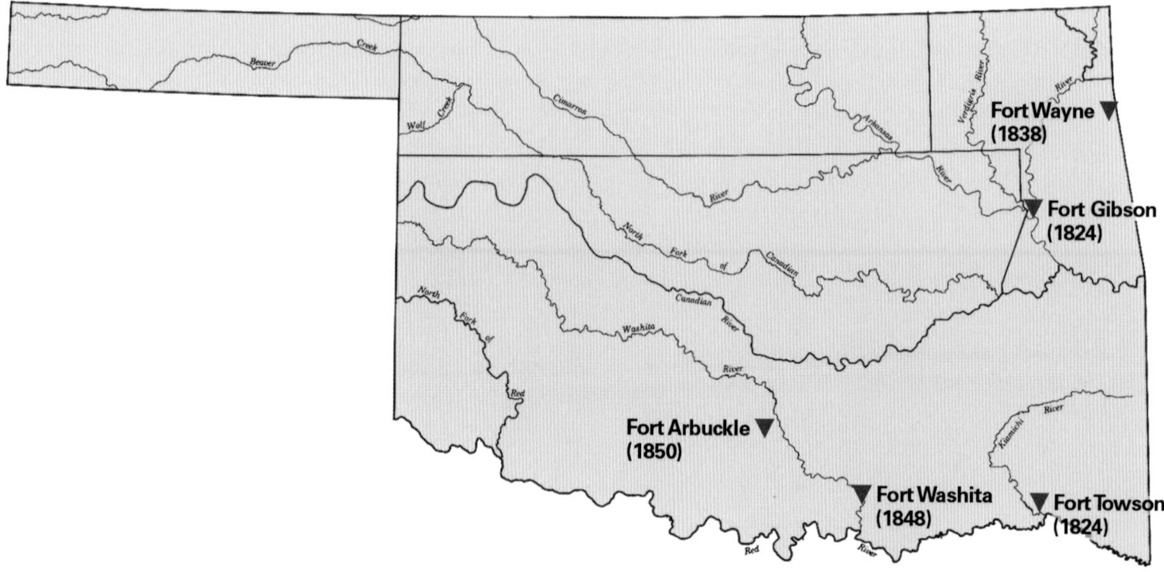

Pre-Civil War U.S. Army Indian Territory forts.

within those tribes. The exodus decimated both the youngest and the oldest of the Natives. A generation would pass before their population balance by age

When the steamboat *Heroine* (similar to the pictured vessel) churned up Red River in 1838, it evoked America's developing industrial power as well as its westward growth, specifically the adjacent Indian Territory. Its sinking after hitting an underwater outcropping illustrated the challenges facing both. The 1999 discovery of the boat's remnants sparked excitement, exploration, restoration, and a window into the little-documented designs of the era's elite watercraft. "In 1830, there were no plans on how to build a boat," explained historian Michael Dean. "You verbally told the boat maker what you wanted and they went by that. There were no known examples of what's designated a western river steamboat. This is the only one in existence."

group returned to normal proportions. Even many of the strong and well-to-do suffered financial, if not physical and emotional, ruin. More than a few wealthy plantation owners made the trek possessing little more than the clothing they wore.

Oklahoma historian Gaston Litton, in his magnum opus *History of Oklahoma,* published during the state's semicentennial anniversary in 1957, well summarized the towering tragedy of the Indian Removal:

1. The U.S. government failed to assess the magnitude of the colossal enterprise, which overwhelmed those assigned to execute it. In general, "Common sense, it would appear, was no more common an attribute in the 1830s than it was before or has been since."
2. The contractors providing the travelers' food and transport failed both the federal government to whom they were obligated to deliver materiel and the Indians who suffered because of this failure. Though the scarcity of available food sources hampered their efforts, often so did their own ineptitude and greed.
3. The weather took a fearsome human toll on the exposed travelers, as it ranged from unusually hot to bitterly cold.
4. Medical attention provided to the Indians proved "little more than an impotent gesture

Well-Intentioned Ethnic Cleansing

The Trail(s) of Tears and the overall subjugation and forced migrations of the American Indian tribes stand as mournful epics in American, even world, history. But a circumspect consideration of these events reveals that the United States government, however misguided and blundering, consistently intended to provide humane treatment and happy destinies for the tribes.

The third president, Thomas Jefferson, spoke of the equality of the Indian with the white "in body and mind." According to him, environment, not racial stock, had retarded the Natives' societal progress when contrasted with Western civilization. Better education, he posited, would result in a better environment. Many Americans cited the Christian religion as a key component of that education, not to mention of the Indians' destinies in the next world. The Natives, so such well-intentioned thinking went, would stand the best chance for all of this coming to pass by possessing their own remote lands, where unprofitable influences on them from white-dominated American society could be limited.

The fifth president, James Monroe, wrote of his Secretary of War (and later Vice President) John C. Calhoun's plan to move the southeastern Indians west to their own "Indian Territory." It would "promote the interests and happiness of these tribes," said Monroe, ". . . [to which] . . . the attention of the Government has long been drawn with great solicitude." Like Jefferson, Calhoun, and other American leaders, Monroe had no desire to remove these tribes from their homes by force, which he declared would be "revolting to humanity and utterly unjustifiable."

[T]he federal government sought first to persuade and reward rather than to compel. It offered cash payments, free land, supply provisions, military protection, and sometimes transportation.

Many other such quotes, as well as actions, prove that through each dismal chapter of Indian removal, relocation, and rights reductions, the federal government sought first to persuade and reward rather than to compel. It offered cash payments, free land, supply provisions, military protection, and sometimes transportation.

Modern Americans wish we could rewrite these pages of our history and infuse them with greater wisdom, vision, justice, and equanimity—with keener adherence to the beatific Christian principles to which many of us adhere. But our own contemporary failures and blindness in social and political matters domestic and foreign suggest the doubtful prospect that we would have dealt with the tribes any better than our white predecessors. For just as those pages reveal tragedy, they also reveal the often misguided but nonetheless honorable intentions of many of our forefathers.

Matthew Arbuckle—Soldier and Bridge Builder (1778–1851)

Were Oklahoma to erect its own Mount Rushmore for American soldiers who, amidst great peril sought not only the welfare of their fellow citizens but that of the benighted Natives they so often matched arms with, this good, perhaps even quietly great, man would take his place on the monument alongside Ethan Allan Hitchcock, Nathaniel Pryor, Sam Houston, A. P. Chouteau, and a select company of others.

in human kindness." The government provided so few physicians that most of the emigrants had none accompanying them.

These factors render all the more remarkable the phoenix rising from the ashes that were the southeastern Indian republics as they stooped and sweated to rebuild their peoples from the nightmare they had lived. They resumed their constitutionally governed and communal lives in Indian Territory, or crafted new laws and built new lives. Many a Cherokee, Chickasaw, Choctaw, Creek, and Seminole even dared to build better

Wayne Cooper's *Washington Irving Meeting the Osage.* "We came upon the banks of the Arkansas [River], at a place (near Tulsa)," Irving wrote in *A Tour on the Prairies.* "We reached a straggling Osage village. . . . Our arrival created quite a sensation. A number of old men came forward and shook hands with us severally; while the women and children huddled together in groups, staring at us wildly. . . . We gave them food, and, what they relished, coffee; for the Indians partake in the universal fondness for this beverage, which pervades the West." Courtesy Oklahoma State Senate Historical Preservation, Inc. and Wayne Cooper.

futures than the now-revered past they and their forbears had lived. Time and providence would reveal whether or not they succeeded.

Trouble in the West

The still-young American nation had all but moved heaven and earth to force the southeastern Indian Republics and other tribes west to its new Indian Territory. A "fly in the buttermilk," however, remained oblivious to all the federal government's best-laid plans—the Plains Indian tribes, and their own mortal enemies, the still-sanguinary Osages. The Plains tribes, which included the Comanches, Kiowas, and Wichitas, thwarted the U.S. government's promised plans of peace for the transplanted woodland tribes of eastern and southern present-day Oklahoma by raiding and plundering them.

The Osages, meanwhile, refused to move north to Kansas from Verdigris River enclaves in the heart of the Cherokee country as earlier agreed upon. They stole both Cherokee and Creek horses, along with other property. All of these tribes also imperiled the travel of American citizens traversing Indian Territory, whether to settle farther west or conduct other business.

Another lingering dilemma was the presence of such small tribes as the Shawnees, Senecas, and

Quapaws, who remained on land overlapping that of recently arrived groups such as the Cherokees. President Andrew Jackson appointed the three-man Stokes Commission, headed by North Carolina Governor Montfort Stokes, to address all these problems. This group succeeded in settling the tribal boundary disputes, but handling the Osages and the fearsome, nomadic Plains tribes proved a greater challenge.

Early outreaches to the Southern Plains tribes bore little fruit. This included an 1832 expedition on which the famed American author and historian Washington Irving (*The Legend of Sleepy Hollow, Rip Van Winkle*) traveled. Irving penned his acclaimed *A Tour on the Prairies* during the journey. A horrifying event the next year, however, helped bring the Plains tribes to the treaty table. A war party of Osages

Comanche Horsemanship

George Catlin's *Comanche Feats of Horsemanship* was part of his eyewitness chronicle in image and words of the daring horsemanship of the "Lords of the Plains":

> Amongst (the Comanche's) feats of riding, there is one that astonishes me more than anything of the kind that I have ever seen, or expect to see in my life: a stratagem of war, learned and practiced by every young man in the tribe; by which he is able to drop his body upon the side of the horse at the instant he is passing, effectively screened from his enemies' weapons as he lies in a horizontal position behind the body of his horse, with his heel hanging over the horse's back; by which he has the power of throwing himself up again, and changing to the other side of the horse if necessary. In this wonderful condition, he will hang whilst his horse is at fullest speed, carrying with him his bow and shield, and also his long lance of fourteen feet in length, all or either of which he will wield upon his enemy as he passes; rising and throwing his arrows over the horse's back, or with equal ease and equal success under the horse's neck. This astonishing feat, which the young men have repeatedly been playing off to our surprise as well as amusement, whilst they have been galloping away in front of our tents, completely puzzled the whole of us; and appeared to be the result of magic, rather than skills acquired by practice.

Wayne Cooper's *Friends for a Day,* based on an episode Washington Irving recounted in his 1832 book, *A Tour on the Prairies: An Account of Thirty Days in Deep Indian Country.* A teenage Osage boy brought a stray horse into the camp of an expedition that included Irving. The Cherokees in the party—typically no friends of the Osages—accused the young man of stealing the horse and suggested flogging him. Irving and others, including young Swiss nobleman Albert de Pourtalès, intervened on his behalf. De Pourtalès hired the Osage as his personal squire. This scene depicts their riding together. The boy soon disappeared, however, possibly due to pressure from his Osage elders. Courtesy the Oklahoma State Senate Historical Preservation Fund, Inc. and Wayne Cooper.

followed a Kiowa trail to Cutthroat Gap in present-day northwest Comanche County/southwest Oklahoma. There lay a defenseless Kiowa village, its warriors away on a hunt. The Osages massacred over one hundred women, children, and old men—committing beheadings and other atrocities—and took away others as captives.

George Catlin's spectacular depiction of an Osage, left, and Comanche, right, warrior duel.

American Soldiers

During the next year, 1834, a historic expedition headed west across present-day Oklahoma from Fort Gibson to treat with the Southern Plains tribes. Federal soldiers now posted in the rugged Indian Territory comprised most of this force. As with the tribes who traveled the Trails of Tears, the Oklahoma country proved new, difficult, and far from home for these American troopers. They manned a series of new forts erected to protect various tribes at various times, and eventually, American settlers. The forts included Coffee, Gibson, Towson, Leavenworth, Washita, Arbuckle, and Cobb.

These soldiers' frequently hazardous service during the antebellum years proved indispensable in fashioning lands for the emigrant tribes much more

General Henry Leavenworth's fateful fall during what became known as the Dodge Expedition, as sketched by G. N. Taylor. Leavenworth died during the trek either from this accident or illness, or a combination of the two. Command of the famous expedition across Indian Territory to treat with Plains Indians then devolved to Colonel Henry Dodge. (www.gntayloroklaart.com)

secure than they would otherwise have been, as well as restraining uncooperative whites and Indians alike. Perhaps no one has depicted the life of these men better than historian Faulk:

> Duty at these posts was hard and dangerous for the soldiers. The men erected their quarters themselves, cutting logs or quarrying stone, moving these to the desired location, and erecting them according to plans drawn by their officers. They fought malaria and bilious fevers, ate government hardtack and bacon, escorted supply wagons, scouted new territory, and sometimes fought Indians or white renegades—all for eight dollars a month.

Dodge and the Dragoons

The aforementioned westward column aimed to meet with the Comanches, Kiowas, Kiowa-Apaches, Wichitas, and other Plains Indian tribes. The assemblage included Stokes, as well as an imposing five hundred-man column of dragoons, a newly constituted formation of mounted infantry. It also included a host of names now familiar in the gallery of American historical luminaries—General Henry Leavenworth, who commanded the column, Colonel Henry Dodge (already a famous soldier who had commanded the first mounted U.S. Army Regulars in history), Stephen W. Kearney ("Father of the U.S. Cavalry"), Nathan Boone (son of Daniel Boone), David Hunter (well-known Civil War general), George Catlin (famed artist whose paintings first recorded present-day Oklahoma), and Jefferson Davis (future U.S. Senator, Secretary of War, and President of the Confederate States of America).

The American military column's epic quest brought drama, glory, death, heartbreak, and a courage that helped write the history of America.

All told, this expedition comprised the most impressive American military force yet assembled in Indian Territory. Their epic quest brought drama, glory, death, heartbreak, and a courage that helped write the history of America. By the time they reached the mouth of the Washita River where it poured into Red River, near present-day Lake Texoma, scores of soldiers—including Leavenworth—had been victimized by heat, typhus fever, and exhaustion. More than a hundred and fifty of them—again including Leavenworth, who suffered a bad fall from his horse—would die. "Perhaps there never has been in America a campaign that operated more severely on man and horses," Dodge concluded.

Artist George Catlin's rendering of Henry Dodge, renowned for his exploits in both the Black Hawk War and Indian Territory, and later governor of and U.S. Senator from Wisconsin.

After Leavenworth fell, Dodge took command and led the column west. Riding through present-day Stephens County, a Sergeant Evans wrote of the "highly romantic and elevated prairies" and large herds of wild horses on Wild Horse Creek between present-day Marlow and Duncan. The dragoons continued into present-day Kiowa County, where they met with Plains tribes' representatives at the Wichita village on the North Fork of Red River. The remaining contingent of soldiers greatly impressed the Natives, as did the former's delivery of Kiowa and Wichita hostages from

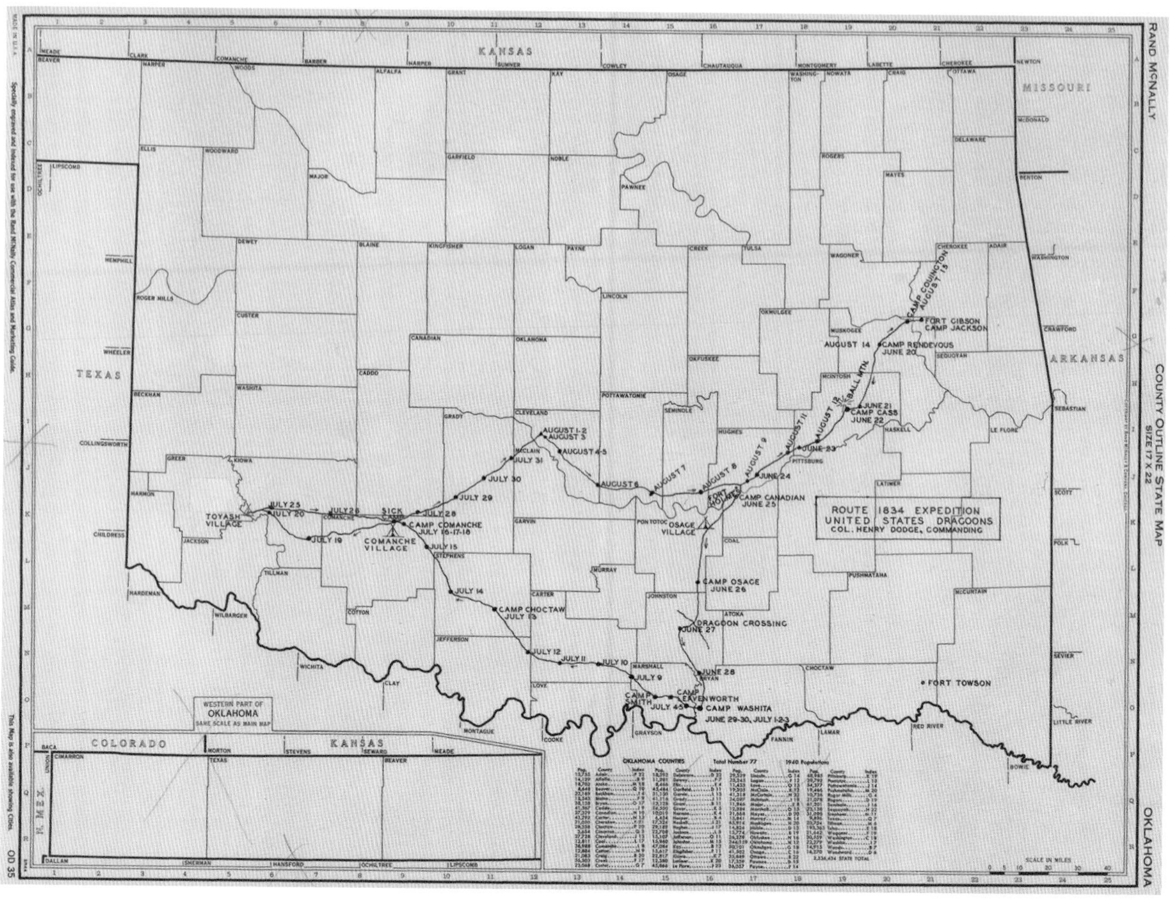

The historic early trek through the teeth of "Indian Country" by General Henry Dodge and his U.S. Army dragoons in 1834. Courtesy Oklahoma Historical Society Map Collection.

the Osages. This meeting led to another a few months later at Fort Gibson.

There, Dodge and other American officials treated with delegates from the Plains tribes, the southeastern immigrant tribes, and even the Osages. All of these tribes, and the U.S. officials, consented to peaceful relations with one another in Indian Territory. The tribes agreed to a treaty council west in the buffalo country in July of the next year, 1835, "when the grass next grows after the snows, which are soon to fall, shall have melted away."

Little Spaniard and the Comanche warriors meeting the Dodge Expedition, as painted by eyewitness George Catlin. "A gallant little fellow," Catlin described Little Spaniard, "represented to us as one of the leading warriors of the tribe . . . half Spanish . . . commanded the highest admiration and respect of the tribe for his daring and adventurous career. We had many exhibitions of his extraordinary strength, as well as agility; and of his gentlemanly politeness and friendship we had as frequent evidences."

That gathering, known as the Camp Holmes Treaty Conference, took place just north of present-day Lexington in Cleveland County. Between six and eight thousand Indians gathered, multiple interpreters translated the many speeches, and on August 24, 1835, the first treaty ever signed between the United States and the Southern Plains tribes was inked. All the major groups of the latter except the Kiowa signed, along with the Cherokees, Choctaws, Creeks, Quapaws, and Senecas who had come from the east.

This landmark peace agreement was not kept inviolate, but two years later the Kiowas signed on. Then when the Osage bands along the Verdigris, acquiescing to the might of American soldiery, retreated north into Kansas in 1839, a historic framework was established that gave hope, after so much suffering, for peace among the many vigorous peoples in the future Oklahoma country.

Indian Republics Rebuild

English poet Rudyard Kipling exhorted young men in his matchless poem *If for Boys*:

> *If you can watch the things you gave your life to, broken,*
> *And stoop and build 'em up with worn-out tools...*

That is what present-day Oklahoma's new tribes set about doing. While hurt, mistreated, frightened, and heartbroken, they wrested much of their new country from the lawless, the wicked, and the heathen and made something special of it, raising their name into the highest ranks of the future Sooner state and even of America.

How that happened varied vastly among the tribes. The Choctaws had arrived in Indian Territory en masse first, by the mid-1830s. They also had the least intratribal factional conflict. They wrote present-day Oklahoma's first constitution, having crafted an earlier one back in Mississippi. They continued their federative system of government, replete with legislative, executive, and judicial branches, as well as mounted companies of law enforcement officers known as lighthorsemen.

The Chickasaws, having governed themselves since at least the 1600s in Mississippi after breaking apart from the Choctaws, chafed at the federal government's coercion of them back under the aegis of their former brethren in the 1837 Treaty of Doaksville. The Chickasaws comprised a fourth Choctaw district and received the requisite elective representation, but lost their autonomy. Inhabiting the westernmost Choctaw district, which reached as far out as present-day Duncan on the future Chisholm Trail, the Chickasaws also faced bloody raids from Comanches and other Plains warriors who frequented the regions just to the west.

The mass of Creeks that arrived in present-day Oklahoma in the mid-1830s settled separately from the earlier arriving McIntosh Creeks, with whom many of them had disputed or even fought back in Georgia and Alabama. The groups cooperated, however, with the McIntosh faction extending advice and capital resources, and the later arrivals integrating with the tribal government and laws already established by Roley McIntosh and his group.

The Seminoles had emerged from the Creeks as a distinctive tribe, similar to how the Chickasaws had separated from the Choctaws. The Florida

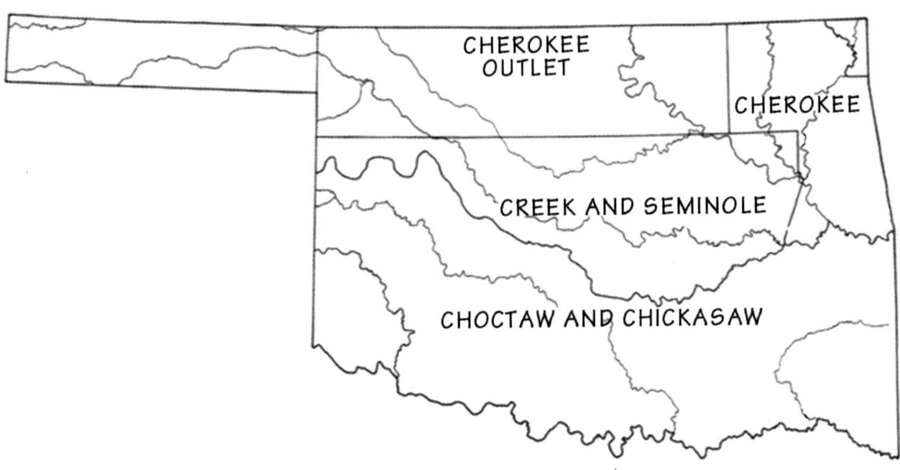

The exiled tribes start over in Indian Territory in Max Standley's Arrival in Indian Territory. (www.maxdstandley.com)

emigrants proved no happier than the Chickasaws when the U.S. government returned them to tribal jurisdiction under the Creeks. The Seminoles, who had come from tropical Florida, also suffered in the colder and harsher Indian Territory climate.

Though the Choctaws, Chickasaws, Creeks, and Seminoles all faced enormous challenges in their new lands, the Cherokees—considered in many ways the most advanced of the five Indian Republics—found the greatest ordeal awaiting them in Indian Territory. Their continuing troubles, along with new ones gathering as Principal Chief John Ross and the majority of the Cherokees labored to settle in, mushroomed mostly from within the tribe itself.

Boudinot Tells Ross Why the Cherokees Must Leave

Elias Boudinot penned a classic rejoinder to Principal Chief John Ross regarding why he believed the Cherokees must accept the U.S. Government's hefty incentives to migrate to Indian Territory for their own blessing, even survival.

> It is a little singular that while you declare the New Echota Treaty to be "deceptive to the world and a fraud upon the Cherokee People," although it was made in the face of day and in the eye of the nation, to prove your assertion, you resort to matters which are deceptive and fraudulent. . . . The fact is, these Cherokees, perhaps, have never spent one moment's thought beyond that of loving and securing the land upon which they live—their whole instructions has tended to that point. According to that instruction, and the impressions produced in their minds by your want of candor and plan dealing, a portion of the Cherokees may be opposed to the New Echota Treaty, but not more than they would be to any other, as long as they understood you as trying to reinstate them in their country. This is the whole secret of this much talked of opposition. Is it right to humor this delusion? Be candid with them—tell that their country cannot be saved, and that you want their authority to sell, yes, to sell it—an authority which you have alleged to the Government you have received, and you will see to where this opposition against a removal will go.

G. N. Taylor's *Distant Relatives,* which portrays a "visit" to migrants from one of the Five Civilized Tribes, right, by roughhewn Plains Natives, left. The latter no doubt seemed very distant relations indeed to the former, who found their violent raids an unexpected additional challenge in a new land already fraught with hardship. (www.gntayloroklaart.com)

Elias Boudinot and Harriett Gold—Cherokee Romeo and Puritan Juliet (1802–1839) (1805–1836)

One of the great martyrs of Oklahoma history is hardly better known than the anonymous leaves that fall from the pecan and persimmon trees in the lovely Green Country he helped secure for his beloved Cherokees. Elias Boudinot—originally known as Gallagina in Cherokee and Buck Watie in English—lived for his family, his tribe, and his Savior, and ultimately he died for them. Yet where his name is still known, controversy and passions boil over with colorful words like "tainted," "traitor," and "bought." Still, his legacy, co-crafted by his first wife Harriett Ruggles Gold, the great love of his life, demonstrates how in the long view of history, one person, though imperfect and fraught with conflict, nonetheless did and can shape the destiny of Oklahoma for the better in a comprehensive fashion affecting every part of an individual's and a people's life.

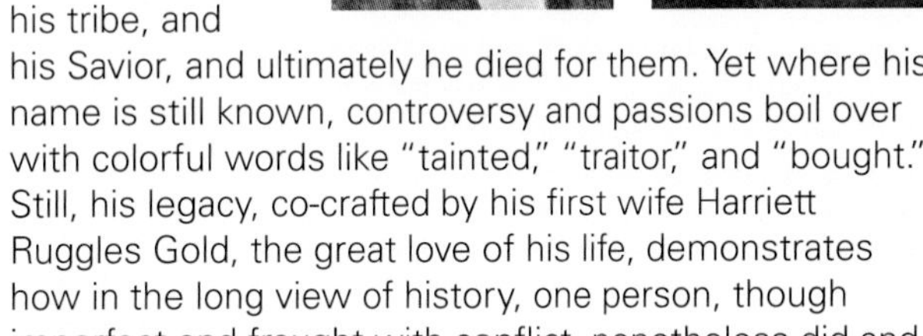

To Marry an Indian: The Marriage of Harriett Gold and Elias Boudinot in Letters, 1823–1839, edited by Theresa Strouth. It contains the letters of Harriett Gold and Elias Boudinot during their dramatic interracial courtship.

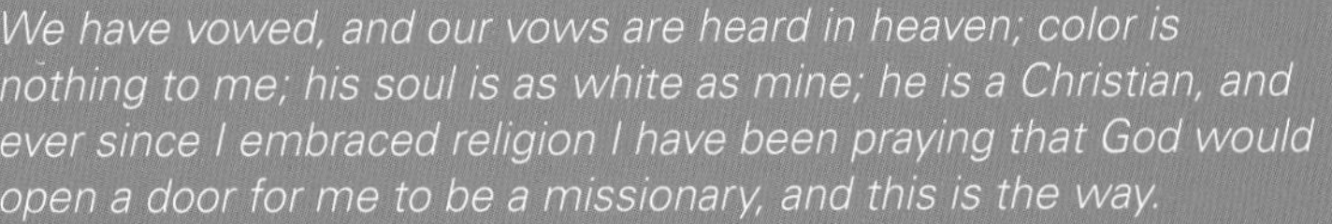

We have vowed, and our vows are heard in heaven; color is nothing to me; his soul is as white as mine; he is a Christian, and ever since I embraced religion I have been praying that God would open a door for me to be a missionary, and this is the way.

—Harriett Gold Boudinot

The modest frame structure where Elias and Harriett Boudinot made their pre-removal home and life in New Calhoun, Georgia.

Who Killed Boudinot and the Ridges?

The unknown identity of those who brutally assassinated Cherokee Treaty Party leaders Major Ridge, John Ridge, and Elias Boudinot sparked hot, sometimes violent debate from the day the killings happened. Treaty Party supporters and others accused supporters of Principal Chief John Ross and in some cases even Ross himself. The accused denied involvement. More than half a century later, however, Ross's son Allen left written, eyewitness testimony with his own grandsons recounting how he and other leaders of the majority Ross Party indeed carried out the plot, though he claimed his father was unaware of their actions and would have opposed them.

The homemade knife used by supporters of Cherokee Principal Chief John Ross to kill Elias Boudinot, according to Ross's son Allen.

For years tension and even outright violence had escalated between those tribal groups that developed into the Ross and Treaty (or Ridge) Parties. The presence of thousands of "Old Settler" Cherokees, including the legendary Sequoyah, who had populated Arkansas and eastern Indian Territory for decades and had long ago established their own self-sustaining communities and government, further complicated matters.

Then on June 22, 1839, three of the most gifted Cherokee leaders who ever lived—Major Ridge, John Ridge, and Elias Boudinot—were brutally executed, all at the hands of fellow Cherokees, who believed they were acting for the good of the tribe and by its rule of law. A fourth man, Boudinot's brother Stand Watie, narrowly escaped that fate. He outraced attackers on a horse named Comet because of its fleetness and loaned to him by Samuel Worcester, who warned him of his peril. These acts, however, would spawn a tragic intratribal civil war that raged through much of the following decade.

Oklahoma has been horse country for a long time. "There is no other animal on the prairies so wild and so sagacious as the horse," wrote artist George Catlin of them in 1834 Indian Territory. "I made many attempts to approach them by stealth, when they were grazing and playing their gambols, without ever having been more than once able to succeed . . . . we saw all the colours, nearly, that can be seen in a kennel of English hounds. Some were milk white, some jet black—others were sorrel, and bay, and cream colour—many were of an iron grey; and others were pied, containing a variety of colours on the same animal. Their manes were very profuse, and hanging in the wildest confusion over their necks and faces—and their long tails swept the ground."

5

1840–1850s

The Cross of Christ

Wheelock Church, built in the mid-1840s by Presbyterian missionary, preacher, physician, educator, and translator Rev. Alfred Wright; his wife Harriett; and their congregation. The sturdy stone structure houses Oklahoma's oldest still-functioning church building. Photo Rhys Martin. (https://rhysfunk.wordpress.com)

1841	Cherokee National Council enacts anti-liquor laws
1842, 1853	Indian slave revolts
1846	Treaty of 1846 reconciles rival Cherokee factions
1850s	Choctaw and Chickasaw cotton plantations flourish
1855	Chickasaws gain independence from Choctaws
1856	Seminoles gain independence from Creeks
1858	Butterfield Overland Mail Trail begins stagecoach service
1858	ABCFM begins defunding non-abolitionist missionaries

> *O what a solemn thought, that they have all of their immortal souls to be saved or lost. How much may be depending on me on the influence that I exert on their souls, what shall be their future state, fearful responsibility! Who is sufficient for these things? Three of my dear pupils have lately hoped that they had given their hearts to the Savior. Pray for them my dear Mother that they may hold out to the end, and will you not pray for me so that I may be fitted for my work. . .*
>
> **—Jerusha Swain, female New England missionary**

What was the situation in which the peoples of Indian Territory—now mostly the southeastern Indian Republics and other tribes forced from the East—found themselves as the decade of the 1840s began? The United States government had labored for years to clear a safe haven for the Five Civilized Tribes upon their arrival in Indian Territory. It also worked to preserve land for smaller tribes threatened by the arrival of the southeastern Indians. The sanguinary Osages were given new land in Kansas, although it took much federal government effort, U.S. troops, and Cherokee warriors to get and keep them there.

Meanwhile, federal forts, a sizable central present-day Oklahoma buffer zone (including the heavily-forested Cross Timbers that runs from Kansas south to Red River), and peace accords such as the 1835 treaty near present-day Lexington helped keep

Robbie Pierce and Don Prechtel's mural *Nathan Boone*, depicting the soldier-explorer son of Daniel Boone leading American Dragoons through the salt flats of the Cimarron River west of present-day Freedom in 1843. Courtesy Alva Mural Society (www.alvamurals.org)

the Comanches, Kiowas, and other Plains Indians away from the immigrant Indians. Still, the men of the Five Civilized Tribes themselves—red, partly or mostly white, and partly or all black alike—tamed the frontier comprising the eastern half of Indian Territory and fashioned of it a land where homes, schools, courthouses, businesses, and churches could rise from the verdant wilderness.

The Cherokees, Chickasaws, Choctaws, Creeks, and Seminoles all owned black slaves. These descendants of Africa, residents of present-day Oklahoma long before the presence of more than a handful of white residents, already exercised a significant role in the building of the future Sooner State. They helped clear paths for the hard journeys, and men like Black Beaver guided travelers along those paths. They planted and raised crops, married and spawned families, and preached the Christian gospel, even creating famous songs to help spread it. Every step of the way, they shared in the suffering, the sacrifices, and the triumphs as pioneers who built an American state.

Traveling Oklahoma

Understanding the means and methods of nineteenth-century transportation through the Oklahoma country—especially navigating its rivers—provides much insight into the history of the state and its various, sometimes competing, groups of people.

Prior to the arrival of European explorers, the aboriginal Indian tribes of present-day Oklahoma got about on foot, although they sometimes utilized dogs to pull belongings and supplies from one location to another.

Coronado and other Spanish conquistadors brought the magnificent horse to present-day Oklahoma and the rest of the Western Hemisphere. The Spaniards' horses brought them unparalleled opportunities to cover vast amounts of territory and provided them, along with their powder ammunition guns and cannon, a decisive advantage in battle with Native tribes who opposed them. The horse then revolutionized the travel and warfare practices of the Indians, depending on who secured and mastered the use of the animal.

George Catlin's 1834 Indian Territory painting of Osage *Shin-ga-wą́s-sa, Handsome Bird.*

Roger Cooke's *The Supply Trail* mural. It depicts the provisioning of Fort Supply in present-day Woods County by horse-drawn stagecoach during the U.S. Army's post-Civil War campaign against the Southern Plains Indians. Courtesy Alva Mural Society. (www.alvamurals.org)

Raymonde Brousseau's striking *L'indienne en canoe* and French explorers repairing their canoe at a wilderness campfire.

The French stood unsurpassed in the handling of dugout canoes, extending back to their vast empire that ranged through Canada and the present-day American North and Midwest. They parlayed their expertise with the craft, along with its ability to penetrate the most foreboding mountains, forests, and thickets, into a means of establishing personal working relationships with often remote Indian Territory tribes. This led to lucrative trading arrangements between the French and the Natives and helped shove the Spanish out of the region. Indians and the emerging American trailblazers employed the canoe as well.

The first full-sized "boats" (fifty to eighty feet long, about fifteen feet wide) utilized for transportation into and across the Indian Territory were keelboats. Most famous for its transporting of many Indian removal bands, the keelboat also carried U.S. troops beginning in the 1820s, as well as mail, other government officials, and some American settlers. This boat stood unique from others through its two main methods of propulsion.

One was "tow-lining," for which a dozen or so men walked along either bank of the channel the keelboat traversed and pulled it forward with a rawhide tow-line fastened to the boat's masthead. The other was "poling." With this method, men stood along both sides of the boat, dropped poles to the bottom of the waterway, and then walked forward, pushing the poles against the bottom and thus shoving the craft forward. Pilots sometimes used sails or oars. But no matter which method was used, keelboat travel proved slow. Typically only twelve to fifteen miles could be covered in a full day. Still, this mode of travel required

Felix Achille Saint-Aulaire's 1830s lithograph of a keelboat that traversed the rivers of Western America.

a draught of only a few inches of water, uniquely fitting it for Indian Territory's shallow rivers and streams.

The superior power and speed of steamboats multiplied the travel along eastern Indian Territory watercourses from the time the *Comet* churned up the Arkansas River in 1820. Although the shallow draft of the area's streams required smallish steamboats, many still sank due to rocks, stumps, and other concealed obstacles. Steamboats—including stern-wheelers propelled by a paddle

Titian Ramsay Peale's eyewitness drawing of the Western Engineer steamship that Stephen Long commanded on his journey (Chapter 2), which concluded on foot across present-day Oklahoma.

wheel in their back—nonetheless elevated the Arkansas and Grand Rivers for a half-century into the central commercial lanes between Fort Gibson and the Three Forks region and the outside world. Only late nineteenth-century railroads altered this preeminence.

Once Captain Henry M. Shreve, working under U.S. government auspices, cleared the one hundred and fifty-mile "Great Raft" tangle from Red River, steamboats regularly navigated that famous stream as well. Their traffic helped propel the entire southeastern Indian Territory region's economy. They provided the slave-worked plantations of Choctaw Robert M. Jones, Chickasaw Robert Love, and others the means for shipping their vast Red River produce. Steamboats also supplied the region—Native settlers, U.S. military, and others—with food, dry goods, and other supplies.

Indian Territory tribes did not welcome the fabled "Iron Horse," which did so much to accelerate the spread of American culture and commercial enterprise across North America. While exercising autonomy over the territory, the Natives kept the railroad out. The fall of the Confederacy—with whom most in the Indian Republics had sided—provided the federal government the excuse it sought to mandate the laying of tracks across tribal land. From the end of the War Between the States in 1865 onward, the government seized increasing control of their territory.

No watercraft able to negotiate present-day Oklahoma's shallow rivers and streams could compare with the speed, size, and power of the railroad locomotive and train. The challenge for the powers in Washington and their large corporate associates was growing Indian Territory's population, despite tribal opposition. They needed enough "customers" to justify the overhead costs necessary to move trains in and out of the region. Punishment for their defeat in the Civil War would solve this challenge, too.

Like many railroad lines running in different directions through present-day Oklahoma, the Fort Smith & Western connected customers and products to markets farther east and north. The FS&W eventually ran through Choctaw coal country all the way to the territorial capital of Guthrie.

Conflict from Within

The conflict and pressure that faced the Five Civilized Tribes continued from multiple sources. Sometimes, trouble flared from within—the Western Cherokees (Old Settlers) already settled in Indian Territory resented sharing their land with the larger (Ross) group that had just arrived, not to mention assenting to their tribal rule. And, within six months of the latter's 1838 arrival, members of that faction killed every Treaty Party leader except Stand Watie, who escaped with the help and horse of his friend, Rev. Samuel Worcester (Chapter 4).

> *The Chickasaws and Seminoles still faced what they considered tyranny from other tribes among the Indian Republics themselves.*

A low-grade, but pitiable civil war—replete with threats, kidnappings, assassinations, and other shootings—seethed for years among the tribe. Finally, Ross and Watie reconciled themselves and their factions in the Treaty of 1846, helmed by a U.S. presidential commission sought by Ross which resulted in a united Cherokee nation. This selfless act of Watie—whose brother, uncle, and cousin had been murdered by Ross Party members—shines as one of the great acts of patriotic statesmanship in early Oklahoma history.

John Mix Stanley's *International Indian Council.* Cherokee Principal Chief John Ross called the 1843 convention in Tahlequah. It drew ten thousand Natives from twenty-one tribes to address the chaotic bloodshed running rampant between tribes including the Pawnees, Caddos, Delawares, Kansas, Osages, Wichitas, and all five Indian republics. Ross's own tribe was immersed in its own guerilla civil war.

The Chickasaws and Seminoles, meanwhile, still faced what they considered tyranny from others among the Indian Republics themselves. As mentioned in Chapter 4, the Chickasaws had earlier separated themselves from the Choctaws. They conducted their own affairs quite well, including battering the French in a war during which that mercantilist European power had attempted to subdue them. Now, however, the federal government, in addition to removing the Chickasaws hundreds of miles west from their ancestral homeland (also described in Chapter 4), was ordering them to participate in, but also subject themselves to, the constitutional governing process of their much more numerous former fellow tribesmen—the Choctaws.

The Chickasaws bristled under this restrictive arrangement, believing—as minority groups often have in America—that the general government was not adequately committed to their interests. As one historian termed it, this "ill-advised arrangement... led to endless contention (that) brought the two tribes to the verge of disorder and violence." Finally in 1855, the Chickasaws secured the agreement of both the Choctaws and the U.S. government to reestablish their own autonomy and self-government, which they did, under a constitutional system much like the Choctaws'.

The Seminoles, a proud tribe who had fought a seven-year war in Florida with the U.S. military, likewise chafed under the federal government's requirement for them to live in minority status among the Creeks, from whom they had chosen to separate themselves. (Nearly fifteen thousand Creeks were forced west to join the approximately twenty-five hundred previously departed McIntosh Creeks, while the government removed less than four thousand Seminoles.)

A host of issues fueled the new discord. First, the Seminoles learned upon arriving in Indian Territory that choice land promised to them by the Creeks near the North Fork of the Canadian River was already settled by that tribe. Then, as mentioned in Chapter 4, they suffered under the harsher and colder climate, which was so different from that of their native Florida. Also, though largely townfolk, they were superb hunters, so they did not like the agricultural life to which the U.S. government attempted to convert them.

Finally, they faced ongoing tension with the Creeks regarding their African-American slaves. Both tribes held slaves—as did all the Five Civilized Tribes—but Seminole slaves generally enjoyed a greater degree of liberty (often virtual equality) than those of the other tribes. Indeed, some of the Seminole blacks had escaped to them back in Florida from other Native tribes or whites. This distinction grew more serious when the Creeks claimed some of these African-Americans as their own, as some white slave owners had done during the Seminole emigration.

During the height of Indian Removal, Fort Gibson housed the largest military garrison in America. Its occupants formed an illustrious roster of nineteenth-century military and political titans. *Fort Gibson 1840* by Oklahoma artist Christopher Nick depicts three men who became leaders of sovereign nations, including Republic of Texas President Sam Houston (brown buckskin jacket and tan hat), U.S. President Zachary Taylor (on horseback), and Confederate States President Jefferson Davis (dark uniform, to the right of Taylor). Other famous "residents" included Robert E. Lee, Henry Leavenworth, Stephen Kearney, and Matthew Arbuckle. Used with permission from the Oklahoma State Senate Collection and the artist. Courtesy Oklahoma State Senate Historical Preservation Fund, a project of Charles Ford.

Restored Fort Gibson troop barracks. Through much of the nineteenth century, the fort (Chapter 4) provided security and a social gathering venue for whites, Indians, and African-Americans alike. General Matthew Arbuckle and other commanders established a gracious spirit of diplomacy and respect with all the area's disparate people groups that prevented much potential violence. The fort's soldiers included future President Zachary Taylor, future Confederate President Jefferson Davis, and Robert E. Lee.

The Seminoles dealt with the threat to their black slaves first by remaining near Fort Gibson for U.S. military protection, and then by settling away from the Creeks along Little River near Wewoka in 1845. Led by legendary chief John Jumper, however, they labored long for independence from the Creeks, finally attaining it in Washington in 1856.

Alone among the Five Indian Republics, the Seminoles never committed their laws to a written constitution. They predicated their government on the local rule of their twenty-five towns. Each of those communities elected their own chiefs and warrior councils, the former serving in an executive capacity, the latter in a legislative one. These leaders met in annual councils and advised their mica (leading chief)—first Micanopy, then Jumper.

Pioneer Oklahoma Roads

Early Roads—American soldiers carved wagon roads and trails out of Indian Territory wilderness in the 1820s and 1830s to connect the emigrant Native settlements and the U.S. forts, especially where rivers did not run nearby. In 1825, troopers pioneered the first road in the territory, a fifty-eight mile wagon route connecting Fort Smith and Fort Gibson. Other such important roads ran from Fort Smith to Fort Towson, Fort Gibson to Fort Towson, and Fort Gibson through present-day Tulsa to the mouth of the Cimarron River.

Texas Road—Blazed from the Grand River Valley by 1) merchants bringing products manufactured up north and back east; and 2) settlers, first heading into the pivotal Three Forks region, and then, especially beginning in the 1840s, south into Texas.

The nineteenth-century Texas Road, generally coinciding with modern U.S. Highway 69.

Gregg Route/California Road—Famously marked out in 1839 by American merchant Josiah Gregg, the great east–west route that ran from Van Buren, Arkansas, across Indian Territory along the Canadian River, and on to Santa Fe, New Mexico, where Gregg was one of the region's most successful traders. A decade later, the onset of the California Gold Rush brought cries from prospectors for military escorts across present-day Oklahoma, in particular the western half, still rife with mounted, hostile Plains Indians. U.S. Army Captain Randolph Marcy conducted an official survey of a Canadian Valley route that largely mirrored Gregg's, and along that swarmed one of the great treks to California. On Marcy's return (east-west) trip, he surveyed what became a more southern California Road route that ran from El Paso across Texas, to Red River at Colbert's Ferry, then northwest to Fort Smith.

Acclaimed photographer Jim Argo's modern capturing of the old California Road that traversed present-day Oklahoma. Historian William Welge recalled that "Wagons journeying along the road left deeply cut wagon ruts in the sandstone of present-day Red Rock Canyon State Park near Hinton."

Butterfield Overland Stage Route—The iconic cross-country western stagecoach route of fact and legend ran, beginning in 1858, from St. Louis and Memphis to San Francisco and Los Angeles. The 192-mile Indian Territory leg cut southwest from Fort Smith, through the Choctaw country, to Colbert's Ferry on Red River. It included fourteen horse-changing rest stops and forty-five hours of travel. One traveler called this rugged trek "two hundred miles of the worst road God ever built." Butterfield stages employed a driver, a rear-stationed guard, additional guards sometimes, as many as nine passengers inside and five more on top, and a team of at least four horses (and more for difficult terrain).

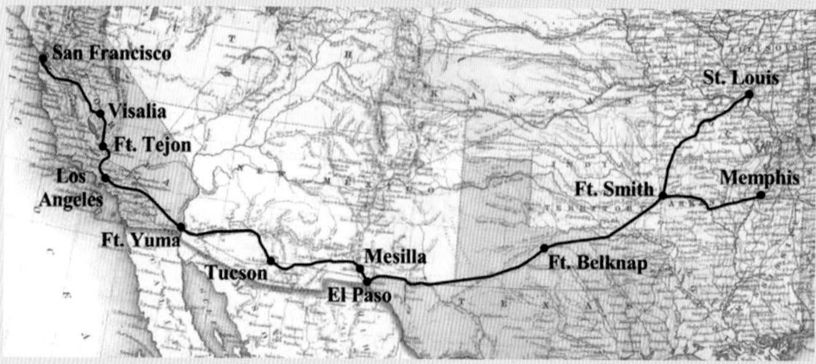

Butterfield Overland Mail Route, 1858–1861.

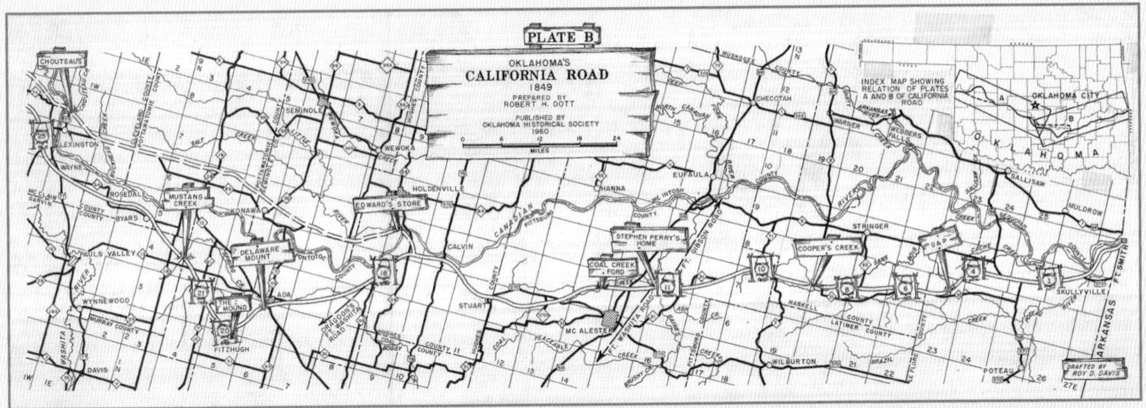

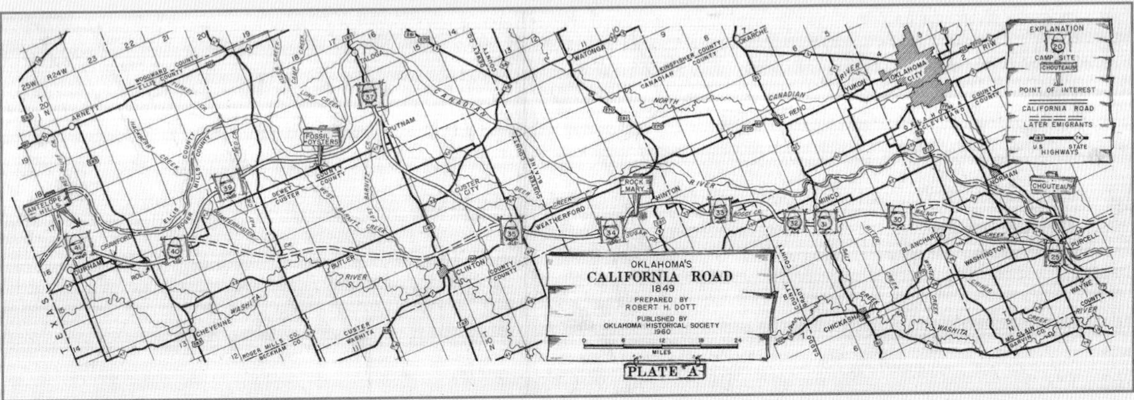

Robert Dott's vibrant map of the California Road (western Indian Territory portion top, eastern Indian Territory below) through present-day Oklahoma, overview inset. The map spotlights stations along the journey against a backdrop of modern communities that provides additional geographical context. Courtesy Oklahoma Historical Society.

G. N. Taylor's *New Year's Eve at Fisher's Station*, as stagecoach horse teams are changed. Fisher's Station, located in present-day Bryan County, was named for its owner-operator Fisher Durant, a Choctaw after whom the town of Durant was also named. It sat astride both the Texas Road and the boundary line between the Choctaw and Chickasaw countries. It was one of numerous stops on the rugged, Indian-threatened 1858–1861 Butterfield Overland stage route through Indian Territory. (www.gntayloroklaart.com)

George Catlin's *Ball-Play of the Choctaw—Ball up*. Sometimes referred to as "the little brother of war," these rough, sprawling contests provided a "civilized" means of settling disputes between Choctaw communities. The opposing goals could lie from one hundred feet to several miles apart. "It is no uncommon occurrence," Catlin wrote, "for six or eight hundred or a thousand of these young men to engage in a game of ball, with five or six times that number of spectators, of men, women, and children surrounding the ground and looking on."

Rising from Ashes

The Choctaws and Chickasaws engineered one of the great feats in American history: a people stared disaster in the face, then defiantly determined to overcome it. As before, mixed-blood tribesmen led the way in commercial productivity, application of the technology spawned from the burgeoning Industrial Revolution, and the harvest of bounty from new tribal lands. If they planted and harvested any crops, the majority of full-bloods limited their seeding to subsistence patches of a few acres apiece.

Led by the brilliant mixed-blood Choctaw Robert M. Jones, Chickasaw Robert Love, and other entrepreneurial mixed-blood planters, the emigrants staged a remarkable recovery from their removal lamentations. Parlaying federal government annuities, profits from their own enterprises, goods purchased from both Native and licensed white merchants and traders, and the labor of black slaves, they extended the Southern plantation system across southern Indian Territory and utilized their own steamboat traffic along the Red, Kiamichi, and Mississippi Rivers to establish the region as a hub of commercial trade with the eastern and southern United States. Men like Jones and Love cultivated some individual cotton and corn fields that spread over fifty acres apiece in size.

Members of the five Indian republics churned out products and produce that included beef, pork, poultry, sheep, eggs, vegetables, cotton, grain, butter, salt, lead, pecans, and wild honey. They provided not only for themselves, but other tribes, U.S. military personnel in the territory, and consumers in surrounding states and back east. The Chickasaws and Cherokees, in particular, raised big, strong horses, racing some and selling others. The Natives established saw mills, grist mills, salt works, cotton gins, and lead mines. They worked as artisans, carpenters, blacksmiths, shoemakers, and tanners.

Historian Arrell M. Gibson described the homes many tribespeople raised up for themselves from the wilderness:

> Indian settlers cleared fields and hewed logs from thick forest stands which they used to construct dwellings. These varied from single-room cabins to double-log dwellings connected by a passage (the "dog trot") between, with porches on both sides of the structure. Back of the cabin were log stables, barns, corrals, and a kennel for hunting dogs. Later, the more successful farmers and stock raisers replaced their log houses with . . . mansions, furnished with carpeting, piano, library, and other fixtures elegant as those of eastern homes.

Socially, the Five Civilized Tribes embraced the Christian faith to a much greater degree than before their removal. They generally favored abstinence from the intoxicating drinks that ravaged so many of their friends' and families' lives.

Cherokee Principal Chief John Ross's Rose Cottage plantation house, near Tahlequah, circa late-1850s.

They built schools considered superior to those of the whites of the time in surrounding states and sent their children back east for college when they had the means. Moreover, they established and supported newspapers such as the *Choctaw Intelligencer* in Doaksville and the *Cherokee Advocate* in Tahlequah. They passionately participated in and supported sports such as the ball play (similar to lacrosse, sometimes featuring over a hundred players at a time), horse racing, and fox chases.

Through all this, tribal property among the five Indian republics remained communally owned, other than the dwellings and improvements created by

Robert M. Jones, Choctaw Plantation King (1808–1873)

Something about the part-Choctaw, part-white boy caught the eye of someone in the white missionaries' party in early-nineteenth-century Mississippi. The man, whose identity is lost to history, sponsored young Robert M. Jones through the local Christian mission school, then to a collegiate-type academy in Kentucky. Upon the completion of his education at that school, a trustee and two teachers gave Jones a letter of reference describing their opinion of him. This excerpt provides a window into a future replete with adventure, accomplishment, heartbreak, and triumph: "(Jones is) a young man of sterling worth, strictly honest and just . . . a high and dignified sense of honor . . . in whom the utmost confidence may be placed, as to integrity and ability on his part to discharge faithfully any duty he would undertake."

Susan Colbert and Robert M. Jones

Page No. 4

SCHEDULE 2.—Slave Inhabitants in the Choctaw Nation in the County of Red River State of ________, enumerated by me, on the 15th day of August, 1860. E. J. Corder Ass't Marshal.

	NAMES OF SLAVE OWNERS.	Number of Slaves.	Age.	Sex.	Color.	Fugitives from the State.	Number manumitted.	Deaf & dumb, blind, insane, or idiotic.	No. of Slave houses.	NAMES OF SLAVE OWNERS.	Number of Slaves.	Age.	Sex.	Color.	Fugitives from the State.	Number manumitted.	Deaf & dumb, blind, insane, or idiotic.	No. of Slave houses.	
	1	2	3	4	5	6	7	8	9	1	2	3	4	5	6	7	8	9	
1		1	9	m	B						1	45	m	B					1
2		1	7	f	B						1	22	m	B					2
3		1	5	f	B						1	40	m	B					3
4		1	3	m	B						1	30	m	B					4
5		1	21	f	m	1					1	40	m	B					5
6		1	13	m	B				3		1	25	f	B					6
7	Leonidas D. Garland	1	33	m	B				1		1	25	f	B					7
8	John P. Garland	1	30	f	m	1					1	16	f	m	/				8
9	12	1	12	m	B						1	25	f	B					9
10		1	9	m	B						1	45	f	B					10
11		1	6	m	B				1		1	25	f	B					11
12	Robert M. Jones'	1	65	f	m	1					1	13	f	B					12
13	Walnut Prairie Farm	1	65	m	B						1	12	f	B					13
14	Reported by G. W. Rowan	1	60	f	B						1	35	f	B					14
15	13	1	45	f	B						1	25	f	B					15
16		1	40	m	B						1	25	f	B					16
17		1	30	m	B						1	25	f	m	1				17
18		1	19	m	B						1	40	m	B					18
19		1	22	m	B						1	18	f	B					19
20		1	16	m	B						1	30	f	B					20
21		1	30	m	B						1 1	30 38	f m	B B					21
22		1	12	m	B						1	21	m	B					22
23		1	19	m	B						1	21	f	B					23
24		1	25	m	B						1	18	f	B					24
25		1	20	f	B						1	18	f	B					25
26		1	20	f	B						1	33	m	B					26
27		1	25	m	B						1	30	m	B					27
28		1	19	m	B						1	45	m	m	1				28
29		1	25	f	B						1	10	m	B					29
30		1	19	f	B						1	8	m	B					30
31		1	38	m	B						1	10	f	B					31
32		1	28	m	m	1					1	10	f	B					32
33		1	35	m	m	1					1	9	f	B					33
34		1	30	m	m	1					1	9	f	B					34
35		1	40	f	m	1					1	6	f	B					35
36		1	24	m	B						1	30	f	B				14	36
37		1	25	m	B					Shawnee Town Farm 14	1	90	f	B					37
38		1	20	m	m	1					1	70	m	B					38
39		1	40	f	B						1	65	m	B					39
40		1	25	m	B						1	60	m	B					40

No. of owners, ____ No. of houses, ____ No. of male slaves, 43 No. of female slaves, 38 Total slaves, . . 81 No. fugitives, ____ No. manumitted, ____ No. deaf and dumb, ____ No. blind, ____ No. insane, ____ No. idiotic, ____

81

A brilliant entrepreneur and shrewd advocate for his tribe's economic and social welfare, Robert M. Jones owned plantations, steamboats, businesses, and the most slaves in Indian Territory. This page from the National Archives' 1860 Slave Schedule shows a portion of the approximately 225 slaves he owned at the time.

individual citizens, and free for development by any tribal member who chose to do so.

Southern Plains

Across Red River to the south in Texas, the war of civilizations had grown unspeakably barbaric. The Texans had already forced the Mexicans from their land. After innumerable deaths, maimings, and

Red River site of Colbert's Ferry, primary nineteenth-century crossing of the waterway on the Texas Road. Photo Jim Argo.

atrocities on both sides, they now determined that every Native in the state would either leave or be killed. By the late 1850s, the tough, relentless Texans, were shoving even fierce tribes like the Comanches and Kiowas northward toward the barren prairies of western Indian Territory.

The U.S. government facilitated this by leasing roughly the southwest quarter of present-day Oklahoma, the Leased District, as a refuge and reservation for these so-called "wild tribes." That did not settle the problem, however, because these Indians preferred the nomadic life of hunting buffalo on the Southern Plains and raiding white settlements in Texas instead of the settled routine of farming and ranching. They blazed war trails south back into Texas and thundered down them to steal, destroy, or kill every vestige of American civilization they could.

Periodically, mounted contingents of Texas Rangers or U.S. cavalry rode into the Leased District and shot it out with the Indians. During one such ferocious battle in 1858, Captain and future Confederate General Earl Van Dorn and his U.S. horse soldiers—including future Texas governor

What the Indians Wore

A Shawnee chief.

A Kiowa girl.

The people of the Indian Territory indulged in a great variation of styles of wearing apparel. The mixed-bloods and intermarried white citizens (whites who married Indians) dressed in accordance with the styles prevailing in the Eastern states. Among the full-blood element, particularly, the hunting shirt of the frontier was common. This costume consisted also of a handkerchief or small shawl, which was usually worn around the head in the shape of a turban. The Indian wore a pair of moccasins on his feet, along with a pair of pants with long leggings of buckskin, fringed at the sides. Wintertime usually brought the addition of a blanket, which was wrapped around the shoulder for extra warmth. The hunting shirts commonly worn by men were usually made of homespun material, except on gala occasions (such as Sundays and holidays), when the hunting shirt might consist of brightly-colored calicos or prints brought from the trader.

The Native women rarely wore a hat or bonnet, even those who dressed in rich silks after the latest of Eastern fashions. Instead, they wore a shawl or handkerchief around their head. Sometimes they carried a parasol instead. A Cherokee woman who traveled over the Trail of Tears as a small child remembered nearly ninety years later details about the clothing they wore then. "I learned to spin when I was a very little girl," she remembered, "and I could make cloth and jeans for dresses and such other garments as we wore. We never any of us wore store clothes and manufactured cloth until after the Civil War." To dye their homespun, the Indians grew their own indigo, gathered sumac berries, found hickory and maple bark, and learned to prepare these and other ingredients to blend colors, which they much preferred over chemical dyes when these became available later.

—Gaston Litton, *The History of Oklahoma*

Earl Van Dorn

Lawrence "Sul" Ross—ambushed and decimated a Comanche raiding party at Rush Springs in present-day Grady County. The battle-hardened Van Dorn himself survived arrow wounds to the arm, stomach, and lungs in the five-hour shootout, and Ross an arrow wound to the shoulder along with a .58 caliber chest wound. The same year, Texas Ranger Captain John "Rip" Ford led a Texan force that chased marauding Plains Indians back across Red River and tracked them down in the Leased District in present-day Ellis County.

Sul Ross

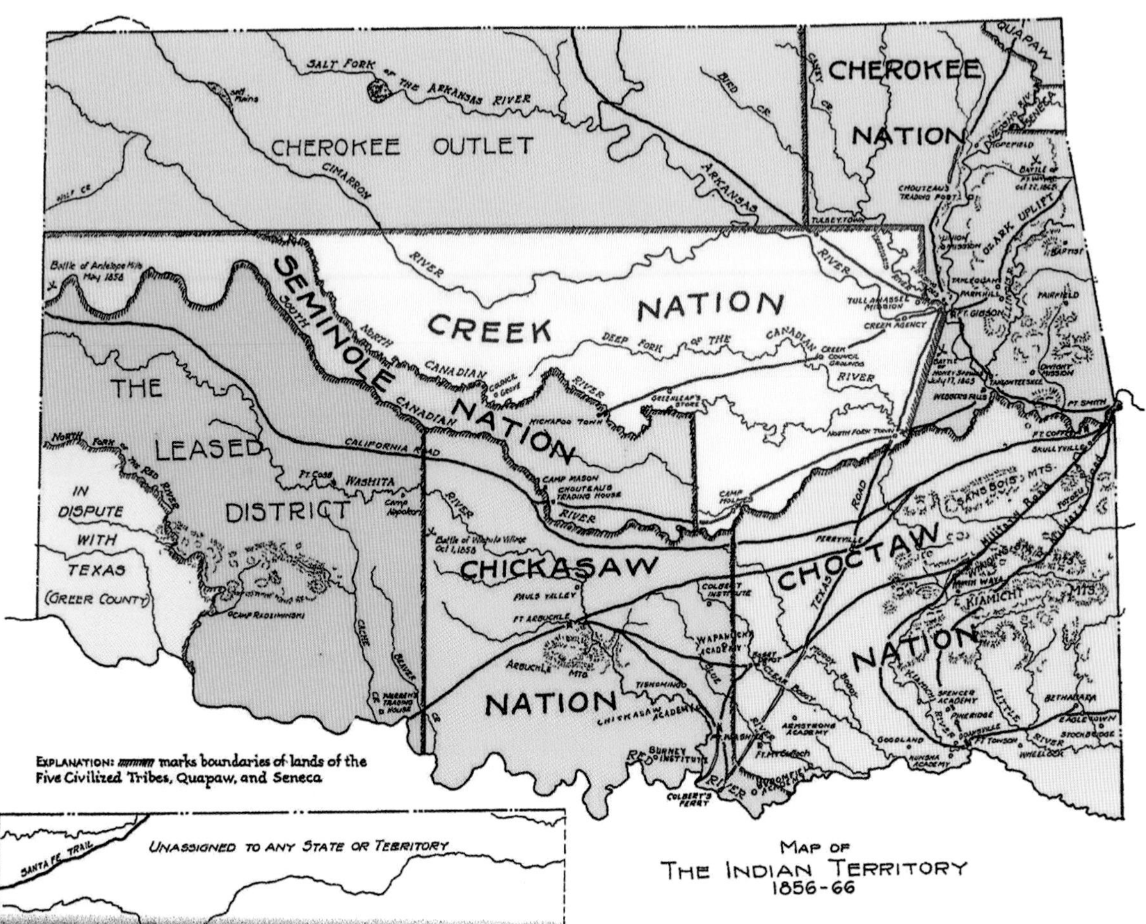

Rip Ford

In a spectacular mounted battle ranging over many miles, the Rangers and some Tonkawa allies, firing Colt .45 revolvers and breech-loading carbines, tore a large Comanche force twice their size to pieces.

When one considers the events and participants of nineteenth-century Oklahoma, the truth emerges that it was the quintessential Old West, American West, and Wild West. It is

Wild Cat (Coacoochee) (c. 1810–1857)

No one in early Oklahoma annals exhibited a more passionate heart for the welfare of his people, nor a more imaginative, resourceful spirit in pursuing it, than Seminole statesman, entrepreneur, warrior, and visionary Coacoochee, whose English variant name was Wild Cat.

Wild Cat.

Wild Cat spearheaded an odyssey of Seminole leaders to Washington, D.C. in 1843 to petition for independence from the Creeks.

where the buffalo roamed, and where cowboys and outlaws, horse soldiers and Indians, rode and fought and made history.

Indian Territory Blacks

As the 1850s wound down and the War Between the States loomed ever larger and more ominous on the American horizon, the population of Indian Territory stood around sixty-six thousand. Indians comprised the bulk of this number, with three thousand white missionaries, traders, soldiers, teachers, Indian agents, and other citizens, many married to Natives. Around eighty-four hundred African-Americans, most of them slaves, formed the remainder of the population. Cherokees owned the largest number of slaves, forty-six hundred by 1860.

Blacks of African descent came to America almost from the beginning of permanent Christian settlement by the Europeans. They came as slaves, captured in Africa by other black tribes who conquered and enslaved them. Those Africans sold them to Europeans and Arab slave traders. The Europeans brought them across the Atlantic Ocean, packed on disease-ridden ships in horrific conditions.

Between one and two million black Africans died on this so-called "Middle Passage." Only a small percentage of their number, between six and eight percent, wound up in the future United States.

Seminole Indians with African-American blood are predominant in this nineteenth-century photo of mixed-bloods.

An African-American Cherokee woman in Native dress.

Most went to Brazil and other Caribbean and South American countries.

Those black Africans whose destiny was America faced a long and difficult journey to societal equality. Many factors contributed to this, not least the pagan beliefs and practices of African cultures, which stymied their spiritual, educational, and social development as compared with Western cultures. This factor, along with the inherent sinfulness of all people and the advent of Social Darwinism in the mid-nineteenth century, spawned racist views among whites and other races in the United States that perceived blacks as originating from inherently inferior racial stock. These unbiblical beliefs led to catastrophic tragedy for African-Americans and, to some extent, all Americans.

The Cherokees, Chickasaws, Choctaws, and Creeks, similar to the inhabitants of the American slave states in the Midwest and South, treated most of their black slaves humanely—notwithstanding the inherent coercion of those who held usually permanent chattel status—and allowed them a significant degree of autonomy beyond the requirements of their work. Also like the slave states of the Union, however, the Indian republics—aside from the Seminoles—established strict social restrictions regarding blacks, slave or free. These included the following: 1) the prohibition of marriage between Natives and African-Americans; 2) any slave who murdered an Indian received the death penalty; 3) a Native who murdered a slave was legally bound to pay the owner of the deceased the financial value of the latter, or suffer execution; and 4) a slave guilty of murdering another slave received a whipping of a hundred lashes, and the murderer's owner had to pay the deceased's owner one-half the value of the victim.

The Cherokees, Chickasaws, and Choctaws also forbade adoption into their tribes of blacks. In addition, they did not allow blacks to hold an office. If a tribal member wished to free his slaves, he could do so, but he had to transport them out of tribal lands.

The Seminoles continued to permit more freedom among the African-Americans among them, including the slave majority. In return for an annual "tribute" of food and other products and services, they could travel at will from their usually separate villages. Many Seminole slaves could read and write and some served as interpreters and office workers.

Churches and Slavery

The complexity of slavery—so simply explained away by modern Americans—evidenced itself in the controversy that arose over the issue even among the great mission-sending organizations of the Christian church. The famed New England-based American Board of Commissioners for Foreign Missions (ABCFM), which sponsored two of the era's prominent denominational missions efforts, the Presbyterian and Congregationalist, denounced slavery and increasingly called for its immediate abolition.

This abolitionist position stood in contrast to the anti-slavery sentiments of most Americans North and South. Anti-slavery supporters desired the gradual cessation of the practice, in conformity with their views of what the United States Constitution, other laws of the land, and even the Bible taught. Many of them advocated financial remittance to the owners whose personal and familial economic survival often depended upon the institution. In contrast, abolitionists demanding an immediate end to slavery often dismissed concerns over the rule of law in that scenario.

During the 1850s, the ABCFM began to require its missionaries in Indian Territory to renounce slavery and even prohibit granting Communion and church membership to supporters of it. Many Cherokees, Chickasaws, Choctaws, Creeks, and even Seminoles, however, felt that releasing their slaves to fend for themselves was an uncharitable, if not unchristian, act. Like other Southerners, they denounced what they considered the hypocrisy of some Northerners, whose region had earlier sold many of its slaves to the South, rather than emancipate them when the practice proved unprofitable in their cooler climate with its shorter growing seasons. The five tribal republics now resident in Indian Territory not only opposed such actions, but they established their own requirements that missionaries working among their tribes *not* be abolitionists.

Some of the greatest missionaries in American history, working in the Indian Nations, opposed the ABCFM's actions. Although many were personally anti-slavery, if not abolitionist, they considered those actions counterproductive to the progress of the Christian gospel in a culture where its propagation now flourished. Like the ancient Roman Empire, slavery was legal and widely practiced, but still roundly considered more humane than in Rome.

Missionary Elizur Butler had suffered imprisonment on behalf of the Cherokees back in Georgia (Chapter 4). When the ABCFM commanded him to withhold the sacraments of the church from slaveholding Indians, he risked his own material livelihood by riposting, "I have members who are slaveholders, who are nearer the Kingdom than I am. I hereby tender my resignation." Legendary Indian Territory missionaries Cyrus Kingsbury and Cyrus Byington—no supporters of slavery—stood with numerous other Christian leaders against the ABCFM's actions that opposed the Five Indian Republics and their spiritual shepherds.

Some Northern missionaries, including Welsh-born Baptist Evan Jones and his son John,

Indian Territory Slaves . . . In Their Own Words

Elsie Pryor

(Former Choctaw slave)

We danced everything that was on the fiddle. The Schottische, Polka, Mazurka, Waltz and the Quadrille. Sometime when the fiddle was all we could get for music, some of the boys would get a pair of bones, horse ribs or something of the kind and keep time beating on a chairback with them to make more time. Then sometimes we'd have a banjo, too. Some would pat and some would whistle and we'd dance. Then sometimes somebody would get drunk and kill somebody and that would break up the dance. After a few years of that, my husband and I decided that this ole world was wicked and that we'd better jine the church. So we jined up with the Missionary Baptist, and then we went to the big turn-outs and meetin's, with the big dinners. Hit got so you wasn't recognized unless you belonged to the church. They used to have big Tom Fuller dinners at them big meetin's.

Lucinda Vann

(Former Cherokee slave)

The married folks lived in little houses and there was big long houses for all the single men. The young, single girls lived with the old folks in another big long, house. The slaves who worked in the big house was the first class. Next, came the carpenters, yard men, blacksmiths, race-horse men, steamboat men and like that. The low class work in the fields. Marster Jim and Missus Jennie wouldn't let his house slaves go with no common dress out. They never sent us anywhere with a cotton dress. They wanted everybody know we was Marster Vann's slaves. He wanted people to know he was able to dress his slaves in fine clothes. We had fine satin dresses, great big combs for our hair, great big gold locket, double ear-rings, we never wore cotton except when we worked. We had bonnets that had long silk tassels for ties. When we wanted to go anywhere we always got a horse, we never walked. Everything was fine, Lord, have mercy on me, yes.

A slave house on a plantation near Talala, Cherokee country, in present-day Rogers County.

Polly Colbert

(Former Chickasaw slave)

When Master Holmes and Miss Betty Love was married dey fathers give my father and mother to dem for a wedding gift. I was born at Tishominge and we moved to de farm on Red River soon after dat and I been here ever since . . . . My mother died when I was real small, and about a year after dat my father died. Master Holmes told us children not to cry, dat he and Miss Betsy would take good care of us. Dey did, too. Day teak us in do house wid dem and look after us jest as good as dey could colored children. We slept in a little room close to them and she allus coon dat us was covered up good before she went to bed . . . .

supported abolition and influenced the mostly full-blood Cherokees and other Indians among whom they worked toward that view. By the eve of America's great and terrible war with itself in 1860, the ABCFM had terminated its financial support of Christian missions in Indian Territory, and most Northern missionaries had abandoned the region.

Slave Revolts

Indian Territory blacks engineered at least two daring escape attempts. One happened in 1842, when about twenty-five slaves belonging to wealthy businessman Joseph Vann and other Cherokee planters and businessmen (including Lewis Ross, brother of Principal Chief John Ross) locked their masters and overseers in their homes and cabins early on the morning of November 15th and fled toward Mexico. The revolters wisely eschewed violence, but they stole animals, food, weapons, and supplies. Ten more Creek slaves joined them farther south. The fugitives fought with and killed two slave hunters in the Choctaw country.

The Fortitude and Charity of Oklahoma Slaves

Slavery had existed among the Southern Indians for some generations before their removal to the Indian Territory. . . . The slaves, in most cases, were well treated, clothed and fed with little distinction as to their color. Wiley Britton, in his study on *The Civil War on the Border*, comments that "the Negroes brought up among the Indians were under such feeble restraint from infancy up that the owners and dealers in slaves in Missouri and Arkansas did not hesitate to acknowledge that Indian Negroes were undesirable because of the difficulty of controlling them."

—Gaston Litton, *The History of Oklahoma*

Wayne Cooper's *S. W. Woodhouse at Lost City* captures the surgeon-naturalist as he records some of the first scientific observations of Indian Territory geology and wildlife during the 1849–50 Creek Indian boundary survey on the Arkansas River just west of modern-day Tulsa. The dramatic limestone outcropping known as "Lost City" appears across the Arkansas near present-day Sand Springs. Courtesy Oklahoma State Senate Historical Preservation Fund, Inc. and Wayne Cooper.

Meanwhile, back in the Cherokee capital of Tahlequah, tribal leaders authorized the eighty-seven-man Cherokee Militia, headed by Captain John Drew, to pursue the escaped slaves. After eleven days of hard riding, the posse caught the runaways seven miles north of Red River. Exhausted and hungry, the fugitives offered no resistance.

The militia took their prisoners back to Tahlequah, where authorities condemned five to execution and ordered others punished. Cherokee leaders blamed armed African-American Seminole freedmen living near the Cherokee slaves at Fort Gibson for provoking the revolt. Just seventeen days after the escape, the Cherokee nation passed a law ordering all free blacks, other than former Cherokee slaves, to leave the Cherokee country.

In 1853, a group of African-American freedmen harassed a series of Choctaw villages, then barricaded themselves on Boggy Creek. Choctaw calls for assistance brought a force of American soldiers from Fort Washita that scattered the freedmen.

Atha Shelby DeWeese's nineteenth-century painting of the original Wheelock Presbyterian Church, near present-day Millerton in McCurtain County. Choctaw tradition says the church rose on the very spot where the tribe's Trail of Tears ended. Courtesy Atha Shelby DeWeese estate.

Christian Missionaries

The towering story of mid-nineteenth century Indian Territory remains the tenacious Christian missionary efforts engineered by Presbyterians, Baptists, Methodists, Congregationalists, Moravians, Catholics, and others. Though some members of the Five Civilized Tribes became Christians prior to removal, many others did not, particularly among the major Muskogean tribes of the Creeks and Seminoles.

The cataclysmic experience of removal left these weary, heartsick tribes in an unprecedented position. They had suffered violent abuse and been forced to move across the country from their ancestral homes by a people who had only lately arrived in the Indians' own lands. Now they faced dangerous challenges in the new country they had been forced to embrace. All these events came at the hands of a people who claimed and even spread the Christian faith.

Resistance, even hostility, rose against that people and its religion, particularly among the Creeks. Sacred fires, "magic" medicines, stomp dances, and pow wows occurred across "The Nations" as Indian Territory was often called. Many in the tribes saw no reason to embrace Christianity after the way its professed adherents had treated them. Nothing less than the spiritual destiny of the Indian republics—whether they would develop as Christian or non-Christian peoples—hung in the balance.

Into this maelstrom of emotion, confusion, bitterness, and uncertainty rode those Christian missionaries. They emerged as one of the most courageous companies in Oklahoma history.

Into this maelstrom of emotion, confusion, bitterness, and uncertainty rode those Christian missionaries. They emerged as one of the most courageous companies in Oklahoma history. Scores of white missionary families, as well as single male and female missionaries, carved an indelible imprint on the Indian republics and the history of the territory and state. Large numbers of Christian Natives and African-Americans took up the banners of this crusade.

Perhaps Joseph's famous words at the end of the epic biblical book of Genesis about men meaning something for evil, but God meaning it for good had an application here. Multitudes of Choctaws, Seminoles, Creeks, Cherokees, and Chickasaws, battered and bereft, turned finally to Christ for salvation, from both earthly and heavenly horrors.

The gradual widespread acceptance of and adherence to Christianity among the civilized tribes corrected many of the Indians' dark ancestral practices. It also enhanced the quality of their lives through the 1840s and 1850s in Indian Territory, even though an increasing vulnerability to liquor (which whites had introduced to them), cast a shadow over them. Even here, Christian missionaries labored in service to the tribes, standing against the consumption of alcoholic spirits, warning about the destruction it brought to so many lives—red, white, and black alike—and giving exhortation to them about the powerful Christian lives they could have when abstaining from it.

Spiritual Warfare

Organized Christian mission efforts to Indian Territory began as early as 1820. The United Foreign Missionary Society (UFMS), a mission organization established in 1817 by a group of Reformed (Calvinistic) denominations, including the Presbyterians, Dutch Reformed, and Associated Reformed, was the tip of the Christian mission spear. The UFMS appointed Job Vinal and Epaphras Chapman to launch a Christian mission effort to Western Cherokees in Arkansas that wound up in Indian Territory.

Supported by congressional funds lobbied for by the UFMS and others, the organization declared its raison d'etre: "to spread the gospel among the Indians of North America." It set about that work in a potently holistic manner, teaching the Bible and the Christian faith as well as a classical Western educational curriculum, along with the skills and knowledge necessary for farming, mechanical arts, and other vocations. It also provided medical services.

From the beginning, the work of Christ among the Indian Nations proved challenging and dangerous. Vinal died before reaching the territory. Chapman headed a company of twenty-one, which included a physician, carpenter, blacksmith, farmer, and women to mentor tribal members in domestic skills. They endured a grueling odyssey to the Osage lands on the Grand River that lasted nearly a year. For decades, Indian Territory missionaries died of disease, found themselves caught in the crossfire of such wars as that between the Osages and Cherokees, and faced hostility from other individuals and groups.

Initially embittered at what they considered the church's collusion in the Native removal from the southeast, the Creeks stood among the most determined opponents of Christianity and its representatives. Conservative Creeks championed laws prohibiting white Christian missionaries from even setting foot on tribal land. They persecuted those who did. Also, they delivered brutal punishment, including fifty lashes with a bullwhip, to Indians and blacks who prayed or worshiped on Creek land.

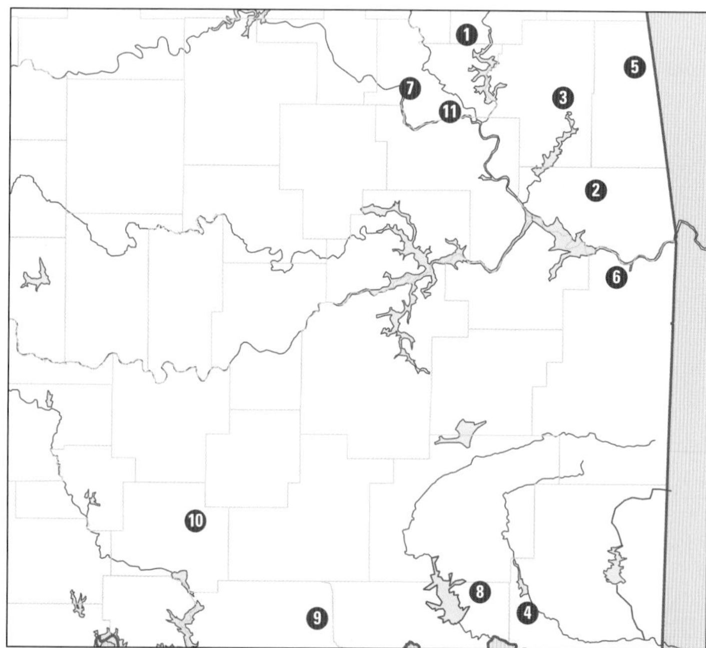

Early Indian Territory Missions

1	Union Mission (Presbyterian)	1821
2	Dwight Mission (Congregationalist)	1829
3	Park Hill Mission (Presbyterian)	1829
4	Wheelock Mission and Academy (Presbyterian)	1832
5	Baptist Mission (Baptist)	1839
6	Fort Coffee (Methodist-Episcopal)	1842
7	Coweta Mission (Presbyterian)	1843
8	Spencer Academy (Presbyterian)	1844
9	Armstrong Academy (Baptist)	1844
10	Wapanucka Mission (Presbyterian)	1852
11	Tullahassee Mission (Presbyterian)	1850

John Mix Stanley's famous 1845 *Osage Scalp Dance*, depicting a traditional battle victory celebration by warriors, who would scalp male Native and white adversaries alike. Women and children might be enslaved or scalped. Here, a chief wearing a peace medal awarded by the U.S. government restrains a warrior from harming the mother and child. Stanley's message supporting American influence on the tribe is clear. Courtesy Smithsonian Institution.

Gradually and inexorably, however, through patience, suffering, and non-violent peacemaking, Christian Creeks began to impact their tribe. They traveled to worship on other tribes' lands when forced to, or endured punishment and persecution for worshiping in their home country. Finally, they won over the great McIntosh family, who, like the apostle Paul prior to his first-century conversion, had been fervent opponents of the Christian faith and its ministers.

The conversion of the McIntoshes turned the tide toward Christianity among the Creeks. Three of martyred Creek Chief William McIntosh's sons became Baptist ministers. Subsequently, despite lingering hostility from some Creek traditionalists, white Baptist missionaries H. P. Buckner and Joseph S. Murrow (Chapter 6) gained renown for their tireless and selfless work over decades of time among the Creeks. Murrow labored among them, the Seminoles, and the Choctaws for *seventy-two* years, never wavering from his declaration in the first sermon he ever preached to the Creeks: "I seek not yours but you."

The Presbyterian missionaries' leading of esteemed Seminole Chief John Jumper to faith in Christ cast a similarly profound influence on that tribe. The Seminoles, too, had resisted Christianity, due partly to their brutal subjugation by the United States, a "Christian nation," during the Seminole Wars back in Florida. Soon, Presbyterian and then Baptist churches multiplied through Seminole lands.

> *I went to the missionary Baptist church where Marster and Missus went. . . . Lots of bad things have come to me, but the good Father, high up, he take care of me. We went down to the river for baptizings. The women dressed in white, if they had a white dress to wear. The preacher took his candidate into the water. Pretty soon everybody commenced a singin' and a prayin.' Then the preacher put you under water three times. There was a house yonder where was dry clothes, blankets, everything. Soon as you come out of the water you go over there and change clothes. My uncle used to baptize 'em.*
>
> **—Lucinda Vann**
> **Former Cherokee slave**

Missionaries and Indians Battle Liquor (Part 2)

by Grant Foreman
Chronicles of Oklahoma

It was in the Cherokee Nation that the temperance movement took form in its most interesting and spectacular aspect. The majority of this tribe was removed through the autumn and winter of 1838 overland through Tennessee, Kentucky, Illinois, Missouri and Arkansas, to their new home in the Indian Territory. About four thousand of them died on the way and the survivors were so impressed by the dreadful effects produced by the sellers of whisky deliberately conceived by the whites to force them from their old home, and by those along their unhappy route, called by them "The Trail of Tears," that they had scarcely begun to erect new homes in the strange country to which they had been forced, when they called temperance meetings to formulate plans for the suppression of the introduction and sale of liquor in their new country.

> *Commencing thus early in life, to march along the path of temperance, these youthful soldiers, now the beauty and hope of our country, and hereafter to become its mothers, fathers, laborers, law-givers, and guides, must exercise an immense influence, and perhaps are those destined to consummate the great cause in which they have enlisted.*
>
> **—William Ross**

Native Schools

It seemed that the Christ-bearers on this final frontier of America always eventually persevered and overcame their challenges. For instance, once Epaphras Chapman and his bold Presbyterian contingent reached the Osage country, they established the first Christian church in the territory—Union Mission—and with it, present-day Oklahoma's first school. Union Mission and its school would eventually minister to hundreds of children, including Osages, Creeks, and members of other tribes.

Indeed, Christian missionary efforts spawned the establishment of dozens of schools across the territory that delivered to Indian young people the unsurpassed educational treasures of Western civilization, beginning with reading and writing English and learning mathematics. Schools, in fact, proved to be an integral component of most Indian Territory mission efforts. In the end, two of the historic contributions of Christian missionaries in the territory to the tribes they served were helping to stabilize and strengthen them after their Trails of Tears, and equipping them to work, produce, and prosper in their new western land.

The Five Indian Republics shouldered their share of the load on the educational front. They channeled most of the funds paid for their lands back East to launching and maintaining schools. In addition, they each elected a commissioner of education to supervise these activities and provide the selection, certification, and training of teachers.

These tribes generally provided kindergarten through grammar school instruction, as well as special education tracks for those with physical disabilities, quality boarding schools for students who advanced to higher grades, and financial support for exceptional students who qualified for college attendance back East. Though all five "Civilized" tribes committed precious resources to educating their youth, the Cherokees and Choctaws left particularly notable legacies in that regard.

The Cherokee National Female Seminary building, students, and staff in Tahlequah, and the Seminary's female faculty. The book, *From the Grassroots to the Supreme Court: Brown v. Board of Education and American Democracy*, well describes the historic significance of the Cherokee National Female Seminary in Tahlequah: "One of the first boarding schools for Native Americans was not created by the federal government, but was founded in 1851 by the Cherokee National Council. . . . Students at the Cherokee Female Seminary took courses in Latin, French, trigonometry, political economy. . . . From Homer to Shakespeare . . . pupils staged dramatic productions, held music recitals and published their own newsletter . . . (the) institution helped shape an acculturated Cherokee identity in which young graduates became educators, businesswomen, physicians, stock raisers, and prominent social workers. One, Rachel Caroline Eaton, earned her PhD in History at the University of Chicago, authored four books on Oklahoma, including two on the Cherokees, and chaired the history department at Trinity University in San Antonio." Courtesy L. C. Handy Studio and Oklahoma Historical Society.

Atha Shelby DeWeese's *Rock Chimney,* the lone remnant of old Fort Towson. The U.S. Army built the fort in 1824 near present-day Fort Towson in Choctaw County to protect emigrating Native tribes from the southeast. A military trail connected it with Fort Smith, Arkansas Territory, 125 miles northeast. Steamboats brought the fort's supplies up Red River, six miles away. Keel boats used a creek to transport them from there.

Numerous people among the tribes who had suffered removal—particularly full-bloods who rejected Western education, religion, and vocational practices—struggled to subsist through the 1840s and 1850s. The Plains Indians in western Indian Territory, meanwhile, continued their predatory, pagan, and frequently brutal existence. Many others among the Five Indian Republics, however, meshed the strength of their race and heritage with the qualities of Christian civilization and built from the devastation of their Trails of Tears what historians christened a "Golden Age."

These stalwart founding fathers of Oklahoma civilization could scarcely imagine that more tears from an even more terrible catastrophe awaited them with the dawn of the 1860s and America's great and terrible war with itself. Forgotten or ignored by typical American chronicles like most other Oklahoma history, the War Between the States would birth its greatest savagery not in a U.S. state, but in Indian Territory.

Greater Love Hath No Man . . .

Missionaries—some of whom have achieved legendary status and fame, though that was not their intent—gave their time, talent, resources, and sometimes their lives to reach the Natives of the Oklahoma country with the Christian gospel. They were predominantly Baptists or Presbyterians, but a healthy number were Methodists and Methodist-Episcopalians or Congregationalists; some were Moravians or Catholics, and many later ones were Mennonites.

Some of the missionaries were men, but at least a couple hundred of them were women, many of whom were single. They preached the gospel, started schools and taught in them, and served as doctors, nurses, counselors, and trainers in various vocations. They translated the Bible and other literature into Indian languages, fixed meals, advised the tribes on matters of law, defended them against the dangers of alcoholic beverages, dispensed precious medicines, and stood with them before American territorial courts and law enforcement officers. Most have been forgotten, but one of the blessings of histories is that they can help to remedy such injustices.

Jerusha Swain and Single Female Missionaries (1822–1862)

In any generation a young, white single female departing an educated and somewhat affluent home in New England (a traditional lighthouse of Western civilization) for a land populated by a different race and culture of people half a continent and two thousand miles away, would represent a notable undertaking. For thirty-year-old Vermont native Jerusha Swain in mid-nineteenth century America, it stood as nothing less than audacious, not to mention dangerous and uncertain by nearly every human measurement.

> *I have become so much assimilated to the people that I feel more like a Cherokee than anything else. I hardly know how I can act in civilized society.*
>
> —Jerusha Swain

Cyrus Kingsbury and His Diary (1786–1870)

The histories of the Choctaw tribe, the state of Oklahoma, America, and the Christian church all would have proceeded far differently if not for the ceaseless devotion of New Hampshire native and graduate of Brown University and Andover Seminary, Rev. Dr. Cyrus Kingsbury. Not one in a thousand modern-day Oklahomans would recognize his name. Yet history once bestowed upon him sobriquets such as "The Prince of Indian Territory Missionaries" and "Father of the Missions" in Indian Territory. The Choctaw people, who loved Kingsbury as a father, called him "Limping Wolf" because he had been lame since childhood. He also established the ABCFM's first mission among the Natives in 1817 for the Cherokees, its first labors of ministry to the Choctaws in 1818, and the Southern Presbyterian Church's first mission effort of any sort in 1861.

> *Lord, revive Thy work in my heart.*
> —Cyrus Kingsbury

Evan Jones, Abolitionist Missionary (1788–1872)

"Big men make big mistakes." So goes a common adage. Whether or not Baptist missionary Evan Jones made big mistakes, he certainly made lots of them. Big quarrels strode through life with Jones like an unshakable plague. So did accusations of financial, political, ecclesiastical, and moral misconduct, including adultery and murder. At various times his legions of foes included the U.S. Government, the Cherokee Treaty Party, Presbyterian missionaries including Samuel Worcester, his own Baptist Mission Board, successive Cherokee Principal Chiefs, and white men opposing the Christian faith in order to enrich themselves at the expense of the Cherokees Jones so loved.

> *These tragic events rendered Jones guilty in the eyes of many, especially among the Treaty Party, and haunted his steps for the remainder of his life.*

Ann Eliza Worcester Robertson, Missionary to the Creeks (1826–1905)

"I said to some ladies the other day, as I showed them a beautiful volume, 'I have just had the crowning joy of my life in receiving the Muskokee New Testament entire,'" Ann Eliza Worcester Robertson reflected. "But I immediately added as I thought of the four children, all of whom God had made earnest workers for himself, 'Should a mother say that?'"

> *Wooster University bestowed upon Ann Eliza Robertson the first honorary doctorate ever awarded to a woman in the United States.*

Historian Althea Bass's biography of famed missionary Samuel Worcester, Cherokee Messenger, includes the following portrait of his daughter Ann Eliza as a young teen.

> Ann Eliza was not yet fourteen when her mother (Ann) died . . . but a single event may seem to bring a child's years to the flower of maturity; Ann Eliza, suddenly motherless and overwhelmed with a feeling of affection and sisterly pity for her smaller brothers and sisters, grew quickly out of childhood into young womanhood. Her father, looking at her with the surprise that every parent feels when he realizes that his child will not always remain a child, saw all of Ann's graces promising to repeat themselves in Ann Eliza.

Bloomfield Academy, established by Methodist minister John Harpole Carr near Achille in present-day Bryan County in 1852 as a Chickasaw girls' school, demonstrated how Christianity and education were so integrally connected in the Native schools of Indian Territory. Courtesy Oklahoma Historical Society.

Wallace and Minerva Willis and *Swing Low, Sweet Chariot*

When slaves Wallace and Minerva Willis traveled the Choctaw Trail of Tears from either Mississippi or Alabama in the early 1830s with their Choctaw owner, Brett Willis, no one knew one of the greatest song composers in American history was moving to the future state of Oklahoma.

Swing low, sweet chariot,
Coming for to carry me home,
Swing low, sweet chariot,
Coming for to carry me home.

I looked over Jordan and what did I see,
Coming for to carry me home?
A band of angels coming after me,
Coming for to carry me home.

If you get there before I do,
Coming for to carry me home,
Tell all my friends I'm coming too,
Coming for to carry me home.

The brightest day that ever I saw,
Coming for to carry me home.
When Jesus washed my sins away,
Coming for to carry me home.

I'm sometimes up and sometimes down,
Coming for to carry me home,
But still my soul feels heavenly bound,
Coming for to carry me home . . .

When Lewis Ross, brother of Cherokee Principal Chief John Ross, discovered a pocket of oil in 1859 while searching for salt water on the Grand River near Salina in present-day Mayes County, he scarcely realized he had launched, with his ten barrels a day for less than a year, the stupendous Oklahoma petroleum industry. Wayne Cooper's *The Magic of Petroleum* preserves the moment for posterity. Courtesy Oklahoma State Senate Historical Preservation Fund, Inc. and Wayne Cooper.

6

1860–1865
Uncivil War

The Federal supply ship *J. R. Williams* goes up in flames after Stand Watie and his mounted Confederate Indian guerillas ambushed, plundered, and fired it in Durant artist Neal Taylor's *Capture of Union Riverboat J. R. Williams.* (www.gntayloroklaart.com)

April 1861	Conflict at Fort Sumter, SC, launches War Between the States
Summer 1861	Five Civilized Tribes ally with Confederate States of America
September 1861–January 1862	Confederate campaign against Opothleyahola and Federal Creeks
July 1862	Federals capture Tahlequah; Chief John Ross joins them
July 1863	Federal victory at Honey Springs
May 1864	Stand Watie becomes only Native general in the war
Sept. 1863	Blunt's campaign crushes Creek Confederates, captures Fort Smith
Sept. 1864	Confederate victory at Second Battle of Cabin Creek
June 1865	Stand Watie surrenders at Doaksville

No portion of the American nation suffered such great hardships during the War Between the States as did the people of the Indian Territory.

—Gaston Litton, *History of Oklahoma*

America's greatest tragedy exploded into war on April 12, 1861, at Fort Sumter, a Federal outpost in the Atlantic Ocean harbor at Charleston, South Carolina. Most Oklahomans do not know that the War Between the American States raged in their state. Yet it proved to be the bloodiest and most destructive epoch in Oklahoma history. It shook the life of every person in the region and affected their destiny and those of their descendants for generations to come, many to this day. It killed a higher percentage of citizens in the future state of Oklahoma than any other event in history.

It is perhaps a testament to the dearth of knowledge, understanding, and wisdom of our modern generation that the ocean of blood and tears—the colossal aggregate of misery, loss, and lamentation our predecessors suffered a mere half-dozen generations ago—remains unknown to us. Also forgotten are the courage, selflessness, and valor the Indian Nations, the territory's African-Americans, and white future Oklahomans from Texas and elsewhere offered up on the altar of their peoples and countries for what they believed, in a supremely brutal nightmare foisted upon them by white America.

The many issues that led the Southern states of South Carolina, Mississippi, Florida, Alabama, Georgia, Louisiana, and Texas (and later, Virginia, Arkansas, North Carolina, and Tennessee) to secede from the United States had brewed for a long time, some of them since long before the states formed the Union. The disagreements included economics (in particular, a protectionist tariff the Southern states realized was disproportionately weighted against them), competing nationalist and regional outlooks on the country's future, and the practice of slavery. Moreover, the North and South squabbled over the intent of the Constitution and nature of the American government, and whether the former posited the locus of power for the latter with the states or the national government. That last question particularly concerned whether those states had the constitutional right to leave the Union they had formed and voluntarily joined.

Such books as *The War Between the States: America's Uncivil War* and *North Against South: The American Iliad* explore these issues at length. Some, including the nationalism vs. regionalism and state vs. national government debates, had direct impact on the Five Civilized Tribes in Indian Territory. Others did not. The institution of slavery exerted small influence in the territory. Many pro-Federal and pro-Confederate Indians alike among the Five Civilized Tribes—especially in tribal leadership—owned black slaves, and such slavery was no factor in the world of the "wild" Plains Indians. Though a significant number of Loyalist Indians among the removed tribes held anti-slavery or abolitionist views, most of these Cherokees, Creeks, and Seminoles opposed the Confederacy due more to their dislike and even hatred of pro-Southern tribal opponents than slavery.

Most citizens of "The Nations," as the five Indian republics, the Osages, and smaller adjacent tribes such as the Shawnees, Senecas, and Quapaws and their lands in roughly the eastern half of present-day Oklahoma came to be called, would happily have remained neutral in the war—and safe. They were, however, left little choice in the matter. Surprisingly, both the United States and the Confederacy deemed the remote, little-developed, and sparsely populated Indian Territory crucial to victory.

The Federals, who abandoned the region when the first Southern states seceded, intended to return. They recognized the area as the perfect launching stage for a back-door invasion of Confederate Texas. It also provided an enormous granary and stockyard for Federal troops in the West.

The Confederates sought access to these resources as well. They suspected the Indian Nations could perhaps supply enough beef to feed the entire Southern military, and enough lead from its mines to supply all the ordnance its soldiers and sailors would need. For the South, also, Indian Territory provided a buffer against Federal invasion.

Moreover, whomever the Nations allied themselves with possessed a decided advantage in maneuvers and supplies related to the burgeoning Kansas-Missouri-Arkansas-Texas theater of operations. And the Native warriors themselves would be hardy, rough-and-ready horse soldiers for whichever side they joined. Yet the question loomed large: would the Five Civilized Tribes, the smaller tribes adjacent to them, and the Plains tribes to the west ally themselves with the Federals, the Confederates, neither, or some with one and some with the other?

North, South, Neutral?

Numerous factors steered most Indian Territory Natives toward alliance with the South. Well before the commencement of war, they grew alarmed over the loud declarations of 1860 Republican Presidential candidate Abraham Lincoln and his primary opponent and eventual Secretary of State William Seward that Indian Territory should be cleared for white settlement. These politically popular utterances came scarcely a generation after the U.S. government's gargantuan—and tragic—effort to remove the southeastern tribes to Indian Territory, where President Andrew Jackson had promised they could live on their own land and govern themselves "as long as the grass grows and the rivers run."

Lincoln and the Republicans' overtures did not occur in a vacuum either, as members of Congress had launched efforts as early as 1854 to prepare the way for white settlement, then statehood. The Chickasaws and Seminoles had not even secured their separate and autonomous lands from the Choctaws and Creeks, respectively, when these efforts began. Wise men among the five Indian republics recognized the specter of history—and "Manifest Destiny"—repeating itself.

The area's tribes grew more unsettled about depending on the United States for security when

Abraham Lincoln.

Indian Territory 1861.

the Federal government removed its soldiers from Indian Territory after the Southern states seceded. The Federals' termination of annuity payments for the Indians' eastern lands, for fear the Confederates would secure the money, generated anger among the tribes, along with increased doubts about U.S. dependability.

The Confederates, meanwhile, proposed favorable remedies and policies for all these tribal concerns and many others. Confederate President Jefferson Davis appointed Albert S. Pike as the new Southern nation's Commissioner for the Indian Territory. Pike had already earned much respect among the tribes in the region, for he had often represented them in litigation battles, a task many white attorneys would not accept. He held the authority to craft agreements, treaties, and alliances with all tribes in the sprawling territory, and was given wide latitude from his government toward that end.

> *The South abolished the U.S.-enforced monopolies held by white merchants over Indian trade and boldly established district courts in both the Cherokee and Choctaw countries.*

Pike enjoyed spectacular success. He relieved the tribes by assuring them the Confederate government would not only protect their rights to their lands and independence, but also invite each of the five Indian republics to send representatives to its Congress. The South, through Pike, also abolished the U.S.-enforced monopolies held by white merchants over Indian trade. These had proven, in the words of one Oklahoma historian, "a pernicious thing for the Indian" and "destructive of all competition and often placed the Indian at the mercy of white men wholly lacking in scruples."

Pike, himself a Massachusetts-reared lawyer, also conferred to the Natives a sweeping slate of enhanced civil rights in the courts, including those related to their personal property, especially in relation to whites. In fact, the Confederates boldly established district courts in both northern Indian Territory (the Cherokee country) and southern (Choctaw). The tribes had long and loudly protested the United States government's refusal to place any courts in Indian Territory, the closest heretofore being across the Arkansas line in Fort Smith.

Albert S. Pike

Durant artist G. N. Taylor's memorable *Confederate Cavalry Charge*. Few mounted military units in history were as formidable as the South's horsemen. As the War Between the States progressed, gray uniforms grew scarce due to the Confederacy's weak industrial capacity and the crushing Federal blockade. (www.gntayloroklaart.com)

Also, the great tribes occupying roughly the eastern two-thirds of the territory had themselves come from the South a generation before. Though Southerners had forced them out, so had Northerners coming for gold and land, along with the Federal government, right up to the term served by President Andrew Jackson. Also, the tribes had no shortage of grievances regarding their treatment in the past by the United States government.

Many of the Natives, especially among the full-bloods, had no particular cultural affinity with any section of America. Many of them did, however, especially amongst tribes like the Cherokees, Choctaws, and Chickasaws. They

John Ross (c. 1790–1866)

John Ross

Though only one-eighth Cherokee, unable to speak the tribe's language, and white in appearance, manner, dress, and social and political acumen, John Ross led his tribe as Principal Chief and held the political loyalty of its majority for the astounding period of nearly forty years. This sprawling epoch included the establishment of a Cherokee constitution and federated government, the struggle against removal, the Trail of Tears itself, the Cherokee "civil war" in Indian Territory, the tribe's "Golden Age" that followed, and the War Between the States, including his alliance with first the Confederates, then the Federals. He lost his wife during the removal, one home before it and another during the Civil War, and was either captured or liberated by the Federal army.

had adopted the agrarian culture of the South, including largely autonomous communities, suspicion of mercantilist industrialization, slave ownership, and a mystical sense of place that superseded mere geography and political organization.

Furthermore, most of the goods the Nations sold to others went to Southern markets and ports, making the South the Indians' chief trading partner. Finally, Indian Territory was geographically—and increasingly religiously—part of the South, especially when viewed in the context of its Confederate neighbors (Texas, Arkansas, Louisiana, and Southern Missouri).

Confederate Indians

As if to clinch the tribes' support, on August 10, 1861, the Confederate army routed the Federals at the Battle of Wilson's Creek, a few miles across the Missouri border from Indian Territory. This victory in the Western Theater's first major battle of the war occurred just weeks following a decisive Southern triumph in the first major Eastern battle at Manassas, Virginia. The electrifying sequence, which stunned the world, convinced most Natives who had remained undecided in their loyalties, that the South could win its independence and should be supported. Besides, the Federals had abandoned Indian Territory, while Confederate men throughout the region were reaching out to the tribes.

The Choctaws and Chickasaws sided almost unanimously with the Confederacy. Creek and Seminole allegiance was split, even though the tribes, guided by pro-Confederate mixed-blood leaders Motey Kennard and Daniel and Chilly McIntosh for the Creeks and John Jumper for the Seminoles, signed treaties with the South. The savvy sixty-three-year-old chief Opothleyahola led the pro-Federal Creek faction, and Billy Bowlegs and John Chupko did the same for the Seminole one. Opinions proved mixed among the Cherokees too, with some not taking any stand on the matter, but most of those with strong feelings, including Stand Watie, urging alliance with the Confederates.

Though both the North and the South counted approximately thirty-five hundred Indian Territory Natives in their service during the war, as many as half of those numbered among the Federals initially sided with the Confederates. Though some shifted allegiance due to conviction, most did so due to hunger, fear for their lives, and the swinging pendulum of fortune once the Federals finally gained the advantage in Indian Territory, along with most of the land in the Cherokee, Creek, and Seminole domains.

Blue-clad Federals and Confederates shoot it out face to face in N. C. Wyeth's *Battle of Wilson's Creek,* from a mural in the Missouri State Capitol. A big early Confederate victory in the Western Theater fought just across the Missouri line from Indian Territory, it helped cement the five Indian republics' alliance with the South. Though Stand Watie did not participate, Joel B. Mayes and others in his Cherokee Mounted Rifles command did. Mayes brought with him his friend William Quantrill, the future guerrilla legend.

Andy Thomas' (www. andythomas. com) vivid sketch of a charging Cherokee warrior.

Principal Chief John Ross—a slave owner like Watie, though he held no strong allegiance to the South as did his old foe—had hoped to keep his tribe out of the conflict. The pressure, however, had for months mounted on him from other Cherokees, particularly Watie and Treaty Party adherents, many of whom were already enlisting as fighting soldiers in the Southern cause.

The unsettling, increasingly violent events unfolding around him also pushed Ross toward alliance with the Confederacy. So did—at least indirectly through its impact on other Cherokee leaders—events occurring more remotely. The tribe's *Declaration by the People of the Cherokee Nation of the Causes Which Have Impelled Them to Unite Their Fortunes With Those of the Confederate States of America* reveals their repulsion over the many harsh, even brutal, acts of suppression already undertaken by the U.S. government against secessionists, as well as those merely deemed not sufficiently loyal, especially in Federal border states like Missouri, Kentucky, and Maryland. No doubt the forced-emigrant Cherokee recognized similarities in these events with their own previous experiences with Washington and its legions. Once the Confederates hammered the Federals at Wilson's Creek, Ross threw his uneasy support behind the South.

Through the diplomacy and gifts of Pike, the Comanches, Kiowas, Wichitas, and other Plains tribes in the West unanimously committed to an alliance with the South. The Confederacy did not ask them to take up arms against the Federals, but only to establish peaceful relations with Confederates—red, white, and black alike. The Five Civilized Tribes would provide soldiers, and already were, though only in the defense of Indian Territory.

The horrors of war with an industrial colossus like the United States would render many Confederate promises difficult if not impossible to maintain. Historian Anna Lewis described why in a 1931 edition of the splendid historical journal *Chronicles of Oklahoma*, which continues publication in the twenty-first century through the Oklahoma Historical Society:

> The Indian Territory was in many respects beyond the pale of civilization. The outlaw bands had a chance and did operate without very much hindrance. The Indians saw their cattle all being driven off by groups of bandits. The dissension among the Creeks and Cherokees caused them to war against

Cherokee Secession

Declaration by the People of the Cherokee Nation of the Causes Which Have Impelled Them to Unite Their Fortunes With Those of the Confederate States of America:

> *Providence rules the destinies of nations, and events, by inexorable necessity, overrule human resolutions. . . . In the States which still adhered to the Union a military despotism has displaced the civil power and the laws became silent amid arms. Free speech and almost free thought became a crime. . . . The mandate of the Chief Justice of the Supreme Court was set at naught by the military power, and this outrage on common right approved by a President sworn to support the Constitution . . .*

> themselves. The Plains Indians to the west had not accepted any bounds to their country. This caused a very disturbing problem. There had always been a fear that the Plains Indians would go on the war path against them, and now conditions seemed very favorable for this to happen.

In addition, the Federals' brutal "Anaconda Plan" blockade of food, medicines, and other life-sustaining supplies from the civilian population of the Confederacy, as well as the South's scant industrial base, would soon render the new nation ill-equipped to feed its own population. Still, all the tribes of Indian Territory now had a new chance at gaining so much of what they had been promised for so long by the U.S. government.

Federal Indians

Indeed, the fighting that occurred in Indian Territory descended to a pattern perhaps unparalleled anywhere else in the war. Several factors contributed to this forgotten fact. For one, this western region was still roughhewn and sparsely settled compared to areas farther east. The rule of law stretched thin in both white and Indian communities. Also, the violent Indian practice of scalping surged—again, among both whites and Indians—as the fever of war spawned a spiraling cycle of hatred and vengeance.

Finally, other theaters of the conflict did not qualify as a true "civil war," which suggests a struggle

Loyalist Creeks and other Natives led by Opothleyahola confront a November 19, 1861 mounted charge by Confederate Colonel Douglas Cooper's white Texans, Chickasaws, Choctaws, Creeks, and Seminoles in Wayne Cooper's *The Battle of Round Mountain.* Courtesy Oklahoma State Senate Historical Preservation Fund, Inc. and Wayne Cooper.

for control of the government. As black economist Walter Williams has written, the American War of 1861–1865 was no more a fight for control of the U.S. government than the American War of Independence had been a fight for control of the British crown. Both were wars of secession and fights for independence—except in Indian Territory and a few other places, notably nearby Missouri. There, brother against brother was a reality, not a myth or song.

In present-day Oklahoma, tribal and even family members destroyed each other's property, burned their homes, and killed one another. The fight in the Indian Nations was a true civil war, among people in close proximity to one another and possessed even at the outset of only modest economic means. It was a historically desperate and brutal bloodletting.

The initial campaign of the war in Indian Territory unfolded with the onset of the winter of 1861. Its confusion, brutality, and lamentations would prove a harbinger of the years of horror looming for the exiled tribes. The afore-mentioned Opothleyahola, formerly the Creek tribal chief, had a half-century of war and tragedy strewn in his wake.

Opothleyahola apparently fought against the Americans as a young teenager in the Creek War theater of the War of 1812. Following that, he swore allegiance to the United States, vowing never again to bear arms against them. He then sided with the U.S. against the Seminoles, rebellious Creeks, and finally, the Confederates. In between, he championed the execution of Creek pro-treaty leader William McIntosh, tried to purchase land for the Creeks in Texas, and traveled the Creek Trail of Tears.

Opothleyahola, along with a faction of Creeks, actually wished to remain neutral in the "white man's" War Between the States. Somewhere between thirty-five hundred and six thousand people—mostly Creeks, with a smattering of black slaves, black freedmen, and Seminoles—streamed to the old chief's plantation. Like other pro-Federal Indians, Opothleyahola worked his expansive lands with slaves, just as the Confederate tribal leaders did.

> *Opothleyahola sent out decoys in one direction while he retreated another. He set prairie fires behind his pursuers' lines that diverted them and covered his civilians' retreat. He used the Confederates' zeal for battle to lure them into fights at times and on ground of his own choosing.*

Former Indian agent Douglas Cooper, now second-in-command to Albert Pike of the Confederate forces in Indian Territory, wanted to negotiate an agreement that would avert bloodshed among the Creeks. Opothleyahola refused even to acknowledge Cooper's overtures. When Cooper learned

Opothleyahola (c. 1798–1863)

This brave and eloquent giant of the Muscogee people evinced many of the best attributes of the Choctaw Pushamataha, the Seminole Wild Cat, and both John Ross and Stand Watie of the Cherokees. He took up arms against the United States to preserve his people's homeland and then fought alongside the Americans against both white Europeans and fellow Natives, even among his own tribe. He strove amongst white and Indian leaders alike for his people's rights to their land, but then he led them out of it when he realized that to stay meant extermination. He upheld the Natives' communal property practices, and the full bloods of his tribe never knew a more trustworthy defender. Yet even though he never learned the English language, he urged fellow Creeks to adopt both the education and culture of the whites, accepting the latter's Christian faith and joining the Baptist church.

Opothleyahola

the Creek leader was seeking military support from Federal forces in Kansas, he felt compelled to pursue him before he ushered a Federal army into the territory that would ignite the region into all-out war.

War and Suffering

Opothleyahola showed the sagacity gathered from that half-century of experience in conflict by leading Cooper's Confederates on a frustrating chase north toward Kansas. He accomplished this while shepherding large herds of livestock and thousands of civilians away from hard-riding Indian Territory Natives and Texas frontiersmen, all amidst the onset of a devastating winter.

He sent out decoy forces in one direction while the vanguard of his assembly retreated another. He set prairie fires behind his pursuers' lines that diverted them and covered his civilians' retreat. He used the Confederates' zeal for battle to lure them into fights at times and on ground of his own choosing. He even parlayed such tactics into victory in the campaign's—and the territory's—first real battle, Round Mountain. This occurred November 19, 1861, near the confluence of the Arkansas and Cimarron Rivers west of Tulsey Town, present-day Tulsa. As Opotheyahola and his throng remained at large and the weather grew colder, the situation worsened for the Confederates. On December 8th, the bulk of the full-blood First Cherokee Mounted Rifles regiment—several hundred men—deserted their commander, John Drew, and joined Opothleyahola. Then on December 19th, the now-Federalist warriors repulsed a second Confederate attack north of Tulsey Town.

At this point, a weary Cooper retreated to Fort Gibson and called for reinforcements from the Confederates' theater command in Arkansas. With commander and Wilson's Creek hero Ben McCulloch gone to Richmond, Virginia, an audacious West Point graduate, James McIntosh (no relation to the Confederate Creek McIntoshes), recognized that the previous month's events might turn the balance of power across the entire Indian Territory to the Federal cause, which only weeks before had seemed doomed in the Nations. McIntosh saddled up sixteen hundred battle-hardened Southern horse soldiers—mostly Texans, with some Arkansans—and rode straight for Opothleyahola.

Texas horse soldiers thunder up a steep hill into the teeth of Federal Indian fire at the Battle of Chustenahlah, the decisive Southern victory of the war's opening campaign in Indian Territory. Sketch by Andy Thomas. (www. andythomas. com)

The wily Creek chief soon attempted to sucker McIntosh into another battle of Opothleyahola's choosing, but McIntosh was no Cooper, and his men were no rookie citizen volunteers. Instead, they were leather-tough frontiersmen, many of them more comfortable on horseback than on foot, and veterans of Wilson's Creek and other battles. Smelling out another Opothleyahola feint on Christmas Day, McIntosh caught up with the main pro-Federal Creek and Seminole force the next day in the Chustenahlah region near present-day Skiatook in Osage County, around twenty-five miles north of Tulsey Town. The latter were arrayed across a high ridge and spread down its front, overlooking Shoal Creek.

Confederate Creek cavalryman Pleasant Porter in 1863.

After the Indians fired on McIntosh's outriders, the Confederate commander called up his main force and unleashed them on a cavalry charge across and up two hundred and fifty yards of open ground toward the ridge above. The Southern horse soldiers thundered across Shoal Creek, over the Creeks on the slope of the hill, and "rushed over (the ridge's) rugged side with the irresistible force of a tornado, and swept everything before it," according to McIntosh. They chased the Federal Natives for miles, over a series of hills and ridges. Three miles away, the Indians gathered for a last stand. The Confederate troopers shattered it and sent the survivors fleeing in all directions.

According to historian Steve Cottrell, around two hundred and fifty pro-Northern Indians died in the battle. The Confederates captured a couple hundred civilians; thirty wagons; hundreds of buffalo robes; hundreds more horses, oxen, cattle, and sheep; and a massive store of food. The complex nineteenth-century social, political, and historical dynamics at work among the five Indian republics evidenced themselves anew during this event that was wrought with supreme passion. The Creeks had lived through a lot with—and sometimes against—one another. Creek commander Daniel McIntosh's own father William had been killed by an opposing faction (Chapter 3). Now, Daniel McIntosh himself reported that the two hundred and fifty killed in the frenzy of combat and vengeance that swept the field at Chustenahlah included numerous women and children.

The situation grew no better for Opothleyahola the next day. The Confederates mounted up and hit the trail before dawn. Cherokee Chief and Colonel Stand Watie and his three hundred Second Cherokee Mounted Rifles now led them. The fifty-five-year-old Watie would rise to become the most famous figure of the war in Indian Territory, and that rise was about to begin. Just missing the pivotal fight of the day before, he and his men now chafed to demonstrate their mettle in battle.

The Cherokees got their chance after about twenty-five miles of pursuit. Watie caught a significant force of warriors, then split his own troopers and charged them. He led one wing and his nephew Elias C. Boudinot, the now-grown son of Watie's slain older brother (Chapter 4) of the same name, led the other. For ninety minutes, the warriors blasted away at each other in desperate combat before the Confederate Cherokees broke through the Creek and Seminole lines and sent them retreating again.

Stand Watie led one wing of the Confederate attack and his nephew Elias C. Boudinot—the now-grown son of Watie's slain older brother of the same name—led the other.

McIntosh decided he and his men had accomplished their mission of breaking Opothleyahola's revolt, and they headed back to Arkansas. Meanwhile, Cooper and his troops, white

Two sons of martyred Creek Chief William McIntosh, Daniel McIntosh (L) and Chilly McIntosh (R), contributed their own mighty deeds to the namesake of a present-day Oklahoma County. Both were Creek political leaders who led regiments of Confederate Creek cavalry through many battles in the War Between the States. Chilly, twenty years older than Daniel, helmed the first group of Creek emigrants on their Trail of Tears, while Daniel led the Southern Creeks at post-war conferences with the Federals in Fort Smith and Washington, D.C.

and red alike, pursued the suffering, freezing Federal Indians all the way to Kansas. There, the refugees suffered a bone-chilling winter in Federal camps. Hundreds perished. Opothleyahola's own daughter died that winter. The old chief himself died later, still a refugee in a Kansas camp. McIntosh, Watie, Cooper, and the Confederates had cleared Indian Territory of Federals and won the region's first campaign of the war.

Federal Counterattack

Indian Territory was too important for the Federals to concede, and they had no intention of doing so. Moreover, thousands of suffering, starving, pro-Federal Native refugees remained in Kansas. The white citizens of that state wanted them out. The Federals employed a two-pronged approach to fight their way back into Indian Territory during the second year of the war. First, during the winter of 1861–62, they determined to wrest Missouri from its considerable Confederate presence, and then move south through Arkansas and Indian Territory to invade Texas.

The major battle of this campaign occurred at Pea Ridge, or Elkhorn Tavern, in northwest Arkansas over a two-day period in early March. The battlefield deaths of a couple of key Confederate commanders, coupled with the Federals' superior artillery, made the difference as they won one of the most important strategic Western Theater victories of the war. The crucial Confederate losses included the commander and famed Texas Ranger Ben McCulloch and now-Brigadier General James McIntosh, whose savvy leadership had turned the tide in favor of the South in their Indian Territory campaign against Opothleyahola a few months before.

No one fought better at Pea Ridge, however, than Colonel Stand Watie and his Second Cherokee Mounted Rifles regiment. The legend of these roughhewn Indian country horse soldiers began to grow during a pivotal sequence in the first day of the battle. They charged headlong into a massed

The explosive presence of Stand Watie and the Confederate Cherokees at Pea Ridge is indicated by the charging Native chief (lower right) and the swarm of Cherokee horse soldiers (higher right) in Kurz and Allison's famous painting of the pivotal 1862 battle.

Federal battery of cannon that had been devastating Southern infantry, captured them, and turned them on the fleeing Yankees. Later, the Cherokees held their positions and provided effective cover for the Confederate retreat. Watie's brilliant field leadership also saved the entire Southern ammunition train from capture.

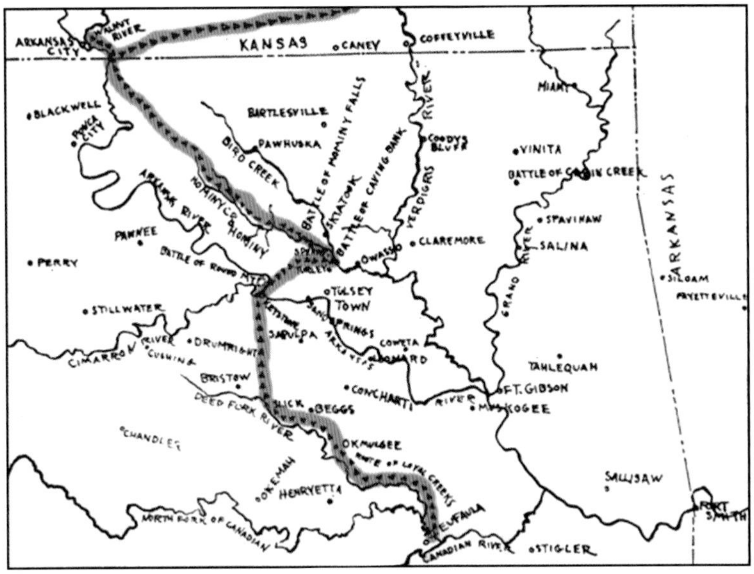

Opothleyahola and the Federal Indians' retreat from Indian Territory into Kansas.

The Cherokee Mounted Rifles' fame took on another element as well—for ferocity and intimidation. The Federals discovered a host of their dead soldiers scalped in the area where the Cherokees had wreaked havoc on their foes. This revelation spawned fury in the North and was an ominous portent of the brutal tactics both sides would employ against the other in the years ahead in the region.

In the end, Pea Ridge did not spawn a Federal incursion into Texas, but it did deliver to the U.S. the upper hand militarily in both Missouri and Arkansas for the remainder of the war. It also denied Southern forces in Indian Territory additional troops they might otherwise have had, and ratcheted up Federal pressure on Confederates in the Nations.

Indian Territory Invaded

The second prong of the Federal strategy called for invading Indian Territory from Kansas at the onset of summer. Brigadier General James G. Blunt, a doctor in civilian life and now the Union commander in that state and territory, assigned Colonel William Weer of the 10th Kansas Infantry to command the campaign. Weer intended to regain control of the region, as well as return the Indian Territory refugees to their homes. Some of those refugees would put on the blue Federal coat and help Weer accomplish both his missions.

> *With (Stand) Watie's troops dismounted and (John) Drew's men still in their saddles . . . the two Cherokee regiments swept forward along with part of the Ninth Texas Cavalry, and the bearded, wild-eyed Texans matched strides through the brush with Watie's warriors. Brandishing shotguns, rifles, tomahawks, knives, and bows and arrows, the Indians charged with wild shrieks and war cries and hit Osterhaus' (Federal) cavalry regulars even before he had a chance to pull his flying artillery back.*
>
> **—Wilfred Knight, *Red Fox***

Blunt chose Weer, however, apparently due more to his common affiliation with the Radical Republican Kansas abolitionist movement than Weer's military credentials. Bloodshed had mounted in the Kansas–Missouri region for years prior to the war, spawning the brutal acts of abolitionist John Brown and other pro- and anti-slavery groups, and even the sobriquet of "Bloody Kansas" for that state. Both Blunt and Weer supported the vicious Jayhawking violence of Kansas Senator James Lane

Andy Thomas's (www.andythomas.com) *Sigel Takes Aim* depicts German native General Franz Sigel commanding the Federal artillery barrage at Pea Ridge that swung the key battle in favor of the North. Here and elsewhere, large numbers of non-English-speaking German natives filled the Federal ranks, no small number of them refugees from the failed Communist Revolution of 1848 or former residents of German jails and prisons.

against pro-slavery families and other Confederates in Kansas and Missouri. Thus, both of these Federal commanders apparently possessed a passionate stake of their own in the war, though some of the Indians siding with them owned their own slaves.

The South's struggle to uphold its pledge of support and protection for the five Indian republics—especially after the strategic setback at Pea Ridge—grew manifest as Weer's far more numerous and better supplied troops took the initiative and marched south from Kansas into Indian Territory. Forces commanded by Weer as well as Charles Doubleday enhanced their advantages with keen scouting, shrewd routes of travel, and a series of startling ambushes of the sparse Confederate forces posted in the northern section of the territory—mostly Cherokee country—to defend as best as they could against Federal invasion.

In one month the sprawling Yankee force of six thousand men advanced nearly a hundred miles; whipped the outmanned and outgunned Southerners at Cowskin Prairie, Spavinaw Creek, and Locust Grove; captured a regiment of Missouri cavalry; took control of the Cherokee capital at Tahlequah; kept Pike's main remaining Confederate force pinned down near Red River for fear of annihilation; and encamped near the crucial Confederate outpost at Fort Gibson on the confluence of the Arkansas, Grand, and Verdigris Rivers.

The icing on the Federal cake was perhaps the greatest mass betrayal of the war, the stunning change of allegiance from Confederate to Federal

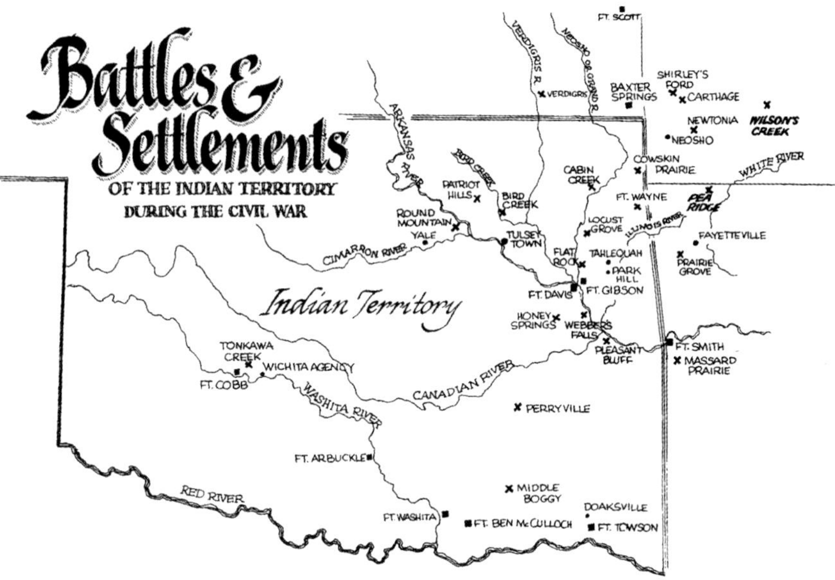

Courtesy Andy Thomas.

by yet another couple of hundred Cherokee soldiers under the command of John Drew. Tasked with defending Tahlequah and protecting their Principal Chief John Ross, these men capitulated at the approach of Weer's army, and Ross greeted the Federals with protestations that the Confederates had forced him into an alliance.

Drunken Reverse

At this point, it appeared as though nothing short of God or Weer himself could slow down the Federal juggernaut. The latter, perhaps prompted by the former, proceeded to accomplish just that. First, however, came a little-remembered skirmish much more important than was at first apparent. When Weer's full column rumbled onto the Arkansas River three miles south of Fort Gibson, they found Confederate Chickasaws and Choctaws under Colonel Douglas Cooper's command camped across the river. Rather than retreat in the face of the overwhelming force, the Confederate Natives stood their ground as their guns blazed back at the Yankees. Only later did the realization grow that this Chickasaw and Choctaw defiance blunted the entire Federal campaign thrust.

Weer decided to pull his men back to their base of operations at Flat Rock, several miles north of Fort Gibson. Flushed with success and on the verge of clearing the reeling Confederate forces clean out of Indian Territory, he retired to his quarters with a supply of whiskey—for ten days. During that time, his sloth rubbed off on much of the rest of his army. His white soldiers chafed under half rations, simmering heat, and a lack of water. Many of his Indians left on extended "hunting trips," many of them never returning. As if all this wasn't bad enough, the dogged Stand Watie rallied the Cherokee Mounted Rifles, who badgered the Federals' supply lines and loomed in and out of the shadows of their own familiar country as a constant threat to the invading force.

While Federal and Confederate armies comprised largely of Indian Territory Natives slugged it out in the eastern portion of the territory, bloodshed drenched southwestern Oklahoma in October 1862 near the Confederates' Fort Cobb Indian Agency. Pro-Federal warriors from an unknown combination of tribes that likely included Shawnees, Osages, and Delawares, attacked the agency, killing whites and Natives alike. They then pursued Tonkawa tribe survivors, whom they accused both of being pro-Confederate and practicing cannibalism. The Native attackers caught the Tonkawas and massacred much of the tribe—approximately 137 men and women, as well as the elderly and children. The survivors straggled to the Confederate Chickasaw Battalion's headquarters at Fort Arbuckle.

D. D. Hitchcock, medical missionary to the Cherokees before the war and Assistant Surgeon in the Federal Army during it.

As historian Cottrell wrote, "What had started out as a splendid campaign on the march to total victory had suddenly decayed into a disastrous expedition on a dead-end road to defeat." Remarkably, the once-unstoppable Federal force advanced no farther. Weer's subordinates finally arrested him and marched his men back to Kansas. Cottrell well described that force as "a mutinous Union army in Indian Territory, apparently cut off from its supply line and slowly becoming encircled by enemy forces."

The Federals accomplished a final act on their way out of the territory. They escorted Cherokee Principal Chief John Ross north to Kansas. He moved to Washington and died, never returning to his people's country, which by the time of his death in 1866 was as ravaged by war as any battleground on the continent.

Missouri and Arkansas

The Confederacy's desperate struggle for survival against the immensely larger and better-equipped Federals spurred Southern commanders in the West to break a pre-war pledge and order Albert Pike and the Confederate Natives out of Indian Territory to Arkansas. From there, they would march north in the vanguard of a Confederate campaign to wrest Missouri—whose Southern section stood staunchly Confederate—from Federal control.

Pike resigned his commission in anger at the latest in a series of CSA orders calling for his Natives to fight outside their own lands. With Cooper now in command, the gray Chickasaws, Choctaws, and Watie-led Cherokees headed into Arkansas, then Missouri. After a series of battles in which both sides won some victories, Federal theater commander John Schofield, who had won the Congressional Medal of Honor as a major in defeat at Wilson's Creek, gathered a gargantuan eighteen thousand-man army dubbed the "Army of the Frontier." Several times larger than the entirety of Confederate troop strength in the region, it shoved the main Southern army out of Missouri and northern Arkansas and back into the Cherokee country.

Blunt's personal heroics keyed a pivotal Federal victory that clinched the campaign.

Blunt's personal heroics keyed a pivotal Federal victory that clinched the campaign. Chasing the retreating Confederates under Cooper and Watie out of Arkansas, he posed as an escaped Southern prisoner and fooled an area woman whose own husband served under Cooper into providing him the location of the main Confederate force in the area. Despite the Federals ambushing the force, the tide of battle swung like a pendulum before massed Northern reinforcements, which included the Third Indian Home Guard under Blunt's tough Scottish regimental commander William A. Phillips, carried the day.

Andy Thomas's (www. andythomas. com) sketch of General James Blunt's famous nighttime charade as a Confederate soldier, which helped carry the pivotal late-1862 Missouri–Arkansas campaign for the Federals.

Andy Thomas's (www.andythomas.com) *They Came Like Demons* depicts a desperate Southern charge at the December 1862 Battle of Prairie Grove in northwest Arkansas, the last time the Confederates possessed sufficient forces to mount a thrust to regain Arkansas and Missouri that had a realistic chance to succeed. "The rebels . . . came sweeping out of the timber in solid column," a Kansas Federal wrote, "lifting their guns with fixed bayonets above their heads. They came on with a yell, like 7,000 demons. . . ." The Confederates battered the Federal forces, and the field was stalemated until the graycoats retreated upon hearing a (false) report that a large Federal reinforcement column was near. Stand Watie's Cherokee Mounted Rifles operated against Federal Pin Cherokees nearby, and his nephew Elias C. Boudinot served Confederate commander Thomas Hindman as an aide-de-camp in the main battle.

> *The 2nd Indian Home Guard had indeed already established an infamous reputation for a severe lack of discipline and tended to pillage and plunder wherever they went. Among the most feared members of the regiment were the Osage warriors. Unlike members of the other tribes serving in the Union Army, the Osages continued to pluck the hair from their heads in the old fashion, leaving only a scalp lock down the center. They were very fearsome in both their appearance and in their manner of dealing with anyone who opposed them. Not only did they take scalps as trophies from their foes, but it was also their custom to decapitate their victims as well. They still adhered to many of their old, primitive tribal ways at this time in their history and simply did not conform well to the white man's style of military life.*
>
> —**Steve Cottrell**
> ***Civil War in the Indian Territory***

The Federal Natives impressed Blunt enough that he sent Colonel Phillips with them into the Nations to wipe out Cooper and Watie's force. Watie had set up operations just west of the Arkansas border, intending to harry Federal supply lines, a strategy for which he had already earned a fearsome reputation. Phillips—like Blunt and Weer, an ardent abolitionist—rampaged southwest through the Cherokee country and into Creek land, burning Confederate military outposts and citizens' homes alike.

Despite his determined and savvy leadership, however, Phillips—like a string of Federal commanders before and after him—could not corral Watie and his Indian horse soldiers, who remained on the loose. As 1862 turned into 1863, it was Phillips and his Federals who returned to Arkansas for the winter. Watie, Cooper, and the Confederates recaptured the Cherokee capital at Tahlequah, and the majority pro-Southern faction of Cherokees elected Watie as Principal Chief. He and his men stayed entrenched in Indian Territory even though they were outnumbered, outsupplied, burned out of homes and land, and their families were exiled as refugees to the Red River Valley. In spite of all that had happened to them, they plotted strategy for another year of war.

1863—Fateful Year

As the war entered its third year, control of Indian Territory, like every other region of the conflict, remained in doubt. Federal manpower and supply resources in Kansas, Missouri, and Arkansas were daunting. On the other hand, the allegiance of so

Stand Watie (1806–1871)

Perhaps never did a man's name better embody the essence of his character. Ever a reluctant hero, Stand Watie, the legendary "Red Fox," stood up for his Cherokees against the U.S. government as it sought to steal their ancient birthright and against his own tribal majority as they clung to their homeland in the face of possible extermination. He also stood up for his family and friends amidst a bitter intra-tribal civil war, and against the invading U.S. government again in the War Between the States. Moreover, he stood up for his exhausted and devastated tribe in his efforts to lead a post-war economic recovery.

> *Only one unit kept the Southern Cause alive in the region with daring raids on Federal camps, patrols, and supply wagons—Col. Stand Watie's Cherokee Mounted Rifles. Watie had become a master of guerrilla warfare, utilizing hit-and-run tactics in countless strikes against his Federal foes and keeping his men supplied with captured Union gear, weapons, ammunition, and raw foodstuffs. His charismatic leadership and little victories in numerous skirmishes kept the spark of rebellion alive in the hearts of many Confederate sympathizers in Indian Territory for the difficult remaining days of 1863. To most Native Americans, and even to many whites in the region, Stand Watie had come to symbolize the fury and defiance of the Southern Cause.*
>
> —Steve Cottrell
> *Civil War in the Indian Territory*

Stand Watie

many Indian Territory Natives to the Confederacy, coupled with the deadly effective guerrilla tactics of Watie and his men, had kept the territory controlled or threatened by the Confederates after successive campaigns by powerful invading Federal forces.

The wartime misery continued for non-combatants among the tribes. Few pro-Union women, children, and aged citizens had regained their homes in Indian Territory by early 1863, since Federal soldiers had once again retreated to Kansas and Arkansas. The civilians continued to suffer—and in the winter shiver and often die in their miserable Kansas refugee camps.

Sarah Watie, eloquent wife of Stand Watie. During the depths of the brutal war in Indian Territory, she wrote and urged him to show mercy to Federal Cherokees: "If you should ever catch William Ross (anti-Treaty Party son-in-law of John Ross and a convert to the Federals) don't have him killed. I know how bad his mother would feel but keep him till the war is over. I know they all deserve death but I do feel for his old mother and then I want them to know that you do not want to kill them just to get them out of your way." A few months later, Watie indeed captured William Ross during an electrifying ambush of Federal Cherokees who were meeting in Tahlequah. He spared his life and Ross went on to become a post-war Principal Chief of the tribe and live to old age.

Historian James L. Huston estimated that meanwhile around fifteen thousand pro-Confederate civilians suffered in the raw, open country of the Red River Valley, many of them in North Texas. Most of these folks had less shelter from the elements than their counterparts up in Kansas. Both groups experienced lengthy separation from their soldier kin and other family, not to mention their homes—many of which had already been destroyed by enemy troops.

Thomas Lewis Rider of the Cherokee Mounted Rifles. He carried mail and other communications between Confederate commanders in Indian Territory. He died during the war and is buried near Durant.

They also encountered difficulty in obtaining food and other basic sustenance for living, along with rampant disease and inadequate medical attention.

As they did in every other theater of the war, the Federals overcame defeats, disappointments, and loss with numerical superiority of men and resources, coupled with relentless—even ruthless—determination. Blunt and Phillips emerged as the prime exemplars of the latter attribute and the vital leaders of the U.S. war effort in Indian Territory. Like successful Federal commanders elsewhere, they proved to be shrewd tacticians and tough-minded leaders, and they kept coming back to fight, no matter the obstacles.

History would record Stand Watie as the only American Indian general on either side in the war. He was the last Confederate General to surrender, nearly three months after Robert E. Lee.

As Union troops again rode deep into Indian Territory, many Cherokees caught behind what would become permanent U.S. lines now switched their support to the North. In return, they received food, clothing, and other supplies, rather than what

The Slaves' War—In Their Own Words

Mary Grayson
(Former Creek slave)

"We slaves didn't have a hard time at all before the war. I have had people who were slaves of white folks back in the old states tell me that they had to work awfully hard and their masters were cruel to them sometimes, but all the Negroes I knew who belonged to Creeks always had plenty of clothes and lots to eat and we all lived in good log cabins we built. We worked the farm and tended to the horses and cattle and hogs, and some of the older women worked around the owner's house, but each Negro family looked after a part of the fields and worked the crops like they belonged to us."

loyal Confederate Indians got—confiscation and often destruction of their property. The Chickasaws and Choctaws remained unanimously Confederate; but the Cherokees, along with the Creeks and Seminoles, continued their own brutal intratribal civil wars, and Indian Territory and its people bled worse.

To consolidate the Federal effort among the Cherokees, Phillips supervised a meeting of tribal loyalists at Cowskin Prairie in February. They formed a second, pro-Union government, in opposition to the one that had elected Watie as Principal Chief. Again in command of Cherokee capital Tahlequah, they also renounced their treaty with the Confederacy, abolished slavery, and declared Watie and the Confederate Cherokees as renegades and fugitives from justice.

Honey Springs

From there, Phillips led the Federals south and shouldered the outnumbered Confederates out of both Fort Gibson and Webbers Falls. After a few Confederate Native warriors murdered a popular Federal doctor headed to treat the Confederate wounded, the Federals burned Webbers Falls to the ground. The Confederates did not stand idle during these setbacks. Cooper, the official field commander of Southern forces in the territory, formed his nation's strongest force of the war in Indian Territory—five thousand men—a few miles south of Federal-held Fort Gibson. Simultaneously, a growing army of Confederates in Arkansas shoved the Federals north toward Missouri.

When the Confederate Indians rustled a slew of U.S. cavalry mounts and nearly overran Fort Gibson, Blunt sent a large column of reinforcements south from Kansas for Phillips. Even this strong contingent got attacked by Watie's elusive guerrillas at the ford of Cabin Creek in northern Cherokee country near present-day Vinita. The outnumbered Confederates decimated one Union counterattack, but the Federals finally drove off the attackers and made their way to Fort Gibson.

Back in late 1862, African-American soldiers of the First Kansas Colored Regiment—some of them from Indian Territory—had seen the first combat of any Federal troops of African descent, according to Oklahoma historian Bruce Fisher. (Ironically, black Confederates fought back east in the Fredericksburg, Virginia, campaign and elsewhere around the same time.) Now they formed the heart of the pivotal Union charge that carried the day at the First Battle of Cabin Creek. A key factor in the Federal success was the rain soaking the Confederate Natives' inferior quality

First Kansas Colored (Black) Volunteers help hold the Federal line during the Battle of Honey Springs. Courtesy Osprey Publishing. (www.ospreypublishing.com)

Mexican-manufactured gunpowder, which prevented it from firing.

A showdown was coming, however. On July 17th the two forces hurtled into one another in a disjointed series of actions at Honey Springs, twenty-five miles south of Fort Gibson. On one side ranged thirty-five hundred to four thousand Texans, Cherokees, Chickasaws, Choctaws, Creeks, and Seminoles, led personally by Cooper. On the other was over three thousand Federals, including white soldiers from Kansas, Wisconsin, Indiana, and elsewhere, along with African-Americans who fought at Cabin Creek and Indians from various tribes.

Though the Federals brought slightly fewer troops to the battle, they owned an overwhelming advantage in firepower. They possessed much more—and much more powerful—artillery, state-of-the-art breech-loading carbines, and multi-shot revolver pistols. At least one-quarter of the Confederates, meanwhile, had no adequate firearms, and many others fielded pieces with much shorter shooting ranges than the Federals'. Moreover, Stand Watie and his men were not present. Cooper chose an unwise time to send the Cherokee Mounted Rifles elsewhere as decoys.

The dismounted Texas 29th Confederate Cavalry amidst desperate front-line fighting at the crucial Battle of Honey Creek, as drawn by Andy Thomas. (www.andythomas.com)

A Federal charge at the pivotal July 1863 Indian Territory battle of Honey Springs. From a sketch by James R. O'Neill. Courtesy Oklahoma Historical Society.

The timing of the battle could not have been more crucial. A three thousand-man Confederate force from Arkansas was only a few miles away from Honey Springs and heading to join Cooper's men for an assault on Fort Gibson. Once again, however, Blunt exhibited spunk and initiative, hitting Cooper and his Southerners before the Arkansas force could reach them. He also possessed the aforementioned decisive advantage in artillery power.

Then, at a climactic point in the battle, the Confederates' wet Mexican-manufactured gunpowder again betrayed them. This time the consequences proved immeasurably greater than at Cabin Creek. When dismounted Texas cavalry charged the center of the Federal line, this ordnance failed en masse on them. It left them exposed to a withering Union volley, which turned the day—and likely, the war in Indian Territory—for the Federals.

Future Creek Principal Chief G. W. Grayson (see page 143) served the South at Honey Springs in the Second Creek Regiment. He blamed the defeat on Cooper, whom he accused of ordering a retreat before many of his men had even reached the battle line, or vice versa, including Grayson's: "By what I have always confidently believed to be bad management, we lost the day here when the enemy came up and engaged us, for Gen. Cooper did not even get all his men out on the firing line, or into any engagement with his adversary before he ordered his forces to retire."

African-American soldiers from the First Kansas Colored again played a pivotal role in the Battle of Honey Springs. They formed the center of the Northern line, whose volley repulsed the Texan charge and thus opened the way to

> *When you first saw the light, it was said of you 'a man child is born.' You must prove today whether or not this saying of you was true. The sun that hangs over our heads has no death, no end of days. It will continue indefinitely to rise and to set, but with you it is different. Man must die sometime, and since he must die, he can find no nobler death than that which overtakes him while fighting for his home, his fires and his country.*
>
> **—Colonel Chilly McIntosh**
> speaking in Creek, to the Confederate Second Regiment before the Battle of Honey Springs

Confederate-held Fort Smith, Arkansas, for the U.S. forces, and secured control of the key Arkansas River east-west transportation route for them. Never again were the Confederates able to mount a strategic threat to Federal control of that portion of Indian Territory north of the Arkansas, which included the Cherokee country. Nor would they again come close to pushing the Yankees out of the Nations.

Decision and Defiance

How close were the Confederates to effecting their junction of forces that, despite ruined gunpowder, might still have provided the margin of victory at Honey Springs? Cooper and his men met up with the Arkansas force just *two hours* after the battle. Then, perhaps possessing one final chance to mount a successful attack against Fort Gibson, their commanders chose instead to split their forces and retreat in different directions.

This did not deter Blunt. Once again, after resupplying and reinforcing his army, he pressed aggressively ahead. By the end of August, 1863, he had driven south and destroyed a small, outnumbered Confederate enclave at Perryville, retaken Fort Smith, Arkansas, to the east, and so splintered the ragged, hungry Creek cavalry that many of them were begging for food at Fort Gibson. His troopers then burned and killed their way through Confederate Indian communities in the Choctaw country, and the masses of pro-South Natives—variously starving, homeless, and disease-ridden—suffered the onset of winter in the open country of the Red River Valley.

Despite the shattered fortunes of the Confederate Indians, Stand Watie's rise as the greatest commander of the war in Indian Territory continued in November as he maneuvered his Cherokee Mounted Rifles around Blunt's main force at Fort Gibson and rode north on an electrifying campaign of raids. With scores of Federal depredations against the Confederate Natives of Indian Territory filling him and his men with rage, they thundered into Tahlequah and burned down much of it, as well as turncoat Chief John Ross's former Park Hill mansion nearby.

From there, the Southern chieftain headed north through Indian Territory and into Kansas, and even Missouri, where he and his men shot it out with other Federal soldiers. Despite commanding a dominant and growing army sitting astride the territory, Blunt had no idea of the whereabouts of Watie and his men, nor where they were headed. Nor would he for the final two years of the war in the bloody hell of Indian Territory.

The year 1863 thus proved decisive in the battle for the territory. Yet the war would drag on for another year and a half. Pro-Federal Natives suffered along with their pro-Confederate opponents. The Yankee army never ridded itself of the deadly presence of Stand Watie's guerrilla-fighting horse soldiers. And it would launch no invasion of Texas through Indian Territory.

Federal Rampage

After Honey Springs, the Federals held the Arkansas River and Indian Territory north of that, the Confederates the country south of that to Red River. No one in the territory was safe, however, as both sides launched murderous raids into the other's lands. The hungry, ragged Confederate Indians waged lethal guerrilla warfare. Watie was the

Double Trouble for Confederates

Two Federal commanders, peacetime doctor and Brigadier General James Blunt and Scottish-born Colonel William Phillips, provided the sagacity, energy, and relentless determination to leverage their larger supply of manpower and resources into gaining the upper hand over determined Confederate opposition in Indian Territory. The campaigns they blazed from one end of the territory to the other between October 1862 and February 1864 turned the balance of power to the Federals.

James G. Blunt

William A. Phillips

mastermind, though many of his own missions and feats possessed more strategic import than that of standard guerrilla, or hit-and-run, actions. His raids and attacks kept the larger, much better supplied Federal forces off-balance for the rest of the war. He and his Southern rough riders captured so many Federal horses at Fort Gibson/Blunt that the Yankee cavalry stationed there became infantry.

Watie's guerrilla exploits provoked Phillips to return to Fort Blunt, and then head down the Texas Road in February with fifteen hundred Federal horse soldiers armed to the teeth on one of the most infamous rampages of the war in Indian Territory. The relentless Scotsman intended through battle and terror to accomplish nothing less than terminating Confederate Native opposition in the Nations.

The war in Indian Territory provided numerous illustrations of African-American Federal soldiers' courage under fire, as portrayed by Andy Thomas. (www. andythomas. com)

Phillips revealed the nature of his mission when he announced to his troopers: "Do not kill a prisoner after he has surrendered. But I do not ask you to take prisoners. I do ask that you make your footsteps severe and terrible."

For the next month, the Federals obeyed their orders, burning every farm, slaughtering every animal, and killing every non-Union man they encountered. The notorious Yankee General William Tecumseh Sherman, who burned all or parts of three state capitals and two states, scarcely accomplished such devastation on a proportional basis to his enemy's population when he scalded his way through Georgia and the Carolinas several months later.

On February 13th, several hundred of Phillips' men equipped with artillery attacked a Confederate supply depot defended by only ninety men with no artillery on the Middle Boggy River in present-day Atoka County, about twenty miles north of Red River. After a savage half-hour battle, the Federals' overwhelming numbers overran the depot. Some of the defenders escaped south to the camp of Lieutenant Colonel John Jumper and his Seminole warriors.

> *Do not kill a prisoner after he has surrendered. But I do not ask you to take prisoners. I do ask that you make your footsteps severe and terrible.*
>
> **—William Phillips**

Hearing the disturbing news of the nearby Federal rout, Jumper ordered his men into the saddle and they galloped straight toward the depot. By the time they arrived, however, the Yankees had already torched it. In keeping with Phillips' directive, they had also left not a single prisoner alive. Though many of the defenders had only superficial battle wounds, the throats of all forty-nine dead had been slit from ear to ear, and many were scalped.

What historian Cottrell termed "the grim Union horde" rampaged nearly to Red River before they turned back. They devastated everything in their path, killing, according to Oklahoma Historical Commission official Whit Edwards, another 110 Confederates—mostly, if not all, Indians—in their homes, because of Phillips's no-prisoners policy.

Did Phillips accomplish his mission of converting or killing all remaining Confederate Natives in the Nations? "He hoped this would be the final blow to the Confederate resistance," Edwards said. "Instead, the brutal treatment of the wounded only served to strengthen the resolve of the resistors."

> *Most (Indian Territory) troops regarded their foes as no better than a pack of rabid dogs that should be exterminated.*
>
> **—Steve Cottrell**

"[Phillips'] mission had failed to break the spirit of the Confederate defiance of Federal authority in Indian Territory," Cottrell concurred. "As a matter of fact, the death and destruction he left in the wake of his march only served to strengthen the resolve of Southern sympathizers to fight back for another year."

Going Down Fighting

Stand Watie, whom one Oklahoma historian called "this redoubtable leader of unsurpassed courage," provides the best—and most dramatic—illustration of the unvanquished Southern defiance. Already renowned for his daring feats against great odds, Watie excelled anything he previously accomplished with his deeds in 1864. He now commanded the newly constituted First Indian Cavalry Brigade in the Confederacy's reorganized Indian Territory Department. Cherokees, Creeks, Seminoles, and a minority faction of Osages comprised this force. Choctaw mixed-blood Tandy Walker, who led the Confederate Natives to victory in the Battle of Newtonia, Missouri, helmed the new Second Indian Cavalry Brigade, which included Walker's fellow Choctaws, Chickasaws, and Caddos.

Walker and his brigade soon found themselves amidst another pitiable display of murder and total war. Sent to Arkansas with Church of Christ minister and Brigadier General Richard Gano and his Texas Brigade, the Indian Territory troopers participated in the successful April 18th ambush and capture of an enormous Federal supply wagon

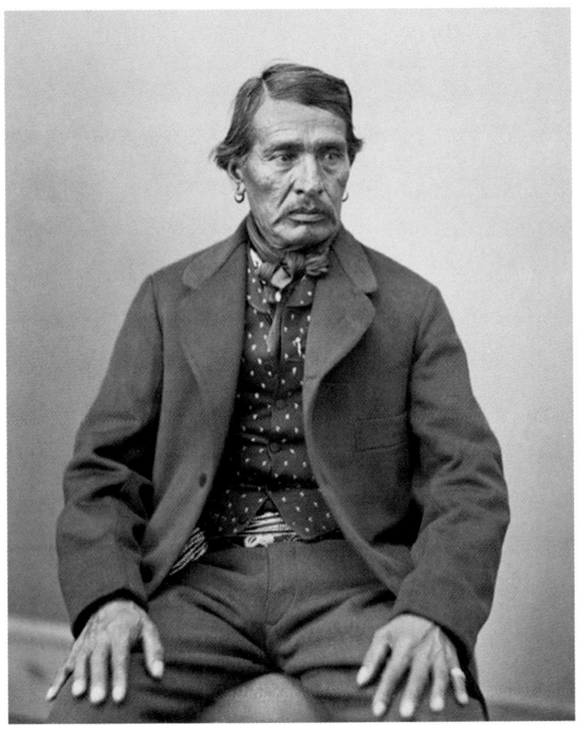

Caddo Chief George Washington, or Showetat, a wise, winsome, and enterprising leader who shepherded his small tribe through decades of dangerous adventure in present-day southwest Oklahoma. He formed the two-company Caddo Frontier Guard, a mounted Confederate rough rider force in 1864-65. He served as its major and commander, and his captains were Caddo Jose Maria and Phil McCusker, a white U.S. Army veteran and future cavalry scout.

train. Among the guards of that train were the First Kansas Colored Infantry, who played crucial roles in the Union victories at Cabin Creek and Honey Springs. The Texans, who considered former slaves fighting for the Federals as murdering traitors, and some of whom had caught the First Kansas' point-blank volley at the latter battle when their own gunpowder malfunctioned, took no African-American prisoners at Poison Springs. They killed every black soldier they saw, including those attempting to surrender. The colored regiment was decimated. The road to freedom was proving a rough one for African-American Federal soldiers in the West.

Watie launched the next in a series of Confederate successes during 1864 with the daring May hijack of the Union steamboat *J. R. Williams* in a shootout on the Arkansas River. The spectacular heist of the largest load of military supplies (approximately $75 million worth in modern currency) ever sent into the territory struck it like a thunderbolt. The thousands-strong Federal force at Fort Blunt was deprived of a colossal supply of provisions, reminding them that Watie and his horse soldiers could strike anywhere at any time.

The capture, plunder, and burning of the *J. R. Williams*, meanwhile, imbued the beleaguered Confederate Indians with renewed hope in their cause after so much suffering and disappointment. The reverberations reached all the way to Richmond, Virginia, where the Confederate States Congress promoted Watie to Brigadier General. History would record Stand Watie as the only Native general on either side in the war.

Watie's greatest feat occurred September 19th, at the Second Battle of Cabin Creek. The campaign began when the Cherokee's scouts reported that a gigantic Federal supply train spanning over three hundred wagons had headed out of Fort Scott, Kansas, toward Fort Blunt. Watie and Gano sneaked around Blunt's army at his namesake fort and thundered

The legendary Cherokee Mounted Rifle.

G. N. Taylor's painting of Tandy Walker, mixed-blood Choctaw Governor and Chief, and regimental commander of the Confederate Second Indian Cavalry Brigade of Choctaws, Chickasaws, and Caddos.

north with eight hundred Indian Territory Natives and twelve hundred Texas horse soldiers.

Along the way, they ambushed surviving First Kansas Colored Infantry as they cut hay for the U.S. mounts. After steamrolling the outnumbered Federals, the battle concluded with another rueful scene of vengeful Texans shooting down surviving black troopers as they fled or tried to hide. The Confederates torched thousands of tons of cut hay and a hay-mowing machine, then rode north up the Grand River Valley to find the supply train.

Watie, orchestrating the determined Texans and Oklahomans like a symphony conductor, ensnared the wagon train and over six hundred U.S. soldiers at a Federal stockade constructed on a bluff next to where the old Texas Road (roughly present-day U.S. Highway 69) forded Cabin Creek in present-day Mayes County. Bringing forward artillery and manpower the Federal commander did not know he possessed, Watie turned the execution of the attack itself over to Gano. That attack, crafted by Watie, was a stunning nighttime charge conducted under a full moon. The Confederates routed the Federal force, thus avenging the previous summer's defeat on nearly the same ground. Then Watie deftly guided his force through a cobweb of pursuing Federal forces, escaping all the way to Texas with enough booty to clothe his entire army and feed every Confederate soldier and civilian in Indian Territory for over a month.

Watie's Second Cabin Creek attack was a stunning nighttime charge conducted under a full moon.

Andy Thomas's (www.andythomas.com) vivid depiction of mounted Confederate *Guerrillas* in the Trans-Mississippi theater of the War Between the States, which included Indian Territory. Brandishing shotguns, rifles, Bowie knives, and four or more Colts pistols apiece, these hell-for-leather Westerners engaged the Federal army in a ruthless war of extermination. Their ranks included legendary warriors such as William Quantrill, Frank and Jesse James, Cole Younger, and Bloody Bill Anderson. Their exploits inspired such memorable motion pictures as *The Outlaw Josey Wales* (Clint Eastwood) and *Ride with the Devil* (Tobey McGuire).

"An Indian Shall Not Spill An Indian's Blood"

Between the time of the surrender of Robert E. Lee and the Army of Northern Virginia and that of the Confederate Natives in Oklahoma, a remarkable council of tribes occurred near present-day Verden, deep in the Choctaw country on the Washita River. As the flame of Southern independence dimmed in the spring of 1865, leaders from Texas, the Confederate Indian republics, the Plains Indians, and the Confederate States all recognized the need for concord among themselves, as well as a cohesive front for negotiating with the United States, following the surrender that loomed.

The Oklahoma College for Women (now the University of Sciences and Arts of Oklahoma) in Chickasha erected this monument to the Confederate and Plains Indians of Indian Territory who counseled together at Camp Napoleon.

Joseph Murrow—"Father" to the Indians (1835–1929)

Joseph S. Murrow

Another in the legion of larger-than-life figures who helped write the history of early Oklahoma, Georgia-born Joseph Samuel Murrow carried forward the legacy of stalwart Christian missionaries while organizing more than seventy-five Baptist churches in Indian Territory; helping ordain seventy Native ministers; baptizing over two thousand people (most of them Indians); founding Oklahoma Masonry, the town of Atoka, and the Baptist Orphans Home for Indian Children; co-founding Bacone College for Indians in Muskogee; living through the deaths of four beloved wives and marrying a fifth at age eighty-six; and ministering among the Chickasaws, Choctaws, Creeks, Seminoles, whites, and African-Americans for nearly three-quarters of a century, his earthly work ending only with his death.

John Jumper (c. 1820–1896)

If ever a larger-than-life character strode the land and history of Oklahoma, surely it was this strapping, great-hearted Seminole chieftain. Towering six feet, four inches tall—proportionate to a modern height upwards of seven feet—and weighing 225 pounds in his prime, his life mirrored and helped forge the history of his people through the bulk of the nineteenth century. The scion of an elite tribal family, he twice shouldered arms against the United States, first in the Seminole Wars of the 1830s and again a quarter-century later in the War Between the States. Yet he not only embraced the faith of white Indian Territory Christian missionaries, he himself became a longtime Baptist pastor.

John Jumper

Requiem

At this point, both sides—their property and possessions destroyed, many of their bravest men dead, and their suffering civilian populaces exiled en masse to Kansas and Texas—quailed at launching major new offensives. Cooper and Watie kept regular patrols in the field to secure beef for their troops and ward off encroaching Federals. But the Yankees had had enough and evidenced no intention of straying south of Fort Gibson. Confederate cavalry ranged north to the Canadian River, but they did not confront the enemy. A jagged stalemate ensued, with the Federals holding roughly the country north of the Arkansas and Canadian and the Confederates that to the south. Other than minor skirmishes, the adversaries fought no more until hostilities officially ended the following summer.

Robert E. Lee's April 9, 1865, surrender of the world-famed Army of Northern Virginia to a Federal army, now five times its size, at Appomattox Courthouse, Virginia, did not end the war. The Confederate government, though fleeing the Yankee tidal wave, had not surrendered, and numerous Southern armies remained in the field unvanquished. But the Army of Northern Virginia was the largest and greatest Confederate force. And the towering esteem his fellow countrymen held for Lee's character and wisdom carried such weight that most of those countrymen thought if "Marse Robert" believed it best to put down his sword, they had best do so as well. Through April and May, one Confederate army after another surrendered, ceased hostilities, or just went home.

Confederate Cherokee Stand Watie, the only Native to attain the rank of general on either side in the War Between the States, was also the final Confederate general of the war to surrender, on June 23, 1865, in Doaksville, Choctaw country, Indian Territory, nearly three months after Robert E. Lee did so at Appomattox Courthouse. Courtesy, Oklahoma State Senate Historical Preservation Fund, Inc. and Dennis Parker.

This included General Douglas Cooper and the white soldiers in Indian Territory. It did not include many of the surviving Confederate Indians, despite the fact that in some tribes, such as the Cherokees, the war had widowed one-third of the married women and orphaned one-fourth of the children.

The Choctaws finally capitulated on June 19th. Stand Watie—feared and pursued for years by Federal armies from all over the West, but never caught—rode into Doaksville on June 23rd. He surrendered on behalf of the Confederate Cherokees, Seminoles, and Creeks, and the Osage Battalion. He was

the final general in the Confederacy to do so. The Chickasaws and the Caddos remained defiant even longer, until July 14th, more than three months after Lee's surrender.

The uncivil war in Indian Territory ended as a slight tactical victory for the North with its larger army, superior resources, and final geographic positioning, but with a strategic advantage to the South. Regarding the objectives of the latter outlined early in this chapter, neither side was able to provision its nation's wider military or populace from the territory's resources. The Confederates, however, led by the costly sacrifice in blood and treasure by the soldiers of the five Indian republics and their families, stopped the Federal campaign to invade Texas through Indian Territory.

George Washington Grayson (1843–1920)

His own people, America, and history swept this wise Creek mixed-blood up and into their own currents, but he rarely failed to answer any of their calls, whether as boyhood protector of his fatherless family, teenage combat commander in the War Between the States, shrewd entrepreneurial genius, presidentially appointed Principal Chief of his tribe, or most of all, advocate for and servant to his great people.

Historian James L. Huston assessed the war's social and economic toll—which he estimated included the loss of ten thousand lives in Indian Territory—on the tribes of Indian Territory:

> It exacerbated long-standing internal divisions and made new ones, and it destroyed needed population and crushed economic advance. Without the war perhaps the tribes might have grown in numbers, in wealth, and in political power. They might then have been better able to ward off later Euroamerican attacks on their land. The only rational assessment that can be made without fear of contravention is that the Civil War crippled the tribes of Indian Territory and took away their strength.

The only rational assessment that can be made without fear of contravention is that the Civil War crippled the tribes of Indian Territory and took away their strength.

—James L. Huston

Indeed, war may have ceased in Indian Territory, but the tribes' troubles had not. And they would have to face the U.S. government with their land devastated and their people decimated more than even they had been after the Trails of Tears. Even with all this tragedy and woe suffered by the Natives, white American civilization was determined to wait no longer to stake its claim on the future state of Oklahoma.

Confederate monument fronting the Bryan County Courthouse in Durant. Photo Susan Thweatt.

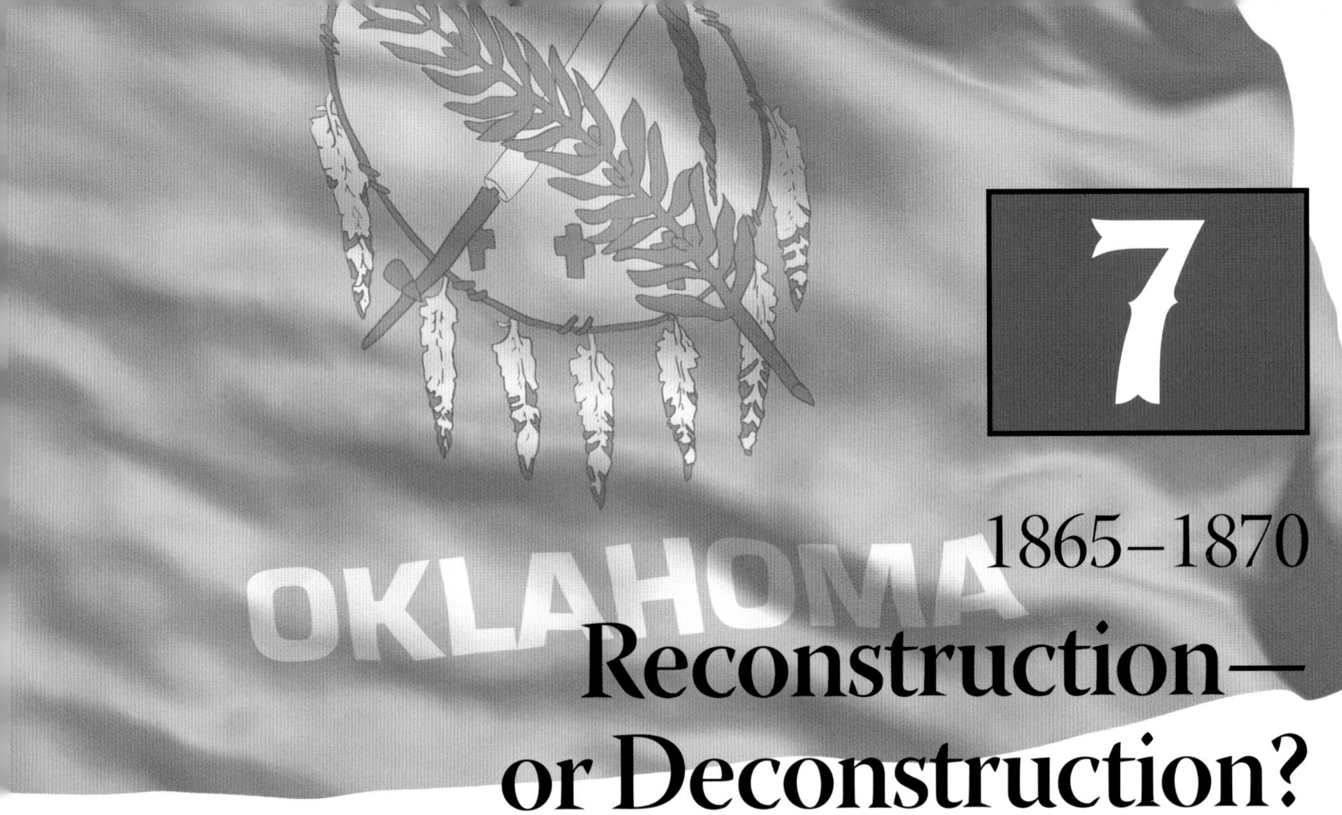

OKLAHOMA

7

1865–1870

Reconstruction—or Deconstruction?

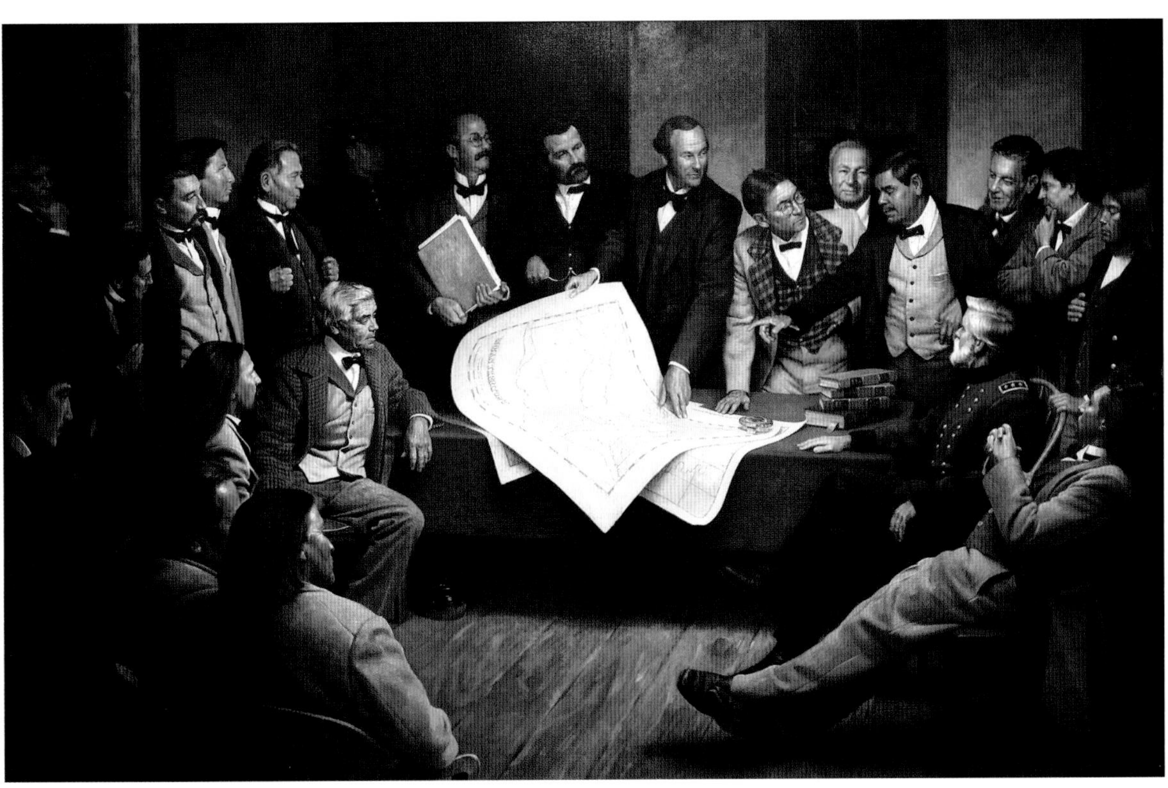

The September 8, 1865, Fort Smith Council, convened at the Fort Smith, Arkansas, military post to renegotiate treaties between the United States and the tribes who sided with the Confederacy during the War Between the States. Tribes represented included the Cherokees, Chickasaws, Choctaws, Comanches, Creeks, Osages, Quapaws, Seminoles, Senecas, Shawnees, Wichitas, and Wyandottes. U.S. representatives included D. N. Cooley, Commissioner of Indian Affairs; Elijah Sells, Superintendent of Indian Affairs; and Colonel E. S. Parker, a Seneca. This painting, *Fort Smith Conference–1865*, is another of Oklahoma artist Mike Wimmer's vibrant work that graces the halls of the State Capitol Building. Courtesy Oklahoma State Senate Historical Preservation Fund, Inc. and Mike Wimmer.

1865	Fort Smith Council
1866	Little Arkansas Council
1867	Medicine Lodge Council
1868	Battle of the Washita
1868–1875	Plains Indian Wars
1869–1887	Chisholm Trail

Using the same stoicism with which they faced removal and resettlement in the 1830s, the (Indians) set about rebuilding homes, fencing land, and plowing and planting, and they began healing the wounds of tribal division during the Civil War.

—Odie B. Faulk and William D. Welge

The war had devastated the Nations. The Cherokee, Creek, and Seminole lands north of the Arkansas and Canadian Rivers were a virtual wasteland. Perhaps as much as twenty percent of the population of the Five Civilized Tribes was dead from battle or disease. Violence such as the Middle Boggy massacre had stained the ground farther south in Choctaw and Chickasaw country. Yet, charity and forgiveness did not characterize the United States government's "Reconstruction" program in the South, and particularly with regard to the five Indian republics.

In addition, the people of Kansas wanted the thousands of Natives residing in that state—many of them pro-Federals long refugeeing there, many others ordered there by the government from other states—to leave, en masse, and had for several years. They planned to replace them with a tidal wave of westward-migrating white settlers. Championing this crusade were two iron-willed Kansas Senators—James H. Lane and Samuel C. Pomeroy. Despite their alliance regarding the Indians, Lane and Pomeroy, according to one Kansas historian, "hated each other with an unexcelled ferocity."

The charismatic but mercurial Lane was famed as "Bloody" Lane and the "Grim Chieftain" of wartime Kansas. While holding his elite office during the war, he had personally led "Jayhawking" Federal irregulars on a bloody trail of vengeance throughout Confederate southern Missouri. Lane's exploits encompassed a series of atrocities, including the plundering and burning of the town of Osceola.

In early 1865, Lane declared to his fellow senators in Washington that support of the Kansas

Kansas Senator James H. Lane

Natives was costing American taxpayers as much as two million dollars a year. In reality, annuities pledged to the tribes during their various removals west covered the cost. The problem for the tribes of Indian Territory was that many of these Indians had not come from there, yet this impending relocation would force them to live in the once autonomous lands of the five Indian republics.

More Loss and Suffering

In September, 1865, the Federals called leaders of the Indian Territory tribes to Fort Smith, Arkansas. There, they informed them they had "lost all rights to annuities and lands" previously provided them in accord with their sorrowful and forced Trails of Tears. The U.S. government would loose a series of reprisals against them—including the requirement that they merge themselves into one government.

The elite Indian delegation sat stunned. They marveled that these same Federals had abandoned them to the Confederates four years before, and that many among the tribes had bled, suffered, and even died for the Union, yet they would be punished along with their Confederate kinsmen. So unresponsive were the Natives, that the Federals adjourned the meeting with little positive accomplished other than the tribes reaffirming their allegiance to the United States.

Unfortunately, a significant amount was accomplished in the meeting that was not positive. With separate pro-Federal and pro-Confederate Cherokee delegations in attendance, the U.S. officials refused to acknowledge late-arriving John Ross as Principal Chief of the Cherokees. When his supporters began to protest that Ross had, in effect, never supported the Confederacy, Elias C. Boudinot—whose father, uncle, and cousin had been murdered by Ross supporters—arose in fury. Now witnessing Ross's attempts to escape the consequences of Confederate loyalty that had cost yet more of Boudinot's family and friends their lives, the nephew of Ross's nemesis, Stand Watie, unleashed such a tirade against Ross that the Federals had to restrain him.

By then, the old scars from passionate differences over removal, culture, war, and to an extent, even

G. N. Taylor's *Guardians of the Herd,* wherein the mighty leaders of one of the vast Southern Plains buffalo herds deal with ravenous wolves. (www.gntayloroklaart.com)

religion tore open—if ever they had healed over. For their part, the Choctaws and Chickasaws rejected Federal suggestions that they had been misled into their alliance with the Confederates; instead, they presented a strong defense for their pursuit of that alliance. Thus, the Council at Fort Smith managed somehow both to alienate the pro-Federal Indians against the U.S. and worsen relations with their pro-Southern kith and kin.

As historian Gaston Litton lamented: "The War Between the States, no less than the War with England in 1812, provided a pretext for a reappraisal of the relations between the United States Government and the Indian nations.... Thus it was that lands originally given to the Southern Indians in exchange for their ancestral territory in the East were now to be carved up and the surplus taken from them on the excuse that they had forfeited their treaty rights."

Through the remainder of 1865 and most of 1866, hunger, disease, poverty, hatred between the Federal and Confederate partisans, and numerous other sufferings beset the tribes of Indian Territory in the extreme. U.S. Indian agent George A. Reynolds wrote: "Now their country is one vast scene of desolation; houses burned, treasury robbed, fences and agricultural implements destroyed, cattle stolen, and their former fields overgrown with weeds."

Reconstruction Treaties

The Federals next called representatives of the five Indian republics to visit Washington in 1866 to work out Reconstruction treaties. The term "Reconstruction" represented the U.S. government's intention to successfully enfold the seceded states and territories—including Indian Territory—back into the Union. Most officials in that government and the people who elected it wished for a resumption of productive antebellum relations between the sections.

Some Northerners—particularly among the now ascendant socialistic, self-termed Radical Republican national political majority—wished in addition for the social, economic, and political practices of the Confederate people to be remade, or reconstructed, more in the likeness of those practiced by the Federal states. Perhaps this application of the word reveals the true designs intended with the colossal program represented by it. Great and lasting strife would only mount because of those latter objectives.

Reconstruction Terms for Five Indian Republics

- U.S. government delays resumption of pre-war annuity payments for the tribes' confiscated southeastern land
- Tribes ordered to sell much land to railroads at low prices and allow them to build across tribal lands
- U.S. government takes back millions of acres of Native land, including much of present-day Oklahoma and eight hundred thousand acres in Kansas
- Slavery ended, with no monetary compensation to Indian slave owners
- Individual tribal governments abolished

The government and the five tribes concluded a series of treaties during 1866. Key provisions included freedom for the Natives' black slaves, membership and equal rights (including as property owners) for these Freedmen in the respective tribes, the right of American railroads to traverse Indian Territory, and most hurtfully, forfeiture of more than half the tribes' lands. The latter involved a significant loss for the Chickasaws, Choctaws, Creeks, and Seminoles—roughly the western half of present-day Oklahoma; nearly a million acres of Cherokee land in Kansas; and Cherokee control over their 7.5 million-acre Outlet, on which the government could now settle other tribes at whatever payment to the Cherokees it set. The Seminoles would lose their entire country for the paltry price of fifteen cents per acre, which forced them to purchase different land parcels altogether from the Creeks.

Indeed, the government intended to pull off a second great feat in Indian Territory by forging its Reconstruction treaties. Part of the punishment for the tribes who offered significant support to the Confederacy involved the loss of their land to other tribes whom the government would now move to the area. In effect, Indian Territory would now serve not as a refuge for the five great southeastern tribes, but as a clearing house for tribes from all over America.

New Tribes Arrive

Over the next decade or so, the Absentee Shawnees, Delawares, Iowas, Kansas, Kickapoos, Miamis, Missouris, Modocs, Osages (whom the government had earlier moved to Kansas *from* present-day Oklahoma), Otos, Ottawas, Pawnees, Peorias, Pottawatomies, Sac and Foxes, Shawnees, Tonkawas, and Wyandottes would come from Idaho, Kansas, Missouri, Nebraska, Oregon, Texas, remote corners of Indian Territory, and even Mexico to take possession of land owned by the five Indian republics.

Plains tribes such as the Arapahos, Cheyennes, Comanches, Kiowas, Kiowa-Apaches, Lipan Apaches, and Wichitas received western sections of the territory. The fame attached to many of these tribes belies their tiny populations and helps explain their engulfment by hundreds of thousands of American settlers whose Christian-based civilization produced higher birth rates, lower infant mortality rates, and longer life spans. The population of these tribes varied from a few thousand in a couple of cases to less than a hundred. Most numbered in the hundreds.

The treaties spelled the end of tribal sovereignty over their own lands and lives, despite the many previous promises in treaties offered by the United States. They also signaled the vulnerability of any autonomy still possessed by the tribes to be eclipsed in the future by the U.S. government. For better or worse, these treaties accelerated the assimilation of most of the Native tribes residing on the North American continent into the United States.

In retrospect, a sensitive question concerns whether the tribes—like the victims of the African slave trade—were perhaps blessed as a people by their eventual melding into American society, even if many of the means accomplishing that end proved unwise and harmful, and significant portions of the tribes at times did not benefit. As one Indian Territory Principal Chief declared, "We try to forget these things, but we would not forget that the white man brought us the blessed Gospel of Christ, the Christian's hope. This more than pays for all we have suffered."

On the other hand—at least regarding some of the tribes, with their already established churches, schools, agrarian practices, strong sense of place and community, and American-influenced culture—perhaps they would have been as blessed, if not more so, to remain on their own, at least until such time as they chose of their own will to join the American body politic.

Mary Jane Ross, daughter of Lewis Ross and wife of Cherokee Principal Chief William Potter Ross.

Cherokee Unity

The five Indian republics battled tenaciously despite challenges old and new to rebuild their lives and country. Division again bedeviled the three tribes—Cherokees, Creeks, and Seminoles—whose lands lay within the frequent reach of the Federal army during the war. Cherokees who opposed John Ross, including Confederates and the earlier Treaty Party faction, seethed with rage as the Federals again rejected their pleas to divide their tribe in two. Instead, they rechristened Ross in 1866 as Principal Chief of a single government that ruled over the Indians.

Ironically, Ross died only days after that decision, yet discord among the Cherokees did not. Ross's nephew William succeeded him as Principal Chief. The younger Ross detested Stand Watie and the Confederate Cherokees—who, unlike the Treaty Party faction, were not a small minority of the

"Oklahoma"

The origin of the name "Oklahoma" can be traced to a specific time, event, and person. Following the War Between the States, as part of its punishment for the "Five Civilized Tribes'" majority support of the Confederacy, the U.S. government initiated a decades-long strategy to force their lands—heretofore self-governed in accord with the Federals' Trails of Tears promises— to merge into a new American territory.

Allen Wright

tribe—and these emotions directed his leadership of the tribe. Not surprisingly, tribal divisions deepened during William Ross's brief tenure.

That tenure proved brief due to the statesmanship and Christian charity of longtime abolitionists and John Ross supporters such as Cherokee Pastor Lewis Downing and white father-and-son Baptist missionaries Evan and John B. Jones. Though these men supported the majority Ross faction—that is, they had long "backed the winners"—Christian unity was of more importance to them. They recognized that the future of the tribe, along with its hopes for happiness and unity, hinged on bringing together the long-estranged factions.

Thus, Downing and the Joneses allied themselves with supporters of both the Ross and Watie-Boudinot factions to form the Union Party. Spearheaded by devout Christians, this group sought to get past the partisan strife of the past forty years to guide the tribe forward in unity toward its potential as a force for good in America.

The genuineness of Union Party leaders shined forth when the majority of both Ross and Watie supporters elected Downing as Principal Chief in 1867. He exercised wise servant leadership in that exalted office until his death in 1872. The Union Party held the office all but eight years till Oklahoma achieved statehood in 1907. Despite the Cherokees' steady loss of autonomy to the United States, a unity permeated the tribe throughout those years that had eluded it throughout the four decades of John Ross's leadership.

Other Indian Republics

The Choctaws and Chickasaws stood most unshakably for the Confederate cause, so only a few of them found joy in the Federal victory. After a year or so of post-war misery, however, their fortunes brightened. Unlike what the Cherokees, Creeks, and Seminoles experienced, fighting had not ravaged their lands.

Yet several factors conspired to cost them dearly. Many of their men had suffered serving the Confederate military effort, not the least the separation from their families, and some had died in the fighting. They had sacrificed the bulk of their wartime stock and produce to the territory's

Choctaw Village, François Bernard's classic 1869 painting of women readying the dye for the color cane strips used in basket-making. Courtesy Peabody Museum, Harvard University.

multi-tribal Confederate army and its civilian refugees. Thousands of these war veterans and refugees remained in the Choctaw country following the war, and some—usually destitute and malnourished if not starving—descended into criminal behavior. Desperate to obtain provisions, African-American Freedmen, including those from Texas, established Red River Valley communities from which they also raided the former Confederate Indians (see page 157).

Such men as Robert M. Jones and Robert H. Love, whose ancestors included the founder of Love's Travel Stops and Country Stores (Tom Love), helped comprise the leadership of the Choctaws' and Chickasaws' post-war rally, what one historian called "mixed-breeds of shrewd discernment, skilled in politics." These savvy frontiersmen built a string of range cattle kingdoms across present-day southern Oklahoma, and resumed, at least to some degree, their antebellum skill in cotton growing and the building of grand plantation homes.

Reconstruction dealt more difficulty for both the Creeks and their cousins, the Seminoles. The U.S. government confiscated the western half of the Creeks' country, over three millions acres of land, for a paltry price of thirty cents per acre. In contrast, the remnant of the Delawares purchased a new tribal domain for themselves from the Cherokees at a dollar per acre. Also, the Creeks endured post-war intra-tribal strife even worse than the Cherokees'. Rival factions of mostly full-blooded traditionalist former Federals and mostly mixed-blooded progressive former Confederates fought—sometimes literally—for power under the tribe's freshly crafted constitution and federated government system.

Creek chief and Confederate veteran Samuel Checote won the election in 1867 as Principal Chief. Traditionalists led by Oktarharsars Harjo (Sands) rejected Checote's leadership. They resisted tribal leadership to some degree—even after Harjo succeeded Checote in that exalted Creek office—all the way till Oklahoma statehood in 1907.

Reconstruction, meanwhile, cost the Seminoles their entire domain. They had to purchase different land from the Creeks and move there en masse. At the same time, they faced their own intratribal strife between generally traditionalist full-bloods led by John Chupco, who supported the Union, and generally progressive mixed-blood former Confederates led by John Jumper.

The Seminole National Capitol building in Wewoka. Built in the late 1860s, it became the Seminole County Courthouse when Oklahoma became a state in 1907.

Unlike the other four Indian Territory republics, the Seminoles had never committed their tribal laws and government to writing, so Chupco and Jumper led, in effect, separate Seminole nations until Jumper's death in 1875. Two years later, the factions finally united in lasting concord under the leadership of Confederate veteran John F. Brown, much as the Cherokees had done under Lewis Downing.

Amidst this long and painful discord, the Seminoles and Creeks suffered much mistreatment by whites. Despite both tribes' earlier resistance to this abuse, the Christian faith originally brought to them by whites took hold of them to such a remarkable degree that by the Reconstruction years, they had become Christian peoples.

Chupco's followers mostly followed the Presbyterianism that predominated in the Northern states, while Jumper and his supporters generally followed pro-Southern Baptist denominations. But both had largely turned from the ancient pagan practices of their forefathers and embraced Jesus Christ in faith, even if they persisted in some of those earlier practices.

Beginning in 1869, the Society of Friends (Quakers) and Catholics established other vibrant and enduring missionary endeavors through churches and schools among the Wyandotte, Seneca, Shawnee, Quapaw, and Modoc tribes in far northeastern Indian Territory.

Recovery and Challenges

The war and its aftermath shook the social, political, and economic foundations of the five Indian republics to a degree not surpassed in some ways even by their Trails of Tears. Not only was much of the country physically destroyed, but tribal institutions faced devastation and possible extinction. Thousands of children who would otherwise have attended tribal schools had missed six or seven years of classes. Some were now too old to attend school. Many missionaries and pastors had been forced, at the threat of their own lives, to leave Indian Territory during the war. Farms, ranches, and businesses lay in ruin.

Now the tribes themselves, along with their churches and ministers—both white and Native—rose up to write their names high in the history and lore of the future Sooner State. The labors of those missionaries and their churches who had accomplished so much before the war accomplished much good after it as well. Presbyterian, Baptist, and other denominational missionaries spearheaded the reopening of the Indians' schools and churches, the birthing of new ones, and the establishment of schools for Freedmens' slaves. These Christian influences played a key role in melting away intratribal feuds among the Cherokees, Creeks, and Seminoles in the years following the war. The afore-mentioned Baptist ministers Evan and John B. Jones and Lewis Downing helped sustain a strong Christian identity within the resurgent Keetoowah Society of Cherokee full-bloods, who might otherwise have been engulfed in the pagan philosophies of their past.

> *The war and its aftermath shook the social, political, and economic foundations of the five Indian republics to a degree not surpassed in some ways even by their Trails of Tears.*

Rugged circuit-riding Methodist preacher John Jasper Methvin, who toiled for a half-century among the Indians of the Oklahoma country, well captured the potent distinctive of this spiritual process:

> There is nothing that transforms life like the gospel of the Son of God. A veneering of civilization may be given or forced upon a people and yet leave them void of the real purposes and high aspirations of life and it soon wears off. Many methods have been tried by the Government and benevolent organizations for the civilization of the Indian and the work done was meant for his good, but not in a single instance have these efforts ever been made effective and abiding without the stabilizing power of the gospel through the ministry of the missionary and without this there has never been any real reform and permanent good.

The Creek National Capitol in Okmulgee, constructed in the late 1870s of native sandstone. Upon Oklahoma statehood in 1907, it served as the Okmulgee County Courthouse.

But other challenges converged on Indian Territory tribes. Their crippled, underfunded civil governments could scarcely function. Consequently, though the law enforcement companies they fielded such as the Choctaw Lighthorsemen—most of them seasoned combat veterans of the war—proved brave and able, the wild sprawling country stretched them far too thin. This bad situation grew much worse through the 1860s as word spread among white, red, and black American outlawry alike that Indian Territory lay open as a virtual colossal criminals' sanctuary from justice.

Soon, outlaws and desperadoes descended on the area from every direction, using it as both a refuge from the law and a staging ground for raids, robberies, and other crimes. From the late 1860s well into the 1890s, Indian Territory hosted a hall of fame of American outlaw legends. Even if Native peace officers did manage to corral a lawbreaker, the few courts they had were not allowed by the U.S. government to exercise justice on whites—even if a white man had murdered or otherwise outraged a local tribesman. Thus, some of the most famous lawmen in American history rose up to challenge the lawless horde of bandits and pistoleros. We shall explore this colorful cavalcade of renegades and peace officers in Chapter 10.

To counter the escalating Indian Territory violence of a scarred, coarsened post-war America and escalating westward migration, the Indian republics formed their own "Lighthorse Police" or "Lighthorsemen," mounted companies of lawmen who rode their respective countries to promote order and restrain lawbreakers. Perhaps the best-known and most diverse Lighthorsemen were the Choctaws. Whites, African-Americans, mixed-bloods, and Natives from numerous tribes formed their hard-riding, sharp-shooting ranks. Many were battle-hardened Civil War veterans.

A Mother's Pride, Richard Luce's painting of a Native woman. Courtesy of Richard Luce. (www.richardluce.com)

Robber's Roost

The 1820 Missouri Compromise allowed slavery in some states and territories but prohibited it in others. Quirks in the legislation left the present-day Oklahoma Panhandle—166 miles from west to east, thirty-four miles from north to south—without governmental jurisdiction. From the 1850s to 1900, many violent outlaws, including "Captain" William Coe and his gang, operated from the remote area that earned nicknames such as "Robber's Roost," "No Man's Land," and "The Cimarron Country."

Coe built an imposing stone fortress, itself called "Robber's Roost," in the mid-1860s. It stood near five thousand-foot-high Black Mesa in the far northwest corner of present-day Oklahoma and overlooked the Santa Fe Trail. He equipped the redoubt for himself and dozens of bandit associates with a stocked bar, piano, and "soiled doves."

For several years, the outlaws attacked U.S. army forts in New Mexico and Colorado, as well as civilian and military travelers and herds. Fact and

The infamous "Robber's Roost" redoubt near Black Mesa in the high plains No Man's Land of the present-day Oklahoma Panhandle. Wayne Cooper's painting depicts a disputed 1867 shootout between the U.S. Army and a large outlaw gang. Courtesy Oklahoma State Senate Historical Preservation Fund, Inc. and Wayne Cooper.

legend blur concerning Coe's fate. The spectacular painting *Robber's Roost* by Wayne Cooper, housed on the fifth floor of the Oklahoma State Capitol, depicts an army force assaulting the enclave in 1867 with rifles and a six-pound cannon. As the story goes, many of Coe's men died or were taken prisoner and then hanged, though he and others escaped.

Old timers in the area doubt a shootout occurred with the army, and no military records record such an event. Beyond dispute is that Coe lived until the next year, then was tricked into capture by, in his words, "A woman, a pony, and a boy." For the third time, he escaped jail. The first two were his doing. But this time, vigilantes hauled him out of the Pueblo, Colorado hoosegow and hanged him from a cottonwood tree.

Blacks in Reconstruction

Ignorance and confusion shroud what little that modern Americans know about slavery, its role in the War Between the States, and the respective positions of the wartime United States and Confederate States concerning the issue. For instance, U.S. President Abraham Lincoln, long revered as the champion of African-American freedom, declared during his first inaugural speech in 1861 that the freeing of slaves was not only inexpedient and impolitic but perhaps even unconstitutional. Several of the states that remained in the Northern Union—Missouri, Maryland, Delaware, Kentucky, and West Virginia—held onto their slaves. The District of Columbia, seat of the Federal government, retained

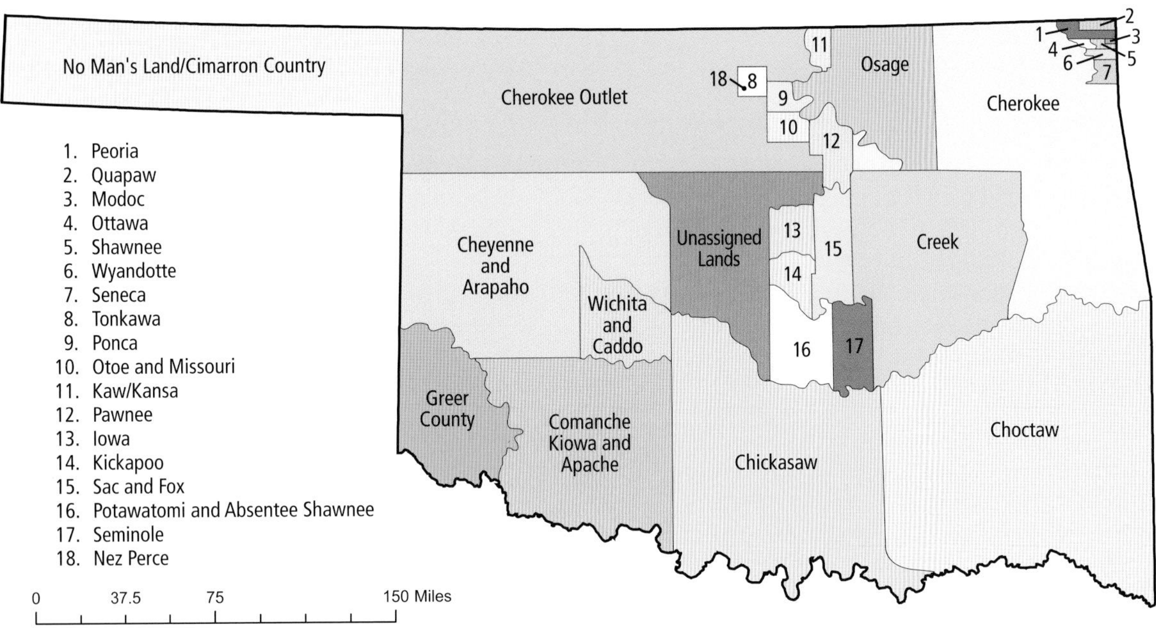

Location of Indian tribes and division of Indian territroy after 1866.

slavery too. In fact, one-third of the states where slavery remained legal throughout the war continued in the Union.

Lincoln announced the Emancipation Proclamation on Sept. 22, 1862. Though traditionally memorialized as an act that freed all American slaves, it actually did not. On the contrary, Lincoln said that as long as the Confederates surrendered to the Union by January 1, 1863, they could keep their slaves. Even when the Proclamation officially went into effect on that latter date, it did not actually free any slaves within the jurisdiction of U.S. governmental authority, just those beyond Federal control in the Confederate states. Although it did lay the groundwork for freedom for all the slaves—which would come with the ratification of the Thirteenth, Fourteenth, and Fifteenth Amendments to the Constitution after the war—for the duration of the war, it left vulnerable to bondage the hundreds of thousands of slaves remaining in the Northern (border) slave states, as well as those living in formerly Confederate areas captured by Federal troops. This included those portions of Indian Territory covered by the Cherokee, Creek, and Seminole countries.

The pro-Federal Cherokee faction freed its slaves in 1863, but the remainder of the tribe and all the other Indian republics still owned slaves after the war concluded. Ideas abounded on how to deal with them. Some people supported sending them away for colonization elsewhere, such as Central America, the Caribbean, or Africa, as Lincoln himself had advocated both before and during the war. Others suggested segregating them in their own towns. Still others proposed incorporating them into the tribes whose members owned them.

One-third of the states where slavery remained legal throughout the war continued in the Union.

African-Americans in Reconstruction Indian Territory faced enormous difficulties. Like everyone who lived amidst the battlegrounds of the South, they now faced a land filled with destruction, death, poverty, fear, and mourning. Most blacks, though, faced the added burden of sharing the struggles looming for their former owners. Halting the southeastern tribes' removal annuities—which they had used to build schools and other institutions, fund business and agricultural pursuits, and support indigent tribal members—as punishment for their support of the Confederacy made a bad situation much worse, for the Natives as well as their former slaves.

Post-War Racial Strife

Ironically, whereas many African-Americans had prospered or at least lived comfortable lives while in bondage, sudden freedom—with most of their former owners financially ruined if not dead—left the majority of them desperate to find ways to support themselves and their families. And in Indian Territory, like elsewhere across the South, many of them faced resentful, bitter, and even hostile former owners and acquaintances, though in the Nations most of their owners had been Native rather than white. Federal General John B. Sanborn wrote from the Fort Smith Council, for instance, that some Choctaws had driven Freedmen "away from their former homes.... One Freedman has been killed at Boggy Depot by his former master and there are rumors of several other cases, and no action has been taken by the Government to punish the guilty party."

But the efforts of Yankee military officers led by Sanborn to regulate "the relations between the Freedmen in the Indian Territory and their former masters" did not cure the blacks' problems. As seen in innumerable other locales across the Reconstruction South, Federal occupation soldiers and carpetbagging interlopers brought haughty attitudes and ignorance of Southern Indian, white, and black folkways alike. Northern white concern for African-Americans, often at the expense of other suffering Southerners—in Indian Territory, the tribes—bred more difficulties for them.

"Almost it might be contended that the United States authorities themselves created the Negro problem in the Indian Territory," said historian Annie Heloise Abel.

> *African-Americans in Reconstruction Indian Territory faced enormous difficulties... a land filled with destruction, death, poverty, fear, and lamentation, along with their former owners' struggles.*

Indeed, one of the great blunders by the U.S. government in American history was simultaneously stripping the rights and freedoms from the formerly Confederate white South in its hour of lamentation while attempting to endow Southern blacks with the political power to join up with carpetbagging white Federals to permanently usurp that power from Southern whites. This helped trigger the rise of the original Ku Klux Klan and other underground Southern resistance groups who opposed the Federal government's harsh military occupation. When that occupation ended, African-Americans faced a white South whose bloodied bitterness had attained historic proportions. They encountered it without the support of the Federal military, which had departed in return for Southern support in the controversial 1876 presidential election.

For the most part, meanwhile, the Indian Territory tribes moved beyond their resentment on their own to begin the difficult work of rebuilding their fortunes yet again. Soon after the war, Sanborn himself found tribal prejudice against blacks to be "rapidly passing away," and he concluded that the Natives' treatment of blacks "had not been so bad and cruel as might be inferred."

Hard times continued for blacks in post-Civil War America. While many African-Americans faced the danger of destitution and even starvation, the Five Civilized Tribes resisted U.S. government pressure to admit them to tribal membership by attempting to bar their ownership of Indian Territory tribal lands. Many freedmen, such as these Chickasaws in Tishomingo, defiantly filed to receive allotments. Courtesy Oklahoma Historical Society.

Independence and Loyalty

The Federals' Reconstruction Era Freedmen's Bureau labored on behalf of African-Americans in Indian Territory, just as it did elsewhere in the devastated post-war South. The Freedmen's Bureau distributed food and supplies among them and required post-war tribal governments to allow blacks the same rights as Natives under the Reconstruction treaties. Still, many African-Americans preferred to make their own way without the help and added tension provided by the U.S. government.

Despite such determination on the part of the sons of Africa in the Nations, however, securing even such basics of life as food and clothing proved to be a daunting challenge after the war. So did the consequences those actions brought, especially when widespread theft by blacks of Choctaw and Chickasaw cattle across the Red River Valley spawned the Indians' hard-bitten, ghost-riding, Klan-like "Vigilance Committees" (see feature below).

A poignant sidebar to African-American life during Reconstruction concerns the desire of many people of African descent to receive full membership in the tribes where they had served. The Cherokees, Choctaws, Creeks, and Seminoles indeed granted many of their former slaves equal tribal status, but here and in other tribes, the process often proved difficult and even impossible. Sometimes, as so often in the history of black people in Oklahoma and America, they suffered the cold heartache of rejection from people and organizations they admired and wanted to join. This excerpt

Indian Territory-born Seminole Freedman Caesar Bowlegs. His late nineteenth-century work among the Seminoles and Seminole Freedmen as an interpreter and medical assistant for some of Indian Territory's first white doctors employing advanced medical practices saved innumerable lives. His tireless efforts also helped gain acceptance for modern scientific principles and medicine among these Seminole groups. In addition, his education and Christian leadership through the Presbyterian church helped guide many Seminoles and Freedmen to function in the developing American society.

from an 1879 petition by African-Americans for Cherokee tribal membership reflects their struggle:

> The Cherokee Nation is our country; there we were born and reared; there are our homes made by the sweat of our brows; there are our wives and children, whom we love as dearly as though we were born with red, instead of black skins. There, we intend to live and defend our natural rights, as guaranteed by the treaties and laws of the United States, by every legitimate and lawful means.

The profound and enduring nature of this debate evidenced itself yet again when, as late as the year 2011, the Cherokees voted overwhelmingly to rescind the tribal membership of blacks, claiming the necessity of Cherokee blood for membership. The African-Americans' struggle to retain membership continues today, even as this book goes to press.

Vigilance Committees

The Chickasaws and Choctaws formed Vigilance Committees in the years following the War Between the States to counter the growing theft of their property by newly freed African-American slaves, many of whom emigrated across Red River from Texas. The Indians' use of Vigilance Committees provide an additional footnote in the lengthy, sobering illumination of the biblical concept of human sin toward both God and one other.

Cow Country

Now one of the singular epics of American and world history rose up from Texas and rolled north across the hills, prairies, and plains of Indian Territory. Born in the wake of the War Between the States was the legendary western cattle drive and range cattle industry. Thousands of these physically-vigorous Texan men of the land left behind ranges uniquely suited by climate, terrain, and land ownership laws to prosper the growth of cattle—a particular sort of cattle.

The Texas longhorn cow emerged from the breeding of lean longhorns—which were introduced from southern Europe by the Spaniards—with bigger northern European cattle brought by Americans. The new breed evinced the best attributes of both its predecessors. It possessed size, strength, endurance, and apparent immunity to heat and hunger, as well as the durability to survive rough marathon treks across the Southern Plains. The beasts could rumble over sixty miles of badlands in heat or cold, with no water.

So tough was this distinctive new American breed, in fact, that when thousands of Confederate soldiers returned to Texas after the war, longhorn cattle had multiplied by the hundreds of thousands across the state's sprawling ranges. The free-market principle of supply and demand, however, meant that even prime fat beeves could draw no more than six or seven dollars a head in the Lone Star State. The same animals, meanwhile, commanded prices up to ten times that in the victorius, economically robust North, where European immigrants were pouring in by the millions. Those populous markets lay hundreds or even thousands of miles away, and the railroads that might provide their speediest transit had not yet reached Texas, or anywhere close.

First Cattle Drives

Visionary Texas cattlemen were determined to bring their beef supply to meet the Northern and Eastern hunger demand by driving their stock in herds to the closest railheads that could transport the cattle north and east. They wasted no time after the war, driving over a quarter of a million head north in 1866, mostly along what became known as

Rush Hour at Colbert's Ferry, G. N. Taylor's rendering of Chickasaw Benjamin Colbert's thriving Red River ferry business as it serviced post-war cattle drives headed north from Texas along the Shawnee Trail. Descended from both Scottish and Chickasaw ancestors, the entrepreneurial Colbert earlier built the southernmost Indian Territory stop of the Butterfield Overland stage route in present-day Bryan County and owned a flourishing antebellum plantation worked by dozens of slaves. (www.gntayloroklaart.com)

Cowboys supping on a trail drive through Indian Territory. The right fifteen drovers could handle a herd of a couple thousand head during the three-month journey from Texas to Kansas. Courtesy Oklahoma Historical Society.

the Shawnee Trail. They moved from central Texas, through the present-day Dallas-Fort Worth area, across Red River, along present-day U.S. Highway 69 through the Civil War Indian Territory battle sites of Boggy Depot and Fort Gibson, to Baxter Springs, in the southeast corner of Kansas.

> *The new longhorn breed possessed size, strength, endurance, and immunity to heat and hunger, as well as the durability to survive harsh treks across the Southern Plains. It could rumble over sixty miles of badlands in heat or cold, with no water.*

This inaugural season of cattle driving proved disastrous to the cowmen. Every conceivable obstacle combined to create a "perfect storm" of misery and calamity for the Texans. They faced rain deluges, swollen rivers, steep hills, and even mountains. Natives demanded toll payments for crossing their lands, and stampedes were initiated by some of the same Indians, who then demanded more money for helping retrieve the cattle. White renegades plied outlawry in the unsettled and generally lawless postwar Nations. And then there was the rough contrariness of the longhorns themselves.

Their perilous adventure grew even worse when the Texans hit the Kansas (and sometimes Missouri) border. There, outraged farmers remembered the fever, mysterious but deadly to bovines, that was apparently left in the wake of small pre-war cattle drives into the area from Texas. Yet the longhorns evidenced no symptoms of the malady, so the Texans felt unjustly accused. Later investigation revealed that the fever—variously referred to as splenic, Spanish, or Texas fever—afflicted Northern milk cows and shorthorns but not the tough Southern cattle, and was transmitted from the latter to the former by ticks. The Midwesterners had little concern for such technicalities, however. Their only focus was keeping the longhorns away.

So, far from home, the outnumbered Texans endured beatings and shootings by self-styled vigilante mobs who would also kill portions of their herds, sometimes nearly their entire herd. The more fortunate drovers turned their herds west and led them across hundreds of miles more of open country to skirt around the Kansans and reach markets in Missouri or Iowa. Only a scant number of the hundreds of thousands of cattle arrived at a profitable destination for their owners.

Tallgrass prairie blue stem in present-day Osage County, part of the rich post-Civil War cattle grazing country of the Cherokee Outlet.

Chisholm Trail

Facing a failure of monumental proportions, the Texans refused to give up, stubbornly driving more cattle north the following year of 1867. Their relentless and physically courageous determination finally paid off when 29-year-old Illinois cattle baron Joseph G. McCoy caught wind of it. He persuaded the new Kansas Pacific Railway to extend its line west beyond both Kansas settlements and Indian Territory communities, whose vigilante mobs harried the Texas drovers. At that new railhead he built a massive cattle depot, shipping center, and hotel, a bustling center of commerce that developed into the town of Abilene—the future boyhood home of U.S. President Dwight D. Eisenhower.

Jesse Chisholm (1802–1868)

Jesse Chisholm, famed Indian Territory frontier trader and mediator between the Plains Indians and the Five Civilized Tribes, the Republic of Texas, and the United States. He is the man for whom the Chisholm Trail was named.

The most famous cattle trail in history appropriately bears the name of the man who founded it—Tennessee-born Jesse Chisholm, son of a Scottish merchant and slave trader and a Cherokee mother. The rugged, durable Chisholm Trail linked disparate cultures while aiding them all by transporting many forward into a future brimming with progress and hope. It reflected facets of this tough, honest man of vision, who played key roles in perhaps more watershed events of the nineteenth-century West than anyone else.

One can almost taste the red dirt dust and feel the earth shaking beneath thousands of cattle hooves in G. N. Taylor's *Chisholm Trail River Crossing*. Millions of head rumbled north on cattle trails from Texas through Indian Territory to railheads in Kansas after the War Between the States. (www.gntayloroklaart.com)

Meanwhile, McCoy contracted with the Kansas Pacific to receive a percentage of all freight charges for Texas cattle shipped from Abilene to the bustling markets at Kansas City and Chicago. Finally, he sent a rider down Indian Territory cattle trails to find herds coming north and urge the owners to bring them to Abilene. Ranchers and cowboys drove cattle north through Texas over hundreds of trails, but most of them began to coalesce into one route that rolled north from Red River up through western Oklahoma.

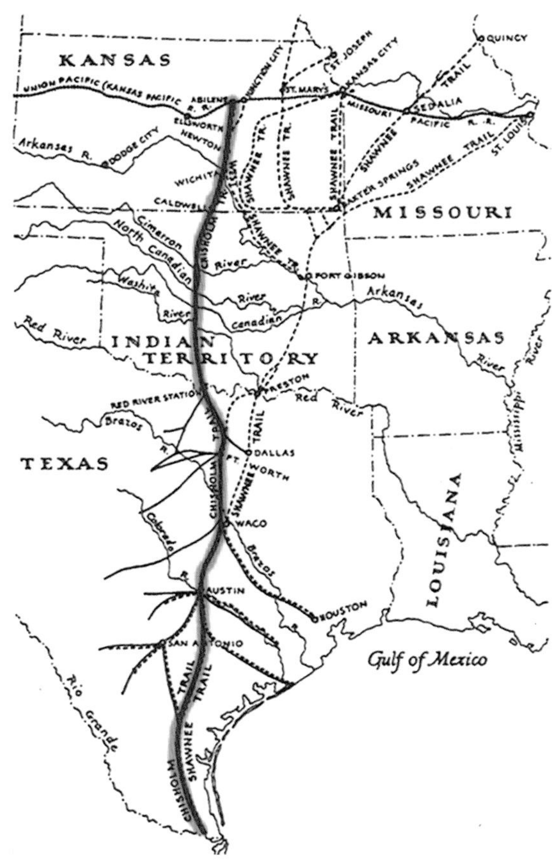

The legendary Chisholm Trail, the predominant path over which Texas cattlemen—many of whom became Oklahomans—drove their beeves north to Kansas, from where new railroads shipped them east to the mushrooming American public. The heart of the trail ran through or near present-day western Oklahoma towns like Duncan, Chickasha, El Reno, Kingfisher, and Enid.

History recognizes that path as the Chisholm Trail. It emerged from a series of trading posts established by legendary scout, trader, cattleman, and interpreter Jesse Chisholm along the road to supply Confederate forces during the War Between the States. Ironically, the Scots-Cherokee Chisholm died in 1868, without having driven any cattle up the trail that made his name immortal.

Joseph G. McCoy, the original "Real McCoy," was the visionary entrepreneur who pioneered the transporting of Texas longhorns—which had been driven up Indian Territory cattle trails to Kansas railheads—on ahead to the mass of Americans farther north and east.

Beginning with Texan O. A. Wheeler and his partners in 1867, however, others drove plenty of stock up the trail that bore Chisholm's name. Thirty-five thousand cattle were shipped to market from Abilene that year; thousands of them had rumbled up the Chisholm Trail. That was a drop in the bucket compared to succeeding years. By the end of 1871, over a million cattle had shipped out of Abilene, and by 1877, five million had.

The Texans forged other famous trails in Indian Territory to the west of the Chisholm (Great Western) and east (West Shawnee). The stream of cattle moving north from the Lone Star State grew so massive that cattlemen began grazing them on the territory's nutrient-rich blue stem and grama grasses. By the end of the 1870s, they paid the Cherokees a hundred thousand dollars a year for grazing rights to the forage-rich Cherokee Outlet in the northern part of Indian Territory.

Thus was birthed the western Oklahoma cattle business, as scores of energetic white cowmen—in particular those who married into a tribe—established their own sprawling spreads. Among them was famed cowboy, lawman, and Oklahoma City pioneer and mayor Charlie Colcord, one of the thousands of Texans who helped settle the territory.

The rise of the Chisholm Trail, coupled with the advent of Fort Sill, adjacent to Lawton in present-day Comanche County, spawned frontier stores that served cowboys and soldiers years before public land openings. Some of them grew into southwest Oklahoma settlements. Ima Jean Scott's painting depicts Scottish trader, intermarried Chickasaw, and pioneer William Duncan and his store, founded in still dangerous country alongside the Chisholm around 1872. It sat on the eastern periphery of what would become Stephens County seat Duncan, eventual birthplace of Halliburton. Courtesy Cova Williams and the Stephens County Historical Museum.

The Old West cattle drive, from Texas through present-day Oklahoma, has inspired some of the greatest works of American fiction. Larry McMurtry's Pulitzer Prize-winning epic *Lonesome Dove* spawned the equally famous film vision of the story about two ex-Texas Rangers blazing a cattle trail from post-Civil War south Texas to Montana. The classic John Wayne film *Red River* chronicled the fictional opening of the Chisholm Trail by the Duke's character and his drovers, former Confederate soldiers returning to his longhorn cattle spread in Texas after the War Between the States.

The Old Chisholm Trail

This famous old cowboy trail song gives a colorful first-person window into the great cattle path of 1870s Indian Territory. It has been sung and recorded by just about everyone, including Oklahoma legend Gene Autry, Roy Rogers, Bing Crosby, Randy Travis, and Michael Martin Murphey.

"On the Chisholm Trail," Oklahoma sculptor Paul Moore's epic monument to the pioneers, cowboys, and cattlemen who helped build Oklahoma, the West, and America. Commissioned by Thomas H. McCasland Jr. for the Chisholm Trail Heritage Center in Duncan, the work stands fifteen feet tall and stretches thirty-five feet long. Courtesy Chisholm Trail Heritage Center (http://onthechisholmtrail.com).

I'll tell you of my troubles on the old
Chisholm trail.

Come a ti yi yippee, come a ti yi yea,
Come a ti yi yippee, come a ti yi yea.

Oh, a ten-dollar hoss and a forty-dollar
saddle,
And I'm goin' to punchin' Texas cattle.

Come a ti yi yippee, come a ti yi yea,
Come a ti yi yippee, come a ti yi yea.

I wake in the mornin' afore daylight,
And afore I sleep the moon shines bright.

Come a ti yi yippee, come a ti yi yea,
Come a ti yi yippee, come a ti yi yea.

It's cloudy in the west, a-lookin' like rain,
And my durned old slicker's in the wagon again.

Come a ti yi yippee, come a ti yi yea,
Come a ti yi yippee, come a ti yi yea.

No chaps, no slicker, and it's pourin' down rain,
And I swear, by gosh, I'll never night-herd again.

Come a ti yi yippee, come a ti yi yea,
Come a ti yi yippee, come a ti yi yea.

Feet in the stirrups and seat in the saddle,
I hung and rattled with them long-horn cattle.

Come a ti yi yippee, come a ti yi yea,
Come a ti yi yippee, come a ti yi yea.

The wind commenced to blow, and the rain began
to fall,
Hit looked, by grab, like we was goin' to lose 'em all.

Come a ti yi yippee, come a ti yi yea,
Come a ti yi yippee, come a ti yi yea.

I don't give a darn if they never do stop;
I'll ride as long as an eight-day clock.

Come a ti yi yippee, come a ti yi yea,
Come a ti yi yippee, come a ti yi yea.

We rounded 'em up and put 'em on the cars,
And that was the last of the old Two Bars.

Come a ti yi yippee, come a ti yi yea,
Come a ti yi yippee, come a ti yi yea.

Oh, it's bacon and beans most every day,
I'd as soon be a-eatin' prairie hay.

Come a ti yi yippee, come a ti yi yea,
Come a ti yi yippee, come a ti yi yea.

I went to the boss to draw my roll,
He had it figgered out I was nine dollars in the hole.

Come a ti yi yippee, come a ti yi yea,
Come a ti yi yippee, come a ti yi yea.

Goin' back to town to draw my money,
Goin' back home to see my honey.

Come a ti yi yippee, come a ti yi yea,
Come a ti yi yippee, come a ti yi yea.

With my knees in the saddle and my seat in the sky,
I'll quit punchin' cows in the sweet by and by.

Come a ti yi yippee, come a ti yi yea,
Come a ti yi yippee, come a ti yi yea.

Second Trail of Tears

As some of the country's toughest outlaws and lawmen shot it out in the eastern half of the territory, the Federal government shifted its martial focus from fighting Confederates to locating—in some cases, relocating—Native tribes from all over the West to the western half. The Pawnees came from Nebraska, Delawares and Shawnees from Kansas, Poncas from the Dakotas, Nez Perce from Montana, and Kickapoos from Mexico, among others.

While launching the one-sided Reconstruction negotiations with the Indian Nations to the east in Fort Smith that would deprive them of so much land and so many rights, the Federals called another meeting, crucial in import. It occurred at the mouth of the Little Arkansas River, near present-day Wichita, Kansas, in October, 1865. Famed frontiersmen Jesse Chisholm and Black Beaver brokered the conference. It involved representatives of four strong, nomadic Southern Plains tribes—the Arapahos, Cheyennes, Comanches, and Kiowas. These tribes' approximate populations ranged from fifteen hundred (Arapahos) to probably between five and six thousand (Comanches), which were large numbers of people being forced to relocate in western Indian Territory. Though comprising mostly people desirous of peace, these tribes had fierce warrior contingents who were rapidly becoming the greatest impediment to the peaceful westward migration of American civilization.

The concurrent Little Arkansas and Fort Smith gatherings provide effective time markers for the two very different dramas that unfolded through the nineteenth century in eastern and western Oklahoma. The U.S. agreed at Little Arkansas to provide the tribes with reserved land, food, supplies, agricultural training, education, and Christian teaching and discipleship. The U.S. army would also restrain white settlers, traders, and others from intruding upon the Natives' lands.

In return, the Indians would relocate to and remain on bounded reservations across western Indian Territory. They would also cease from raiding white American pioneer settlements in northern Texas, western Kansas, and eastern New Mexico. As a lamentable Second Trail of Tears unfolded in western Indian Territory, almost nothing that elements of either "side" did to antagonize the other ceased, any longer than it took those assembled to break camp.

Most members of the other tribes getting corralled to the west—despite suffering uprooting, travel hardships, separation, exposure, bad food, poor medical care, disease, homesickness, and death—pursued customary but peaceable ways. Meanwhile, those minority contingents of the Arapahos, Cheyennes, Comanches, and Kiowas continued to ride, roam, hunt, raid, and kill in Texas and Kansas. They had no intention of kowtowing to the white man by laying down their weapons and taking up farming.

As white hunters, spurred on by the U.S. government and its military enforcement arm, began to thin out the once colossal buffalo herds that fed and clothed the Plains Indians, these warlike tribes were compelled to travel farther to find sustenance for themselves and their dependents—sometimes at the expense of white settlers. At times, government Indian agents also unwittingly contributed to the Natives' bloody rampages by depriving the Kiowas and others of rations in order to force their obedience to U.S. policy. Desperate warriors sometimes responded by taking to the war trail against whites in order to feed their families. Less noble aims fueled some of these raids.

Massacring the Cheyenne

Something else was at work that caused the resistance of the Plains tribes—their experiences past and (unfortunately) present with the United States Army. The Native republics of eastern Indian Territory, the powerful Plains tribes, and smaller tribes throughout the region lost much trust in the Federal government when it abandoned Indian Territory—and its promised payments to the Natives—to the Confederates at the dawn of the War Between the States. As chronicled in chapter 6, many of these Indians then fought with the Confederacy against the United States in that war.

Against this troubled backdrop near the end of November, 1864, occurred a seminal event in the unfolding conflict between the U.S. and Plains Indians, one of the worst atrocities ever committed

Pawnee Scout, Richard Luce's rendering of the intrepid Natives who skillfully helped the American army fight their many tribal enemies, including the Comanches. Courtesy Richard Luce. (www.richardluce.com)

on American soil. It happened on a trickling stream in eastern Colorado named Sandy Creek, as the War Between the States raged in full fury across the continent. There, living in relative peace, were Black Kettle, leading chief of the Southern Cheyennes, and several hundred of his tribespeople.

Enraged at crimes by some Cheyenne warriors such as stealing the life-sustaining supplies of white miners in the region, a cadre of civilian and military Federal leaders had deceived Black Kettle and his followers into moving away from a U.S. fort where they had been promised safety, and out into the unprotected open. Key among those leaders was former Methodist circuit-riding preacher and Colonel John Chivington, who towered over most men with his strapping build and six-foot, four-inch height, as well as his bluff and commanding presence. Chivington also possessed military renown as the hero of the Federals' stunning Civil War victory two years before at Glorieta Pass, New Mexico. That battle thwarted the Confederacy's entire Far West military campaign that had been successful until that point.

For months, Chivington had badgered state officials to declare war between the white settlers in Colorado and the Cheyennes and Arapahos. He got his wish when the governor commissioned him to lead a mounted seven hundred and fifty-man column of short-term militia recruits that one historian called "an ignorant army" on a forced winter trek through banks of snow toward the Cheyennes at Sandy Creek.

The perspective of this rowdy band of marauders is recorded by military historian and Brigadier General S. R. A. Marshall in his vibrant chronicle of the Plains Indians Wars, *Crimsoned Prairie*: "The newcomer to early Denver (and eastern Colorado) did not have to be an Indian hater to settle there, though it was a qualification that made him more congenial to the society."

Such was the mindset of the communities that filled the ranks of Chivington's not-so-immortals. When asked prior to the attack about its potential danger to Cheyenne women and children, Chivington infamously responded, "Nits make lice."

The bluecoats thundered into the Cheyenne camp at dawn after an all-night ride through feet-high piles of snow. They found a sleeping village, most of whose warriors had departed on a hunting expedition. The Yankee horse soldiers did not fret over such technicalities. Though they did not kill the four to five hundred male warriors Chivington

> *Formed out of Blue and (to a lesser extent) Gray veterans, with a large leavening of newly arrived immigrants, chiefly Germans and Irish, (the U.S. cavalry in the Plains Indian Wars) was battle-seasoned in many parts and its average file had signed on because the excitement of war was to his liking, and he wanted more of it. . . . It was also a rowdy army. . . . A large portion of its enlisted people were habitual drunks and few of the officers shunned the bottle."*
>
> **—Historian S. L. A. Marshall**

claimed, they did slaughter around thirty men—and over a hundred women and children. As mournfully recounted by historian Bruce Cutler in OU Press's *The Massacre at Sand Creek*, they took out "their bowie knives to... hack at the scalps, to take off fingers three at a time and get at the rings, to take the noses, take the ears, take the lips... cutting out the private parts of squaws and... throw papooses in the air and stick them." Then they paraded through Denver as though in Roman triumph, showing off their scores of carved-off scalps.

Such remembrances jolt the sensitive reader, but they demand recounting so that America, along with Christ's church, might learn from their mistakes and blindness. For as Black Kettle himself declared, even as he risked and finally lost his life for peace between his people and the U.S.: "The white men make two wars. One to kill us. And one to make sure no one will remember." The Cheyennes and other Plains tribes indeed committed innumerable atrocities of their own against white Americans—including women, children, and babies—which provides vengeful context to Sand Creek. But the teachings of the church declare that "savages" act as they will—but the followers of Christ must not.

White Voices Protest

Captain Silas Soule, who had ridden to glory with Chivington during the War Between the States at Glorieta Pass and Apache Canyon, commanded a hundred regular soldiers at Sand Creek, but refused to allow their participation in the massacre. He furiously protested against the attack and testified against a shouting Chivington for two days in the military trial, which led to the colonel's resignation from the Army. "A preacher who wanted to kill the innocent, up against an infidel who wouldn't," Soule wrote to the famed poet Walt Whitman. "What do you make of that?"

Soule, whose own motivations and actions Chivington's defenders have condemned then and since, wrote to his mother that Chivington was determined to kill him, too, for his defiance. Soon, only weeks after his wedding, Soule was indeed murdered in Denver while with his wife, under

Reservation Indian women and children butcher a "beef issue" cow. They would subsequently transport the meat to the reservation campsite. Courtesy NAA-Smithsonian Institution.

circumstances suspicious toward Chivington. A subordinate officer hauled in the suspect, then the officer was poisoned to death.

Chivington, meanwhile, gloried in his recollections of Sand Creek to the *Denver Inquirer* newspaper:

> How reviving to a soul... to know that God has given invincible might to quell the wicked of the earth and given dominion to the good, the wise, the just—the true believers! This world is delivered to our hand, sir, delivered for dominion! Our Savior bids us make His excellence supreme!.... Oh the Indian... he's dumb, sir, dumb as a dog, he's ignorant of what can lift him! What will save him? Offer him salvation! Offer life! As he is, he'll never read a word you're writing. I will! *I* am what conversion means!

The *Inquirer*—the largest newspaper of the era in the Rocky Mountain region, took a different view:

> The uniform of these United States should ever be the emblem of humanity and justice. The colonel (Chivington) broke the honor of that trust. He planned and put in hand a massacre so foul it would have set to shame the veriest "savage" of all who were victims of his cruelty. The toll of the Indian Wars is not the count of bodies only. It is invisible. It attacks the mind and heart. It puts the soul to trial by asking, "This nation under God? How shall it grow from roots so deeply set in wrong?"

Plains Indian Wars

Word of the sensational crime at Sand Creek spread throughout the West. Never again would the Cheyennes or any other tribe trust the words or actions of the Yankee army and its government. The Cheyennes, Sioux, and other tribes rose as one, wreaking bloody bedlam on pioneer wagon trains, homes, and settlements, not to mention U.S. military detachments attempting to shield westward American settlement. Even white Coloradoans who initially cheered the Sand Creek massacre perceived the Natives' accelerated aggressiveness and disowned Chivington's slaughter, as did the U.S. government.

Just one example of the blowback was the Fetterman Massacre, which occurred two years after Sand Creek. It happened just to the Wyoming side of that territory's border with Montana, and very near the site of the later, Battle of the Little Big Horn. Cheyenne Chief Red Cloud—who ranked, along with the Apache Geronimo, the half-white, half-Comanche Quanah Parker, the Nez Perce Joseph, and the Cherokee Stand Watie, among the greatest Indian war chiefs of the American

General Winfield Hancock in John Paul Strain's painting of the Civil War Battle of Gettysburg, *You Will Soon See Them Tumbling Back* (www.johnpaulstrain.com). Hancock's legacy of valor and competence from that conflict suffered through his later actions against the Plains Indians.

West—led a massive Cheyenne and Sioux war party that obliterated nearly a hundred U.S. cavalry and infantry protecting the famed Bozeman Trail for pioneer travel.

One scene from that battlefield revealed the brutal and desperate nature of the mushrooming Plains Indian Wars. Two civilian scouts for the U.S. cavalry—both Civil War veterans and sharpshooters shouldering Henry repeating rifles—died in the battle. Around their bodies were sixty separate frozen pools of blood from the bodies of the Indians that the two of them had shot down. One of the scouts had 105 arrows in his body.

> *The toll of the Indian Wars is not the count of bodies only. It is invisible. It attacks the mind and heart. It puts the soul to trial by asking, "This nation under God? How shall it grow from roots so deeply set in wrong?"*
>
> ***—The Denver Inquirer***

A tragic new chapter of cross-cultural madness followed in 1867, spawned in part by the enduring legacy of Sand Creek. This involved another Yankee leader from the War Between the States, one possessing far greater accomplishment and fame than Chivington. General Winfield Hancock had carved out one of the most glittering records of any Union general during the war. Not only did he gain plaudits for his leadership in many famous battles, but in doing so, he exhibited steady judgment and humane restraint that was lacking in many Federal generals.

As commander of the federals' post-war Department of Missouri, the confident Hancock determined to settle the "Indian question" himself. In the process, he committed a series of blunders that demonstrated anew the dangerous inclination toward unwitting arrogance and blindness that success—especially born of violence—can spawn. Hancock mistakenly accused Cheyenne and Arapaho chiefs of postponing their meetings with him. When the tribes' women and children fled out of fear that his aggressive army would repeat Chivington's actions, he overreacted by incinerating their entire camp, the value of whose possessions ran into the low millions of dollars in twenty-first-century currency.

Hancock, headed toward the Democratic Party nomination for president the following year, had received wise counsel against many of these actions from the Southern Cheyenne chief living in Indian Territory, Henry Roman Nose. When the general ignored this advice, the worst suspicions of the Cheyennes and surrounding tribes were confirmed regarding their blue-coated nemesis. Not only the Cheyennes suffered, but as historian Gaston Litton wrote, "Hancock's action precipitated unrest that resulted in the loss of scores of lives of settlers, freighters, immigrants, and soldiers and which cost many millions of dollars."

Medicine Lodge Treaty

All of these remarkable acts influenced the thinking and actions of the Plains tribes living in western Indian Territory, not least their bloody rampages into Texas and Kansas. A distressed Congress, with its post-war army concentrated in Indian Territory and the rest of the Great Plains, called for another summit with the Plains tribes. This one took place just north of the territorial line in Medicine Creek Lodge, Kansas. The recent bloodletting with Hancock had not stolen from the Natives their usual habit of winter hibernation. It took the savvy diplomacy of famed mixed-bloods Jesse Chisholm and Black Beaver, as well as peacemaking Army officer Edward Wynkoop, to bring them in.

They came, finally, in astonishing numbers—seven thousand Apaches, Arapahos, Cheyennes, Comanches, and Kiowas. And they came grim and suspicious. A government feast cheered them, but then they grew sullen and threatening. Sensing violence and perhaps a fresh massacre afoot, U.S. commanders formed their men into a hollow square around the peace commissioners and then aimed a Gatling gun at the Indians. The immediate threat melted away, but soon the Indians learned that the federals intended for them to remain on their western Indian Territory reservations—and those reservations now shrank.

Ten Bears' Words at Medicine Lodge

Comanche Chief Ten Bears delivered these eloquent words at the 1867 Medicine Lodge, Kansas, peace conference between the United States and the Plains Indian tribes.

> *My heart is filled with joy when I see you here, as the brooks fill with water when the snows melt in the spring; and I feel glad as the ponies do when the fresh grass starts in the beginning of the year. I heard of your coming when I was many sleeps away, and I made but few camps before I met you. I knew that you had come to do good to me and to my people. I looked for benefits which would last forever, and so my face shines with joy as I look upon you. My people have never first drawn a bow or fired a gun against the whites. There has been trouble on the line between us, and my young men have danced the war dance. But it was not begun by us. It was you who sent out the first soldier and we who sent out the second. Two years ago, I came upon this road, following the buffalo, that my wives and children might have their cheeks plump and their bodies warm. But the soldiers fired on us, and since that time there has been a noise like that of a thunderstorm, and we have not known which way to go.*

Rarely has the historical record preserved more eloquent lamentations from such ferocious warriors. Charismatic Kiowa chief Satanta, still fearsome after a half-century of years, told the vast assemblage: "I love to roam over the wild prairie, and when I do it I feel free and happy, but when we settle down, we grow pale and die. . . . A long time ago this land belonged to our fathers, but when I go up the river I see a camp of soldiers, and they are cutting my wood down or killing my buffalo. . . . When I see it my heart feels like bursting with sorrow."

Battle-hardened Yamparika Comanche chief Ten Bears, immortalized in Forrest Carter's novel *Gone to Texas* and the classic Clint Eastwood film *The Outlaw Josey Wales* it spawned, declared, "I was born upon the prairies, where the wind blew free, and there was nothing to break the light of the sun. I was born where there were no enclosures and where everything drew a free breath. I want to die there, and not within walls."

Kiowa chief Satanta, standing right of the horsebacked Indian on the left, addressing the United States Peace Commissioners in Hermann Stieffel's painting of the 1867 Medicine Lodge Treaty Council. An array of U.S. military and political officials gathered with thousands of Plains Indians to address the seminal issues of post-Civil War American–Native conflict in the West. Courtesy National Museum of American Art, Smithsonian Institution.

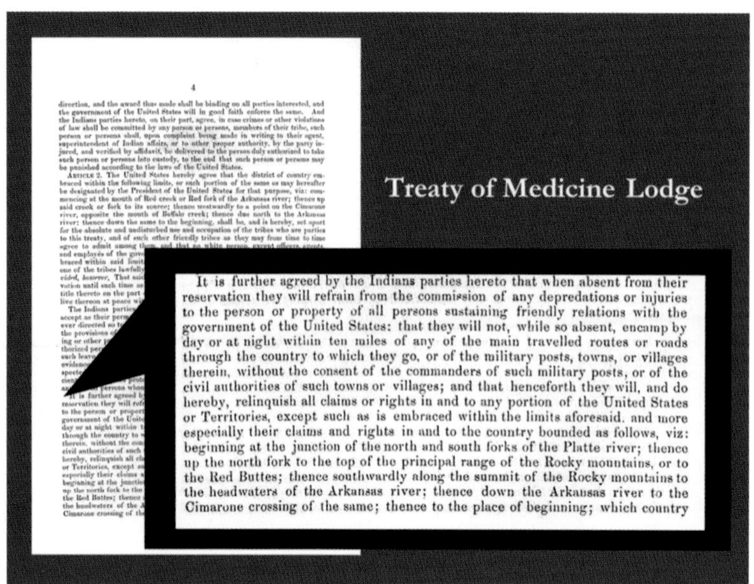
Treaty of Medicine Lodge

It is further agreed by the Indians parties hereto that when absent from their reservation they will refrain from the commission of any depredations or injuries to the person or property of all persons sustaining friendly relations with the government of the United States: that they will not, while so absent, encamp by day or at night within ten miles of any of the main travelled routes or roads through the country to which they go, or of the military posts, towns, or villages therein, without the consent of the commanders of such military posts, or of the civil authorities of such towns or villages; and that henceforth they will, and do hereby, relinquish all claims or rights in and to any portion of the United States or Territories, except such as is embraced within the limits aforesaid, and more especially their claims and rights in and to the country bounded as follows, viz: beginning at the junction of the north and south forks of the Platte river; thence up the north fork to the top of the principal range of the Rocky mountains, or to the Red Buttes; thence southwardly along the summit of the Rocky mountains to the headwaters of the Arkansas river; thence down the Arkansas river to the Cimarone crossing of the same; thence to the place of beginning; which country

A portion of the Treaty of Medicine Lodge, describing the restriction of the Plains or "Wild" tribes to their new reservations in western Oklahoma. Courtesy Research Division, Oklahoma Historical Society.

Battle of Washita

All the Treaty of Medicine Lodge seemed to accomplish was to provide the Plains tribes with enough food to energize their young (and sometimes not-so-young) warriors to mount and ride anew the vengeance trails to Kansas and especially Texas, where lived the people so hated by these tribes that they considered them a separate, inferior, and more brutally violent species from other Americans.

These acts of vengeance exhausted the patience of William Tecumseh Sherman, famed Union Civil War champion now in military command of all territories west of Missouri. He ordered Major General Philip Sheridan, the decorated wartime Yankee cavalry chieftain who replaced the failed Hancock as head of the Department of Missouri, to launch a military campaign into Indian Territory. Sheridan's mission: to force the Plains tribes onto their reservations and out of the path of westward American migration to the north and south. The fiery little Irishman built a fort (Camp Supply) in present-day Woodward County between Kansas and the reservations. He then sent fellow Yankee horse soldier legend George Armstrong Custer and the 7th Cavalry after Sand Creek survivor Black Kettle and the Southern Cheyennes, who were indeed off their reservation.

> *I love to roam over the wild prairie, and when I do it I feel free and happy, but when we settle down, we grow pale and die.*
>
> **—Satanta, Kiowa chief**

The rugged, cocksure Custer drove his men relentlessly through the bitter winter cold and sprawling drifts

A Comanche warrior, exhibiting the élan that helped birth the subriquet "Lords of the Plains" for the tribe.

In "the most important conflict between soldiers and Plains Indians ever fought in Oklahoma," Custer caught the Natives sleeping at dawn. Over a hundred Cheyennes—men, women, and children—died in the desperate fight, as did twenty soldiers.

of snow toward the Cheyennes, whom he found encamped along the Washita River, near the present-day northwestern Oklahoma town and Roger Mills County seat of Cheyenne. In what historian Edward Everett Dale called "the most important conflict between soldiers and Plains Indians ever fought in Oklahoma," Custer caught the Natives sleeping at dawn, November 27, 1868, and unleashed a blazing slaughter on them. Over

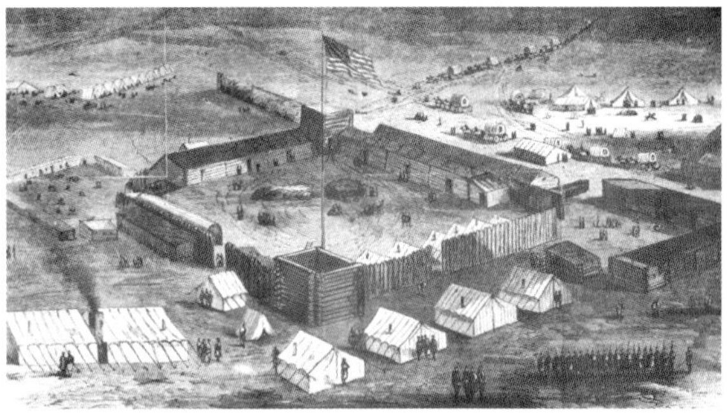

Camp Supply, key U.S. Army outpost established in 1868 in present-day Woodward County as General Philip Sheridan's base of military operations against the Southern Plains Indians.

Charles Schreyvogel captured the larger-than-life bravado, courage, and arrogance of General George Armstrong Custer in *Custer's Demand*, his epic painting of the U.S. Army–Kiowa confrontation in present-day Oklahoma. Legendary artist Frederic Remington, despising the rise of Schreyvogel, humble son of German immigrants, who rivaled his own greatness, criticized the supposed inaccuracy of this work. Yet Custer's wife Libbie, his officers, and even President Theodore Roosevelt defended Schreyvogel's research and authenticity. Courtesy Thomas Gilcrease Institute of American History and Art, Tulsa.

a hundred Cheyennes—women and children, as well as warriors—died in the desperate fight, as did twenty soldiers.

The Battle of the Washita deepened the enmity of the Plains tribes toward the U.S. government and army. The relentless campaign ramrodded by Sheridan and Custer, however, forced nearly all these Natives onto their reservations—whether temporarily or permanently—by 1870. Most of them went only by compulsion, and scattered, unvanquished bands such as Quanah Parker and his Quahadi Comanches remained at large. On the reservations, the Indians faced trouble from a debauched assemblage of white renegades and outlaws who tempted them with whiskey, gambling, and stolen horses.

On the reservations, the Indians faced trouble from a debauched assemblage of white renegades and outlaws, who tempted them with whiskey, gambling, and stolen horses.

History, that silent observant sentinel, would disapprove of many acts committed by the United States against the aboriginal tribes of North America. In the same manner, it would recognize that the fierce Plains tribes had stolen, kidnapped, raped, tortured, and murdered their own way to preeminence across the American West—over the dead and mutilated bodies of weaker tribes, as well as whites—and continued to do so. Some of those other Natives shed few tears over the conquest of the warrior tribes. Some aided the American army and settlers with that conquest.

The Plains Indian Wars cast a giant shadow of legend and lore over American history, in part because they pitted two determined juggernauts of willful and violent martial power—the Apaches, Arapahos, Cheyennes, Comanches, and Kiowas, and the United States military and armed frontier citizenry—against one another. Such formidable companies form both parent and child for much of the distinctive American character and its history. These relentless adversaries displayed on a sprawling canvas, across decades of national life, all the courage, sacrifice, loyalty,

The Battle of the Washita

It was a very unChristian-like war of extermination in which both sides committed atrocities. One of the most notorious was the Battle of the Washita in 1868, the biggest shootout of the Plains Indian Wars in present-day Oklahoma. There, George Armstrong Custer—who had earned the hatred of many Southerners for his brutal tactics in the Shenandoah Valley during the War Between the States—and his 7th Cavalry regiment thundered into a snow-blanketed Cheyenne village on the Washita River in northwestern Oklahoma.

George Armstrong Custer's 7th Cavalry defeating the Cheyennes in the pivotal battle of the Plains Indian Wars in present-day Oklahoma, the *Battle of the Washita*, as classically illustrated by Charles Schreyvogel. Courtesy Thomas Gilcrease Institute of American History and Art, Tulsa.

Cheyenne Chief Black Kettle, who survived the Sand Creek Massacre, but not the Battle of the Washita.

George Armstrong Custer (1839–1876)

Of all the larger-than-life characters who emerged from the War Between the States and the nineteenth-century American West, few have eclipsed George Armstrong Custer as an enduring icon. The changing perceptions of him have in many ways reflected the shifting societal views of the American public. Was he the gallant and selfless hero whom Errol Flynn unforgettably portrayed in the 1941 film classic *They Died with Their Boots On*? Or the silly prima donna played by Richard Mulligan in the 1971 movie *Little Big Man*? Or the brave but arrogant fool embodied by Gary Cole in the 1990 motion picture, *Son of the Morning Star*? Or some of each?

initiative, passion, great-heartedness, and valor we Americans so yearn to claim as our own. And they evidenced the vanity, greed, pettiness, brutality, cruelty, arrogance, and small-mindedness we disclaim even while struggling not to practice these sins in our own lives.

Grant's Peacemakers

Ulysses S. Grant emerged from the War Between the States as the most triumphant war captain of the conflict. His successes in both the Eastern and Western Theaters stood unmatched. Victories like Shiloh, Vicksburg, Richmond, and Appomattox Courthouse endure among the most famous and significant in American history. With so illustrious a resumé, it is small wonder that both major political parties sought him as their presidential candidate in 1868, the first such post-war election.

Peacetime hopes soared when Grant's reputation as a humble, honest, self-effacing military champion won him election to the White House over recent Indian fighter Winfield Hancock. Moreover, Grant—along with various national political luminaries, religious leaders, and other humanitarians—sought the peaceful conversion of the Plains Natives to Christianity and other American ways. Such conversion, they hoped, nurtured by a few decades of segregated reservation life, would also ease the westward path of American migration and business.

Grant soon ran aground, however, with congressional leaders from his own Republican Party. Protecting their own patronage prerogatives, they prevented him from appointing his military associates as agents for the tribes in Indian Territory, the Plains, and elsewhere. Grant countered by calling on several of the country's prominent Christian denominations to provide those representatives. In doing so, he dared his rivals in Congress to oppose the American church. They did not, and an array of Christian ministers soon arrived in present-day Oklahoma to lead the agencies established to serve the reserve tribes.

Ulysses S. Grant

Good, sometimes godly government-appointed Indian agents like Quakers Lawrie Tatum and John D. Miles faced formidable challenges. They spearheaded efforts both to encourage the Americanization of the Plains tribes and discourage the latter's continued pursuit of practices dangerous to themselves, other Natives, and American pioneers. All of this occurred within a context of tribes who were sullen, dejected, and sometimes violent, yet held in high esteem by the government's own peace commissioners:

> Naturally, the Indian has many noble qualities. He is the very embodiment of courage.... If he is cruel and revengeful, it is because he is outlawed and his companion is the wild beast. Let civilized man be his companion, and the association warms into life virtues of the rarest worth. Civilization has driven him back from the home he loved; it has often tortured and killed him, but it never could make him a slave. As we have so little respect for those we did enslave, to be consistent, this element of Indian character should challenge some admiration.

Reminiscent of the Christian missionaries who had served the five Indian republics following their Trails of Tears, some agents labored for years amongst the Natives, championing the first schools that educated the Plains tribes' children. The quality of these schools proved of sufficient excellence that many young people graduated from such acclaimed Indian colleges as Carlisle in Pennsylvania, alma mater of the legendary Olympic athlete and Sac and Fox of Indian Territory, Jim Thorpe.

The agents also orchestrated training for Natives of all ages in vocations encompassing both agricultural and skilled trades. Many of the Indians, parlaying their work in higher education, succeeded in commercial, governmental, and ecclesiastical vocations. And the agents coordinated ministry efforts toward the Natives' spiritual and physical needs through the planting of Baptist, Methodist, Mennonite, Episcopal, Presbyterian, Roman Catholic, Church of Christ, Quaker, and other denominational churches.

Despite many unhappy stories such as those previously recounted, the sacrifices of numerous white Americans, coupled with the Indians' trust and desire that their children might benefit from full participation in and acceptance from an onrushing American society of awe-inspiring power, wealth, and opportunity, produced innumerable happy tales of Indian success and Christian conversion. "The religion of our blessed Savior is... the most effective agent for the civilization of any people," the Board of Indian Commissioners concluded. But these events occurred amidst an uneven road of racial prejudice and the sometimes rough and forcible discarding of not only the Natives' pagan beliefs and practices, but also many of the morally neutral cultural ones that distinguished them.

Plus, the truth remained that two proud and strong peoples had locked in a fight to the death over land, resources, and a way of life. Thus proceeded their tragic cycle. Even though the aggressor among them professedly followed in the way of the "Prince of Peace," both peoples stood undaunted, unwilling to yield to their adversary unless compelled to do so by sheer force of armed might. Unfortunately for the weaker and less numerous Indians, they posed the greatest obstacle of the postwar era to westward American migration. The U.S. government would spend years hunting, fighting, and corralling them onto restricted reservations. The well-intentioned Lawrie Tatums would accomplish much good. And they would face bitter disappointment and betrayal.

Quaker Lawrie Tatum with Mexican children he redeemed from the Comanches after their capture. Tatum orchestrated the rescue of numerous captives from both the Comanches and Kiowas during his four years' service as agent.

8

1870s
A New Invasion

Wayne Cooper's *First Coal and the Katy Railroad*, his vibrant depiction of the 1872 union of the Katy Railroad, the frontier coal industry, former Confederate Colonel J. J. McAlester's vision of Indian Territory commercial development, and McAlester's namesake new town. Courtesy Oklahoma State Senate Historical Preservation Fund, Inc. and Wayne Cooper.

1868–1875	Plains Indian Wars
1869–1887	Chisholm Trail cattle drives
1872	Katy Railroad enters Indian Territory
1872	J. J. McAlester launches Indian Territory coal industry
1872	Chickasaw Oil Company founded
1874–1875	Red River Campaign
1875	Cherokee Orphan Asylum founded
1875	Fort Reno built
1877–1878	Northern Cheyennes' forcible relocation, escape
1879	Elias C. Boudinot's "Call to America" published

I think we should lose no time after the hot season in securing claims in the nation along the lines of the R. R. (railroad) which will *be built.*

—Elias C. Boudinot

When the 1870s came to Indian Territory, change was coming with it—change even more momentous than that wrought by the bloodbath of the War Between the States. After the war, the stream of American citizens pioneering west for land and destiny gushed like a tidal wave. The frontier that possessed property unclaimed by other citizens was quickly narrowing. The largest portion yet remaining was Indian Territory. There, approximately a hundred thousand people—the great majority of them Natives—lived on nearly seventy thousand square miles of land. In comparison, New York had around 4.3 *million* people living on forty-seven thousand square miles.

Now began in earnest, at least into the territory's eastern environs, the armed migration of whites from the States and many other lands. Their sometimes roughhewn genius and relentless drive would most shape the character and destiny of the Oklahoma country, as they had done everywhere else in the United States. Thousands of white pioneers and other immigrants—many of them vigorous, enterprising, and energetic—wanted Indian Territory land. So did the century's titan of nineteenth-century industry—the railroads.

Due to the government's punishment of the Confederate Indian republics, the railroads now held the right to lay track through tribal lands. These corporations possessed power, land, and capital. All they needed was people who wanted to settle the very lands the railroads now prepared to build across. Concerning the dearth of Indian Territory customers, one railroad official described his corporation as the first ever to lay tracks "two-hundred and fifty miles through a tunnel."

Free, formerly-enslaved African-Americans continued migrating to Indian Territory from Texas and elsewhere. Thousands more remained in the territory, no longer under bondage to their former Native owners. The Treaty of Medicine Lodge and the U.S. government continued drawing weary, sullen Southern Plains Indians as well, their numbers mounting into the tens of thousands. A climactic and violent showdown between defiant factions of Comanches and other Natives and the American army loomed. And, in the post-war moral slough common to the aftermath of all marathon slaughters, the multiracial outlaw enclave mentioned in Chapter 7 grew into fearful expanse. Adventure, opportunity, and trouble beckoned in every corner of present-day Oklahoma.

Railroads, Mines Partner

Despite the devastation wrought by the War for Southern Independence, along with the Yankee government's harsh Reconstruction treatment of the pro-Confederate Indian republics, an economic renaissance blossomed in the Nations as the 1870s progressed. The Missouri, Kansas, and Texas (Katy), as well as the Atlantic and Pacific, built rail lines across them. That encouraged the mining of coal—and later, lead, zinc, and other minerals—in the territory, since both the railroads and their vast host of customers back East would gladly pay for these necessities. Indeed, the train locomotive engines burned mountains of coal, so the railroads proved to be some of the coal companies' best customers.

Simultaneously, vast amounts of additional coal traveled east on the trains, making the coal companies among the railroads' best customers. This mutually profitable combination spurred some of the railroads to launch their own coal companies.

Thus, though white soldiers, teachers, and missionaries continued to come, now so did thousands of seasoned coal miners. The Cherokees and Choctaws, who owned the lands where most of the coal fields lay, had first shot at working them, but they refused to do so. Then occurred a providential confluence of events that triggered an epic new chapter in Oklahoma's history. The Katy Railroad reached the heart of the coal country at McAlester in 1872, the eve of the infamous Panic of 1873, perhaps the worst financial depression in American history prior to the Great Depression of the 1930s.

J. J. McAlester (1842–1920)

Only one man rose from Arkansas poverty, commanded Confederate troops in some of the War Between the States' greatest Western battles, built the coal industry of present-day Oklahoma, played a key

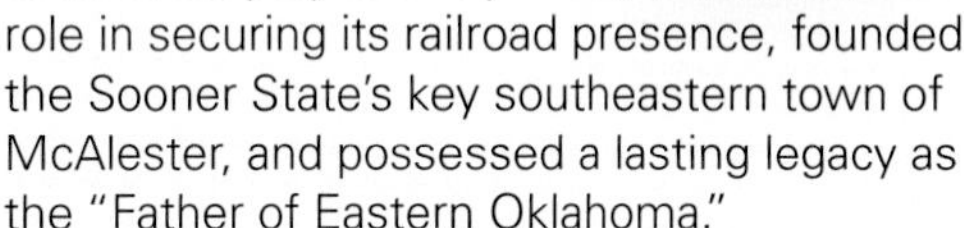

role in securing its railroad presence, founded the Sooner State's key southeastern town of McAlester, and possessed a lasting legacy as the "Father of Eastern Oklahoma."

The East's corruption- and greed-spawned economic disaster, however, proved to be Indian Territory's blessing as another exodus of American migration began. Rugged but unemployed white miners from coal fields in such states as Pennsylvania and Illinois poured into the new land. The white tidal wave grew international, when even that onslaught proved insufficient for the mining opportunities. Mining companies recruited hundreds and eventually thousands more miners from Ireland, Scotland, Wales, and England.

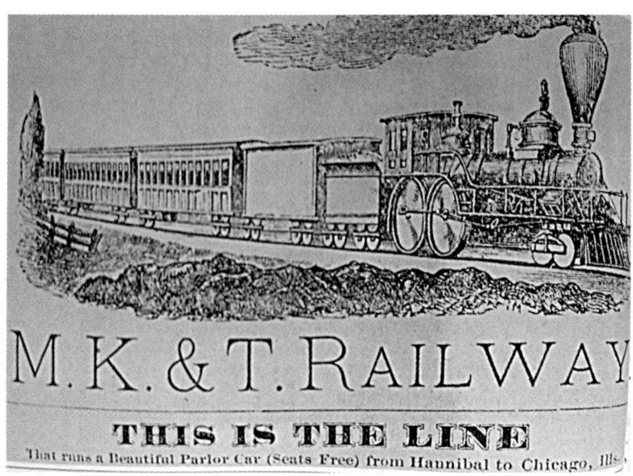

A newspaper advertisement for the Missouri, Kansas, and Texas (Katy) train line, which pioneered rail travel through Indian Territory in the early 1870s.

Other Daring Entrepreneurs

Thousands of other white men pursued employment opportunities in eastern Indian Territory, some spawned by the tribes' need to replace the labor of former slaves freed after the Civil War. Many of these arrived, lived, and worked through one of three legal avenues: 1) as federal government employees; 2) as licensed traders; or 3) through permits issued by the tribal governments to provide needed labor for them. Others came illegally and without invitation.

J. J. McAlester, a former Confederate officer from Arkansas, hauled freight across the territory for the U.S. Army, but learned of coal deposits in

The face of American free enterprise comes to the Indian Territory frontier with J. J. McAlester and his mercantile store in McAlester.

southeastern Indian Territory. Shrewd and visionary, he was now married to a Choctaw woman, which secured him tribal membership. This in turn qualified him to obtain land in the area; establish a store there in 1872, which later became his namesake town; and parlay the coal discovery into the territory's first coal mine. This launched what would become one of the mightiest industries in the territory by the dawn of the twentieth century. McAlester then persuaded the Katy Railroad to run a new line through the region.

The company gained a valuable customer to help cover its early investment into the territory. McAlester turned unused minerals laying in plain sight on the ground into the beginnings of a

The Railroads

Railroads endure as the titanic industrial marvel of the nineteenth-century United States. They embodied many of the pillars of the American character that created them—courage, vision, perseverance, ingenuity, energy, greed, ruthlessness, and violence. Nowhere did they more dramatically impact the destiny of a people than post-Civil War Indian Territory.

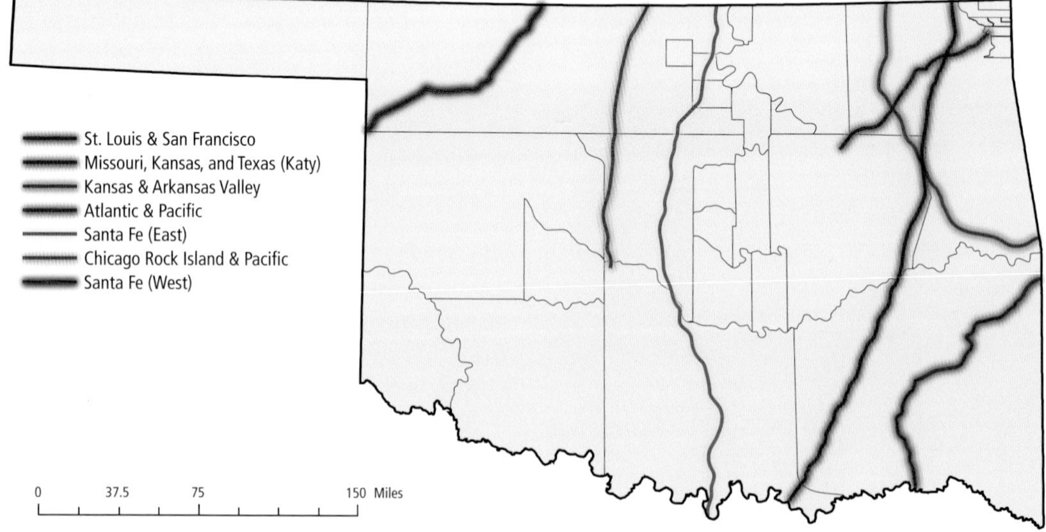

Post-Civil War American migration into present-day Oklahoma, coupled with decreasing tribal sovereignty, triggered an Indian Territory railroad boom.

Chickasaw Oil Company

Oklahoma's first petroleum firm, the Chickasaw Oil Company, was established in 1872. This enterprise was the brainchild of Robert M. Darden of Missouri. In February of 1872 he and nineteen Chickasaw and Choctaw citizens organized the business under Missouri laws, with Darden as president. Stock certificates were issued to investors.

Darden's partners included former Chickasaw Governor Winchester Colbert, a resident of Pontotoc County in the Chickasaw Nation. Oil was believed to be located near Colbert's residence, and it was there that the company sought to acquire leases on quarter sections of land. It had been agreed that the company would assume operational costs. In return, Darden and the investors would divide the proceeds equally.

The Chickasaw Oil Company, however, was short lived. Commissioner of Indian Affairs Francis Walker and Secretary of the Interior Columbus Delano opposed Darden's speculation in Indian Territory and disallowed his venture. Moreover, the coal-powered Missouri, Kansas, and Texas Railway (Katy) entered Indian Territory in 1872 and focused regional attention on coal mining.

—Jon D. May
Oklahoma Historical Society

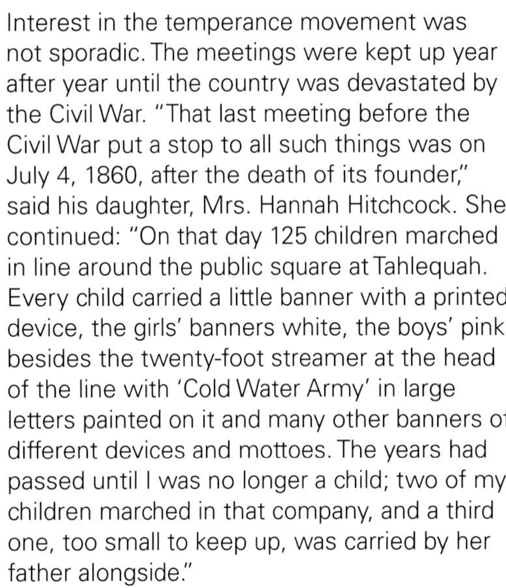

Missionaries and Indians Battle Liquor (Part 3)

by Grant Foreman
Chronicles of Oklahoma

Interest in the temperance movement was not sporadic. The meetings were kept up year after year until the country was devastated by the Civil War. "That last meeting before the Civil War put a stop to all such things was on July 4, 1860, after the death of its founder," said his daughter, Mrs. Hannah Hitchcock. She continued: "On that day 125 children marched in line around the public square at Tahlequah. Every child carried a little banner with a printed device, the girls' banners white, the boys' pink, besides the twenty-foot streamer at the head of the line with 'Cold Water Army' in large letters painted on it and many other banners of different devices and mottoes. The years had passed until I was no longer a child; two of my children marched in that company, and a third one, too small to keep up, was carried by her father alongside."

personal fortune, while myriads of Americans back in the States benefited from coal for heating, fuel, and other uses. Other white entrepreneurs began to build in Indian Territory as well, and different men came—often bringing their wives and children—to work for them as miners, farm laborers, ranch hands, and in many other roles.

Another illustration of 1870s entrepreneurial flair in eastern Indian Territory was the birth of present-day Oklahoma's first oil company, Chickasaw Oil. Its founding partners included former Chickasaw Governor Winchester Colbert. Illustrative of the many actions through the years that slowed the future Sooner State's economic development, especially in contrast with surrounding states, the federal government disallowed the venture due to its speculative nature within the Indian Nations.

Throughout the decade, the government also attempted to corral the original southeastern tribes into a single governmental entity with which it could deal, thus further eroding individual tribal sovereignty. Amidst the nascent but burgeoning free-market American economy in the region, the tribes warded off this unification effort, but their autonomy was fading into the past. From now on, for instance, the U.S. government would enter into "agreements" rather than treaties with the tribes—agreements that could be adjusted or scrapped whenever it suited the government.

Reservation Troubles

As white and mixed-blood entrepreneurs launched the first significant efforts to mine the commercial potential of eastern Indian Territory, the reservation system to the west proceeded uneasily. By the end of the decade, upwards of fifteen thousand Natives would reside on these tracts. Despite incompetent and sometimes corrupt actions from

Legendary Kiowa war chiefs, defiant till the end. Left to right: Satanta, Lone Wolf (the elder), and Satank.

the government agencies with whom they dealt, life improved for many of these Indians, at least as the years passed. The food they gleaned from their own farming and government provisions, though inconsistent, especially early on, eventually proved more

Office Kiowa Agency
5 mo 30, 1871
Jona Richards,
Ind Agent,
On the 27 inst
Satanta with several
other Chiefs, women & children
& a few young men came
after their rations, Before
receiving them the Chiefs
& some of the young men came
into the Office, & Satanta
made, what he wished
understood to be a "Big
Speech," in which he said
addressing me
"I have heard that you have
stolen a large portion of our
5

The first page of Quaker Indian Agent Lawrie Tatum's 1871 letter to colleague Jonathan Richards, which describes Kiowa war chief Satanka boasting to Tatum of having led a deadly ambush on a Texas supply wagon train. Courtesy Research Division, Oklahoma Historical Society.

reliable than that garnered from increasingly paltry buffalo hunts. They also faced less probability of death—sometimes accompanied by torture—in battles with opposing tribes. An ever-increasing host of them learned to read and write, many of their sons and daughters assimilated into American society, and, most significantly, large numbers of them placed their spiritual faith in the Christian God.

At the same time, many Natives detested their constrained new lives. They felt pressure from white teachers, missionaries, soldiers, and others to learn a new language, new vocations, new dress, new grooming, and a galaxy of other unfamiliar social practices. Meanwhile, they faced taunting and sometimes worse treatment from roaming companies of Quahadi Comanches. The most doggedly defiant of the five Comanche bands toward American settlement and culture, and accompanied by some Kiowas and Cheyennes, the Quahadis boasted they would never submit to white rule unless compelled to do so by force of arms. And an infuriating band of white horse thieves bedeviled the reservation Indians throughout most of the remainder of the century.

Most of the Natives exercised forbearance amidst these and other difficulties, some with the patience learned through their new Christian faith, others through sadness and resentment, and still others through the numbing escape of alcoholic spirits. As mentioned, though, some resorted to the art of war they had long mastered. In addition to the Quahadis, several Kiowa chiefs, including

Satanta, Satank, Big Tree, and Lone Wolf (the elder), waged a particularly destructive—and deceptive—campaign against white settlements in north Texas. These battle-hardened killers, abusing the confidence of trusting, often pacifist Indian agents like the Quaker Lawrie Tatum, spent time on the Indian Territory reservation, then sneaked away to hunt, raid, or both, whereupon they returned to the reservation, feigning innocence of all mischief.

Forcing a People to Change

- Housing—The government built a house for a chief who had seven wives. He housed his dogs and stored buffalo hides in the structure, and he and his wives continued living in their separate tepees.
- Animals—Indians often took farm animals and stock supplied by the government for cultivating herds and used them instead to hold feasts for friends and family.
- School—The tribes had no clocks, so their children struggled to attend white schools because they never had set times for going to bed or getting up.

Blood and Hate

The Texans' blood feud with the Plains Natives was breathtaking in its violent intensity, a true war of extermination between two civilizations stretching back half a century. They lambasted the federal government for unleashing harsh Reconstruction policies against the Lone Star State while not protecting it from the recent Native rampages. For instance, the feds and their carpetbag state administration feared the Texas Rangers due to their renowned feats before and during the War Between the States, and disbanded them after the war (until ex-Confederate Democrats regained control of the state government in 1874). The Rangers had wreaked havoc on the Comanches and other fighting tribes before the war, clearing them out of large swaths of Texas.

A Cheyenne chief ponders whether to attack an encampment of white settlers who have circled their wagons for protection while passing through western Indian Territory in G. N. Taylor's *Time of Decision*. (www.gntayloroklaart.com)

The often-unreconstructed Texans suspected, with some justification, that the Yankee government they had fought so bitterly against felt no great concern over their welfare. "If I had a choice between living in hell or Texas, I would live in hell and rent out Texas," declared General Philip Sheridan, Union war hero and now military commander over the Great Plains. A Texan replied, "Every man to his own country." The Quaker Indian Agent Tatum, meanwhile, finally caught on to the Indians' subterfuge and called on William Sherman—now commanding general of the U.S. Army—to come and straighten things out.

The situation grew clear for Sherman when he nearly got himself killed in an ambush launched by Satanta and the Kiowas against a wagon train rumbling out of Fort Richardson in north Texas. When Sherman reached Fort Sill, the major southwest Indian Territory military outpost adjacent to Lawton in present-day Comanche County, and Satanta boasted of having led the bloody attack, the army commander ordered him hanged and his confederates Satank and Big Tree thrown into prison.

For a while, tensions with the Southern Plains Indians eased, partly because the army had sidelined the leaders of the Kiowa warrior faction. But though most of the Kiowas remained on or returned to the reservation, the Quahadi Comanches and other Kiowas, along with some Southern Cheyennes, remained in the field. And white buffalo hunters, spurred on by the U.S. government in ways large and small, continued to decimate the bison, further kindling the unvanquished Natives' fear and anger. By mid-1873, the hunters were slaughtering their prey all through the prohibited western Indian Territory and hundreds of miles down into Texas. The Quahadis and Southern Cheyennes exploded into action.

War in West

Over the next year, often using western Indian Territory and even their own reservations as both staging grounds and places of refuge, these rugged Natives unleashed enough firepower that the Southern Plains grew more rather than less violent for American settlers—and the railroads. Then on June 27, 1874, several hundred Comanches, Cheyennes, and Kiowas—including legendary Comanche Chief Quanah Parker and Kiowa Chief Lone Wolf (the elder)—thundered into the buffalo hunting operation at Adobe Walls, in the Texas Panhandle. There they shot it out with a small but well-armed band of tough white frontiersmen that included future Dodge City Sheriff legend Bat Masterson and some of the most accomplished buffalo hunters in America. It was a sight as fearsome as it was unparalleled—hundreds of the toughest warriors ever to ride, from the most dangerous tribes, uniting in a concerted campaign to wrest control of the Southern Plains from the white man.

Oklahoman Billy Dixon, whose legendary rifle shot ended the Battle of Adobe Walls.

The latter and their .50-caliber buffalo guns stacked up numerous Indian corpses, wounded scores more—including Quanah—and the shattered attackers scattered across the north Texas plains. It was a singular feat by one of the defenders that finally sent the Natives packing after three days of determined assaults and siege. Scout and buffalo hunter Billy Dixon, who lived the last many years of his life in Cimarron County and was one of eight civilians ever honored with the Medal of Honor, used a Sharps .50-90 rifle to fire the most famous shot in the history of the American West. It killed a mounted Comanche on a rise nearly *one mile* away.

The enraged, heartsick Indians exploded in a summer-long rampage of vengeance, robbing, raping, murdering, and torturing from southern Colorado to the Rio Grande. Nearly two hundred white men, women, and children perished. Buffalo hunting, stage coach travel, railroad expansion, westward settlement itself were imperiled. At long last, the U.S. government, corporate America, and the American people alike, clear to the Atlantic, reached their breaking point. President U.S. Grant himself unleashed the armed might of the nation's western armies against the remaining hostile Indians.

The government had devoted much of its attention for the past decade to "reconstructing" the South. Historian Clyde A. Wilson described what now happened with the Red River War:

> Until late in the game, most Indian fighting was a private and local enterprise and many white men, women, and children made the ultimate sacrifice. Only in

the last phase of settlement did the U.S. government turn its mighty military machine from suppressing Southerners to suppressing Indians—not because the Indians were killing white men, women, and children but because they were retarding railroads, mines, and other sources of corporate profits.

Hard Tack: Diet of Frontier Soldiers

This article material appeared in the Teachers' Guide that accompanies the Oklahoma Historical Society's education trunk on forts in Oklahoma. Schools throughout Oklahoma can access trunks on subjects containing a wide range of items related to the trunk's subject.

The chief diet for U.S. soldiers on the march in 1860s and 1870s Indian Territory was a hard bread known as hard tack or hard crackers. Lack of refrigeration and other proper food storage during the 1800s made spoilage common. Hard tack produced from unleavened flour proved the logical solution, since it had an infinite shelf life. In fact, American troops received hard tack baked during the War Between the States as late as 1898 during the Spanish-American War—thirty-three years after the end of the earlier war!

Red River War

This epic confrontation proved to be the single most important campaign in the United States winning the American West. Following a prelude of years, even decades, it took place over many months from the summer of 1874 through April of 1875, across tens of thousands of square miles in five states and territories including present-day Oklahoma, and with thousands of combatants. When it concluded, no doubt remained as to which civilization ruled by its might of armed power the Southern Plains and most of the Southwest.

Sherman, Sheridan, campaign commander Nelson A. Miles, and the War Department crafted a masterful strategy to clean out the Quahadi Comanches, Southern Cheyennes, and any other Natives who remained armed and in the field. Five columns of infantry, cavalry, and artillery, totaling three thousand men, converged on western Indian Territory and the Texas Panhandle. They rode out from forts in four different states and territories: Fort Dodge, Kansas; Camp Supply and Fort Sill, Indian Territory; Fort Concho, Texas; and Fort Bascom, New Mexico.

The army and the Natives fought at least fourteen and perhaps as many as twenty battles during the Red River campaign. Well mounted, well armed, well supplied, and well taught from their many past fights with the Plains Indians, the army rumbled in on them from all sides, fighting as they came, careful to leave no path of escape.

The bluecoats ground down their foe, killing or taking the Natives' horses, capturing the tribes' women and children, and hauling them to the reservations. The pursuing force included the Fort Sill, Indian Territory-based 10th Cavalry African-American troopers known as "Buffalo Soldiers." One

Former slave and sharecropper, U.S. Army sergeant, buffalo soldier, and Medal of Honor winner Emmanuel Stance leads his men into battle in Don Stivers' thrilling work *The Redoubtable Sergeant* (www.donstivers.com).

The Buffalo Soldiers

Among the most audacious figures in Oklahoma history were the post-Civil War African-American troopers—some of them former slaves, all of them victims of a prejudiced society—known as the Buffalo Soldiers. One or more of the Plains Indian tribes apparently bequeathed them their legendary moniker after claiming that with their curly, dust-coated black hair, the "Negro Cavalry" resembled the rugged bison with which they shared the Southern Plains. From 1867 through most of the 1870s and 1880s, the Buffalo Soldiers marched and rode in the United States military vanguard for Indian Territory and the rest of the Southwest.

The African-American Buffalo Soldiers' wide range of duties included guarding stagecoaches that carried passengers, mail, gold, and other valuables through Indian Territory and other perilous western territories.

African-American Buffalo Soldiers based at Fort Sill comprised both infantry and cavalry regiments in the post-Civil War West, including these 25th Infantry soldiers.

Dashing Henry Ossian Flipper rose from childhood slavery to become the first African-American graduate of the United States Military Academy and the first black officer in the 10th Cavalry "Buffalo Soldiers," stationed at Fort Sill in the late 1870s. After a controversial discharge from the army, he excelled in private life as an engineer, businessman, and government official.

> *The notion that the trouble with Plains Indians was entirely due to white men was spectacularly wrongheaded. The people who cherished it, many of whom were in the U.S. Congress, the (corrupt) Office of Indian Affairs, and other positions of power, had no historical understanding of the Comanche tribe, no idea that the tribe's very existence was based on war and had been for a long time. No one who knew anything about the century-long horror of Comanche attacks in northern Mexico or about their systematic demolition of the Apaches or the Utes or the Tonkawas could possibly have believed that the tribe was either peaceable or blameless.*
>
> **—S. C. Gwynne**
> ***Empire of the Summer Moon***

or more of the Southern Plains tribes apparently coined this sobriquet when they compared the appearance of the enemy black troopers' curly, dust-coated beards and hair to the coats of Great Plains buffalo. The newly reconstituted Texas Rangers roared back into action as well. They ranged between army columns, fighting Indians, preventing their escape, and providing reconnaissance.

> *The Red River War proved to be the single most important campaign in the United States winning the American West.*

Mackenzie and Palo Duro

The climactic shootout took place in late September in Palo Duro Canyon, near present-day Amarillo in the Texas Panhandle. There, U.S. soldiers and their Texan and Tonkawa scouts cornered the largest remaining vanguard of defiant Comanches, Southern Cheyennes, and Kiowas, who had stockpiled massive food and supplies to bivouac for the winter.

Colonel Ranald S. Mackenzie, a renowned, six-times-wounded Federal cavalry chieftain in the War Between the States and battle-hardened Southern Plains campaigner, commanded this key American column, which had pursued many of the Indians from the south. "Three Fingers Jack" Mackenzie did not arrive at Palo Duro unprepared or by chance. For years, he had intrepidly studied, pursued, and engaged the Comanches where no other American commander had—across the vast and terrifying expanses of the Llano Estacado high plains of northwest Texas, the deepest sanctuary of Comancheria.

He had learned their tactics, their routes and cycles of travel, their preferred redoubts, even their watering holes. He had winnowed down their manpower during a host of skirmishes and battles, including his stunning 1872 ambush of them at the Battle of the North Fork (of Red River) near present-day Lefors, Texas. That audacious feat included the capture of one and possible two of Quanah Parker's wives and the virtual destruction of the Comanches' Kotsoteka band.

One statistical comparison illustrates the impact that Mackenzie and his horse soldiers made in opening the American southwest to secure white settlement. The number of Comanches they killed in the Battle of the North Fork alone would have been equal, on a proportionate basis, to the United States losing one-third of all Americans who died in the four years of the War Between the States in *one battle*.

To draw upon the words of Comanche chronicler S. C. Gwynne, Mackenzie had largely brought about the tribe's reckoning at Palo Duro "by daring to go where white men had not gone, by using his Indian scouts well, and then by attacking in force the moment he had intelligence of the camp (and he) attacked with fury." Gwynne also cited the restraint, especially for such a brutal war, of Mackenzie and

Pre-1960s American histories often emphasized Native atrocities against white Americans, such as in Charles Shreyvogel's *In Safe Hands*, while post-1960s works often reversed the emphasis. In reality, both sides killed thousands of the others' non-combatants in a tragic, desperate centuries-long war for the continent across which the United States of America now stretches. Courtesy Thomas Gilcrease Museum of Art.

Ranald Mackenzie—America's Greatest Indian Fighter (1840–1889)

The capricious nature of historiography is well illustrated by the fact that America's most famous Indian fighter, George Armstrong Custer, perished in the most breathtaking defeat the United States ever suffered in the Old West, while the courageous man who, in the saddle, led the defeat of the most powerful Plains Tribes north and south died already forgotten by the nation whose westward expansion and growth he as much as any one person made possible.

Palo Duro, the second largest canyon in America, near Amarillo in the Texas Panhandle. Here, in September 1874, Colonel Ranald Mackenzie and U.S. cavalry under his command routed a much larger Native force in the climactic battle of the Red River War.

his disciplined troopers in their humane treatment of enemy women, children, and elderly men.

Final Showdown

Mackenzie's organization and savvy paid historic dividends during the climactic 1874–75 campaign. His cavalrymen caught a Mexican Comanchero headed to meet, probably on gun running business, with the Indians that Mackenzie was pursuing. Mackenzie forced the outlaw to reveal the location of the Native resistance—the Palo Duro, second largest canyon in North America.

Mackenzie not only arrived at the Indian redoubt undetected after a grueling twelve-hour night ride in which he eluded Comanche scouts, he got nearly all of his six hundred-strong force, leading their horses down a narrow buffalo trail, to the canyon floor before Comanche chief Red Warbonnet spotted them. The chief sounded the alarm, but it was too late, and an army sharpshooter killed him. Mackenzie and his troopers stormed through the miles-long camp of teepees in an electrifying charge that routed their foe, after the Indian warriors made a determined stand to shield the escape of their women and children.

Following a several mile-long running fight, the Natives scrambled up the canyon walls, then spread out and surrounded the troopers from above. Eight hundred to a thousand feet high on the canyon rim, they unleashed a barrage of rifle fire down on the bluecoats. "How will we ever get out of here?" one rattled trooper cried out. "I brought you in," Mackenzie curtly replied as bullets whistled past. "I will take you out." He then led his men straight for the Indians in an awe-inspiring rush back up the canyon walls and drove them into open country, now on foot.

The soldiers destroyed fourteen hundred Indian ponies, took scores of non-combatants back to Native reservations in Indian Territory, and set about, with the other American columns that included the 10th Cavalry Buffalo Soldiers, to track

down the scattered warrior survivors. "The black smoke marked the end of Quanah's (Parker) hopes, as the retreating Indians saw it rise from far out on the prairie," wrote historian T. R. Fehrenbach. Relentlessly pursued by Mackenzie, Quanah led the last of them, his dauntless Quahadis, into Fort Sill the next June to surrender.

Sheridan ordered dozens of tribal leaders shackled in irons and transported by rail to prison in faraway Florida. There they remained for three years, at which time Army Captain Richard Henry Pratt invited some of them north to the Indian school at Carlisle, Pennsylvania. Unexpected blessings flowered through this marathon of suffering and tragedy. Pratt's humane, biblically sourced ethos led many of the former war captains to forgive their white enemies, embrace the whites' (and blacks') Christian faith, and return to Indian Territory to influence their people toward the same path. Some of the exiles even shouldered leadership roles in the church as pastors and missionaries to their own people, including the Cheyenne warrior Making Medicine. He became an esteemed Episcopal priest known as David Pendleton Oakerhater. Volume 2 of this work will profile him.

Not surprisingly, Sheridan appointed Mackenzie commander of Fort Sill following the Red River War. There, the Comanches, Kiowas, and Apaches he had long fought all gained respect for his tough but fair ways as they attempted to adjust to their new, more sedentary life on their present-day southwest Oklahoma reservations. The peaceful emissaries whom Mackenzie wisely sent to Quanah had finally persuaded the warrior chief and his remaining Quahadis to lay down their arms and come in. After they did, Quanah himself credited Mackenzie with respecting and befriending him, providing him opportunities to rise as a leader in both the Native and white societies, and even teaching him American manners and social graces.

After the stunning, world-famed massacre of George Armstrong Custer (Chapter 7) and his U.S. Seventh Cavalry at the Battle of the Little Bighorn in Montana, Sheridan sent Mackenzie and his now-elite Fourth Cavalry north to deal with the powerful and unconquered coalition of Northern Cheyennes and Lakota Sioux who had vanquished Custer and threatened American settlement across the Northern Plains. Within months, Mackenzie did what no other United States commander could do. He defeated Chief Dull Knife and the Northern Cheyennes, forced Crazy Horse and the Lakota to surrender, and ended the Great Sioux War. "You are the one I was afraid of when you came here last summer," Dull Knife told Mackenzie after he surrendered. Mackenzie thus led the U.S. Army to victory over its most intrepid Indian opponents in the

The Comanches and a Thousand Deserts

"One by one, the children and young women were pegged out naked beside the camp fire. They were skinned, sliced, and horribly mutilated, and finally burned alive by vengeful women determined to wring the last shriek and convulsion from their agonized bodies."

This contemporaneous nineteenth-century account of *female* Comanche atrocities against white captives in Texas illustrates what one prominent chronicler of the tribe's history terms its systematic "demonic immorality" (prior to its subjugation by the U.S. Army and Texas Rangers) toward its legion of captured adversaries, most of whom were actually other Indians or Mexicans.

Small Tribes, Great Men

Chief Joseph (1840–1904)

"Of one Indian leader—and one only—nothing but good has ever been written," wrote historian S. L. A. Marshall. "Chief Joseph of the Wallowa band of the Nez Perce, although his story has been debunked and rebunked almost endlessly, still stands higher than his legend. . . . Devoted to peace, without prior military experience, he became the central and leading captain in the most trying and skillfully conducted Indian war ever to engage the United States Army."

Standing Bear (c. 1829–1908)

"An Indian is a person under the meaning of the law." When Federal Judge Elmer Dundy ruled as such in the landmark 1879 legal battle *Standing Bear vs. Crook*, he assured a historic and well-deserved legacy for the wise, selfless, longsuffering Ponca chief whose name adorned the case.

American West, on both the Northern and Southern Great Plains.

One final significant outbreak of U.S.–Native violence erupted from western Indian Territory in 1877. After the Northern Cheyennes' battlefield defeat to Mackenzie, the government forced them, over their vigorous protests, more than a thousand miles across country from Montana to join their southern cousins on their present-day Oklahoma reservation. Within months, many of the unhappy emigrants died.

The following year, as dramatized in the John Ford Western film *Cheyenne Autumn*, a few hundred Northern Cheyennes led by Dull Knife and Little Wolf left the reservation and headed for home. Even though women and children accompanied them

This 1891 painting depicts Fort Reno, built in 1875 near the Darlington Indian Agency on the old Cheyenne-Arapaho reservation a few miles northwest of present-day El Reno. The historic U.S. Army outpost was named for Jesse Reno, a Mexican War and Civil War hero killed by a Confederate sharpshooter at the Battle of South Mountain. It provided a bulwark against the 1875 Plains Indians uprising, helped buffer the Five Civilized Tribes from the Plains tribes' raids, and finally helped American troopers protect Native lands from Boomer incursions. Courtesy Oklahoma Historical Society.

Elias C. Boudinot, who took up his father's mantle as a bold, imaginative, and controversial visionary for Cherokee—and Oklahoma—progress and prosperity. Courtesy Oklahoma Historical Society.

and they suffered through withering winter weather conditions, they sustained a marathon flight from a gauntlet of army pursuers. Some of the younger male Cheyennes murdered numerous white civilians, which were criminal acts the older chiefs renounced. Though most of the exiles were captured, some made it all the way home. The U.S. government eventually allowed the Northern Cheyennes permanent sanctuary in their Montana homeland.

The Boomers

As the 1870s concluded, the U.S. military controlled Indian Territory, and American pioneers exerted increasing influence and land ownership. Some of

The Cherokees continued to set a shining standard for Natives and whites alike with their care for "the least among these." They built the Cherokee Orphan Asylum in 1875. It accommodated 135 people at a time and served the blind and mute, as well as the insane. Courtesy Oklahoma Historical Society.

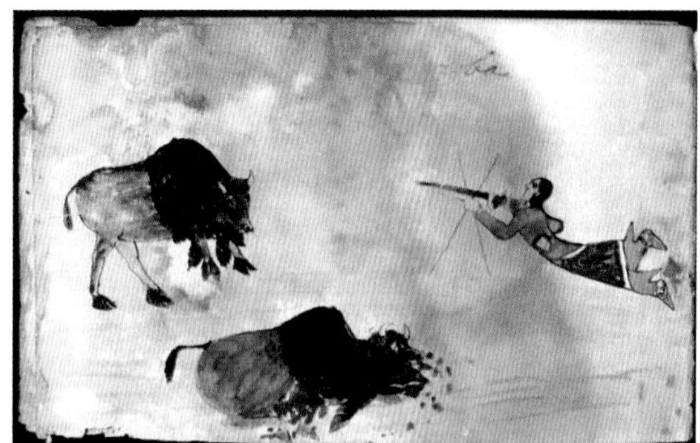

Seventy-two Southern Plains Indians who surrendered in 1874–75 following their defeat by the U.S. Army in the Red River War were shipped to prison at Fort Marion, in St. Augustine, Florida. Viewed as leaders in the Native resistance to government reservation policies, they spent three years incarcerated there. During that time, however, Captain Richard Henry Pratt encouraged their pursuit of various American artistic and academic pursuits. These included ledger art, the practice of drawing and painting on a variety of surfaces, especially government and business ledger paper. Koba, a young Kiowa man, produced some of the best ledger art, including: (top) Kiowas hunting buffalo, (center) discovering a column of U.S. Cavalry, and (bottom) being confined to the reservation in 1875. After Fort Marion, Koba attended Hampton Institute in Virginia, as well as Carlisle Institute in Pennsylvania. Courtesy Research Division, Oklahoma Historical Society these pioneers, known as "Boomers" because they were booming or trumpeting the settlement of Native lands, sought to expedite that process. A famous name in Oklahoma history rose up anew as their standard bearer. Elias C. Boudinot, whose father had defied the dominant powers of his Cherokee tribe to bring his people to Indian Territory, himself now defied the ruling powers of the whites and Natives alike. In early 1879, Boudinot fired a written shot heard round the world in the editorial pages of the large and influential *Chicago Times* newspaper. In it, he challenged

Quanah Parker (1852–1911)

This famed warrior, peacemaker, and champion of the Comanches endures in many ways as a human metaphor for the state that rose from the shortgrass country hallowed by him and his people. Born of a legendary Indian chief and equally famed white woman (and Comanche captive), he taunted fellow Natives who settled in post-Civil War Indian Territory reservations, then he fought to the bitter end in the Red River War. By the time he died, however, just a few years before World War I, he had parlayed innate business savvy into a formidable estate, gained celebrity status in the popular American culture, and nudged his people toward the Christian faith he once detested.

The Man Who Killed the Buffalo

Philip Sheridan

"Let them kill, skin, and sell until the buffalo is exterminated, as it is the only way to bring lasting peace and allow civilization to advance," famed Civil War general and commander of the post-war Army in the West Philip A. Sheridan told the 1875 Texas Legislature. Members of that body had complained about rampaging buffalo hunters who piled up thousands of carcasses at a time with intentions to utilize only small portions of the magnificent beast, if any portions at all. They wanted Sheridan to stop the practice.

General Phil Sheridan's famed ride during the War Between the States from Winchester to rally his bloodied, retreating Federal troops turned the tide at the Battle of Cedar Creek, won the 1864 Shenandoah Valley Campaign for the Yankees, ended the final Confederate invasion threat to the North, helped secure Abraham Lincoln's presidential re-election, and made Sheridan a national hero in the Union states.

Buffalo—The Indians' Commissary

The magnificent American bison, better (if less accurately) known as the buffalo, provided the Native tribes an array of provisions so vast that it met most of their subsistence needs. William D. Welge, Director of the American Indian Culture and Preservation Office and longtime archivist for the Oklahoma Historical Society, provided the information for the adjacent illustration, which well illustrates why the buffalo was known as the "Indians' Commissary" and why the U.S. Government warring with the tribes worked so hard to exterminate the animal.

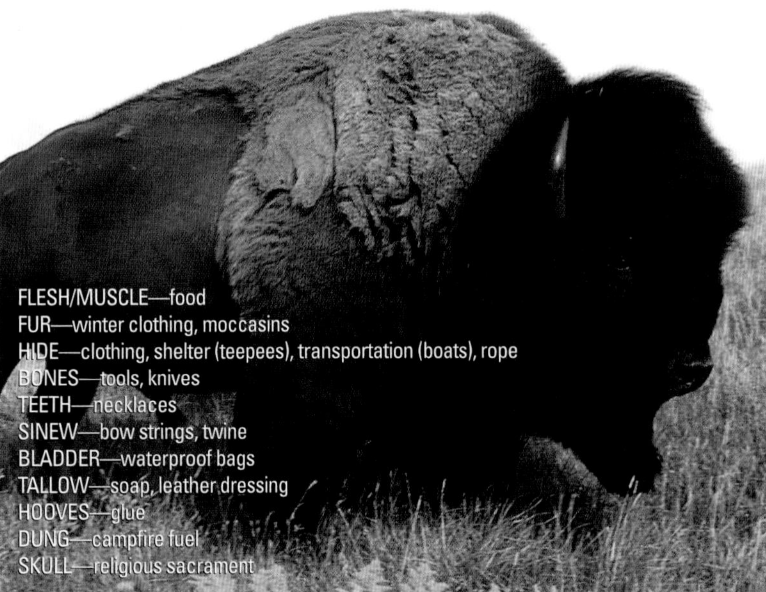

Buffalo skinners had plenty of work in late 1860s–early 1870s Indian Territory. U.S. Army Commander-in-Chief Philip Sheridan green-lighted the massacre of the majestic titan of the plains in order to starve out the tough Southern Plains Natives, who posed a threat to the railroads and the rest of westward American expansion. Courtesy Oklahoma State Senate Historical Preservation Fund, Inc. and Gordon Snidow.

the U.S. government to open to the American populace as public domain the lands it took from the Indian republics in 1866, as he claimed that federal homestead laws demanded.

Would-be settlers poured into southern Kansas and southwestern Missouri, as well as the Red River Valley of north Texas, preparing to stake their claim in what Americans increasingly called the "Oklahoma Lands" or "Oklahoma" (Chapter 7). A swashbuckling Union Army veteran named Charles Carpenter who sported Custer-like long hair and buckskins rallied hundreds of them around himself and served notice that the birth of a new state loomed—with him as its apparent leader. Government officials intimidated Carpenter into backing off in 1879, and the army burned out early settlements of Boomers near present-day Oklahoma City.

As the 1880s arrived, however, a sea change roiled in Indian Territory. Gone were the buffalo and the rule of the Natives. Coming or already there were the U.S. Army, the railroads, white entrepreneurs, and a tidal wave of new boomers. Maybe the government—earnestly attempting to honor its latest commitments to the Indians—could turn back Carpenter, and perhaps even David Payne, the Boomer leader who followed him. But U.S. industry and the American people now had their sights trained on the Oklahoma country. And history has shown many times that once that happens, for better or worse, there is no turning them back.

Don Stivers' poignant *The Promise*, the portrait of an African-American Buffalo Soldier leaving his forlorn wife to serve the America he was helping build (www.framery.com).

9

1880s

White Oklahoma

Staking His Claim, Run of '89, G. N. Taylor's rip-roaring portrait of the first Oklahoma land opening, the Unassigned Lands Run of 1889. It encompassed the future communities of Oklahoma City, Norman, Moore, Edmond, Yukon, El Reno, Mustang, Del City, Midwest City, Noble, Stillwater, Guthrie, Lexington, and Kingfisher.

1880	Cherokees lease Outlet to Texas cattle ranchers
1880	David Payne begins Boomer raids
1880	Mennonites launch Darlington mission to Arapahos
1880–1889	German, Italian, Russian, Eastern European, Mexican immigrant coal miners
1885	President Cleveland orders cattle herds off Plains reservations
1887	Dawes Severalty Allotment Act
1888	H. A. Faucett strikes oil at Clear Boggy Creek
1889	Unassigned Lands Run
1889	First Indian Territory federal court at Muskogee
1889	Edward Byrd sinks four oil wells in Cherokee country

I've seen beauty enough, known earth's joys and delights;
Still the lure of that far prairie home
With its wild, simple life and its matchless expanse
Holds my heart strings wherever I roam.

—J. L. Hefley, from *My Home on the Plains*

Perhaps Edward Everett Dale, the dean of Oklahoma historians, best described the "Continental Divide" that now appeared in the timeline of Oklahoma history:

> In the period from 1867 to about 1883 a large number of tribes were brought to the lands ceded by the Five Civilized Tribes in 1866. With the arrival of the last of these tribes, what may be called the "Indian Era" of Oklahoma history came to an end. Six years later, the first white settlers arrived, and the second epoch of the history of the state, that of the white man, got under way.

In one of the great paradoxes of Oklahoma history, the Native population of Indian Territory reached its zenith at the very time white and black Americans began en masse to set their sights on the region for settlement. By the early 1880s, as the final horde of exiled tribes arrived in the territory, the American citizenry was rising up to engulf the Indians and their lands in a titanic tidal wave of humanity.

The Boomers had succeeded both in gaining the attention of the U.S. public and pushing Congress toward a reassessment of its plans for the remaining (northern, central, and western) open lands of Indian Territory—and even those not open. Also, the era's industrial giant—the railroads—now crosshatched eastern Indian Territory. By the end of the 1880s, the Union Pacific's Missouri–Kansas–Texas

A Sunday service in the open country for Boomers readying to enter the Oklahoma Territory for land in 1881, years prior to federal approval. *Frank Leslie's Illustrated Newspaper* equaled *Harper's Weekly* as the foremost illustrated publication of the era.

John Seger and the Arapahos (1846–1928)

This man, who marched to the sea with Sherman amidst flames, slaughter, and crime, was accused of never spelling a word the same way twice. Even though he came to the Cheyenne-Arapaho reservation as a carpenter and mason, it did not appear likely at first that he would forge one of the great educational and job training efforts for Natives, nor stay at the task for over half a century, nor have it written of him, "No other white man ever lived who had the confidence as well as the good will of the Indians of the Plains." But Ohio-born John Homer Seger did.

Cheyenne and Arapaho young men learning to brand cattle in 1900 at the Seger Colony's Indian School in Washita County.

(Katy) line ran south along the Texas Road from southeast Kansas to Red River; the Frisco, southwest from Fort Smith, Arkansas through southeastern Indian Territory to Red River between Hugo and Paris, Texas; the Santa Fe, south from Kansas through the Unassigned Lands in the center of the territory, near modern-day Interstate 35; the Rock Island, south from Kansas to Texas along the Chisholm Trail. Numerous other rail lines ran through sections of the territory.

By the 1880s, armed Indian resistance to American settlement was over. In 1886 even the legendary Apache chief Geronimo had laid down his rifle for good in Arizona—again to the forces of master Indian fighter Nelson Miles. Now he sat imprisoned in Fort Sill, located adjacent to the present-day southwest Oklahoma town of Lawton. The way was cleared for the railroads, the cattlemen, and American settlers.

American Free Enterprise

The railroads knew (Chapter 8) that the Native population alone could never make their immense investment in the area profitable. They wanted U.S. citizens in the territory as much as the latter wanted in. Commercial partners multiplied for the railroads.

Spurred by enterprising mixed bloods and an increasing stream of resourceful white entrepreneurs (some immigrating legally, some illegally) finding ways to establish business undertakings in the area, new mining, lumbering, and petroleum

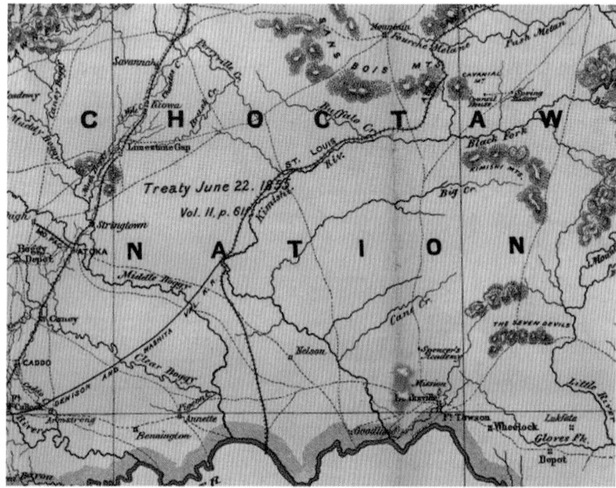

An 1887 map illustrating the freshly laid Frisco Railroad's path across the Choctaw country and Kiamichi Mountains that formed present-day southeastern Oklahoma. The historic advance triggered the Indian Territory logging industry, fostered American immigration to the area, and birthed towns from one end of the line to the other.

endeavors also unfolded in the eastern parts of the territory. They joined the expansive ranching empires of the Chickasaws, Choctaws, and Cherokees. The latter tribe retained possession of whatever portion of the sprawling Cherokee Outlet the government chose not to assign to other tribes or otherwise dispose of. And by 1888, the Cherokees were earning two hundred thousand dollars per year—equating to millions in twenty-first century currency—in leasing fees from white cattlemen from Texas and elsewhere, including Scotland (Matador Land and Cattle Company) and England (Cattle Ranch and Land Company).

The increased cattle prices these ranchers garnered after fattening their herds in the Outlet were helping to spread the cattle industry across the territory. Battling brutal weather, harsh terrain, wild animals, and periodically violent Indians, the cattlemen shrewdly pooled their efforts for common defense and shared resources. Then they proceeded to build some of the greatest cattle empires in American history. The Comanche Pool, for instance, headed up by such men as Charlie Colcord and his father William, encompassed six thousand square miles of range in northern Indian Territory and southern Kansas. The cattlemen served customers as varied as New York City restaurants and the western Indian Territory reservations now hosting thousands of Natives.

Meanwhile, the coal mining industry, though one of the most dangerous on earth, surged forward in eastern Indian Territory. So rich were the deposits around towns such as McAlester, Krebs, Hartshorne, Coalgate, Lehigh, Wilburton, and Adamson that another onslaught of immigrants streamed forth to join the thousands of Americans, Irish, Scottish, English, and Welsh already toiling away.

Comanche Pool cowboys, part of one of the greatest cattle empires in history. The Comanche Pool covered thousands of square miles during the 1880s in southern Kansas and northern present-day Oklahoma.

The new wave hailed from continental Europe, including Italy, Poland, Russia, Germany, Lithuania, Slovakia, Belgium, and France, as well as Mexico. Some African-Americans, mostly descendants of Choctaw and Chickasaw slaves, toiled in the mines, too. By 1894 the U.S. Mine Inspector for Indian Territory reported over three thousand men employed in coal mining, and the number rose steadily from there.

Apparently, the recent consolidation of German and Italian states into forcibly unified empires had not proven ideal for many. The steady increase of German miners, coupled with the influx of Mennonites taking the gospel of Christ in word and deed to the Plains Indians in the west, birthed a significant German community in present-day Oklahoma. According to historian Richard Rohrs, the Germans came for land ownership, economic opportunity, and a reunion with friends and loved ones already there from the old country. By the end of the 1880s, over seven hundred German-born people lived in Indian Territory in addition to their American-born children. By the end of the 1890s, the number of German-born people exceeded five thousand, which did not include those of the increasing company of children born to them in America.

Meanwhile, Italians formed the bulwark of the burgeoning Choctaw country mining industry. They raised up a host of towns in that region in the 1870s and 1880s, including Krebs, Hartshorne, Wilburton, Haileyville, Coalgate, and Stringtown. Soon they impacted the territory not only through mining, but in the operation of restaurants and even breweries.

Immigration—Legal and Otherwise

A major twenty-first century debate concerns the enormous number of illegal immigrants—mostly Hispanics—entering the United States and how to deal with this phenomenon. Few advocates on any

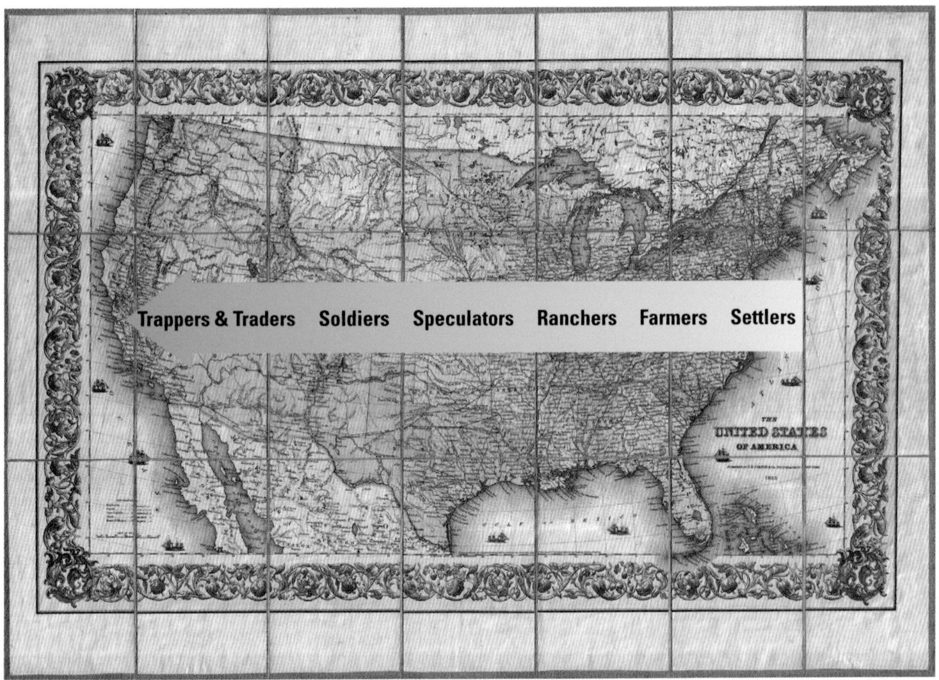

Waves of westward American migration. Courtesy Oklahoma Historical Society Executive Director Bob Blackburn.

side of the conflict realize the major role played by late nineteenth-century illegal immigrants—mostly white—in transforming an underpopulated, non-industrialized, outlaw-laden Indian Territory into the vibrant modern state of Oklahoma.

Until the U.S. government broke up the communally owned tribal lands in the 1890s and 1900s, non-Natives had only three legal avenues (all work-related) for settlement in Indian Territory. These included federal government employment, work as federally licensed traders, or temporary work permits granted by one of the tribal governments. But tens of thousands of whites, along with some blacks, swarmed into the territory illegally in search of work or land or both. In 1886 federal Indian agent Robert L. Owen, a part-Cherokee future U.S. Senator from Oklahoma, left his memorable assessment of this cohort as "intruding cowmen, farming intruders, coal and timber thieves, tramps, vagrants, refugees from justice, professional thieves and whiskey peddlers."

Intruding cowmen, farming intruders, coal and timber thieves, tramps, vagrants, refugees from justice, professional thieves and whiskey peddlers.

—Robert L. Owen

The skeleton crews tasked with immigration enforcement faced innumerable difficulties in dealing with the intruders. Many proved difficult to distinguish from legally sanctioned workers. Others claimed Indian citizenship, either through blood or marriage. Still others moved about, remaining beyond the short and thin arm of the law. Evidence was difficult to collect. Citizenship and other cases could take months or even years to settle, and many were never settled.

As with the modern tidal wave of illegals into America, people invading

Non-Native Indian Territory Population 1889*

Permit system workers (farm and manufacturing workers), their families	45,000
Intruders (criminals, refugees), their families	35,000
Licensed traders, federal employees, railroad & mine workers, their families	25,000
Claimants to tribal citizenship	4,000
Others (prospectors, visitors, etc.)	3,000

* Prior to land runs in western Indian Territory (Gaston Litton, *History of Oklahoma*).

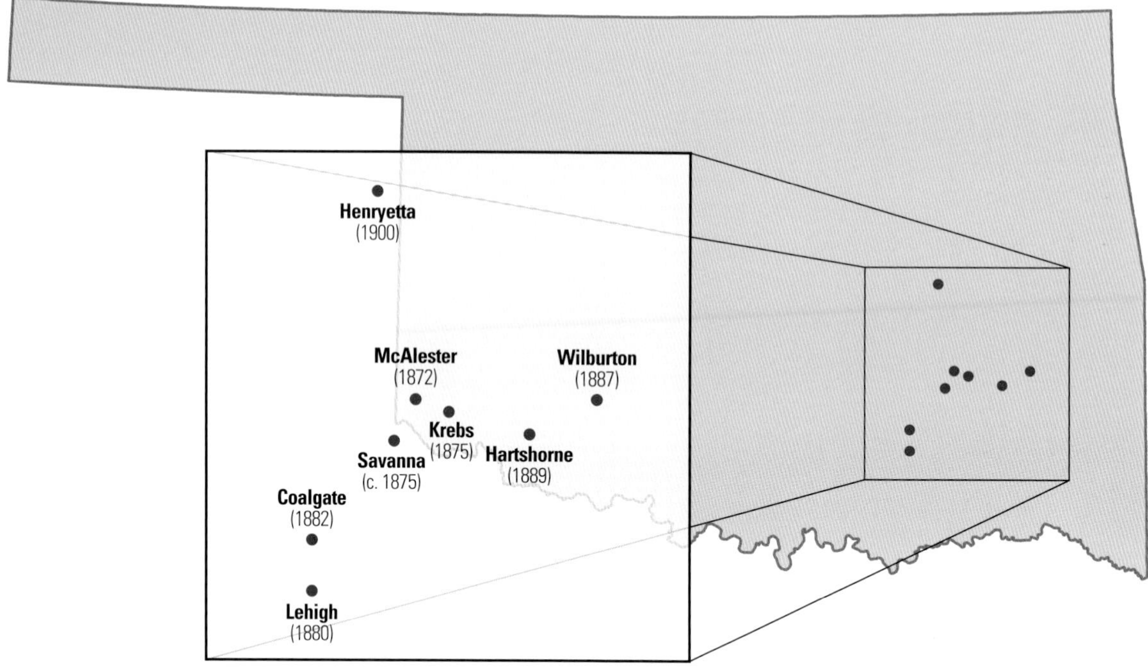

Early southeastern Oklahoma coal towns.

Indian Territory committed many crimes, transformed both the literal and figurative complexion of the society, and helped build that society into something more than it would otherwise have been.

Oil Seepings Spotted

The petroleum products that have catapulted Oklahomans to fame and staggering fortune evidenced themselves long before people assayed not only how to draw them out of the ground, but to then transport them to markets where they could be sold. Back in 1853, Chickasaw agent A. J. Smith declared the presence and early uses of petroleum deposits in southwest Indian Territory:

> The oil springs in this nation are attracting considerable attention, as they are said to be a remedy for all chronic diseases. Rheumatism stands no chance at all, and the worst cases of dropsy yield to its effects. The fact is, that it cures anything that has been tried. A great many Texans visit these springs, and some from Arkansas. They are situated at the foot of the Wichita Mountains on Washita River. There is one or two of great medical properties.

The Natives also lighted their camps and council gatherings with underground gas, by placing a tube or gun barrel into the ground to control it and then lighting it on fire. Then in 1859, still decades before automobiles, airplanes, and other machines revolutionized the uses for petroleum products, longtime Cherokee Principal Chief John Ross's brother Lewis inadvertently drilled the first well in the territory—and one of the first in America. Seeking to enhance his salt mining efforts, he sank a water well into the Grand Saline salt spring in the Grand River in present-day Mayes County. His "strike" tapped a vein of oil and churned out ten barrels a day for a year, but he had no way to transport it to market.

As chronicled by Oklahoma historians Muriel H. Wright in *Chronicles of Oklahoma* and Kenny Franks in the *Encyclopedia of Oklahoma Culture,* the telltale greenish-black slick appeared elsewhere around Indian Territory throughout the second half of the nineteenth century. Reported sightings included north of Tahlequah (New Spring Place), northeast of Ardmore (Boyd Springs), northwest of present-day Caddo in Bryan County, along Sand Creek in present-day Osage County, and present-day Pontotoc County, where a Choctaw businessman used it to grease a machine he owned that was one of the first in the Southwest to mow grass. Jacob Bartles, who founded the future oil center of Bartlesville, spotted it southeast of present-day Vinita when riding past with the Federal Sixth Kansas Cavalry during the War Between the States.

Oil Drilling Begins

In the years following the War Between the States, the federal government—in particular, the Department of the Interior—strove to keep white-owned commercial enterprises from opening up the Indian country. This policy thwarted the 1870s Chickasaw Oil Company, discussed in Chapter 8. The momentum did not begin to shift until 1883, when a determined New York oil promoter named H. W. Faucett parlayed the support of railroad officials and leadership of both the Cherokee and Choctaw tribes into the first determined effort at oil exploration in present-day Oklahoma.

Faucett persuaded the Cherokee and Choctaw leaders to form companies through which they could lease tribal land, which he subleased from them for oil exploration. He labored for years—first gaining, then losing, and then regaining the support of the tribes. He secured production, transportation, and refining rights to all thirteen million acres of tribal land. He raised and spent enormous amounts of money, struggled to deliver the necessary equipment to drilling sites, and lost key New York investors. Indomitable in spirit, however, he pioneered ways to bring in equipment, secured new investors from St. Louis, and rekindled the support of tribal leaders.

Never giving up, he battled all the way to 1888, when he drilled a fourteen-hundred-foot well that struck oil in the Choctaw country alongside Clear Boggy Creek, west of Atoka. In perhaps a fittingly bittersweet epitaph to Faucett's uniquely American story, he died of typhoid fever shortly before the strike.

White cattleman Edward Byrd, married to a Cherokee, remains the other stalwart name in the oil annals of old Oklahoma. In 1886 Byrd tracked some stray cows toward Spencer Creek, near present-day Chelsea in Rogers County. There or nearby, he spotted a shiny green slick atop water. He leased ninety-four thousand acres in the area from the Cherokees and set about forming an oil drilling partnership, which in 1889 drilled four wells by literal horsepower. The first went thirty-six feet deep and none more than a hundred, but all produced a modest amount of oil. Leasing regulations stymied further efforts by Byrd, but they did not keep him from preparing the way for one of the great industries in American history.

First Presbyterian Church of Beaver, the first church built (1887) in what became Oklahoma Territory. Courtesy Oklahoma Historical Society.

Booming Oklahoma

David Payne proved not nearly so simple for the federal government to get rid of as Charles Carpenter (Chapter 8). Tall, strikingly handsome, brimming with restless energy, able to fire up crowds tiny or large, impossible to intimidate, and according to some Oklahoma historians a "moral reprobate," he did not even arrive on the scene until after Carpenter's demise. Yet he had hundreds of eager pioneers lined up to "boom" the Oklahoma lands before the next year (1880) ended.

For years Payne led at least two wagon trains of settlers per year south from Kansas into Indian

David Payne and the Boomers (1836–1884)

Throughout the 1880s, public pressure to open Indian Territory—gradually gaining recognition as the "Oklahoma" country—spawned an increasingly robust private sector movement to make that happen. Elias C. Boudinot, son of the murdered newspaper publisher and Treaty Party leader, and nephew of Stand Watie, led the initial charge. He wrote influential newspaper editorials in the *Chicago Times* and elsewhere that caused American public interest in the area to skyrocket.

David Payne, adventurer, entrepreneur, soldier, visionary, Boomer, and enigmatic "Father of Oklahoma." Courtesy Oklahoma Historical Society.

Territory. Every time, bluecoated soldiers, enforcing the will of a well-intentioned but increasingly ambivalent government, removed them. The Army threatened, arrested, jail, fined, and physically roughed up Payne, and destroyed his property. But millions of immigrants continued to pour into America from Europe, swelling Northeast and upper Midwest cities. Millions of native and immigrant Americans wanted their own land. Boudinot's writings, famous throughout the nation and beyond, fueled these desires.

The name "Oklahoma" became a byword for the final frontier of America. And Payne's colorful and charismatic creativity depicted the territory for the colossal audience whose attention Boudinot had helped gain as not just that, but as a verdant Garden of Eden too. Not only did the multiplying ranks of would-be pioneers seek the opening of at least the Unassigned Lands and Greer County—if not the Cherokee Outlet and some of the western Indian Territory reservations—so too did the railroads, merchants in neighboring states, and wholesale organizations farther north and east who sold to those merchants.

Ranged against this unusual alliance was an even stranger one. It included the resident Indians, who knew the white race well enough to suspect that even if they settled only the Unassigned Lands today, they would soon own the rest of the territory; white cattlemen who did not want their sprawling ranges—whether fenced or open—chopped up by farms and towns; a gaggle of federal bureaucrats, contractors, and suppliers, as well as illicit whiskey peddlers, all of whom feared losing revenue or influence or both from lost tribal sovereignty; and white church leaders, missionaries, and other humanitarians disgusted with the long train of broken promises dealt the reeling Natives by forked white tongues.

Celebrated photographer C. P. Wickmiller, who founded present-day Oklahoma's first drugstore in Kingfisher, photographed David Payne (center left in hat and mustache) and a Boomer contingent in "Stopping to Cross Deep Fork," (of the North Canadian River) in an 1883 incursion. Courtesy Research Division, Oklahoma Historical Society.

Fort Reno soldiers secure arrested Boomers with ropes. Note the racial diversity evidenced in early Oklahoma. Both white and Indian soldiers corral white, Hispanic, and African-American Boomers. Courtesy Research Division, Oklahoma Historical Society.

The battle waxed fierce for years. By the summer of 1885, the Boomer cause appeared doomed. The iconic Payne had dropped dead of a heart attack while breakfasting with his common-law wife. The leaders who succeeded him faced charges of treason. Scores of would-be pioneers left the Oklahoma country for home. But now the balances of the world turned upon the irresistible weight of Manifest Destiny toward opening the lands.

Only two months after Payne's stunning death, Secretary of Interior Henry M. Teller, besieged by mounting pressure from every conceivable quarter, declared his support for opening the lands. Then the U.S. cavalry began running out the cattlemen whose ranges swept across the Cheyenne and Arapaho reservations. President Grover Cleveland cancelled the government's contracts for them to supply beef. The government, undoubtedly influenced by the gargantuan economic and political power of the railroads, had changed course. As if to put a providential exclamation point on the destruction of the opposition, one of the worst winters in history then decimated the cattle kingdoms in northwest Indian Territory.

Soon, Creek leader Pleasant Porter and his tribe, from whom land use rights to most of the Unassigned Lands had been purloined, shrewdly divined the

Cowboy Talk

All hands and the cook: A cattle-range phrase meaning everybody—the whole outfit, including the ornery cook.

Arbuckle: A generic term for coffee, from a trade-name brand common at that time.

Balling up: Referred to bunching up of cattle at a river crossing or entrance to a corral.

Bean-master: The cook (also known as belly cheater, biscuit-shooter, grub spoiler, hasher).

—Mike Adkins, from his teachers' guide for the Oklahoma Historical Society education trunk for teachers entitled "The Long Drive."

Cook's Office, Xiang Zhang's portrait of perhaps the most revered spot on the trail. (www.xiangzhangart.com)

Natives such as these Caddos and Kickapoos comprised around 10 percent of all cowboys in late-1800s Indian Territory, and African-Americans accounted for 20 percent. Courtesy Western History Collections, University of Oklahoma Libraries.

> *I knew the wild riders and the vacant land were about to vanish forever... and the more I considered the subject, the bigger the forever loomed. Without knowing how to do it, I began to record some facts around me, and the more I looked the more the panorama unfolded. Art is a she-devil of a mistress, and if at times in earlier days she would not even stoop to my way of thinking, I have persevered and will so continue.*
>
> **—Frederic Remington**

inevitable and decided that they might best sell for top dollar while they could. As financial negotiations with the Creeks and Seminoles proceeded, the cattlemen and ranchers stalled the inevitable. The Bureau of Indian Affairs commissioner urged settlement of the Chickasaws' black freedmen, who had never been accepted into the tribe, on the Unassigned Lands. His plea was rejected. But by the end of the decade, whites and some African-Americans would raise a new society from the Oklahoma lands.

Cowboy Clothing

The typical cowboy of that era wore heavy woolen trousers; a woolen shirt whose sleeves were held up by sleeve garters; a large hat that protected him from rain, snow, and hot sun; a neckerchief knotted around his neck to be pulled up to cover his nose in wintry cold or blowing dust; and boots that fitted well into stirrups. Only in winter did the cowboy don a coat, for it tended to bind his arms and hold in the heat. Instead he wore a vest in which he kept his watch, his tobacco, and any coins he might possess. He took great care in selecting the gloves he wore year-round, which usually were of buckskin. His boots were a source of great pride, although he tended to be awkward in them when not on horseback. Finally, he wore chaps made of heavy leather and fitting as a second pair of trousers, to protect his legs from thorns. Somehow chaps became a symbol of the trade to newcomers, who wanted to "look like cowboys."

—Odie Faulk and William Welge
Oklahoma, a Rich Heritage

Mennonites—The Quiet of the Land Speak Loudly

Mennonite leader Daniel Krehbiel evidenced that no amount of terror, bloodshed, hatred, and loss in the War Between the States could staunch the valiant Christian outreach to the Natives of Indian Territory: "My heart is so full of joy it can find no adequate words to express the innermost feelings. As a river hurls itself against an unbreakable dam, so my emotions in vain seek to express themselves in words. Yes, the everlasting true and all-governing God and Father has at last brought it to pass that the banner of the Cross shall also be erected by Mennonites among the Indians."

From 1880—nearly three decades before statehood—Mennonite Christians, themselves driven out by persecution from Germany, Switzerland, Holland, and Russia, pioneered mission efforts among the Plains Indian tribes in present-day western Oklahoma. Mennonites built this church in 1894 at the Canadian County town of El Reno. It was added to the National Register of Historic Places in 1979.

The Indian System of Land Ownership

Clara Nash and Erma L. Taylor depicted in their history of Bryan County the system of land use and ownership practiced by the agrarian Indian republics of eastern Indian Territory. The Choctaw system closely resembled those of the Cherokees, Chickasaws, Creeks, and Seminoles.

> *The Choctaw domain was held in common. Any citizen of the nation had the right to make his home anywhere in the country. He could fence the surrounding land for fields and pastures, "as long as it was no closer than 'a hog-call' (about 1/4 mile)." They could not trespass on the already-fenced lands of another Choctaw. Any citizen could sell his improvements such as houses, barns, and fences, but could not sell the land. If he abandoned the farm for a period fixed by law, usually three years, it reverted to public domain. They paid no land taxes since they didn't own the land, so other sources of revenue for their government had to be found. None of them were very successful.*

Hardy German Mennonite immigrants, persecuted in Europe and then Russia for their devout, pacifist ways, bequeathed present-day Oklahoma and the Southern Great Plains region one of its greatest gifts in the 1870s and '80s with the Turkey Red wheat strain. Tough and winter-resistant, Turkey Red proved capable of producing flour for bread. It helped modern Oklahoma climb to the coveted status of second-most productive American state for winter wheat and fourth for all wheat.

Dawes Act

The beginning of the end of Native rule over the lands given to them a half-century previously—"for as long as the grass shall grow and the rivers flow"—occurred when Congress passed the Dawes Severalty Allotment Act in 1887. This historic blow to tribal sovereignty eliminated the reservations in western Indian Territory—and the Plains' and other tribes' control over them, such as it still was. Though Dawes did not immediately encompass the five Indian republics in eastern Indian Territory, the die was cast, and within a few

Dawes Commission officials working near Okmulgee in the 1880s to enroll Creeks so that they could receive individual land allotments as the U.S. prepared to break up the tribal lands. Courtesy Oklahoma Historical Society.

years their tribal land ownership and control would cease as well.

Many factors combined to spawn the Dawes Act and the accelerated stripping of Indian sovereignty. Most American civic and political leaders, including well-intentioned reformers seeking the Natives' welfare, viewed their brightest future as one wherein they embraced the individual land ownership practices of Western civilization, which would supposedly cement nuclear family relations and produce economic co-dependency.

U.S. Senator Henry L. Dawes of Massachusetts spearheaded a group of Eastern humanitarians who began meeting in 1883 to assess and offer wisdom regarding "the Indian problem." Illustrating the perils of American do-goodism based more on zeal than knowledge, Dawes remarkably sided against the Indians he sought to help when describing to his fellow Easterners a visit to Indian Territory:

> The head (probably Cherokee) chief told us that there was not a family in that whole nation that had not a home of its own. There was not a pauper in that nation, and the nation did not owe a dollar. It built its own capitol . . . its schools and its hospitals. . . . Yet . . . they have got as far as they can go, because they own their land in common . . . there is no enterprise to make your home any better than that of your neighbors. There is no selfishness, which is at the bottom of civilization.

> *There is no selfishness, which is at the bottom of civilization.*
>
> **—Massachusetts Senator Henry L. Dawes, about Oklahoma Indians**

As famed Oklahoma historian Angie Debo recorded in *And Still the Waters Run*, her landmark exposé of U.S. dealings with the state's Indian tribes, Dawes and his comrades "based their opposition purely upon theoretical belief in the sanctity of private ownership rather than upon any understanding of the Indian nature or any investigation of actual conditions." As time and the Natives' loss of their individual lands would prove, they perhaps also lacked understanding of their fellow whites' nature.

Non-Native Settlers

Tens of thousands of white and African-American eastern Indian Territory settlers harbored their own motives for Indian allotment by the end of the 1880s. The production they generated from the land and its resources surpassed anything ever before witnessed in the region. Their multiplying population put into play vast stretches of territory whose surfaces had never before been scratched.

Some of these settlers, mostly those who possessed either partial Native blood or an Indian spouse—or both—capitalized on the white American's flair for enterprise and diligence by turning it into a business or property bonanza. Many others immigrated to Indian Territory and contracted with tribal members to clear, cultivate, and work their land for them. Some did so for a few years, and then they contributed the land's improvements, including structures, to the owner and established similar situations elsewhere. Others continued working the land as long-term tenants, or renters. Still others continued working it as sharecroppers, paying the owner 20 to 35 percent of the crop or the proceeds from it. Many of these arrangements and others like them survived for decades, finding dramatic resolution in the Great Depression and Oklahoma farm crises of the 1930s and 1940s.

Yet not only did these non-Native immigrants possess no access to the region's tribal schools for their own children, they could not own land either—even that which they worked, improved, and made profitable. Nor did they have fire, police, sanitation, electrical or other services that were commonplace in other American communities, even though they paid taxes to the Indian governments. Also, they could be expelled by their host tribe for reasons good or bad.

Unlike other Americans, the non-Natives had little protection from the hordes of violent, gun-blazing criminals—red, white, and black alike—who threatened to forge the territory into a vast outlaws' refuge smack in the middle of the now continent-wide nation. In fact, the Indians struggled to protect their own people from these renegades. Author Debo pointed out an additional factor that gradually intensified the desire of both African-American and white settlers for the overthrow of Native rule in Indian Territory:

> Less spectacular than the frequent commission of serious crimes, but more annoying to the hundred thousand white residents of the Indian Territory was the complete absence of civil law. There was no way of enforcing the payment of debts, and people who had a dispute over property had no recourse except to "shoot it out," or to refer it to the arbitration of the Indian Agent.

Business Building Oklahoma—Hitch Enterprises

James K. Hitch

In 1884, bold and enterprising Tennessee native James K. Hitch launched the beginnings of a ranching and agriculture empire in No Man's Land, the present-day Oklahoma panhandle, that still survives. Hitch outlasted high winds, bitter cold, scalding heat, failed crops, piteous droughts in an already dry land, violent Old West outlaws in a country without laws, the exodus of more than two-thirds of the region's settlers, and the death of his wife, who had spurred the birth of the area's first church.

He did it all on a frontier so dangerous it was also called the Cimarron Country, Spanish for wild and unruly. Then his son Henry, grandsons Ladd and Paul, great-grandsons Jason and Chris, and other family members carried forth the Hitch legacy, building today's three-state cattle and pork producing, agricultural, feedlot, and meat packing dynamo.

Allen Allensworth escaped from slavery and joined the Federal army during the War Between the States. He served as a nursing assistant and then joined the U.S. Navy. Following the war, parlaying the reading and writing skills he learned from white owners as a boy, he attended a theological seminary. After gaining ordination as a minister, he served as a Republican National Convention delegate. In 1886 he secured an appointment as a military chaplain to the Buffalo Soldiers regiment at Fort Supply in Indian Territory. Convinced that a basic education would enhance black soldier performance, Allensworth taught them U.S. history and English along with the Bible. He later crafted a curriculum and teaching practices booklet for African-American servicemen. He retired from the Army in 1906, the first lieutenant colonel of his race in the U.S. Army. He subsequently founded the all-black town of Allensworth, California.

The Marlow Brothers and The Sons of Katie Elder

The five hard-riding Marlow boys of old Indian Territory could scarcely have dreamed their exploits would lead to a namesake Stephens County town, help blaze the dramatic Old West legacy of Oklahoma, and inspire a popular John Wayne film nearly a century later, a hit Johnny Cash song, and even a modern Australian rock music group. But they did.

The Marlow boys, circa 1887: George, Boone, Alfred, Llewellyn, Charles. Courtesy Robert K. DeArment.

Two of the five Marlow brothers, Charles and George. Courtesy Robert K. DeArment.

The U.S. government partially addressed the innumerable complaints over this situation in 1889 by finally establishing an Indian Territory federal court in Muskogee. Designed for Natives and non-Natives alike, this court handled cases other than serious crimes punishable by death or hard labor imprisonment. Two more federal courts, desperately needed especially in light of the exploding white population, would follow the next year.

Did the Indians have a right to retain their Indian Territory lands in communal ownership and rule, especially since they were already forcibly moved there by the American government and people with promises of perpetual sovereignty? Yes. Did the more than one hundred thousand white and black Americans living there by 1890, most at the behest of the U.S. government, American business, or the Natives themselves, have a right to expect protection, services, and political representation by others, even though the Indians had not deceived them about the absence of these? Yes. Thus does the complex drama that forms the history of Oklahoma often defy simple analysis.

Run of '89

In 1889, the federal government designated slightly more than the western half of Indian Territory—including "No Man's Land" or the Panhandle—as a separate territory, the Oklahoma Territory. The latter contained the Plains and other Indian reservations, but possessed far sparser settlement—black,

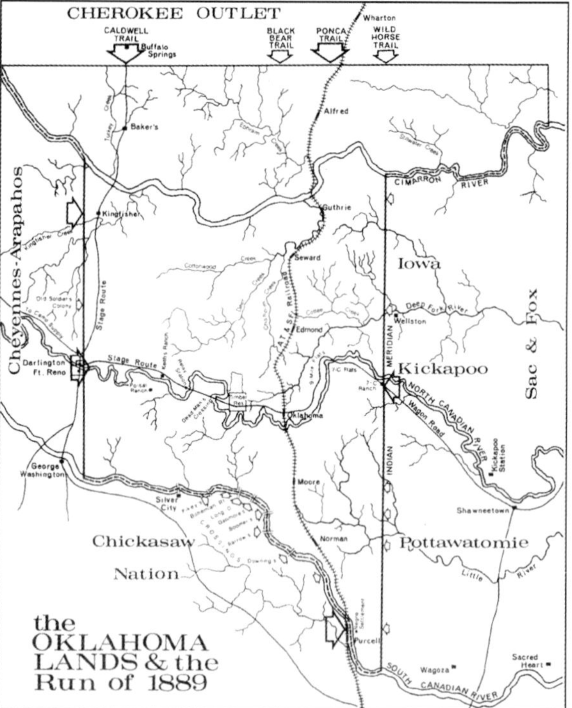

The Unassigned Lands Run of 1889, the first opening of free federal land in Oklahoma Territory, which comprised roughly the western half of the original Indian Territory. Around fifty thousand people raced for property in six present-day Oklahoma counties. It encompassed Oklahoma City and Norman, the first- and third-largest cities in the twenty-first century state.

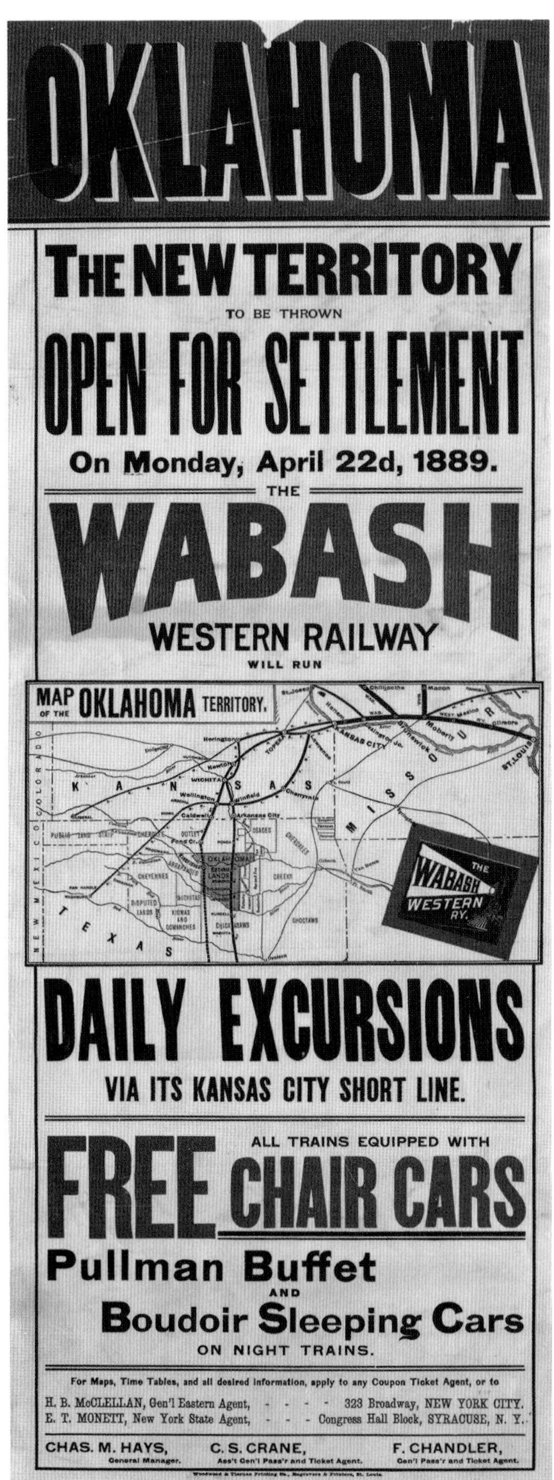

A poster that helped draw tens of thousands of pioneers to the 1889 "Oklahoma Lands" run. Courtesy Research Division, Oklahoma Historical Society.

Boomers fill Purcell, Indian Territory, in present-day McClain County, just south of the country opened for settlement in the Unassigned Lands Run of 1889. Purcell was a major portal for Texans and other Southerners. Photograph by William S. Prettyman. Courtesy Dickinson Research Center, National Cowboy & Western Heritage Museum, Oklahoma City, Oklahoma.

white, and Native alike—even than its neighbor to the east, and had no such advanced constitutional law as did the five Indian republics. In the span of a few decades, American civilization had swarmed across the continent, claiming virtually all other arable land between the Atlantic and Pacific oceans. The Oklahoma country had become the final American frontier, the last chapter of the settling of the West.

> *The Oklahoma country had become the final American frontier, the last chapter of the settling of the West.*

On April 22, 1889, in the first of a series of such acts over the next several years, Congress opened a chunk of Oklahoma Territory, which was wrested in 1866 from the Creeks and Seminoles, to settlement, while continuing strict regulation of Indian land in Indian Territory. The nation's legislative branch accomplished this through the Springer Amendment to the Indian Appropriations Act, sponsored by Illinois Representative William Springer. President Benjamin Harrison signed a proclamation setting the date and other details.

This singularly American event gained lasting renown through the method of its implementation.

A Boomer family on the Kansas–Oklahoma border east of Arkansas City preparing for the 1889 Unassigned Lands Run. Courtesy Oklahoma Historical Society.

No photograph exists during the 1889 Unassigned Lands Run, but this shot captured a vast host of wagons and horsemen arrayed south of Buffalo Springs, minutes before U.S. troopers launched the run. Courtesy Oklahoma Historical Society.

The Spirit of '89, G. N. Taylor's paean to the pioneer woman. The dauntless settler packs a six-gun, cartridge-loaded belt, rifle in her scabbard, and claim flag—and a horse with a loose girth. (www.gntayloroklaart.com)

The federal government split the two million acres into hundred and sixty-acre tracts. Word was shouted through the Western world that at noon on the 22nd of April, anyone with the guts and wherewithal to do so could rush into the Unassigned Lands in the center of present-day Oklahoma and claim their own spread—upon the sound of a shotgun fired by a U.S. cavalryman.

Fifty thousand people—including nearly a thousand African-Americans—from every state in the Union descended on the area to do just that. When the shotgun sounded, they thundered across the line on horseback, mule, bicycle, and foot; in wagons; and even inside, outside, and on top of trains churning in from Texas and Kansas. Some got land, while others didn't. There were fistfights, shootouts, and court battles. Many sneaked in early and claimed some of the best hundred and sixty-acre tracts and town lots. These energetic folks earned the label "Sooners."

By sundown on April 22, however, the entire country was settled, including the present-day towns of Oklahoma City, Norman, Stillwater, Kingfisher, and Guthrie, the latter designated as the territorial capital. And Elias C. Boudinot, David Payne, Charles Carpenter, and many others won supreme vindication.

Pioneers, Populists, Progressives

Something else loomed on the horizon of Oklahoma—and U.S.—history. A welter of influences swirled, soon to coalesce into the first of two pivotal movements (one on the heels of the other), which would permanently change the social, economic, political, and even religious fabric of the American republic. The 1890s would bring Populism and the next decade Progressivism.

> *"Unlike Rome, the city of Guthrie was built in a day. To be strictly accurate in the matter, it might be said that it was built in an afternoon. At twelve o'clock on Monday, April 22d [sic], the resident population of Guthrie was nothing; before sundown it was at least ten thousand. In that time streets had been laid out, town lots staked off, and steps taken toward the formation of a municipal government."*
>
> ***—Harper's Weekly***

Legendary University of Oklahoma history professor Edward Everett Dale (1879–1972), commonly acknowledged as the dean of the state's historians. Dale himself pioneered "Old Greer County" in the shortgrass country of future southwest Oklahoma with his family as a teenager. He rose from a cowboy on that remote prairie to a school teacher to a Harvard-educated historian, and longtime OU history chair. He mentored fellow Oklahoma historian Angie Debo and wrote a gaggle of classic Oklahoma history books, including *The Range Cattle Industry, Cow Country,* and *Frontier Ways.* Courtesy Western History Collections, University of Oklahoma Libraries, Dale 1.

Peter Pearson and a Dr. Aker, Kansas friends of William S. Prettyman, hold their town lots as Guthrie town fathers on April 22, 1889 in Prettyman's photograph. Courtesy Dickinson Research Center, National Cowboy & Western Heritage Museum, Oklahoma City, Oklahoma.

These movements would continue and expand the watershed innovations brought to the Republic by Abraham Lincoln, the War Between the States, the Radical Republicans, and Reconstruction.

> *It was the pioneer settlers who won the West when the wooing was difficult and sometimes dangerous, and most of them now sleep in its soil.*
>
> **—Edward Everett Dale**

Lest we forget, however, that people—men, women, and children—of many and varied ideologies and philosophies birthed Oklahoma and made it what it is today, perhaps it is appropriate to end this chapter as we began it, with the sage words of historian Edward Everett Dale:

Run of '89—Remembrances of Those Who Ran

We got in line ready to make the run when the signal was given. Then, real excitement began—everybody yelling, horses' hoofs clattering, all in a hurry. Mother applied the whip and the horses started running. She didn't try to guide them until we came to land on which very few people could be seen. She stopped the horses, jumped out of the wagon and stuck up her stakes. (This claim was one mile east of Crescent.) Mother then looked over her claim for a likely place to pitch our tent. She found a wide rocky canyon and a good spring of water.

—Mrs. Welling Haynes, daughter of a widowed, sharecropping Kansas mother and "'89er"

. . . the pioneers who came to the West (sought) for that most precious of all human material possessions, a home. Largely speaking, this home seeker is the forgotten man in the annals of the American West . . . Yet he was by far the most important factor in the conquest and development of our American empire.

His way of life has vanished and is largely forgotten by all but a comparatively few people. It is, however, a part of our social history and as such should be preserved and cherished. It was the pioneer settlers who won the West when the wooing was difficult and sometimes dangerous, and most of them now sleep in its soil.

We have been broken up and moved six times. We have been despoiled of our property. We thought when we moved across the Missouri River, and had paid for our homes in Kansas we were safe. But in a few years the white man wanted our country. We had made good farms, built comfortable houses and big barns. We had schools for our children and churches where we listened to the same Gospel the white man listened to. We had a great many cattle and horses. The white man came into our country from Missouri and drove our cattle and horses away across the river. If our people followed them they got killed. We try to forget these things, but we would not forget that the white man brought us the blessed Gospel of Christ, the Christian's hope. This more than pays for all we have suffered.

—Charles Journeycake,
Principal Chief of the Delawares,
Baptist pastor in Oklahoma who
preached in five different languages

The legendary Frank "Pistol Pete" Eaton, inspiration for the longtime mascot of the Oklahoma State University Cowboys. Long before that, Eaton played a mean fiddle, carried Pony Express mail through rain, hail, sleet, snow, and the pitch dark of night from Ponca City to Kansas, and helped clear outlaws from the Twin Territories as a U.S. marshal for Isaac "The Hangin' Judge" Parker. He chased Apache Chief Geronimo, too, and later befriended him. A ninety-six-year-old Eaton, still sporting a Colt .45 pistol on his hip, a nimble gait, and long, braided hair and cowboy hat, told an *Oklahoma Today* magazine reporter shortly before his death in the 1950s that Geronimo was "a gentleman" who "fought for his people" and "loved the Plains." When asked by a reporter what he thought of Oklahoma, he responded, "What would you think of a land that had been your home for ninety-two years?" Courtesy Oklahoma State Senate Historical Preservation Fund, Inc. and Harold Holden.

'Twere a boon just to be a lone pioneer
With courage rare and strong
To go out and over the farthest frontier
Away from conventional wrong,
And to fall in the quest of a fine, larger truth,
Then to sleep and dream of that song.

—J. L. Hefley, from *The Pioneer*

Downtown Oklahoma City, looking west on California Street, May 2, 1889, ten days after the Run of '89. Courtesy Oklahoma Historical Society.

This poster promoted one of Gordon "Pawnee Bill" Lillie's famed Wild West shows. A human whirlwind of talent and giftedness, Lillie worked as a trapper, teacher to the Pawnees with whom he had a lifelong relationship, and interpreter at their Indian agency. He also carved out fortunes in oil, real estate, and banking. His captaining of the Boomer movement in the 1889 Land Run and his leadership of four thousand settlers into present-day Kingfisher County garnered him national acclaim, which led to his forming the greatest of all Wild West shows with William F. "Buffalo Bill" Cody. He championed automobiles and modern highways in Oklahoma, yet was also the foremost defender of the American bison, the best exemplar in his opinion of Oklahoma and the American West. He built his own herd on his Pawnee ranch, lobbied Congress to protect the animal, and paved the way for the Wichita Mountains National Wildlife Refuge, where thousands of buffalo now live in safety. Courtesy Oklahoma Historical Society.

Oklahoma City

From the high-noon carbine shot that unleashed "President Harrison's Hoss Race on April 22, 1889" till that midnight, more than twelve thousand pioneers poured into a prairie railroad station sporting less than ten structures near the dry banks of the North Canadian River. They came on foot, mounted, in wagons, on trains, even pedaling bicycles. They founded a lusty (Chapter 12), rough-hewn cow town that promoted a distinctive blend of Southern, Western, and Midwestern culture. Oklahoma City did not begin, nor would it ever be like any other city.

A great American city rises from the open prairie in Wayne Cooper's *Oklahoma City—April 29, 1889, Seven Days After the Land Run of 1889.* Courtesy Oklahoma State Senate Historical Preservation Fund, Inc. and Wayne Cooper.

The first school in Guthrie, capital of Oklahoma Territory, seven weeks after the 1889 Unassigned Lands Run. Courtesy Dickinson Research Center, National Cowboy & Western Heritage Museum, Oklahoma City, Oklahoma.

"Where the antelopes sported in the morning an election for city officers was held in the evening and 10,000 ballots cast." Trumpeting the newly birthed town of Oklahoma City's first Fourth of July celebration in 1889, this poster emerged from the Century Chest buried in the First Lutheran Church of Oklahoma City in 1913 and opened a century to the day later. Reflecting the spirited Western character of the pioneer community, the festival's itinerary included "horse racing, feats of horsemanship, sack racing, Indian war dances, infantry drills, a baseball game, and a gun tournament."

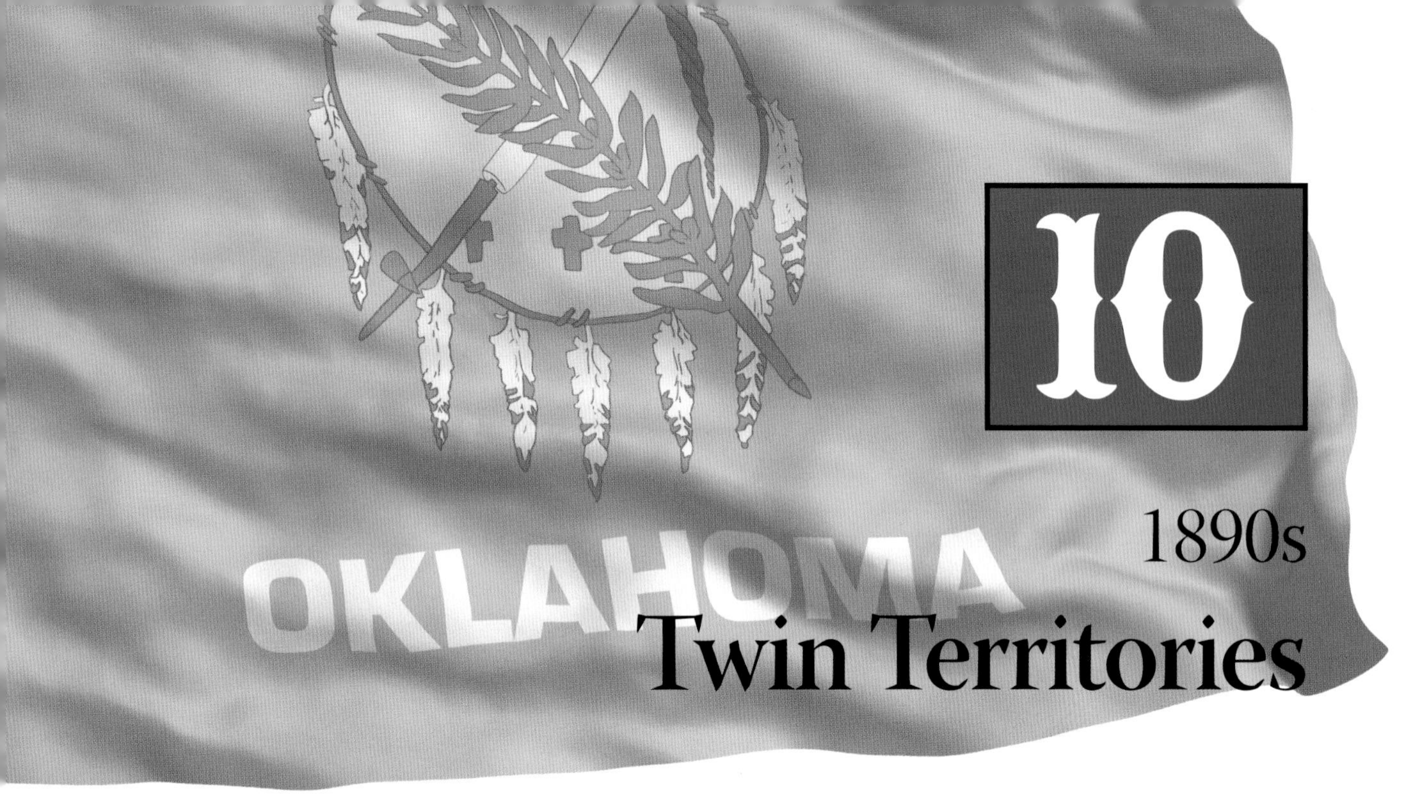

10

1890s
Twin Territories

Dugout Soddy on the Prairie, by Wayne Cooper, depicts homesteading life in a post-land runs western Oklahoma largely devoid of timber and other standard home building components. The earthen structure is partially built into the ground for support against high winds and other elements, as well as insulation against summer heat and winter cold. It rests alongside a water source. Mama feeds chickens, Papa plows, Grandpa saws, and the daughter plays with her dolls as befits a traditional American family scene. Courtesy Oklahoma State Senate Historical Preservation Fund, Inc. and Wayne Cooper.

1890	Organic Act divides Indian Territory in two
1890	First three colleges founded
1891	Lead and zinc industries launched
1891	Absentee Shawnee-Sac and Fox-Potawatomi-Iowa land run
1892	Osage Coal and Mining Company disaster
1892	Cheyenne-Arapaho land run
1893	Financial Panic of '93 spurs Populist movement
1893	Congress establishes Dawes Commission
1893	Cherokee Outlet land run
1895	Kickapoo land run
1897	Nellie Johnstone No. 1 Oil Strike
1897	Langston College founded for African-Americans
1898	Curtis Act

> *There's never been anything like it since Creation. Creation! That took six days. This was done in one. It was History made in an hour—and I helped make it.*
>
> **—Yancey Cravat, in Edna Ferber's *Cimarron***

The Run of '89 was the beginning, not the end, of settling the vast, sweeping prairies and plains of western and northern Indian Territory with American citizens. But the territory did prove to be the final chapter of large-scale land settlement in the United States. The government declared the American frontier effectively closed in the 1890 national census. As has often happened in the nation's history, though, Oklahoma was overlooked, because the frontier was not yet shut here.

Recognition of these facts, coupled with the electrifying excitement generated over the Oklahoma country by Boudinot, Payne, and other Boomers, along with whatever distinctions perhaps animated the American pioneer ("Frederick Jackson Turner and the Frontier," p. 218), raised the stakes in the game and multiplied the hosts of settlers converging from every direction, every state, and many foreign countries.

The Organic Act

In 1890 Congress passed the Oklahoma Organic Act, which legally divided Indian Territory in two—the Twin Territories. Oklahoma Territory now comprised roughly the western half of Indian Territory, that portion to the west of the five Indian republics' lands and the smaller tribal enclaves to the northeast. In response to the settlers' petition, the Organic Act also established a republican form of representative government for Oklahoma Territory, complete with legislative, executive, and judicial branches. The act called for Republican President Benjamin Harrison to appoint a territorial governor, judges, and other officials, and for the people to elect a territorial legislature.

Farther west, the Organic Act also folded the rough-and-tumble Panhandle (then variously called

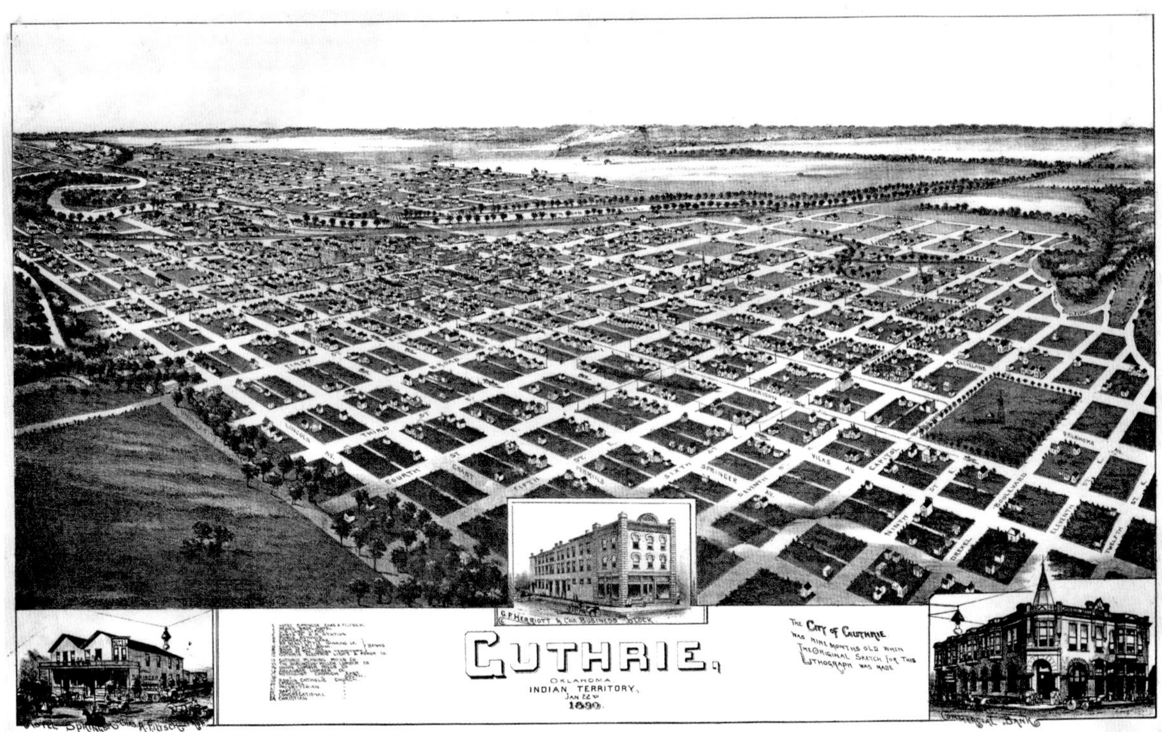

Guthrie, bustling new capital of Oklahoma Territory, the year after its land run founding.. Courtesy Oklahoma Historical Society.

No-Man's Land, the Public Land Strip, the Cimarron Country, or Robber's Roost), into Oklahoma Territory. A haven for outlaws and fugitives until cowboys, cattlemen, and settlers cleared them out, its law-abiding citizens had applied unsuccessfully for territorial status as the Cimarron Territory. Now the government opened it for settlement under the provisions of the 1862 Homestead Act.

Greer County (comprised by present-day Beckham, Greer, Harmon, and Jackson counties), formed the extreme southwest portion of Oklahoma Territory. Now known as Old Greer County, Texas and the United States had contended for ownership of its one and a half million acres since the 1819 Adams-Onis Treaty (Chapter 2) was negotiated, and its official status lay in doubt. Texas ranchers and pioneers had already settled much of it, many of them receiving 640-acre land certificates for serving in the Texas Revolutionary Army and/or the Confederate Army. The Organic Act, however, ordered the U.S. Attorney General to file suit with the U.S. Supreme Court to settle once and for all the area's ownership. The case would take half a decade to decide.

Present-day Oklahoma's longtime distrust of and displeasure with the distant national government at Washington, D.C., roared to life when settlers caught wind of Ohio and Indiana native Harrison's selection of high territorial officials. Harrison's Republican Party stood at the time synonymous with the more liberal Northern political party, as opposed to the largely Southern, more

The Organic Act and Oklahoma Territory

- Presidentially appointed territorial governor
- Bicameral territorial legislature elected by citizens
- Presidentially appointed territorial judges
- Two sections in each township reserved for public education efforts
- $50,000 toward temporary public school system
- Temporary capital at Guthrie

In 1890 the first Legislative Assembly of Oklahoma Territory green-lighted three territorial colleges. They included Territorial Normal College in Edmond, now the University of Central Oklahoma, top, and the Agricultural and Mechanical College of Oklahoma Territory in Stillwater, now Oklahoma State University, bottom. OSU's renowned Old Central building, pictured, opened for classes on the northern Oklahoma prairie in 1894 and has served the school ever since. UCO, meanwhile, was the first institution of higher education ever to hold classes in Oklahoma Territory, beginning in 1891. Two years later, Old North Tower, pictured, started hosting classes that trained Oklahoma teachers, including the assembly seated on the lawn fronting it. During the same era, numerous privately supported Christian institutions began, including Bacone College, as well as the forerunners of Oklahoma Baptist University, Oklahoma City University, Phillips University, Southern Nazarene University, and Tulsa University. Courtesy Oklahoma Historical Society.

Frederick Jackson Turner and the Frontier

The famed historian Frederick Jackson Turner, whose legion of disciples included Edward Everett Dale and other Oklahomans, crafted in his lengthy essay "The Significance of the Frontier in American History" at this time an enduring theory of American Exceptionalism. This is the notion that the American people and country are not merely different from others as Germany, for instance, is from Brazil, but singularly and qualitatively set apart from all others.

conservative Democrats. Only two of Harrison's seven appointees even lived in the Twin Territories. Of the remaining five, only one hailed from the South. As these and other men from distant regions came and then left at the end of their terms or never came at all, frustration and fury against them mounted among non-Northern Republican Oklahomans. The same pejorative attached itself to them that had labeled similar opportunists who flooded the South during Reconstruction—*carpetbaggers*.

Other Land Runs

Through the 1890s whole new towns bustling with thousands of people rose up overnight from the Oklahoma prairie in a series of epic land runs, lotteries, auctions, and even a U.S. Supreme Court battle with Texas. In each case, the federal government apportioned members of the tribe who owned the land to be allotted their own quarter-section

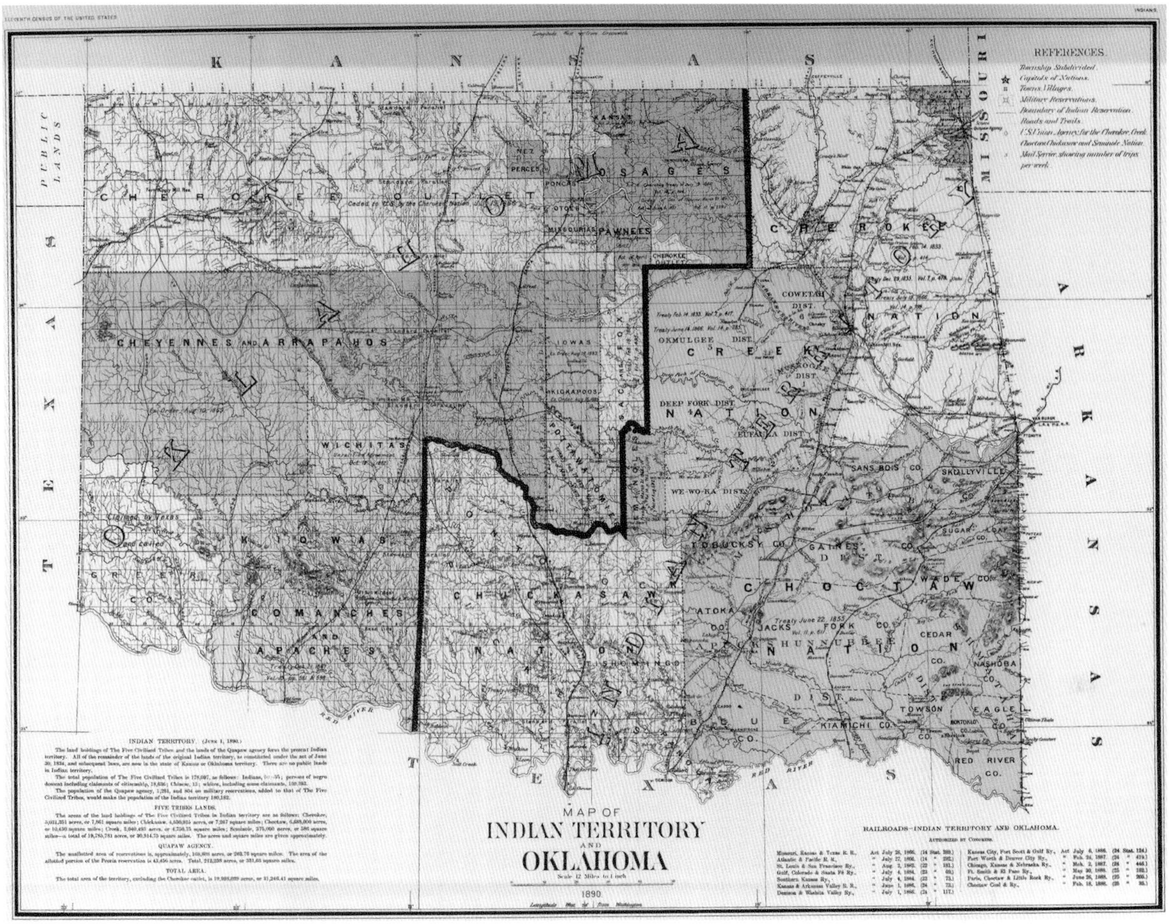

The "Twin Territories" of the 1890 Oklahoma Country, produced by the Organic Act of Congress, carving Oklahoma Territory from the western portion of Indian Territory and opening it to American settlement. Courtesy Oklahoma Historical Society.

(160-acre) land parcel. Settlers received the remaining (surplus) lands.

After the epochal Run of '89 that settled the Unassigned Lands in the center of old Indian Territory (Chapter 9) came the September 22, 1891 land run immediately to the east in the Absentee Shawnee, Iowa, Potawatomi, and Sac and Fox country. Over twenty-thousand pioneers raced for land, but only six thousand succeeded in securing it. These included William H. Twine, future African-American publisher as well as political and legal chieftain in Muskogee. Perhaps as many as a thousand blacks, including many residents of the all-black Oklahoma Territory town of Langston founded the previous year from land opened in the first run, sought claims in the 1891 event. It opened present-day Lincoln and Pottawatomie counties

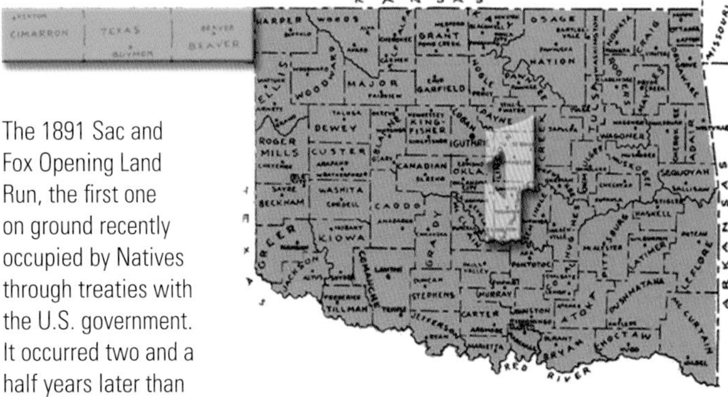

The 1891 Sac and Fox Opening Land Run, the first one on ground recently occupied by Natives through treaties with the U.S. government. It occurred two and a half years later than and immediately east of the first run in 1889. Courtesy *Oklahoman* newspaper and the National Cowboy Museum.

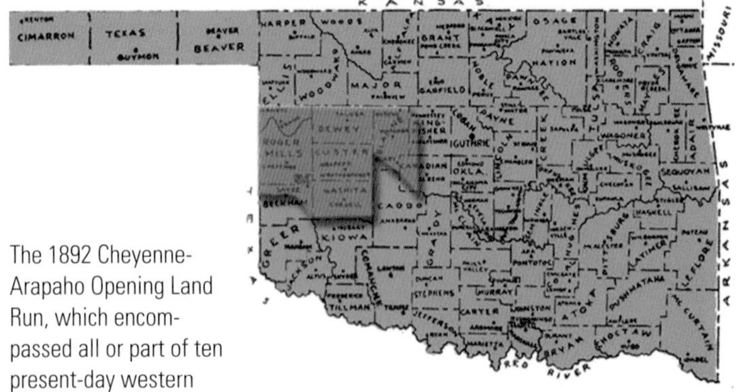

The 1892 Cheyenne-Arapaho Opening Land Run, which encompassed all or part of ten present-day western Oklahoma counties. Courtesy *Oklahoman* newspaper and the National Cowboy Museum.

Pioneers hoping for land prepare to ride in the 1892 Cheyenne-Arapaho land run—twenty-five thousand participants vying for 3.5 million acres of land. Much of it was agriculturally unworkable, and nearly three million acres were not claimed. Courtesy *Clinton Daily News*.

and portions of present-day Cleveland, Logan, Oklahoma, and Payne counties.

Just seven months later, on April 19, 1892, twenty-five thousand Boomers thundered over the three and a half million acres of surplus Cheyenne and Arapaho country in the Great Plains of western Oklahoma. This sprawling charge encompassed an area larger than Connecticut and Rhode Island combined. It remains as singular as it is forgotten. The participants included a hot air balloon and a six-horse team pulling a house. The well-known Kiowa chief Big Tree, by now a Christian and advocate of peace between the Natives and whites, witnessed "as many (people) as the blades of grass on the Washita in the spring."

Government officials reeled when no one claimed nearly three million acres of this land. A long and devastating drought, absence of railroads or any other roads, harassment by cattlemen who wanted the range, lack of building materials, scarce food, poor water, the barrenness of the land for crop growing, and worry about the fierce—and sometimes still threatening—Cheyennes all contributed to this rejection of free property.

"About the only sure crop was the rattlesnake" went the saying. By the end of the decade, however, rugged pioneers of German, Irish, Scottish, Russian, English, African, and other stock had braved all challenges, often to the point of death, and carved their mostly forgotten names high in the annals of Oklahoma and American history to settle the area.

Cherokee Outlet Run

The greatest land run in history shook the earth across the Cherokee Outlet in northern Oklahoma the following year, on September 16, 1893. One hundred thousand pioneers poured into this vast sweep of land that stretched from the main Cherokee country in northeastern Indian Territory to No Man's Land, the present-day Oklahoma Panhandle. It encompassed not only the sprawling grazing lands the Cherokees leased to white cattlemen but also the small tribal enclaves of the Pawnees and Tonkawas, the latter numbering around seventy members.

Two factors generated drama in the Cherokee Run of a magnitude not found in any other

A survey crew for the 1893 Cherokee Outlet Run. Courtesy Research Division, Oklahoma Historical Society.

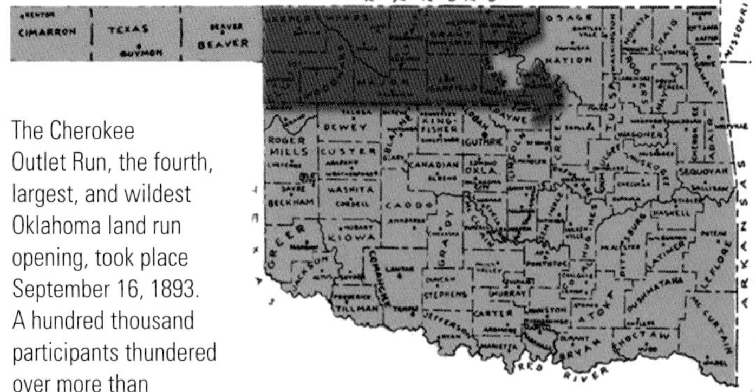

The Cherokee Outlet Run, the fourth, largest, and wildest Oklahoma land run opening, took place September 16, 1893. A hundred thousand participants thundered over more than 6,300,000 acres of formerly Cherokee-owned northern Oklahoma land. Courtesy *Oklahoman* newspaper and the National Cowboy Museum.

Just two of the many women who rode for land in the Cherokee Outlet Run.

Oklahoma land opening. One was its sheer size, double the participants of the next largest, the Run of '89. The other was the tense context in which it occurred. Historian Alvin O. Turner well described how years of drought across the South and Midwest, inadequate agricultural prices, and a national depression—the Panic of 1893—brought thousands of desperate Boomers to the region, many of them financially destitute and many others close to starvation.

As the date of the run neared, the federal government required them to wait in line, often for days, in scalding heat just to register for the right to participate. Boomers, suffering from thirst, hunger, and sunstroke fell ill, and some died in these lines. Twenty thousand still waited when federal officials closed down the registration booths.

Many Boomers endured mistreatment and even violence at the hands of soldiers and deputies tasked with controlling the enormous throng. Others suffered injuries and a few were killed when a chain reaction of stampedes broke out just prior to the start of the run. The great majority of the participants behaved well, and many displayed generosity and assistance toward one another. Enough did not, however, that the threat and sometimes the reality of violence hung over the entire proceedings like a dark cloud.

> *Countless individuals were injured in the frantic (Cherokee Outlet) races following the starting guns or when mobs fought to board the trains or individuals jumped from the trains as they neared town sites.*
>
> **—Historian Alvin O. Turner**

As towns such as Ponca City and Blackwell sprang from the Oklahoma prairie within hours,

Seconds after the gargantuan Land Run of 1893 commenced. Courtesy Oklahoma Historical Society.

The unconquerable pioneer spirit of Oklahoma, as illustrated in Edward Everett Dale's *History of Oklahoma*. The same location appears in all four photos of "the evolution of an early Oklahoma town" as: 1) a prairie cornfield; 2) the initial settlement twenty-four hours later; 3) the beginnings of a community two weeks later; and 4) a bustling town twelve months later.

cheating Sooners snatched many of the best claims, and most of those daring Boomers who made the Cherokee Outlet Run did not even get land. For those who did, the challenges had only just begun, as Turner recounted:

> The chaotic process of settlement continued to affect the region's development long after the land run. Towns were over-built; farmers went broke on land unsuitable for farming . . . many claims were abandoned by the end of the year. There were, of course, success stories just as there had been instances of neighborly actions, generosity, even gallantry during the run. Yet even those who managed to secure good land soon learned that farmers' opportunities were limited. The new towns, dependent on the farmers' business, faltered in a changing American economy where the growth of industrialization had redefined the meaning of opportunity.

Different Land Openings

The final land run opened the Kickapoo country on May 23, 1895. This tiny tribe—fewer than three hundred members, possessing around two hundred thousand acres—did not desire to be assimilated into white American culture. Their refusal to negotiate a treaty with the U.S. Government on allotment delayed the process for years. The Kickapoos could forestall the inevitable no longer than May 23, 1895, however, when ten thousand more Boomers and Sooners charged into the area to claim a homestead or town lot. Wellston and McLoud are among the present-day towns that emerged from this run.

Once again, only a minority of the runners, which included numerous independent females as did previous runs, succeeded. More than ever before, though, due in part to a lack of race officials, Sooners foiled the Boomers. Perhaps as many as half the land seekers sneaked in early, although scores were arrested and fined a thousand dollars apiece, an enormous sum in that day. Still, "Soonerism" had mushroomed to take a large enough toll on the available land, trigger enough law suits, and generate such a wealth of anger and even violence that the government terminated land runs as a means of releasing the remainder

America's greatest race for free land, the 1893 Cherokee Outlet Run, has been memorably captured in several motion pictures. Three renderings stand out. First was the initial film version of Edna Ferber's landmark novel of early Oklahoma, *Cimarron* (upper left). A breathtaking accomplishment for its time, the movie won the first Academy Award for Best Picture in 1931. Next was a new, color version of *Cimarron* in 1960 (above) that starred Glenn Ford. Most recently was *Far and Away* (left), Duncan native Ron Howard's 1992 epic of Irish immigrants coming to Oklahoma Territory. Tom Cruise and Nicole Kidman starred, at the height of their careers.

of surplus Indian lands. The lottery and the auction would serve as the methods for future openings.

One other piece of the territory, the long-contested Plains country in the far southwest corner, Greer County, came into the present-day Oklahoma fold in 1896. The U.S. Supreme Court ruled that the southern stream of Red River was its main course through the region—and thus was the original boundary of the Louisiana Purchase and now, Oklahoma Territory. This delivered the 1.5 million acres between it and the northern stream from Texas, which had claimed and partially settled it, to Oklahoma. Present-day towns such as Altus, Frederick, Hobart, Mangum, and Hollis would have been located in Texas had the verdict gone the other way.

The final and smallest land run opened 183,000 acres of present-day Lincoln, Oklahoma, and Pottawatomie counties land belonging to the tiny Kickapoo tribe. Courtesy *Oklahoman* newspaper and the National Cowboy Museum.

Panic and Populism

Great events such as the land runs and settlement of the Oklahoma country occur within intersecting currents of history, as do smaller events. One such current rising to the forefront of American life at the beginning of the 1890s, when the nation's people and government consolidated control of the region, was the Populist movement. It involved distinct social, economic, and political convictions.

In the broadest sense, the Populist movement sought government intervention to harness the expanding power of big business and industrial combines. This contrasts with most modern

Oklahoma Land Openings

No Man's Land
Cherokee Outlet
Tonkawa
Ponca
Kaw
Osage
Oto-Missouri
Pawnee
Peoria
Quapaw
Modoc
Ottawa
Wyandotte
Seneca
Shawnee
Cherokee Nation
Cheyenne & Arapaho
Unassigned Lands
Iowa
Sac & Fox
Kickapoo
Creek Nation
Wichita & Caddo
Seminole Nation
Greer County
Comanche, Kiowa, & Apache
Pottawatomie & Shawnee
Big Pasture
Chickasaw Nation
Choctaw Nation

Lands Opened By Allotment
1891 - Tonkawa
1892 - Pawnee
1904 - Ponca
1904 - Oto-Missouri
1906 - Osage
1906 - Kaw

Lands Opened By Run
April 22, 1889 - Unassigned Lands
September 22, 1891 - Iowa,
- Sac & Fox,
- Pottawatomie & Shawnee
April 19, 1892 - Cheyenne & Arapaho
September 16, 1893 - Cherokee Outlet
May 23, 1895 - Kickapoo

Lands Opened By Lottery
July 9 to August 6, 1901 - Wichita and Caddo
- Comanche, Kiowa & Apache

Lands Opened By Sealed Bid
December 1906 - Big Pasture

Courtesy National Cowboy Museum.

American populist movements that brandish the "populist" name and argue for the interests of the common people yet seek a reduction rather than an increase in government power. Also, the financial Panic of 1893, a four-year national financial calamity and depression, created enormous turmoil that helped trigger the decade's Populist outpouring.

Late nineteenth-century Populists, including the People's Party they had formed, aimed to allow smaller enterprises, as well as individual workers and their families, to enjoy a larger portion of the gross national product—and through more satisfactory means. Widespread perception that the poor and near-poor were growing poorer and the rich much richer at the poor's expense fueled the Populist phenomenon.

Once the former Ohio farm boy David Ross Boyd stepped off the train in pioneer Norman and became president of the spanking new University of Oklahoma—which he had yet to see—the school, town, and state were never the same. In addition to building curriculum and faculty, within months he was planting trees at his own expense on the prairie expanses around sixty-nine student OU. Thus was forged the legacy of the Seed Sower (see likeness in clouds of painting) of knowledge and nature alike, which is central to the school's seal, campus, and mission.

He also gave from the bounty of his devout Presbyterianism, holding school chapel services every morning that included Scripture readings and short sermons. He exhorted Sooner students to be faithful followers of Christ. For sixteen years, Boyd shepherded OU forward with passion and vision. Sacked for political reasons in 1908, he was later named president emeritus and served as president of the University of New Mexico. Courtesy Oklahoma State Senate Historical Preservation Fund, Inc. and Mike Wimmer.

A Warm Welcome for the Territorial doctor as he makes a house call that could be so vital on the hard frontier, especially in a driving blizzard. Painting by G. N. Taylor. (www.gntayloroklaart.com)

The train of events leading to it stretched back at least to the War Between the States. Rarely examined by U.S. histories are the colossal aggregates of crime, vice, and wickedness perpetrated by and against Americans during our many and nearly continual wars. Even supposedly "good" wars like the American Revolution and World War II wrought pitiable consequences for decades to come in the lives of participants and their offspring. So did the Civil War.

Next, a decade of post-war "Reconstruction" birthed financial overspeculation in the railroad industry, carpetbaggers, scalawags, robber barons, the Black Friday Stock Market Crash, the most corrupt presidential administration in U.S. history, the Gilded Age, the Ku Klux Klan, the Union League, and lasting enmity between the black and white races in the South.

The war, Reconstruction, and the emergent American Industrial Revolution also spawned a big business phenomenon crucial to that war effort and largely unregulated by the government. This, coupled with its gargantuan financial bonanza, led it to develop, in the words of historian Gregg Singer, "an attitude of irresponsibility toward its thousands of employees and the public in general, which was not conducive to a sound economy or social structure."

Causes of Populism

The railroads, the industrial titans of the age (Chapter 8), represented the most readily blamed culprit for transgressions—real, imagined, and misinterpreted—against the common man. What was not imagined or misinterpreted was that greed-triggered financial calamities during the final three decades of the nineteenth century, mechanization, competition on the world market, and other factors

Louis Dalrymple's patriotic cartoon of the United States, as embodied by Uncle Sam, throttling another in a series of national financial calamities, the Panic of 1893.

were lowering farm prices and gradually reducing the number of farmers needed to produce foodstuffs far exceeding what the country required. In addition, barren plains in the path of westward migration challenged farmers to extract a living from the earth *in extremis*.

Falling prices further harmed farmers because they had—unwisely then and in later generations—succumbed to government enticements toward debt, and debt payments remained perhaps the only items for which prices did not fall. This triggered another major conflict between farmers and the national political and business establishments—particularly, in the farmers' eyes, debt- and mortgage-holding big banks.

To escape falling prices and choking debt, farmers wanted the nation's currency either backed, or equaled, not just by its supply of gold, but by silver, and issued in the now familiar, easily traded paper form. They reasoned that this would increase the amount of currency in circulation, thus lowering its value—and that of debt payments—while increasing the value of the farmers' land and other capital. Thus, it would create inflation. Moreover, farmers and industrial laborers alike grew yet more vulnerable because larger business concerns could cut their own expenses by hiring employees elsewhere from the abundance of available labor.

Even modest farmers in remote lands observed and suffered the consequences of the Black Friday Stock Market Crash of 1869, the financial Panic of 1873, the nationwide Long Depression of 1873–79,

American civilization churns forward across the Twin Territories in the form of a Katy locomotive near the turn of the century. Courtesy Oklahoma Historical Society.

the Panic of 1893, and the mushrooming monopoly frenzy. Also, they caught wind of the corruption, bribery, and other misbehavior that fueled many of the colossal fortunes accruing in the North and East, sections that had triumphed in the late war.

Iowa Senator Ross Grimes, himself of both the North and the dominant Republican Party, well summarized the situation: "The war has corrupted everybody and everything. It is money that achieves success... nowadays. Thank God, my political career ended with the beginning of this corrupt political era."

A New Liberalism

Whereas most twenty-first century American populist efforts lean toward the right, or conservative, end of the political spectrum, the late-nineteenth-century Populist movement leaned toward the left, or liberal, in the modern sense of the term and even toward socialism. As so often has occurred in Oklahoma and American history, questionable solutions arose to address legitimate, unsolved problems. Populists put forth a compelling case, no one more so than Kansan Mary Elizabeth Lease:

> Wall Street owns the country. It is no longer a government of the people, by the people and for the people, but a government of Wall Street, by Wall Street, and for Wall Street. The great common people of this country are slaves, and monopoly is the master. Money rules... Our laws are the output of a system which clothes rascals in robes and honesty in rags. The parties lie to us and the political speakers mislead us... the politicians said we suffered from overproduction. Overproduction when 10,000 little children, so statistics tell us, starve to death every year in the United States, and over 100,000 shop-girls in New York are forced to sell their virtue for the bread their niggardly wages deny them. The West and South are bound prostrate before the manufacturing East... Kansas suffers from two great robbers, the Santa Fe Railroad and the loan companies. The common people are robbed to enrich their masters.

Such passion and pitiable events were not easily ignored by the nation's industrial and governmental elites, along with its dominant Republican and Democrat Parties, despite their frequent efforts to do so. Indeed, Populism helped propel the U.S. in the same direction as the other great industrial power of the age, England—away from the classical liberalism that had served as a pillar of its growth and greatness, and toward modern liberalism.

The classical, economic, or nineteenth-century, liberalism of Adam Smith and America's Founding Fathers emphasized personal liberty and responsibility coupled with limited government power and intrusion. Both forms of liberalism sought happiness, freedom, and justice for the individual, but the modern variant no longer thought that end possible for the great masses of the public without intervention by a formidable power outside the marketplace and its dominant forces. Modern liberalism deemed government as the means, rather than the hindrance, to that end.

Populists for President

Populism crashed into the center ring of national politics in 1892 with the formation of the People's Party, a third-party challenge of "the working man" to the Republicans and Democrats. The party's Preamble threw down the gauntlet:

> We meet in the midst of a nation brought to the verge of moral, political, and material ruin. Corruption dominates the ballot box, the legislatures, the Congress, and touches even the ermine of the bench... The fruits of the toil of millions are boldly stolen to build up colossal fortunes for a few, unprecedented in the history of mankind... From the same prolific womb of governmental injustice we breed the two great classes—tramps and millionaires...

The upstart party swept approximately 10 percent of the presidential vote and a dozen seats in Congress. It unnerved the dominant parties; the Democrats resorted to illegal and sometimes brutal tactics to maintain electoral control in the South. The Populist voting surge continued through the 1894 and 1896 election cycles, but the major parties'

As Oklahoma Territory grew, so did the businesses established to serve its people. D. I. Brown's store provided the supplies that early-Yukon-area farmers needed, and his grain elevator stored their wheat before shipment. Courtesy Western History Collections, University of Oklahoma Libraries.

organization, financial resources, political acumen, and control of the electoral machinery stymied the People's Party from further electoral gains.

The Republicans and Democrats may have won these battles, yet by the end of the new century, either the American electorate or government or both would embrace nearly every People's Party objective. So would the Founding Fathers of the nation's forty-sixth state as they wrote its constitution in 1906. That document would exert profound impact on Oklahoma even to the present day.

Social Darwinism

A final and decisive component in the birth of Populism and its successors was the profound impact on American intellectual and religious thought by Charles Darwin's evolutionary innovations. "Social Darwinism," which applied the theories of Darwin, English philosopher Herbert Spencer, and others to human society and institutions, spawned both conservative and reform versions. The former, fueled by the colossal production of the American Industrial Revolution, generated monopolies, trusts, business-political cabals, and unprecedented financial fortunes.

Meanwhile, reform Darwinism sought to correct the concomitant fruits of unharnessed conservative Darwinism—poverty, abusive labor practices, political corruption, and social inequities—through mobilizing the power of both the federal government and the masses of the voting public. That movements from both ends of the political spectrum could germinate from one source indicates how potent and pervasive a force in American society Social Darwinism became. So does its continued influence into the twenty-first century.

The Populists dragged many legitimate questions of social and economic justice out into the light of day. Opinions regarding their solutions varied. They drew immense support from farmers and some among industrial laborers. Partly because the U.S. was growing more urban and Populist sentiment was centered in rural areas, however, they failed to sustain a lasting organization or party.

As mentioned in the preceding passage, however, they did birth a philosophical movement that would steer American civic life in a new and enduring direction. Within a few years that compelling juggernaut, which evolved into the more broad-based Progressivism, captured the soul of

Darwinism and Populism

Charles Darwin's 1859 *On the Origin of Species* and 1871 *The Descent of Man* suggests the natural survival of the fittest, strongest, and most competent among living creatures of all sorts, along with humanity's evolution from apes or similar creatures. These landmark treatises permeated every arena of national thought—particularly in the victorious, economically expansive Union states of the North—including the social arena, from the 1860s onward.

both major political parties. As Chapter 12 will demonstrate, it also guided the brains and pens that authored the Constitution of the State of Oklahoma.

Tribal Rule Ends

As land runs and the Greer County ruling gradually opened Oklahoma Territory to white and African-American pioneer settlement in the 1890s, the federal government continued urging the Native republics of Indian Territory toward allotment. In 1893 a congressional act established the Dawes Commission, headed by Henry L. Dawes, the now-retired U.S. senator who superintended the 1887 Dawes Act (Chapter 9) that launched the allotment process in what became Oklahoma Territory. The Dawes Commission became the tip of the government spear aimed at the heart of the remaining tribal lands in the region, particularly those of the five Indian republics in Indian Territory.

Other than a few entrepreneurially inclined men like Elias C. Boudinot, the tribal leaders despised the two landmark reversals of treaties that allotment would create: loss of sovereignty over their own lands and termination of tribal governments and self-rule. In 1895 Congress gave up trying to persuade the Natives and proceeded with Indian Territory tribal land surveys and crafting of citizenship rolls.

Still the Indian republics stalled, resisted, and persuaded. On June 28, 1898, the federal hammer blow fell with the Curtis Act. Ironically sponsored by Kansa Indian and Kansas Senator Charles Curtis, this law officially abolished tribal courts and law, subjecting the Natives to U.S. legal jurisdiction. It also cleared the way for the U.S. government to survey and incorporate towns, as well as establish public schools. Unless the tribes crafted their own plans for enrollment of tribal members and allotment of tribal lands to the people and for towns, the government would do it for them.

As happened during the Trails of Tears and later, many of the tribes' most brilliant leaders persuaded their people toward their own allotment plans in order to exercise what little autonomy they still could. Some of these men had done so for a few years. By 1902 the Cherokees, Chickasaws, Choctaws, Creeks, and Seminoles had all worked out supplemental agreements with the federal government that included modestly more favorable provisions than the Curtis Act contained.

> *No church assembly now passes resolutions against a violation of our treaties, the abrogation of our government and an invasion of our right of property.*
> **—1890 Cherokee tribal delegation to U.S. government**

Despite all these concessions, had tribal leaders foreseen the mountainous aggregate of greed, corruption, bribery, theft, extortion, and even murder that accompanied the eventual disposition of their lands (Chapter 11), they might yet have resisted the government. Some might even have advocated war.

This plaintive cry from an 1890s delegation of Cherokee leaders in Washington should disturb an American church whose actions have often belied

Built at Tishomingo in 1898 out of red granite from the Pennington Creek quarry of Chickasaw Governor R. M. Harris, the Chickasaw National Capitol Building in Tishomingo housed the tribal government until Oklahoma statehood in 1907. It now hosts a Chickasaw museum.

"We Were a Happy People"

Tribes who lost their land and sovereignty left eloquent testaments to their trials. An 1895 Cherokee delegation to the federal government in Washington, D.C., directed these remarkably prophetic words to their chief, S. H. Mayes:

> *East of the Mississippi we were a happy people. The United States wanted our country there; reluctantly we parted with it, and to this day have not received all that was promised us for it... the terms of the agreement... were changed by act of Congress without our consent, and yet, after changing those terms to its own liking, the Government has not complied with them. And now, they want us to enter into another agreement—an agreement with the Dawes Commission. But what assurance have we, even if we were disposed to come to an agreement with that Commission, that the terms of such agreement would not be swept aside and others, to which we could never assent, imposed upon us? We think it would be but fair on (the) part of the Government to comply with the agreements already made with our people, before asking us to enter into others of a nature more serious in their character than any hitherto proposed.*

its stated beliefs and scriptures, whether regarding slavery; war; imperialism; deification of government; race and civil rights; materialism; family, marriage, and sanctity of life issues, or other accommodation to worldly cultural mores:

> Even the pulpit, which some time ago, was so exuberant of love for the slave has no good word to speak in behalf of the Indians of Indian Territory. No church assembly now passes resolutions against a violation of our treaties, the abrogation of our government and an invasion of our right of property.

Early Black Oklahomans

Late nineteenth-century America proved not to be the panacea for people of sub-Saharan African descent that abolitionists prophesied would ensue following emancipation. Successive post-war Republican presidential administrations and Congresses, often hailing from the party's socialistic Radical wing, had used African-Americans—and their newly won voting rights—in the South to help exert political and social power over the region's conservative white Democratic majority. Pitted against one another by a triumphant Yankee Republican government that wielded overwhelming power over both, Southern blacks and whites fought desperately—oftentimes literally—for survival, oftentimes against one another. Thus was multiplied a racial enmity not yet healed more than a century later.

African-Americans possessed more legal rights in some Northern states, but several of these states voted to deprive them of basic rights such as voting. Everywhere in the North and the developing West,

Choctaw Governor Wilson N. Jones, who led the tribe from 1890–1894, by G. N. Taylor. A brilliant entrepreneur, Jones's sweeping vision for his people included endowing a tribal hospital, establishing the Jones Academy boys' boarding school, the Tushka Homma Academy for girls, and the Tuscaloosa Institute school for black **freedmen**, and designating the old Armstrong Academy as an orphans' home. (www.gntayloroklaart.com)

a raging racial prejudice advanced with succeeding generations, as it had since the Africans' arrival on their horrifying cross-Atlantic slave ships long before the founding of the nation.

The Oklahoma country, however, appeared to present a historic opportunity for this benighted and longsuffering race. By 1890 nearly nineteen thousand blacks resided in the Twin Territories. That number grew to over thirty-six thousand in 1900 and eighty thousand—more than the total Indian population—by 1907, the year of statehood. Some of them held exalted positions in the white-dominated society. Green I. Currin, who gained Kingfisher County land in the Run of '89, won election to the first Oklahoma Territorial Legislature in 1890. David Wallace of Logan County, an African-American Republican like Currin, won election in the next session.

African-American U.S. Twenty-Fourth Infantry at Fort Reno, circa 1890.

School recess on the frontier takes place for Indian, African-American, and white children in Sonya Terpening's *The Community of Boling Springs*. Racial harmony apparently reigned in the no longer extant multi-ethnic, late-1800s community of Boling Springs, located in present-day Craig County. Courtesy Oklahoma State Senate Historical Preservation Fund, Inc. and Sonya Terpening.

Green I. Currin (c. 1842–1918)

Green I. Currin possessed talent, intelligence, courage, and an Irish grandfather. He served as a U.S. marshal, staked land in the Run of '89, was appointed a college regent, and won election to the first Oklahoma Territorial Legislature. All these and others of his accomplishments cast a shining light across Oklahoma history. They do all the more because of one other remarkable fact—his book of days turned in an era of harsh prejudice and discrimination against African-Americans, and all his other forbears were black. Courtesy Oklahoma Historical Society.

What explains this remarkable surge by early Oklahomans of African descent, who faced obstacles of every imaginable sort? Regarding the eastern portion, still called Indian Territory, historians Bruce Fisher and Larry O'Dell cited the Indian allotment process. The tribes' loss resulted in unprecedented opportunity for their former slaves. When the U.S. government surveyed Indian Territory tribal lands and divided it among the individual Natives, they reserved tracts for black tribal members and former slaves of the tribes as well.

Allotments for African-Americans, recorded with a "C" for colored or "N" for Negro, lay adjacent to one another. Now owning sweeping blocks of land unparalleled anywhere else on the continent, these folk transformed many such areas into all-black towns and communities. This provided social cohesiveness as well as collective security from whites or Indians who might wish ill on individual members of the community.

Edward McCabe and African-American Oklahoma (1850–1920)

No better saga of the spirit, triumph, heartbreak, and audacity of the early Oklahoma pioneer endures than that of Edward P. McCabe. This African-American "Exoduster" roared into the territorial capital of Guthrie in 1890 with a grand vision for nothing less than establishing an American state where blacks could own vast property and wield enormous influence. Many observers believed he intended for Oklahoma to become the first black, or black-controlled, state.

All-Black State?

In the western portion of present-day Oklahoma, now called Oklahoma Territory, two key factors spurred African-American initiative and hopes. Brilliant black clergyman, farmer, businessman, civil magistrate, and Oklahoma pioneer Samuel R. Cassius cited the first of these as the belief of many African-Americans that the U.S. government would reserve land (probably the Unassigned Lands opened in the 1889 Land Run) for blacks that was forfeited to it by defeated pro-Confederate tribes. This widely held belief—yearned for by African-Americans, but feared by whites—suggested that Indian and Oklahoma Territories would birth an all-black, or at least black-dominated, state.

"When the colored people heard this report," Cassius recalled, "they all started to Oklahoma, some walking, some on the train, some in oxcarts and some in wagons. No thought was given to money. In fact, the most of them had no money to think of; all they wanted was to get there."

The second factor Cassius suggested involved the exalted claims of African-Americans who won land during the first run and declared it "only a day's walk to the original Garden of Eden." It teemed with game, so the story went, such as "wild turkeys and deer . . . so plentiful that a man had to carry a Winchester and a large club when he went out hunting, the club to be used in beating the deer and turkeys back while he loaded his gun."

The notable entry into Oklahoma of Edward P. McCabe, a black man who possessed enormous charisma and energy and had held statewide elected office in Kansas, heightened the climate of anticipation. It only escalated as he tirelessly promoted African-American migration to Oklahoma. He also helped found the all-black town of Langston, near Guthrie, in 1891, as well as a "colored" college of the same name in 1897.

Social and political opportunities in Oklahoma Territory appeared bright for African-Americans throughout the 1890s due to their own energy and ambition, as well as their alliance with the white-dominated Republican Party. The "Party of Lincoln" needed black votes against the growing power of the Democratic Party, whose conservative

"The Black Man in Oklahoma, 1896"

"The negro may look awful bad after he has wrestled with a cyclone, or had a tussle with a blizzard, but when he looms up in a cotton patch he is a thing of beauty and a joy forever. A bay steer in a fodder stack would not inspire the lover of art with more reverence than would the average colored farmer standing amid the white sea of cotton. It has long been conceded that Oklahoma was made for the colored man, and the colored man for Oklahoma. Here it is he will demonstrate to the world his fitness for an equal show with the dominant race. Already he has assumed the responsibility of making Oklahoma the most prosperous land in America, for without a dollar or team, hoe, plow, or in fact anything but his wife, children and dogs, he has snatched this country out of the jaws of famine and the hand of ruin by raising over three million dollars' worth of cotton."

—Samuel Robert Cassius

Langston University

Oklahoma Territory in 1897 loomed as both an inhospitable, sometimes dangerous place for African-Americans and one that offered greater economic and political potential for them than anywhere else in America. Into this enigmatic context and following the U.S. Supreme Court's 1896 *Plessy v. Ferguson* decision, which mandated separate but also equal educational facilities for blacks, rose the Colored Agricultural and Normal University, the future Langston University.

An early Industrial Shop class at Langston College.

One of the first Langston student body photos.

African-American freedmen at a dance during their enrollment with the Dawes Commission at Fort Gibson in the 1890s. Courtesy Oklahoma Historical Society.

white Southern supporters grew more numerous in the territory each year.

Those Democrats, though, already formed a strong political majority to the east in Indian Territory due to the many Natives and whites alike who held Southern ancestry and pro-Confederate, limited-government sympathies. And they possessed their own dreams for a new start in the Oklahoma country. These included working land that was not worn out like elsewhere in the South. They also concerned finding a country free from the boot of federal military might that had oppressed their fathers after the catastrophic War Between the States. Free, too, from the African-Americans the federal government had used as a wedge to try and wrest political power for the Republicans in Dixie from white Southerners. Trouble was coming in Oklahoma between the black and white races.

The Lawmen

Despite its youth and modest population, Oklahoma has not only embodied many of the preeminent features of the American character, but has done so in exaggerated, sometimes larger-than-life, form. Americans as a whole are a religious Christian people; Oklahoma has many times been called the buckle of the Bible Belt. Americans are a generous, compassionate people; the consensus opinion of observers inside and out of the state is that friendliness there trumps all other characteristics of its people. Americans, as earlier noted regarding Frederick Jackson Turner's Frontier Thesis, are a restless people with a pioneering spirit as alive in the development of new computer chips as the discovery of new valleys and mountains; Oklahoma's history is layered with boom and bust stories of dreamers, schemers, and risk-takers large and small.

Moreover, Americans have always been a violent people, despite their protestations to the contrary in their histories and odes to themselves as peace lovers. We have been engaged in one war or another almost from the birth of our republic, far more often engaged in bloody arms than most nations. Oklahomans, meanwhile, are known

Bass Reeves (1820–1910)

If anyone in Oklahoma's colorful history rises up like a figment of a Hollywood scriptwriter's imagination, surely it is Bass Reeves. Yet this tall, powerful former slave with keen perception and cool nerve gained renown as one of the greatest lawmen and deadliest guns in one of the most dangerous lands in nineteenth-century America, all in an era of rampant, even lethal, racism against African-Americans. He proved anything but fanciful to the many outlaws and bad men he stalked during a law enforcement career stretching across a third of a century.

The Three Guardsmen

From where did the ultimate tribute come that was paid to the greatest triumvirate of lawmen in American history? It came from the very outlaws whom erstwhile Confederate boy soldier Heck Thomas, buffalo hunter Bill Tilghman, and Danish-born Chris Madsen eradicated from the badlands of the old Twin Territories. The notorious villains of the Old West christened them "The Three Guardsmen." Those renegades themselves included some of the most infamous names in American outlawry.

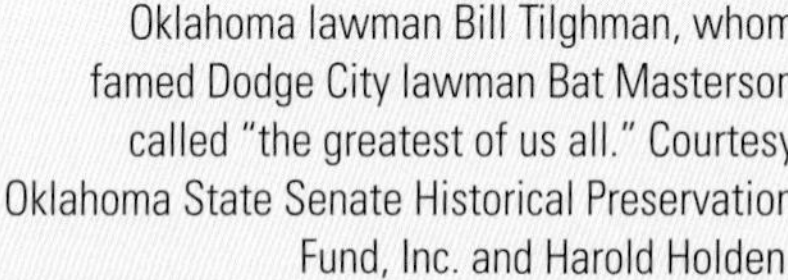
Oklahoma lawman Bill Tilghman, whom famed Dodge City lawman Bat Masterson called "the greatest of us all." Courtesy Oklahoma State Senate Historical Preservation Fund, Inc. and Harold Holden.

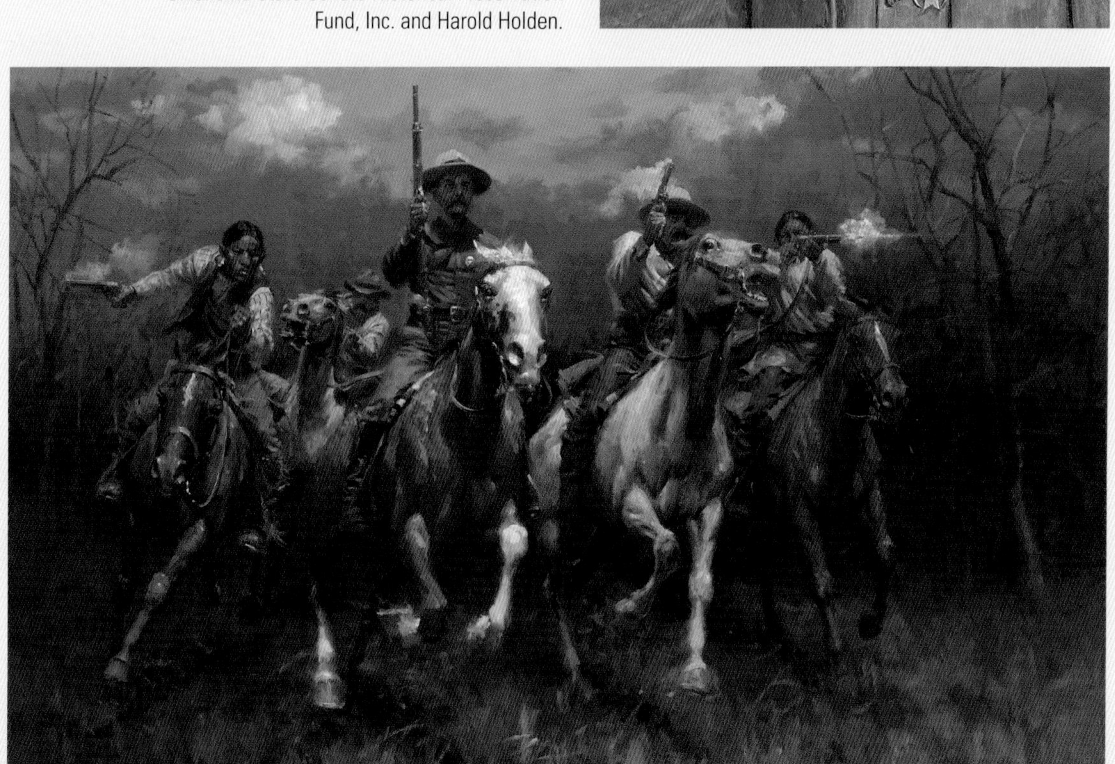

The legendary Heck Thomas, brought to life by Andy Thomas. From the time he volunteered as a twelve-year-old Confederate courier in the War Between the States and Robert E. Lee ordered him to return deceased Federal General Philip Kearney's horse to the latter's widow, to the epic *True Grit* novel and uncanny screen portrayals of the closely resembled lawman Rooster Cogburn, Heck Thomas, the co-founder of Lawton, has retained a larger-than-life stature. Courtesy Andy Thomas (www.andythomas.com).

by the world as a pioneer people, a cowboy people, and a people of guns—whether they are frontier six-shooters or modern automatic weapons. No state supports the U.S. Constitution Bill of Rights' Second Amendment right to own and bear personal firearms in higher proportion than Oklahoma.

Like America, Oklahoma was birthed in a mystical solution of guns and Bibles. Cherokees clashed with Osages, Federals with Confederates, and Comanches with Texas cowboy pioneers. And a violent, motley band of marauders descended on the land in the late 1800s, using it as a refuge, hideout, and staging ground for more mischief, due to its dearth of law enforcement among the thinly populated Indian republics. A popular nickname for Indian Territory was "Robber's Roost," because the bandits pouring in from the north, east, and south threatened to turn the territory into a permanent redoubt of robbery, murder, and terror.

From the late 1860s well into the 1890s, Oklahoma hosted a hall of fame of American outlaw legends, including Cole Younger and his brothers, the Dalton Gang, the Doolin Brothers, Belle Starr, Blue Duck (of *Lonesome Dove* fame), Sam Bass, Ned Christie, and even occasionally the

The Old-Time Religion

African-American historian Jimmie Franklin's words focused on the black church in the days of the Twin Territories, but their principles set the context for the most powerful societal influence of the era: "In Oklahoma the church played a leading role in fostering a sense of place, while it also cushioned blacks against some of the difficulties of segregation and discrimination. Except for the possible exception of the school within the black community, the church fostered the healthiest notion of a sense of place."

St. John the Baptist Catholic Church in Edmond, built in Oklahoma Territory, June 1889.

Legendary Comanche Chief Quanah Parker tells German-born Mennonite missionary pastor Henry Kohfeld, mounted behind another Comanche, that he may build "Jesus House" on the site of this post oak tree in rough Comanche reservation country east of present-day Cache, Comanche County. From discouraging beginnings, the thriving Post Oak Mennonite Christian mission rose here among the Comanches. Kohfeld and other Mennonites exhibited a humble, servant-hearted approach that honored both Christian teachings and Comanche traditions and helped transform the tribe. Post Oak continues its work in the twenty-first century. Oklahoma-born artist Michelle Noah drew on the influence of Kiowa Ledger Art (Chapter 8) for this original painting, *Here, Build Jesus House*, commissioned for *The Oklahomans*. (www.MichelleBNoah.com)

legendary former Confederate guerilla and U.S. government resistor Jesse James.

Rising to challenge them were some of the most famous lawmen in American history, including Heck Thomas, Bill Tilghman, Charlie Colcord, Chris Madsen, Bass Reeves, and Zeke Miller. Remarkably, both Reeves and Miller were African-American, so their deputation was unheard of in an era when most blacks had only recently gained citizenship and few could even vote. Notable as well was Isaac Parker, the famous "Hanging Judge" whose Fort Smith, Arkansas, jurisdiction included the Twin Territories. Other familiar names in U.S. history had ridden the territory hunting buffalo, including "Buffalo Bill" Cody, "Wild Bill" Hickok, and Pat Garrett, famed slayer of William "Billy the Kid" Bonney.

John Jasper Methvin, Methodist missionary among the Kiowas and Comanches. Here he is with a group of Kiowa girls (c. 1894). Methvin rode the bicycle. Courtesy Western History Collections, University of Oklahoma Libraries.

Mining Drama

By the 1890s, more than three thousand men worked in the coal mines of Indian Territory. The companies paid their workers better than those back east, and coal mining had become the most important industry in Indian Territory after the railroads, whose arrival, transportation, and purchase of coal had established the industry in the territory.

Working conditions, however, proved to be bad, even abominable for miners. No state or federal law governed their work and environment like elsewhere in America. The rugged hands of the miners themselves accomplished nearly every facet of the mining process. Without realizing they were helping to found an American state, they labored in uncomfortable and even miserable positions, such as stooping, kneeling, or standing in water, sometimes for most of their nine and a half-hour work day. They endured explosions—intended and unintended—choked on coal dust and powder from dynamite detonations, and gagged on underground air barely fit to breathe.

In keeping with the same, all-too-common commercial ethos of the era that triggered the Populist movement, they also labored

J. J. Methvin and the "Wild Tribes" (1846–1941)

"I did not anticipate that I was one of the missionaries to be sent," Reverend J. J. Methvin recalled of his historic appointment to a suffering field as a man in his early forties. "Inasmuch as I had a wife and five young children I did not judge myself eligible for so difficult but glorious a task. So I was startled into quickened heart beats when I heard Bishop Galloway in his clear, musical voice read, 'Missionary to the Western Tribes, J. J. Methvin.'"

I have seen rugged old Indians who, many a time have been on the warpath and jerked the scalp from many heads, under the preaching of this gospel come forward and with quivering forms and streaming eyes confess their sins and ask for help, and I have seen them transformed by this power alone and lead new lives. And this has been the power that wrought the change in our so-called wild who are no longer wild, and while there is much ahead to be done yet, wonderful has been the change that has taken place since the first missionary work was begun among them years ago.

—J. J. Methvin

Oklahoma pioneer William Harrison Odor believed a round barn would withstand the area's tornadoes. So in 1898, he, along with his family and neighbors built one near the Deep Fork River in Arcadia. The lower level housed hay, and the upper level or loft sheltered farm stock and hosted barn dances. Way more than a century later, the Round Barn still stands, a familiar landmark to Route 66 and Interstate 44 travelers. Courtesy Linda Tuma Robertson and the Oklahoma State Senate Historical Preservation Fund.

for companies who apparently placed a much higher premium on cheap, quick coal production than they did the comfort or even safety of their employees. Regardless of one's opinion of later labor unions and their corruption and violence, such callous treatment of the employees whose blood, sweat, and tears built financial kingdoms for many coal companies leaves little doubt as to why those unions rose to such power and influence.

Indian Territory coal miners endured explosions, choked on coal dust and powder from dynamite detonations, and gagged on underground air barely fit to breathe.

Accidents, which were sometimes fatal, abounded until the early 1890s. The crowning debacle occurred on January 7, 1892. An Osage Coal and Mining Company shaft exploded, killing nearly a hundred men and crippling and maiming a hundred and fifty others. The outcry from this tragedy at long last provoked the appointment of a federal mine inspector for Indian Territory. His diligent supervision of mine conditions helped lower the death and injury toll in Indian Territory coal mines, beginning in 1894.

Another historic milestone in Oklahoma's coal mining history occurred after an exhausting five-year regional strike that ran from 1899-1903. Coal miners and the "Big Four" Southwest operators— the Kansas and Texas Coal Company, the Atoka Mining Company, the Osage Coal Company, and the Choctaw Coal

Oklahoma miners load coal in the strip mining pits of Wilburton, Indian Territory, in 1898.

Company—disagreed over wages. When the miners walked out, the companies brought in African-American strikebreakers from Alabama and West Virginia to replace them. These actions magnified the tension and added a racial component to it. Miner leader Peter Hanraty's patient, circumspect, determined leadership unified the miners' efforts and led both to the establishment of the United Mine Workers as a powerful collective bargaining organization in Indian Territory and development of a favorable wage resolution.

Coal was not the only valuable mineral that spawned a commercial mining industry in the late nineteenth-century Twin Territories. A major discovery of lead and zinc at Peoria in 1891 launched those industries in present-day Ottawa County. Overnight, Peoria was transformed from a remote rural outpost to one of the region's busiest mining camps, playing host to fifteen hundred miners. A phalanx of additional camps spread throughout the area in subsequent years.

The Kiamichi Mountains and other forests covering the Choctaw Country in southeastern Indian Territory stoked another late nineteenth-century industry—lumber. It had grown stronger in the area ever since the War Between the States. Steam-powered lumber mills, pioneers' construction needs, and the railroads' massive consumption of wooden ties and bridges all contributed to the growth of the lumber industry.

Oil Business Born

The biggest event of the nineteenth century's final years in the Twin Territories occurred on April 15, 1897. It involved a Nebraskan of uncommon talent and determination and an Oklahoma pioneer who had spotted an oil seepage near present-day Bartlesville over twenty years before. The latter, George B. Keeler, emigrated to Indian Territory in

Pete Hanraty and the Mining Industry (1864–1932)

Like so many pioneer Oklahomans, especially those opposing the powerful on behalf of the powerless, the road proved a hard and sometimes unforgiving one for Peter Hanraty, the great-hearted champion of Sooner miners. A son of Scotland and founding father of Oklahoma, he risked his nine-year-old life in his native country's coal mines and eventually lost both legs in an Oklahoma coal mining accident. In between, however, he spearheaded the future state's greatest human rights legislation for manual laborers, championed its ultimately successful campaign for women's suffrage, served as mayor of one of its most important cities, and helped lead the state's constitutional convention as its vice president.

Gushing Nellie Johnstone No. 1, April 15, 1897, at present-day Bartlesville, Indian Territory/Oklahoma's first commercially viable oil well. Inset, its beautiful part-Delaware namesake, daughter of William Johnstone, the intrepid man who helped drill the historic well. Courtesy Oklahoma Historical Society.

1871, when the only settlement between Coffeyville, Kansas, and a cow camp near present-day Sapulpa was the Osage Agency near present-day Pawhuska.

Keeler later related how bears, wolves, panthers, wildcats, and Natives constituted nearly all the inhabitants of present-day Bartlesville when he arrived. In 1875, while herding cattle along Sand Creek, he stopped to refresh his horse at a watering hole, but the animal refused to drink. Keeler noticed a rainbow-colored sheen of oil topping the water in the tank. Over the next several years, he opened a trading post in the area with William Johnstone and Bartlesville town founder Jake Bartles. Then in 1884, with Johnstone, he established the first store on the present site of the town. Bartles himself had spotted oil seeping from the ground southeast of Vinita when he rode past with the Sixth Kansas Federal Cavalry during the War Between the States.

Meanwhile, Omaha resident Michael Cudahy, whose family came to America from Ireland during its catastrophic potato famine, had been drilling wells on a two hundred thousand-acre leasehold in the Creek country since 1894. Despite once drilling into oil sand and even tapping into small amounts of oil on another occasion, he experienced repeated disappointments at locations as far away as Muskogee. Then Keeler, Cudahy, and Johnstone pooled their resources and talents. Keeler leased the sort of quality drilling location that had for years eluded Cudahy—including the very site where his horse had long ago refused to drink the water. Cudahy, meanwhile, ramrodded a financing effort and tribal (Osage) authorization, which Keeler had been unable to accomplish. Johnstone and another pioneer, Frank Overlees, provided additional capital and petroleum-rich ground.

As the winter of 1896–97 grew numbingly cold, yet another Cudahy drilling attempt failed near Red Fork on the Caney River. Together with his new partners, Cudahy ordered his drillers, A. P. McBride and C. L. Broom, to haul his rig to the Caney just north of Bartlesville and near Keeler's old spot. For nearly three weeks, McBride, Broom, and their crew fought their way across the icy countryside. They had to carve out a path for their wagons through the frozen Arkansas River.

They launched drilling in late January, 1897. At 3 p.m. on April 15, a crowd witnessed the making of history as Keeler's stepdaughter, Jennie Cass, dropped a "go-devil" torpedo down the shaft that trigged an explosion of nitroglycerin. From a depth of 1,320 feet, the Nellie Johnstone No. 1—named for Johnstone's

Frank (far right, in suit) and Montgomery (center, in suit) Frantz's Hardware and Tin Store, an Enid hardware and lumber company. They opened it following Frank's return to the Oklahoma country after the Spanish–American War.

daughter, a descendant of Delaware Chief Charles Journeycake on her mother's side—came in, and commenced producing fifty to seventy-five barrels of oil a day. However, the nearest railroad, which was necessary to transport the crude oil to market, had not yet reached Bartlesville. Cudahy managed to cap the Nellie Johnstone to preserve its precious reserves.

In one of a myriad of early-day petroleum fiascos, leaks from the well ignited two years later when a group of young ice skaters built a bonfire nearby on the frozen Caney. Fire touched off the exposed oil and destroyed the Nellie Johnstone. Despite this setback, Cudahy and his partners were as determined as ever as they sank new wells in the area. Keeler, now a leader in the region's burgeoning banking industry, spearheaded financing for completion of the railroad into Bartlesville. An army of other oilmen—including Frank and L. E. Phillips, who built the Phillips Petroleum dynasty—swarmed into the area with the railroad. Thus, one of the great oil booms of the American West was born around Bartlesville.

Meanwhile, the refurbished Nellie Johnstone No. 1 proved worthy of the sacrifice, investment, and faith that had birthed it. It pumped over a hundred thousand barrels of Oklahoma crude in its half-century life of production.

The first American officer killed in the 1898 Spanish–American War, during which the two sides battled for control of Cuba and other Spanish possessions, was Oklahoman Allyn Capron (left). He led one of three troops recruited in Oklahoma and Indian Territories that comprised the First U.S. Volunteer Cavalry Regiment, whose second-in-command was future President Theodore Roosevelt. The tall, lean, athletic, and handsome Capron died leading an American charge up a hill against the Spaniards at the Battle of Las Guasimas, Cuba. He posthumously won the Silver Star. Roosevelt called him "the ideal of what an American regular army officer should be . . . a first-class rider and shot . . . he looked what he was, the archetype of the fighting man." He was, the future President declared, "the best soldier in the regiment."

Frank Frantz and the Rough Riders (1872–1941)

Illinois native Frank Frantz and his brothers pioneered the Cherokee Outlet in Medford following the region's epic 1893 Land Run. His renown began after he volunteered for Theodore Roosevelt's Rough Riders in the Spanish-American War in Cuba. After a battlefield promotion by Roosevelt upon the fall of another officer, Frantz led the Rough Riders up Kettle and San Juan hills in the pivotal battle of the war. Roosevelt's enduring devotion to Frantz—who thrice knocked him out in "friendly" boxing matches at the White House after "Teddy" became President—led him to appoint the Westerner final governor of Oklahoma Territory.

Oklahoman Frank Frantz, on horseback, leads the Rough Riders up San Juan Hill, Santiago, Cuba, in the bloodiest and most famous battle of the Spanish-American War. Courtesy Oklahoma State Senate Historical Preservation Fund, Inc. and Timothy Tyler (http://tctyler.com).

11

1900–1905

New Century, New Land

The thrill of an oil strike that could make poor folks rich overnight on the early Oklahoma prairie in G. N. Taylor's *Oklahoma Wildcatters*. Such gushers launched the modern era of Oklahoma history. www.gntayloroklaart.com

c. 1900–1916	Progressive Era
1900–1910	Crazy Snake Rebellion
1901	Kiowa, Comanche, Apache, Wichita, and Caddo land lotteries
1905	Sequoyah Convention
1905	Glenn Pool Field oil strike

I hear the Government is cutting up my land and is giving it away to black people.... It can't be so for it is not in the treaty.... They are negroes who came in here as slaves. They have no right to this land.... It was given to me and my people and we paid for it with our land back in Alabama.

—Chitto Harjo

The Twin Territories churned into the twentieth century with all the muscle and fire of the locomotives now cross-hatching the region. People, industry, and ideas poured in. During the decade of the 1900s, the combined population of Indian Territory and Oklahoma Territory exploded from 790,391 to 1,657,155, the greatest ten-year gain in history for the land comprising the present-day Sooner State. Between 1900 and 1910, Oklahoma's Founding Fathers birthed in their own words, "not just a new state, but a new kind of state." Tens of thousands of white and black pioneers and settlers raised up a vibrant new American state from the sprawling Southern Plains, and from the land loved by so many of those people ushered forth one of the greatest oil booms in history.

The American population mushroomed during this decade due to increased immigration and high domestic birthrates. The nation's vast frontier was mostly secured by the dawn of the new century, despite the fact that much of the South was still stymied by the devastation of the War Between the States and its aftermath. Thus, the sweeping tracts of free land, moderate climate, and opportunity to build new families and a new state alike in the Oklahoma country gleamed like a beacon of last chance-hope and paradise to whites and blacks alike across the United States and even other nations.

These events, meanwhile, seemed more like the final curtain closing on their history and culture to many of the Twin Territories' tribal members.

Old meets new as motor cars line up along dirt roads in downtown Drumright in early 1900s Indian Territory.

Perceiving that the approaching juggernaut of American statehood was at hand, but hoping to retain as much autonomy as possible, the leaders of the five republics held a constitutional convention in 1905. They aimed to establish the state of Sequoyah, which they did not intend to include Oklahoma Territory. Natives—whether full blood, mixed blood, or intermarried whites—would comprise a high percentage of Sequoyah's population, even more so among its leadership.

The U.S. presidential administration of Republican Theodore Roosevelt, however, possessed its own agenda, which was quite different from the Indians'. It rejected entry into the Union of the strongly Democratic Sequoyah. Instead, it approved the single statehood of Oklahoma, comprising both the Oklahoma and Indian Territories. It hoped the higher quotient of Republicans in Oklahoma Territory would swing the single state into the Republican political column.

But Southerners—Democrats, nearly all—raised for generations to detest the "Party of Lincoln" that had burned down much of their Confederate country during the war and oppressed it during Reconstruction, poured into the Oklahoma Territory from Texas and elsewhere during the latter runs, lotteries, and allotments. Now both territories were strongly Democratic, still the conservative party of that generation, at least regarding issues such as social relations, religion, and race. So would be for a long time the forty-sixth state of the Union—Oklahoma.

Path from Indian Republics to American State

1887 Dawes Allotment Act ends tribal ownership of Native lands except for the Five Civilized Tribes

1890 Organic Act creates Oklahoma Territory from the western half of Indian Territory, governed by U.S.—not Indian—laws

1893 Dawes Allotment Act applied to Five Civilized Tribes

1898 Curtis Act abolishes tribal rule and subjects all Indian Territory residents to federal jurisdiction

1906 Oklahoma Enabling Act orders Indian Territory and Oklahoma Territory to elect delegates to a constitutional convention tasked with creating the American state of Oklahoma; remaining tribal government authority ends

1907 Oklahoma becomes the 46th American state; all its land and people—including Natives—subject to United States laws

Crazy Snake Rebellion

Now unfolded the sad concluding chapter in the long and bloody tragedy of war between red and white Americans. Following the 1898 Curtis Act (Chapter 10) that mandated land allotment and the end of tribal rule, Pleasant Porter, the wise, great, and final Principal Chief of the Creeks (1899–1906), feared three possible tribal responses to allotment.

Merle St. Leon's view of Crazy Snake eluding lawmen.

These included 1) armed resistance, leading to certain destruction; 2) abandonment of the country, which would result in the loss of their homes and the likelihood of not finding new ones; and 3) peaceful non-cooperation, which he reckoned would accomplish nothing but more suffering for the Creeks.

Most members of the five Indian republics followed Porter's counsel to cooperate. Yet minority factions in each did not. Most famous of these efforts was that of the conservative Creek full bloods—perhaps as many as five thousand of them, close to one-third of the tribe. Led by Chitto Harjo, whose name translated in English means "Crazy Snake," they formed their own shadow Creek government, including

Cheyenne and Arapaho young men branding cattle in 1900 at the Seger Colony (Chapter 9) in Washita County.

Lighthorsemen. These armed riders carried out punishment, including land and property theft, intimidation of white landowners, and beatings and whippings of fellow Creeks who supported or even grudgingly accepted allotment or hired/rented land to whites.

In rapid succession, the Creek National Council requested help against Harjo and his followers; a shootout between "Snakes" and white lawmen shed blood; and a troop of U.S. cavalry arrived to deal with the rebellion. Then, Deputy Sheriff Grant Johnson and his Creek interpreter Bernie McIntosh calmly rode out, captured Harjo and two of his confederates, and brought them in.

Sadly, intratribal incidents and threats instigated by some of Harjo's followers, along with a growing white population that grew increasingly alarmed and frustrated by what the Snakes faction might do, all contributed to a mounting tension in the area through the decade of the 1900s. Thrown into the uneasy mix were African-Americans, many of them unhappy with their prejudiced plight and not above robbery to supply their needs.

In fact, a series of thefts by blacks and Creeks triggered a second and final tragic chain of events in 1909–10, sometimes known as the "Smoked Meat Rebellion." Lawmen and territorial militiamen set out to deal with African-Americans suspected in a number of stolen meat incidents. The long-simmering tensions and agitation generated among anti-allotment Creeks by Harjo's continued defiance provoked McIntosh County Sheriff William L. Odom to obtain a warrant for his arrest and then pursue him with an armed posse. Over the next several days, several white lawmen (including Odom), Snake Creeks, and blacks died in confused ambushes and shootouts.

With non-Snake Creeks and whites in the area near panic and ready to commence a shooting war, the mayor of Checotah declared, "Crazy Snake must

Chitto Harjo and the Crazy Snakes (1846–1911)

This full-blood Muscogee Creek devoted his life to carrying out his role as tribal "gatekeeper." Finally, he gave that life in doing so. He never capitulated to the U.S. government's assimilation program for the Creeks and other Oklahoma tribes. He refused to accept a land allotment, complained that black former slaves were receiving tribal land, helped form a rump Creek government in defiance of the federal takeover of that authority, then died beyond the reach of the U.S. authorities from a gunshot wound suffered in a shootout with Oklahoma lawmen.

Frank Canton, who overcame an early criminal career in Texas to become one of the West's greatest lawmen. He led the successful pursuit of Chitto Harjo.

go.... His people are dangerous to the community.... It is necessary that (the Snake Indians) be cleaned up or else they will eventually depopulate this part of the country of Whites.... The situation is critical."

This chaotic sequence electrified newspapers across the world. Frank Canton, who rode many a trail with Heck Thomas and promoted himself as one of the Oklahoma country's most famous lawmen, decried the media's trumping up of the situation. However, he also said, "While a great many sensational reports have been sent out regarding the Snake uprising and correspondents have painted exaggerated pictures of the situation, the fact is not altered that the Snakes are a dangerous lot and should at this time be suppressed once and for all."

A white lawman finally shot Harjo in one blazing gunfight. This ended significant Snake resistance, although the determined Creek eluded posses large and small, even the one including legendary Oklahoma lawman Bill Tilghman. Harjo was never found until after dying from his

Pleasant Porter—Creek Leader (1840–1907)

Irish-American John Porter Snodgrass lay dying, full of days, in his home on the Arkansas River near Clarksville in present Wagoner County. He had fought the Creeks with Andrew Jackson, but later stood up to save the tribe from extermination. He was adopted by them but excommunicated by his own family. He brought his wife and children with the exiled Indians to Indian Territory and then joined his friend Sam Houston in the Texas Revolution. Now family members ringed his deathbed. He placed his hand on the head of one of them, his seven-year-old grandson Pleasant, whose dark skin evinced his Native blood. "He will do more than any of you," the dying man declared with signal prophecy.

Chief Porter: Should Oklahoma Control Allotment?

Few people of any race brought a more circumspect, humble, and balanced perspective to the 1906-07 United States Senate Select Committee to Investigate Matters Connected with Affairs In the Indian Territory and its deliberations over tribal allotments and the governance of that challenging process than Creek Principal Chief Pleasant Porter. He recognized both the many wrongs committed against the Natives and the advantages—even urgency—of statehood for the Oklahoma country. He also knew about the land and property laws requisite for the latter. His agonized words pose disturbing challenges through the years to observers on either side of the matter.

wound in 1911 while hiding out in the Kiamichi Mountains of the Choctaw country. The specter of violent Native opposition to allotment passed into history with the demise of Chitto Harjo.

Grafting

Many twenty-first century Oklahoma Indians' lack of enthusiasm for the 2007 Statehood Centennial becomes understandable considering—beyond the Trails of Tears, Reconstruction, and the allotment process—the twentieth-century phenomenon of grafting. In short, grafting involved the acquirement of Natives' allotted lands, whether through legal or illegal means, both of which abounded during the decades following allotment.

Oklahoma historian and pioneer Angie Debo's landmark work *And Still the Rivers Run* chronicled the astounding effects of grafting on the Indians of the five (disappearing) republics. The following paragraphs reveal, in Debo's words, a portion of the many unintended consequences wrought by the forced allotment of tribal lands. They do not represent isolated incidents.

Agricultural leases—"One man secured the appointment as guardian of a large number of (allottee) children; he then leased the land at a very small figure to a real estate dealer with whom he was in collusion; and the real estate dealer sub-leased it to farmers at an enormous profit.... The child (often) received nothing for his allotment."

Forced marriage—"A state law... conferred majority upon married (but underage allottee) minors. An unprincipled man or woman would be employed to win the confidence of the young Negro or Indian; the marriage would take place in the real estate office and the deed would be signed immediately after; and the charmer would walk out of the office, never to be seen again by the allottee."

African-Americans—"Guardians hastened to unload the land of Negro and mixed-blood children through the county court.... Seminole freedmen who had been tricked into giving deeds under the impression that they were signing other instruments had helplessly remained in their old homes and had been arrested and placed in jail for trespass. 'The days of... the good-for-nothing lazy criminal n----r, are numbered in Seminole County,' wrote a local newspaper."

Children—"The most revolting phase of the grafter's activities was his plundering of children.... Every minor possessed an estate varying in value from an average farm to the great and speculative wealth represented by an oil allotment. No other children had ever been so rich or so defenseless... (grafters) controlled the children's land through guardianships, and awaited only a legal opportunity to dispossess their wards through purchase."

Orphans—"Orphans received the most generous educational provision by the tribal governments. But when the land was allotted, the average parent was entirely irresponsible in dealing with his children's property; he was ready to sign it away for any bauble or appropriate the entire income for family expenses... parents... innocently leased their children's land, possibly to several different parties, and spent the money.... Many heartbreaking cases were uncovered of wrongs done to orphan children... a practice so general as to be almost universal."

Kidnapping—"Many young allottees were virtually kidnapped just before they reached their majority. They were put on the train, spirited from place to place, kept in hotels under constant surveillance, and induced to sign deeds at midnight on the morning they became of age."

Murder—"Murder became very common. Some spectacular crimes occurred, such as the dynamiting of two Negro children as they slept, in order that the conspirators might secure title to their Glenn Pool property by forged deeds; and many sinister stories were told of Indians who died under suspicious circumstances after bequeathing their property to white men.

"An epidemic of deaths broke out among aged Choctaws... Federal officials became convinced of an organized plot whereby the Indian made out a will to the land dealers in return for a ten-dollar monthly pension for the remainder of his life. A

Author and Oklahoma pioneer Angie Debo, by renowned Oklahoma painter Charles Banks Wilson.

suspicious fatality followed the making of such wills, and in several cases carbolic acid or ground glass was found on the premises. Several prominent real estate dealers were arrested, but the mystery of the Choctaw murders was never solved."

Even wealthy allottees, such as part-Cherokee Robert Owen—one of Oklahoma's first tandem of U.S. Senators—suffered. They often lost large tracts of land that exceeded the allotment limits on which they had built, cultivated, and improved. This increased the temptation for them to break either the letter or the spirit of the law, or both, to retrieve their valuable holdings.

The Cast Grows

Nor were whites the only culprits. Numerous Natives and African-Americans threw themselves into grafting enterprises. Many forgery gangs included black or Indian members who impersonated allottees of their own race. Elsewhere, as historian Debo chronicled, one Creek freedman signed away his own oil-rich allotment any time he needed cash, at prices ranging from fifty cents to a thousand dollars. He apparently sold the allotment forty-three times before he came of legal age. Years of contentious, expensive court battles ensued over the land once he did become an adult. Scores of such legal sagas occurred over land allotments.

Though many federal agents labored for a just execution of the allotment process, an "astounding" number of swindlers arose from their former ranks. The Natives received little help from atop the government either. Despite his "progressive" *bona fides,* Theodore Roosevelt, President from 1901-09, stood out for having been repeatedly called upon by the five Indian republics for assistance—and rarely if ever providing it.

Roosevelt's four-volume saga, *The Winning of the West*, provided abundant clues regarding his views dealing with the red race:

> No other conquering and colonizing nation has ever treated the original savage owners of the soil with such generosity as has the United States.... No treaties, whether between civilized nations or not, can ever be regarded as binding in perpetuity.
>
> All men of sane and wholesome thought must dismiss with impatient contempt the plea that (America) should be reserved for the use of scattered savage tribes, whose life was but a few degrees less meaningless, squalid, and ferocious than that of the wild beasts with whom they held joint ownership.... I don't go so far as to think that the only good Indians are dead Indians, but I believe nine out of every ten are, and I shouldn't like to inquire too closely into the case of the tenth.

I don't go so far as to think that the only good Indians are dead Indians, but I believe nine out of every ten are, and I shouldn't like to inquire too closely into the case of the tenth.

—President Theodore Roosevelt

A youthful Thomas P. Gore, around the time of his 1907 election as one of Oklahoma's first two senators. His stature grew through the years and decades as a defender of Indian rights.

Allotment: Missionary vs. Politician

As the United States Senate Select Committee to Investigate Matters Connected with Affairs In the Indian Territory considered the issue of Indian allotment in the Twin Territories and whom should control the process, Joseph Murrow, famed Baptist missionary to the Creeks, Choctaws, and Chickasaws, engaged in a memorable exchange with Colorado Senator Henry Teller during Murrow's testimony. Historian Angie Debo wrote, "Dr. Murrow expressed the most solemn warning against turning the problem over to local control—a warning that viewed in the light of subsequent events seems charged with prophetic insight. When Senator Teller urged his favorite thesis that the evils of the system were only temporary and that the proposed state of Oklahoma would soon correct all abuses, . . ." Murrow challenged him, and the rumble unfolded for the world to witness.

Cheyenne and Arapaho council members meet with a Bureau of Indian Affairs agent at the John Seger Colony in 1900.

Nor did territorial and state legislators as a whole gain an honorable legacy through the process of allotment and grafting. Still, some Oklahomans shine with unsullied brilliance through the mists of time for their remarkable wisdom in these affairs and their respect for both the law and the dignity of their fellow human beings. Notable among them are reformer Kate Barnard, missionary and pastor Joseph S. Murrow, and the other member of that inaugural tandem of U.S. Senators, Thomas P. Gore. All these, and numerous others, fought with vigor against a tide of slings and arrows for the powerless and the "least among these."

Indian Territory Confederate Cherokee war veterans at a 1903 reunion.

Benefits of Grafting

Alas, real history seldom allows its students simple accounts or answers. As Bartlesville oilman William Johnstone, who drilled the Nellie Johnstone Number One well (Chapter 10), stated regarding allotment restrictions, "There are two sides to that question. There is the Indian side to it and there is the commercial side to it. There is the side that affects the Indians and there is a side that affects the material progress of the country."

Further toughening the debate was the reality that "the material progress of the country"—though often meaning the opportunity for the very rich to grow very richer—also involved the survival of vast hosts of white, black, and red Americans and their families. Even Chief Court Clerk Nelson H. McCoy of Ardmore, who supervised the appointment of guardians, told a U.S. Senate committee in 1906, "These men called 'grafters' are not such bad fellows.... They spend a lot of money in getting these allotments made to these ignorant Indians."

> *There is the Indian side to it and there is the commercial side to it. There is the side that affects the Indians and there is a side that affects the material progress of the country.*
>
> **—William Johnstone**

So, numerous factors stood in support of the general practice and culture of grafting. For one, without grafters millions of acres of potentially productive allotted lands unclaimed by full bloods and other Indians would have laid useless, perhaps permanently. Also, a few thousand Natives had possession, under compulsion by white Americans, of tens of millions of acres of land. Meanwhile, amidst a series of Gilded Age financial recessions, panics, and true depression, hundreds of thousands of African-American and white American settlers—many of them willing to work their hearts out to build a life for their families, and in doing so, build a great American state—owned little or nothing.

Moreover, as previously discussed, Indian Territory shouldered the richly deserved sobriquet of "Robber's Roost" due to its endemic outlawry and the tribes' inability to curb it. Even Creek Chief Pleasant Porter, no supporter of allotment, admitted that white law enforcement was needed to rein in a lawless element that came in many different skin colors.

Indeed, at least one respected Oklahoma historian declared Debo a "muckraker." This term denotes a person who attempts to find and expose real or alleged corruption, scandal, or the like, especially in politics. That historian also contrasted her revisionist, anti-establishment perspective in her book, *And Still the Rivers Run,* written during the 1930s—amidst that benighted era's questioning of traditional American free enterprise and capitalism—with her pro-capitalist, pro-Oklahoma "boosterism" of the patriotic World War II-dominated 1940s.

Elderly Choctaw Full-Blood Speaks Against Allotment

"Surely a race of people, desiring to preserve the integrity of that race, who love it by reason of its traditions and their common ancestors and blood, who are proud of the fact that they belong to it may be permitted to protect themselves, if in no other way by emigration. Our educated people inform us that the white man came to this country to avoid conditions which to him were not as bad as the present conditions are to us; that he went across the great ocean and sought new homes in order to avoid things which to him were distasteful and wrong. All we ask is that we may be permitted to exercise the same privilege. We do not ask any aid from the Government of the United States in so doing. We do ask that we may be permitted, in a proper way, by protecting our own, to dispose of that which the Government says is ours, and which has been given us over our protest against the distribution, to the end that another home may be furnished, and another nation established."

—Jacob Jackson

So, were most of Oklahoma's "Founding Fathers" corrupt, selfish hypocrites, as Debo accuses and other state historians deny? With the passage of a century of time, perhaps these assessments may be reasonably offered: 1) corruption did grip some Oklahoma founders; 2) the work of Debo and others suggests such corruption grew somewhat more widespread—including among the founders—than earlier suspected; and 3) a long train of unwise, uncharitable, and immoral actions by the American government and people produced an allotment situation with so many layers of wrongdoing that no plan, regardless how well-intentioned (which this one was), could have produced happy results for both the allottees and the settlers. As witnessed many times in more recent American history, after a certain number of foolish decisions, no satisfactory solution remains possible.

Blacks Seek Rights

Horizons remained bright for African-Americans in the Twin Territory days of the early 1900s. According to historian Jimmie Franklin, sourcing

Cowboy Bill Pickett and Bulldogging (1870–1932)

Cowboy Bill Pickett in late 1900s bulldogging action, biting the lip of a bull.

This rugged Texas native couldn't even participate in most rodeos due to the color of his skin. Yet he pioneered the practice of bulldogging that led to modern steer wrestling, helped catapult the Miller Brothers' 101 Ranch Wild West Show near Bartlesville to world fame, became a silent movie star, and left a lasting testament to the prominence of African-American cowboys in the Old West.

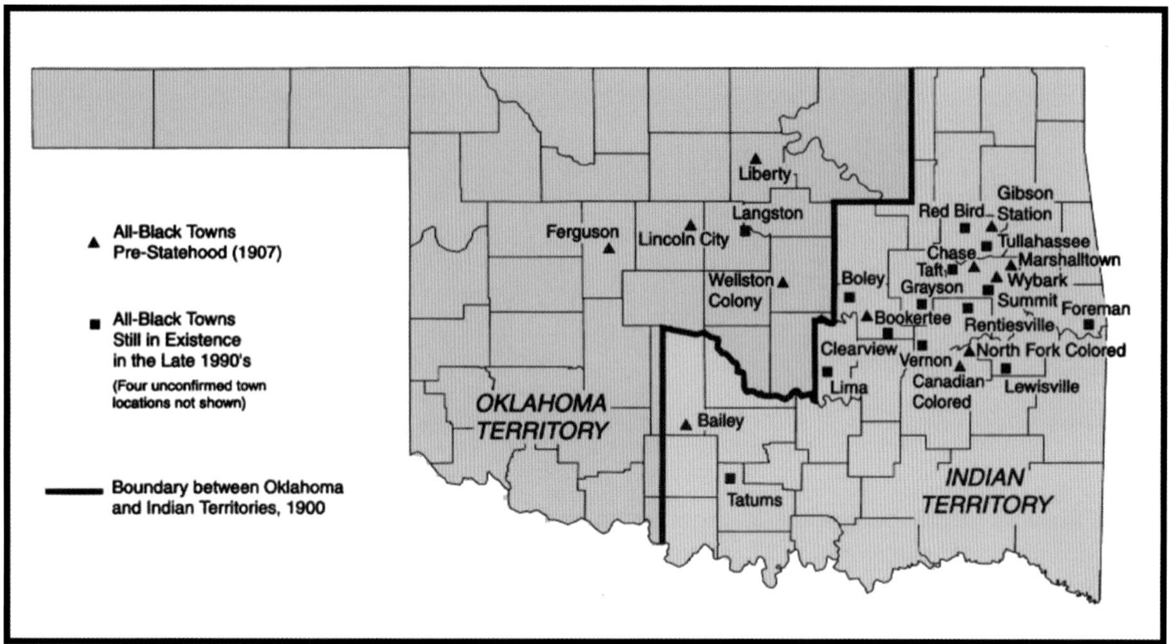

Oklahoma's all-black towns. Courtesy, Oklahoma State University Cartography Service.

the U.S. Bureau of the Census regarding the 1910 census, blacks owned more than 1.5 million acres of land in future Oklahoma by 1905. This represented an amount perhaps rivaling the total of African-American-owned land in the remainder of the United States!

Far from cowering in servility during this pioneer era, numerous bold, innovative, and courageous black entrepreneurs weathered the enormous obstacles of a developing Jim Crow society and built a galaxy of businesses that served their own communities and sometimes whites and Indians as well. Oklahoma City's Deep Deuce, Boley's downtown business district, as well as sections in other towns such as Muskogee, Wewoka, and Ardmore, and in particular Tulsa's Greenwood area, gained national renown as bastions of African-American enterprise, community, and spirit. Such flourishing redoubts were few and far between elsewhere on the North American continent at the time.

> *You kin talk about your cities with their steeples in the skies,*
> *Their nice paved streets and their business enterprise;*
> *We ain't got no sidewalks, and there's nothing here to see,*
> *But the little town of Boley is plenty big enough for me.*
>
> **—Samuel Robert Cassius**

In addition, many blacks employed vigorous and comprehensive strategies within the developing American legal system to fight for the interests of themselves and their families. Tribal freedmen exemplified this in a series of momentous legal actions against their tribes. Chickasaw freedmen won congressional approval for partial (40-acre) land allotments identical to those of their Choctaw peers, despite lacking tribal status. Tribal freedmen then sought enrollment onto tribal rolls so they might gain full (320-acre) land allotments, although the Natives warded off these efforts in court.

Other African-Americans secured the full Creek land allotments (160 acres) granted Creek freedmen by claiming through the courts the same identity. Principal Chief Porter wryly commented on the dubious nature of many of these claims to Creek freedmen status: "Our freedmen have increased wonderfully.... They come from the four quarters of the earth and employ a lawyer

Bootstrapping it in Boley. African-Americans build their own Okfuskee County town in the 1900s, without white or government help. The 1907 Town Council, left, and Farmers and Merchants Bank executives, right.

here to assist them, and they and the lawyer will get up the proof that slides them through."

Meanwhile, the Inter-Territorial Negro Protective League labored to protect the restrictions on the five Indian republics' allotments in order to protect the holders—which included African-Americans, Natives, and various red, white, and black mixed-blood combinations—as best as possible from wheeling and dealing land speculators and outright land swindlers that might, and ultimately did, maneuver much of the land away from the allottees.

After conducting painstaking research, historian Franklin determined that by the early 1900s, as many as twenty-seven all-black towns grew across the Twin Territories and then the new state. Rather than escaping from or surrendering to the American society around it, they flourished in it. "The Negro in the all-black community," write William B. Bittle and Gilbert Geis in *The Longest Way Home*, "was in no sense a retreat from the American standards and values which (blacks) had learned to cherish, nor was it an anachronistic revival of Africanism, but rather it constituted an attempt to develop fully and to exploit completely the American culture." Franklin went further, suggesting the opportunities and responsibilities gained in such enclaves fired up many African-Americans to apply their skills and experience in the full society.

Meanwhile, just as white pioneers across the future Sooner State ventured all they had to pursue

Streetcar-laden Main Street, Tulsa, Indian Territory, 1900.

W. H. Twine—"The Black Tiger" (1864–1933)

If any man could live up to the larger-than-life moniker of "The Black Tiger," it was this African-American pioneer who claimed land in the 1891 Sac and Fox Land Run, founded the first black law firm in the Twin Territories, built his own brick office building in Muskogee, crusaded against the Ku Klux Klan and others with his *Cimiter* newspaper, and even appealed in person to President Theodore Roosevelt against the statehood he believed to be founded upon an unjust constitution.

Despite the sorrowful chapters involving Natives and whites in Oklahoma history, the grand triumph of unity is their heritage of mutual Christian worship, including this circa-1900s Sunday school gathering in Indian Territory.

their dreams—whether it was the devout family staking, clearing, planting, harvesting, living, birthing, and dying on their earthly "Promised Land," or Marlow town father John O'Quinn helping found the State National Bank with the proceeds from a winning poker hand—blacks risked, labored, and bled for the vision of a free and prosperous future few of their race had experienced. They vied for leadership in the white-dominated territorial governments and founded newspapers across the state. Bold entrepreneurs like Guthrie grocer Sidney Lyons and Wewoka attorney and oilman J. Coody Johnson began amassing financial fortunes.

> *African-Americans vied for leadership in the white-dominated territorial governments, they founded newspapers across the state, and bold entrepreneurs began amassing financial fortunes.*

Ironically, the towering event celebrated and so long strived for by the Twin Territories' white majority population—statehood—triggered a series of events that would so set back the cause of African-American human rights, it would require better than half a century to return to its pre-statehood status.

Oil!

Indians in the Nations as early as Lewis Ross in 1859 (Chapter 5) had found oil on their land. A lack of technology and transportation, however, kept it in the ground until the early 1880s, when drilling began near Atoka on Choctaw land and by the Illinois River in the Cherokee country. An increasing number of discoveries peppered Indian Territory for more than twenty years. Then in 1901, daredevil wildcatter Robert Galbreath and others struck oil in the new Red Fork field, four miles west of the Arkansas River, across from the Creek-spawned village of Tulsa.

The international publicity triggered by Red Fork far outstripped its actual production, which proved modest. Yet the sensation spawned a new land run as exciting in its own way as those of 1889 and 1893. Thousands of drillers, speculators, investors, service people, roughnecks, and other business people and workers—including railroad employees—swarmed to the area. Red Fork did not need most of their talents, but another field of inestimably greater magnitude soon would.

Galbreath, demonstrating the eye for the deal and the nose for riches inside the earth that was already catapulting him into the front rank of early Oklahoma entrepreneurs, suspected a lot more oil lay to the south of Red Fork. With his partners Charles Colcord and Frank Chesley, he secured a gaggle of leases in and around the area ten miles south of Tulsa owned by Robert and Ida Glenn and her family. Shrewdly tracking the federal government's evolving policy on land leasing from its Native allottees, Galbreath delayed drilling there until restrictions on drillers softened. Satisfied that they had, he drilled nearly fifteen hundred feet

Red Fork and Glenn Pool—Oklahoma's First Oil Strike and Boom

Charles Colcord, legendary Oklahoma pioneer, shared his first-hand account of Oklahoma's first real oil strike, the Red Fork Field, which led to the future state's first true oil boom at Glenn Pool:

Oklahoma's first great oil boom, the Glenn Pool Field near Tulsa in old Indian Territory. Courtesy Oklahoma Historical Society.

In the spring of 1901 the Federal government sold at auction the town site of Red Fork, a new community on the Frisco line which was then building about three miles west of Tulsa. Robert Galbreath, representing Colcord, Galbreath and C. G. Jones, attended this sale and purchased twenty-five or thirty lots. On a lot near these lots, where he lived, Doctor Bland was drilling for water and struck a small gas well. A number of other parties from Oklahoma City had bought lots . . . and we all began drilling about the same time. Years later I heard stories of several fellows who drilled the first oil well in Red Fork, but for all these years I have felt that we were the first to strike oil there.

A Glenn Pool oil field gusher, around 1905.

down, where he believed oil was, and brought in the Ida Glenn Number One in late 1905. He sank well after well, and brought in the famed Glenn Pool field, one of the mightiest on record. It generated more revenue than the California Gold Rush and Colorado Silver Rush combined.

This epic play, which mushroomed from eighty acres in size to eight square miles, launched the careers of Harry Sinclair (Sinclair Oil) and J. Paul Getty (Getty Oil) and spurred pioneer stalwart Dennis Flynn's infant Oklahoma Natural Gas to pipe gas to Oklahoma City—which helped build both ONG and OKC. The massive oil boom also triggered construction of thousands more miles of gas pipeline into the Oklahoma country, secured millions of dollars of investment capital and jobs for the territory/state, birthed such towns as Sapulpa, Jenks, Glenpool, and Mounds, and established Tulsa for half a century as "The Oil Capital of the World."

Oklahoma was churning out over forty million barrels of oil a year while not yet a state. By the end of the decade and for twenty years after that, it stood as the greatest oil-producing state in America, and ever since as one of the top two or three. For once, here was a country that lived up to the stuff of the Hollywood legends it spawned. As historian and pioneer Angie Debo wrote, "The oil industry was a free for all scramble, with the great Mellon and Standard interests, the young oil worker who could scrape together enough money to drill a well of his own, and the gambler who must try one more 'sure thing,' all entering into the most unrestricted rivalry."

The early twentieth-century Oklahoma oil boom lives as one of the greatest discoveries of natural resources in history. It made fortunes, helped build and sustain a state, and spawned a gallery of larger-than-life legends. These were men and women with the cunning derring-do of riverboat

Epic shot of oil boom in Cleveland, Pawnee County, 1905.

gamblers, the leather-tough perseverance of frontier preachers, and the steel-nerved calm of Old West gunfighters. Most of the boom, though, occurred on land owned by the five Indian republics and then that of their individual members. Historian Debo again speaks through the years in a manner akin to a still, small, penetrating voice of reason and protest against the blindness, folly, and injustice that can taint even the most exciting, revered events in American history:

> The Federal administration of the tribal estates had not always been to the best interests of the owners, but there was a genuine desire to protect the individual allottee. As the Federal officials began to realize the vast helplessness and inexperience of the average Indian, they began, through a blundering process of experimentation, to try to guard his property. But because of the lack of a definite and constructive policy, and most of all because of the inherent difficulty of the task itself, the general effect of allotment was an orgy of plunder and exploitation probably unparalleled in American history.

The early twentieth-century Oklahoma oil boom lives as one of the greatest discoveries of natural resources in history. It made fortunes, helped build a state, and spawned a gallery of larger-than-life legends.

Robert Galbreath, Patriarch of Oklahoma Oil (1863–1953)

After this shrewd pioneer sniffed out oil on the Glenn spread, he coolly waited years for federal regulations on the land to relax, then sunk the wells that ignited the historic Glenn Pool Field strike. That catapulted Oklahoma into America's largest oil producer, simultaneous with its statehood; established the nearby city of Tulsa as the Oil Capital of the World; and bequeathed Galbreath his lofty status as the patriarch of the Sooner State energy empire.

Later Land Openings

Around 3,500,000 square acres of Comanche, Kiowa, Apache, Wichita, and Caddo land in southern

Oklahoma Land Openings

Lands Opened By Allotment
1891 - Tonkawa
1892 - Pawnee
1904 - Ponca
1904 - Oto-Missouri
1906 - Osage
1906 - Kaw

Lands Opened By Run
April 22, 1889 - Unassigned Lands
September 22, 1891 - Iowa,
- Sac & Fox,
- Pottawatomie & Shawnee
April 19, 1892 - Cheyenne & Arapaho
September 16, 1893 - Cherokee Outlet
May 23, 1895 - Kickapoo

Lands Opened By Lottery
July 9 to August 6, 1901 - Wichita and Caddo
- Comanche, Kiowa & Apache

Lands Opened By Sealed Bid
December 1906 - Big Pasture

(Courtesy Oklahoma Historical Society)

Oklahoma Territory, along with nearly 2,000,000 acres of Osage, Ponca, Kaw, and Otoe-Missouri land in northern Indian Territory, remained unallotted to the resident tribes and unapportioned to American settlers at the dawn of the twentieth century. Congress remedied this with several more great land openings. Land runs, for all their epic historical drama, had proven to be logistical, administrative, and legal nightmares. The final land giveaways occurred through lottery and sealed bid.

In 1901 came the Wichita and Caddo lands around present-day Caddo County and the Kiowa-Comanche-Apache (K-C-A) lands around present-day Comanche and Kiowa counties. Over 135,000 prospective homesteaders and town citizens registered for 160-acre tracts, hoping to hear their names called among the listings of 13,000 lots pulled from large boxes.

Following the awarding of these lots, town lots in the new county seats of Anadarko (Caddo), Lawton (Comanche), and Hobart (Kiowa) commenced. Nearly seven hundred and fifty thousand dollars in sales financed construction and improvement of roads, bridges, and courthouses in these counties.

At least two legendary Oklahomans—future U.S. Senator Thomas P. Gore and famed lawman Heck Thomas—put down stakes as thousands of people raised the new town of Lawton up from the southwest Oklahoma plains on the day of its birth, August 6, 1901. The two men developed a close friendship. Though he was blind, Gore's recollection of the signal experience, when he and Thomas at first lived in tents on the heretofore wild and dangerous prairie, provides an enduring window for future generations into pioneer Oklahoma:

> I located at Lawton before there was any Law-ton. There were only two little shacks on the town-site when I located my tent on the Eastern Boundary which was then called 'Goo-goo' avenue. The blue grass was waist high on most of the town-site, particularly where there were "hog-wallers." The hard mesquite occupied part of the town-site.

In 1904, much smaller portions of Ponca, Otoe, and Missouri lands were allotted to individual tribal members. Settlers purchased the remaining fifty-one thousand acres. Osage and Kaw Indians received individual allotments of their tribal lands in 1906, with none left for settlers. At the end of 1906, the federal government auctioned off 480,000 acres of K-C-A range along Red River through a sealed bid. This "Big Pasture" had served as a hunting and grazing reserve for these tribes since the 1901 allotment and sale of their remaining southwest Oklahoma lands.

As might be expected of a region in which some of the most feared Plains Indian tribes as well as rugged white ranchers and cowboys had lived, the Big Pasture did not prove to be cordial to the influences of either big government or big business.

As might be expected of a region in which some of the most feared Plains Indian tribes as well as rugged white ranchers and cowboys had lived, the Big Pasture did not prove cordial to the influences of either big government or big business. Historian

The first and greatest Oklahoma Territory land lottery, for the Kiowa, Comanche, and Apache reservations.

Edward Everett Dale, who as a young cowboy lived in the Big Pasture, considered the people of this area to be significant contributors to Oklahoma's historic populist influence.

Repeating a recurrent theme of Oklahoma history, such epic events spawned opportunity and thrilling history, as well as injustice, loss, and sorrow. Dust clouds billowed and the earth shook when thousands of horses, mules, wagons, and other vehicles thundered across the prairie toward new homesteads and the building of an American state during the K-C-A opening. Yet Christian missionaries who had labored among the Comanches, Kiowas, and Apaches on those enormous reservations, "lamented the high crime rates, drunkenness, unsanitary conditions, and diseases" strewn in these pioneers' wake, according to historian Benjamin R. Kracht.

Numerous white voices joined the Indians in opposing the K-C-A opening. They included Indian Agent James Randlett, Fort Sill Cavalry Commander Hugh Scott (namesake of Lawton's Mount Scott), Texas cattlemen who grazed herds there, and Baptist, Presbyterian, Mennonite, Roman Catholic, and Methodist Episcopal, South missionaries.

Kiowa Chief and Christian convert Lone Wolf (the younger adopted son of famed warrior and Chief Lone Wolf, the elder) mounted a brilliant, years-long legal battle with the federal government over the K-C-A opening that roared all the way to the U.S. Supreme Court. That body ruled against the Kiowas, citing the Fifth Amendment of the Bill of Rights for their remarkable admission that "the power exists to abrogate the provisions of an Indian treaty."

Progressivism

Progressivism emerged from the Populist movement (Chapter 10) of the late 1800s, but expanded far beyond that movement's rural base. It seized the affections of Republican leaders as it already had many Democrats and endured as a permanent influence in the American republic. At the dawn of the twentieth century, it guided in diverse ways the hearts, tongues, and pens of most of the men who birthed the state of Oklahoma.

Progressivism served as the vehicle by which the classical or economic liberalism of the eighteenth and nineteenth centuries gave way to the modern liberalism of government intervention to achieve individual freedoms and opportunities. For

An Otoe woman. Otoe land was allotted to tribal members and sold to settlers in 1904. Courtesy Oklahoma Historical Society.

whites—if not Indians or blacks—the earlier traditional sort of liberalism, which America's Founding Fathers largely supported, strongly advocated limited government, personal liberty, and free-market economics, and placed much authority in the citizenry on both state and local levels. The historic sea change of progressivism evidenced itself not only in Oklahoma but across America, in Britain, and elsewhere. Charles Haskell, soon to be the state's first governor, declared the 1906–07 Constitutional Convention's intent "not just to create a new state, but to create a new kind of state."

> *Progressivism evolved into a broad social and political philosophy of activist government, but its adherents proved to be diverse and inconsistent in their practice of it.*

In the early 1900s, those pursuing progressive ideas sought through expanded governmental power—especially on the national level, but in Oklahoma as well—to correct the ills of a fast-growing nation and economy for which the Industrial Revolution had produced both new products and new problems, not least the perception of a widening chasm between the rich and powerful, and the poor. Progressives (although this term did not initially convey the full import of the previous statement) took aim at correcting the ills of other nations as well, as Presidents like Roosevelt, William McKinley, and Woodrow Wilson launched the U.S. into the global imperialist sweepstakes long pursued by the European powers.

Varieties of Progressivism

The philosophy varied according to its proponents. Some people aimed for economic reform through government control of big business or promotion of farmers' and laborers' rights. Some sought social change, such as the vote for women, protection of working children, or prohibition of the alcoholic spirits that were destroying so many lives. Others desired to replace republican processes of representative government according to constitutional statutes with direct democratic decisions by popular majorities. Progress to others meant codifying separation of the white and black races through segregation and Jim Crow laws.

An Oklahoma pioneer family, the Prestons, around 1900 in Cimarron County, so far west it lies in the Rocky Mountain Time Zone.

Adding to the confusion, proponents of these "progressive" notions often opposed one another. As just one of many such examples, a white female suffragette and an African-American male farmer seeking social and political rights might both have claimed progressive interests, yet both might have opposed the other's aims.

No one has better explored the dangers of suggesting a rigid test of orthodoxy for "progressivism" than historian Kenny Brown. For instance, he cited the variance in definitions for such entities as trusts, monopolies, and special interests. Also, how Oklahomans as diverse as political leaders, oil men, and tenant farmers often supported in practice some of the various entities or actions they opposed in public.

According to Brown:

> As elsewhere, in Oklahoma there was no unified group of people with common goals who called themselves progressives. There were several separate interest groups that arose and used the prevailing anticorporate sentiment to achieve their ends. In particular, Oklahoma farmers and labor union members convinced politicians to draft provisions in the constitution and legislation favorable to agriculture and labor. Legislators also approved laws designed to restrict the actions of various types of corporations. But the language, goals, and results of this political activity were contradictory, inconsistent, and vague.

Merle St. Leon's send-up of the competing interests of white women, disenfranchised from voting until 1920, and African-American men, disenfranchised in Oklahoma beginning in 1910.

The twenty-first-century Tea Party phenomenon perhaps provides a modern if distinct analogy to progressivism. In modern terms, progressivism stands to the political left or liberal side, and the Tea Party to the right or conservative. Both "movements," however, possess populist roots, feature an array of often self-serving politicians speaking to particular issues with no little demagoguery involved, address multiple issues, and encompass citizens and groups with a variety of grievances. In both cases many of the issues, upon closer examination, stand at cross-purposes with one another and are more difficult to solve than the typical slogans suggest.

In the end, progressivism—whose primary era Brown suggests as 1900–16—evolved into a broad social and political philosophy of activist government, but its adherents proved to be diverse and inconsistent in their practice of it.

Reasons for Progressivism

At its root, progressivism had much in common with another familiar but amorphous term, socialism, in that it sought greatly enhanced governmental control of American society and institutions for the good of the citizenry. Numerous factors set the stage for the turn-of-the-century reformist impulse that gripped civic leaders on the local, state, and federal levels. These included:

1. The social and economic sea change of the American Industrial Revolution
2. Widespread corruption and moral breakdown stemming from the War Between the States, especially its latter stages, and continuing through Reconstruction
3. Political and governmental corruption on an unparalleled scale during the 1870s-1890s "Gilded Age," including within a U.S. presidential administration (Ulysses S. Grant's)
4. Massive governmental collusion with corporate giants such as railroads through exorbitant protective tariffs, colossal land giveaways, and other mercantilist practices
5. Suppression of American Indian tribes
6. Raging racial prejudice and continued denial of constitutional rights to African-Americans
7. National financial calamities, most notably the four-year depression that began as the Panic of 1893
8. Hard economic struggles for millions of people within the working classes (farming, laboring, factories, etc.)
9. Fading societal impact of the Christian gospel the further American society migrated west
10. Upstaging of that gospel with a social gospel predicated on the perfectability of man rather than the perfection of God

All of this occurred as a group of industrialists centered in the Northeast compiled financial fortunes never imagined in previous American history. Historian Brown recounted that in 1897, the United States had only twelve huge corporations, capitalized at $1 billion. Just six years later, in 1903, those numbers had mushroomed to three hundred five and $7 billion, respectively.

Roosevelt co-edited *The Outlook*, a key Progressive Party publication. The *Outlook* chastised the supposedly less progressive Woodrow Wilson and Democratic Party for their accused allegiance to early Christian creeds such as the Nicean, the biblical doctrines of the Reformation, and the U.S. Constitution. Progressive leaders called instead for "a new theology, a new science, a new sociology, a new politics . . . men who have faith in themselves" in America. They declared, "The Constitution is the political wisdom of a dead America."

> *The Constitution is the political wisdom of a dead America.*
> **—Walter Edward Weyl**

Progressivism—Pro or Con?

Many historians question key underlying premises for progressivism. They acknowledge legitimate criticism of many practices of railroads and other large corporations of the day, but they also suggest those critics often frame their attacks too broadly, skewering free enterprise and capitalism in the process. The excesses and corruption of Gilded Age "robber baron" industry grew not from classical laissez faire economics, they say, but rather from the mercantilist-fueled (Chapter 1) movement away from it.

Thomas E. Woods, Jr., for instance, suggested that select and unfair governmental collusion with favored industries and corporations through high protective tariffs and subsidies, not the rapacious acts of unregulated business, fueled the monopoly problems of the Gilded Age and Progressive Era. The weighty evidence for this notion casts the progressive movement as a swirl of efforts to better balance the growing powers of government between the interests of the nation's powerful institutions and the vast sweep of citizens with little means.

Such supposed "predatory" monopolists as John D. Rockefeller and Andrew Carnegie actually accelerated the production of manufactured goods, reduced the prices of those goods to American consumers, entered into voluntary mergers and acquisitions with competitors that made many of the latter rich, and donated billions of dollars (in early twentieth-century value) to charitable and public causes. Rockefeller—a devout Baptist teetotaler—gave away more than half a *billion* dollars of his personal fortune.

Shifting law-giving authority from the legislative branch of government to the (current) popular majority, as progressives urged on many fronts, again broke with the Founding Fathers' vision. And although two millennia of Christendom offered no gleaming record on the issue of slavery—racially based or otherwise—the "survival of the fittest"-influenced Social Darwinism (Chapter 8) that opposed theistic Christianity and fueled both populism and progressivism did anything but advance the rights of African-Americans in Oklahoma or other states. In fact, the ascendance of progressivism arguably set back the social, political, and economic rights of blacks for at least a half-century in Oklahoma.

> *The ascendance of progressivism arguably set back the social, political, and economic rights of blacks for at least a half-century in Oklahoma.*

Indian State?

As leaders of the five great Indian republics realized the impossibility of regaining control outside the Union of American States over their lands, people, and institutions, they determined to make the best of their situation. For years they petitioned the Dawes Commission, the Interior Department, Congress, and President Theodore Roosevelt himself to honor the United States' long and oft-repeated promise regarding their self-governance. "As a people we have kept our faith with the United States government," they wrote Roosevelt, urging him to support Indian Territory statehood apart from that of Oklahoma Territory. "You know our hopes and ambitions; and we appeal again to your sense of justice and fair dealing."

As though the wise and insightful voice of Elias Boudinot still sounded among them, the Five Tribes also recognized the awful carnage wrought upon them by alcoholic spirits. They passed prohibition laws long before any American state did. This issue further fired their determination to remain unhitched from their neighbor to the west. As recalled by Oklahoma pioneer Angie Debo, "They objected strongly to the open saloons that carried on such a thriving business in Oklahoma Territory... (and) preferred the (prohibition) system to the arrogance with which the liquor traffic dominated the life of Oklahoma (Territory)."

Carnegie Saloon in Caddo County, circa 1900. Indian Territory had long outlawed such establishments with their recreation and vice, and Oklahoma Territory would do so as well at statehood.

Working together with white leaders of Indian Territory, these Natives—most of them mixed-bloods—convened the 1905 Sequoyah Convention in Muskogee. They aimed to establish the new state of Sequoyah (named in honor of the legendary Cherokee linguist and educator, Chapter 3) and remain separate from whatever white-dominated state might evolve from Oklahoma Territory to the west. They believed that this was their best chance to gain a strong voice in the area's future American state(s). According to historian Bob Blackburn, "The Sequoyah Convention was the voice of the Indians and their desire to have their own state to serve the needs of their own people."

(The Indians) objected strongly to the open saloons that carried on such a thriving business in Oklahoma Territory... (and) preferred the (prohibition) system to the arrogance with which the liquor traffic dominated the life of Oklahoma (Territory).

—Angie Debo

The Sequoyah assembly included many of the pillars of early Oklahoma, including no less than four future governors. Two men, though, towered over both the gathering and early Oklahoma—Charles N. Haskell, who emigrated from Ohio in 1901, and William H. "Alfalfa Bill" Murray, who came from Texas in 1898. Ironically, both of these magnetic founding fathers of Oklahoma were white, though Murray qualified as an intermarried Chickasaw citizen, having been betrothed to Mary Alice Hearrell, beautiful niece of Chickasaw Governor Douglas Johnston.

Haskell, already a heavyweight in the railroad, legal, and petroleum fields, possessed such stature that he would soon do ferocious personal—and very public—battle with an American president, while a three-time presidential candidate rose to his defense. Although Cherokee lobbyist James Norman first heralded the idea of an Indian Territory statehood convention, Haskell parlayed the concept into reality. Exhibiting the vision, shrewdness, and judgment of character that illumined his career, he persuaded

Principal Chiefs Pleasant Porter of the Creeks, William C. Rogers of the Cherokees, and Green McCurtain of the Choctaws to see the merits of such a convention. Later, Creek Chief John F. Brown also assented, though Chickasaw Principal Chief Johnston opposed the effort.

> *The Sequoyah Convention was the voice of the Indians and their desire to have their own state to serve the needs of their own people.*
>
> **—Bob Blackburn**

Sequoyah Convention

Privately, Haskell doubted the possibility of statehood for Indian Territory, though not because the notion lacked merit. The territory's population had ballooned to around seven hundred thousand people, nearly twice that of the previous most populous American state to join the Union. Congress fast-tracked Nevada to statehood in 1864 with a population of only thirty thousand. Why? Wartime President Abraham Lincoln and his Republican congressional colleagues feared Lincoln would not win re-election without additional votes against Democratic opponent and military hero George McClellan, who wanted to negotiate an end to war and a return to the Union for the South.

This time, however, the Republicans running Washington were determined to keep out a territory boasting over twenty times the population Nevada had claimed. Southern Democrats filled Indian Territory and had grown increasingly dominant in Oklahoma Territory as well since around 1898. No matter how many requests the Indians made of him, President Roosevelt—a progressive, an activist, and no great admirer of the South nor its politics—had no intention of allowing the Oklahoma country to send two sets of likely Democratic senators and representatives to Washington to oppose the Northern-dominated Republicans' agenda. Haskell perceived all this, but he also believed that without statehood for Sequoyah, tribal leaders would consent to single statehood for the Twin Territories, which he did not oppose.

Carriages park outside the Missouri, Oklahoma & Gulf passenger train station in pre-statehood 1900s Muskogee. Charles Haskell's leadership built this rail line, from Missouri through Texas, as it did many other businesses.

Indian Territory voters confirmed Republican concerns by sending an overwhelmingly Democratic congress of delegates to the Sequoyah Convention. There, Porter won election as president and chairman of the convocation. Each of the five Indian Republics provided a vice president. They included mixed-blood chiefs Rogers of the Cherokees, McCurtain of the Choctaws, and Brown of the Creeks, as well as Haskell for the Creeks due to his leadership qualities and Porter's chairmanship, and Murray in place of his uncle Johnston for the Chickasaws. Delegates also tabbed Haskell as convention vice-chairman. Famed Creek poet Alexander Posey served as secretary.

The Sequoyah delegates labored to craft the framework for an American state. The searching light of history testifies they accomplished that audacious mission—though not for the state they intended. Even as friendly U.S. congressmen introduced bills to admit the state of Sequoyah, Roosevelt declared his implacable opposition to the two-state plan. Congress shot down all dual-statehood bills, and the Hamilton Statehood Bill passed both legislative houses to pave the way for the forty-sixth state of Oklahoma's entrance into the Union.

The lasting legacy of the Sequoyah Convention lay elsewhere. The forty-five thousand-word constitution they authored under "Alfalfa Bill" Murray's leadership set the tone for the following year's penning of the Oklahoma Constitution. And the men who wrote it captained that later, more important

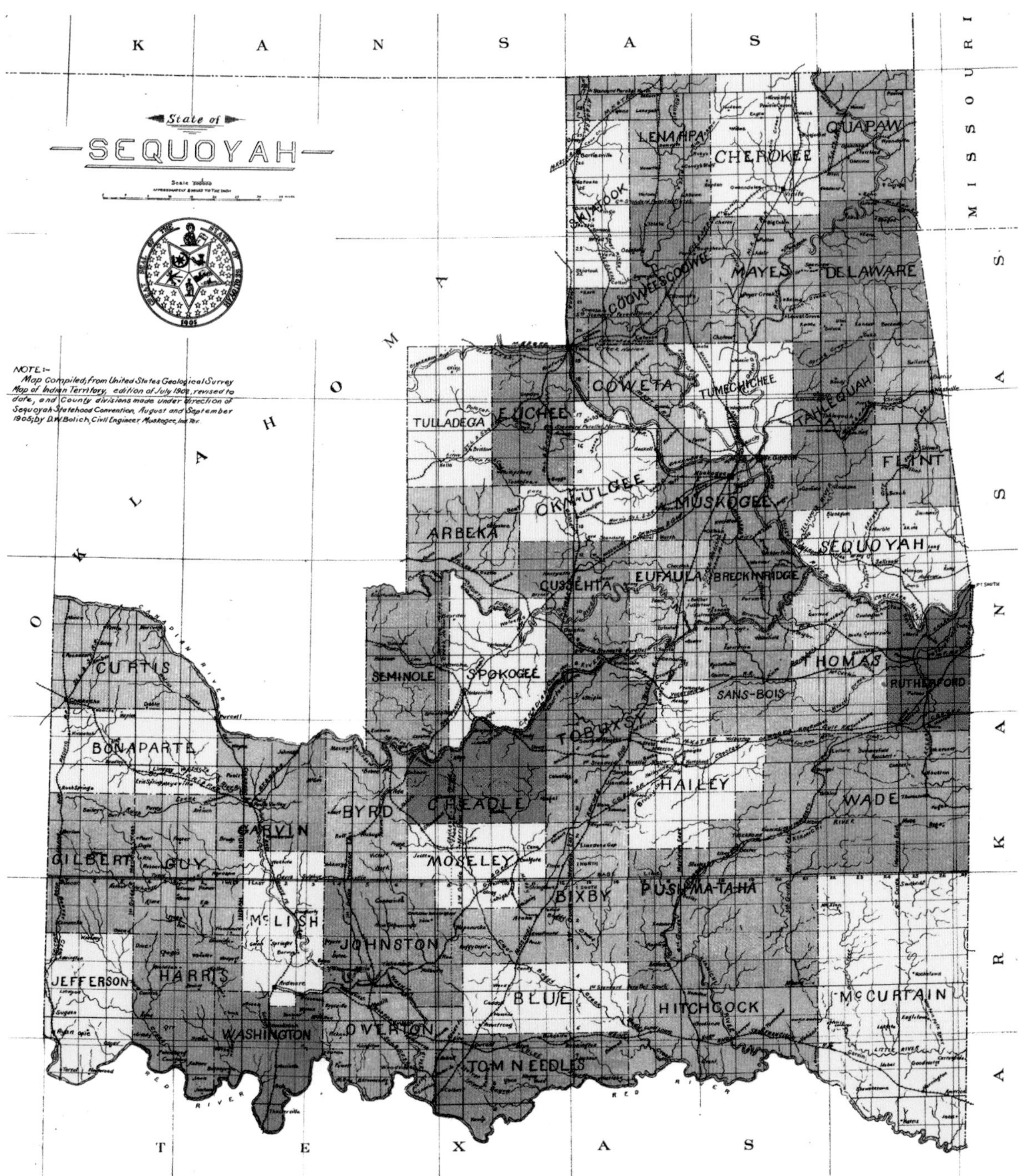

effort. The assembly believed America's surging industrialization was littering the country with the debris of the common man, who they believed no longer had the wherewithal to maintain his rights—nor at times even his physical survival—against a government-favored oligarchic juggernaut and a corrupted, money- and power-grubbing one at that. So Sequoyah planned for a state, not where government would rule, but where the majority possessing humble means could again access and utilize that government for its rights as they believed America's founders had intended—to serve and represent not only the powerful few, but all the people.

Theodore Roosevelt—Cowboy President (1858–1919)

This legendary President left a lasting footprint on the world, the United States, and singularly on Oklahoma, where he made a couple of memorable personal visits and played a key role in the drama of statehood during the decade of the 1900s. No political label sufficed for him, whether Progressive, Bull Moose, or Republican. Regarding the latter, had he lived a generation later he would likely have been a Democrat. Had he lived a century later, he may have been a Republican again. Through his power of personality and vision, he transformed the office of President into a more powerful one than it had been before, and, more than any other individual, he did the same for the U.S. as a nation on the world stage.

Teddy Roosevelt and the Great Wolf Hunt

"The big white horse, Sam Bass, came bucking over the bluff and there was the wolf, dead ahead, heading for rough ground. One greyhound left in the chase, Catch 'Em Alive Jack Abernathy's own, right on the wolf's heels. Snapping a glance back, Jack caught one glimpse of the rider behind him, a flash of big white teeth and glittering eyeglasses, and then the flying white horse was down in the flat."

Perhaps no other hunt in Oklahoma or anywhere else ever assembled a cast with the stature of the 1905 Oklahoma Territory bare-handed wolf hunt near Frederick, OT. It included cowboy and wolf hunter Jack "Catch 'Em Alive" Abernathy, standing in center clutching a dead wolf; President Theodore Roosevelt, standing second from the right, Comanche Chief Quanah Parker, kneeling left of Abernathy; and Texas-Oklahoma cattleman Samuel "Burk" Burnett, standing far right.

Oklahoma cowboy and wolf hunter John R. "Jack" Abernathy and President Theodore Roosevelt on their great 1905 hunt near Frederick. Abernathy exhibits his bare-handed catch.

Also, a company of Natives, at least of the mixed-blood variety, rose to lead the new state. And for the first time in American history, Indians and whites teamed up in a large and concerted cause toward a mutual objective. The agreements, differences, biases, and disputes they faced forged them into a united assembly that dominated the Oklahoma Statehood Convention. After Sequoyah, they knew how to work together as a team and when to act to push their goals forward.

Catch 'Em Alive Jack and the Abernathy Boys (1876–1941)

Whether it was "Catch 'Em Alive" Jack leaping from his horse in the Oklahoma Territory short-grass country and taking down a vicious 125-pound wolf with his bare hands as President Theodore Roosevelt watched, or the rugged cowboy's grade school-aged sons crossing America on horseback by themselves, the Abernathy family's dauntless deeds remind us that the legends of the Old West were oftentimes fact.

President Theodore Roosevelt, Frederick, OT, Oklahoma artist Mike Wimmer's captivating depiction of Jack Abernathy and President Theodore Roosevelt in Frederick, Oklahoma Territory, during the famed 1905 wolf hunt. Used with permission from the Oklahoma State Senate Collection and the artist. Courtesy Oklahoma State Senate Historical Preservation Fund, a project of Charles Ford.

The Glass Mountains, located in Major County, northwest Oklahoma.

The men of Sequoyah bided their time as necessary, forged ahead as able, and determined to outlast what they and the sweep of Oklahomans viewed as arrogant, unwelcome carpetbaggers ruling them from afar without sensitivity or understanding of their ways and culture. Soon, Haskell and Murray and others knew Oklahoma would be their state—not Roosevelt and his party's. Most whites in Oklahoma applauded, believing their rights championed. Most blacks did not, seeing many of theirs discarded. Twin Territory Democrats assayed the political landscape well. Their attitudes toward their political (and in many ways cultural) foes have, rightly or wrongly, endured as part of their heritage among the people of Oklahoma, even into a new century.

"It's no lie. I did it with my hatchet"

Merle St. Leon's depiction of temperance advocate Carrie Nation. Famed for smashing whiskey barrels with her axe, the nearly six-foot Missourian headquartered in Guthrie during Oklahoma's constitutional battle over prohibition.

The Carpetbaggers

"There was a universal protest against the "carpetbag" administration, arising partly from the natural desire of a large American population to be self-governing, and partly from a vast hunger for the spoils of the many Federal agencies in the Territory that were monopolized by Northern Republican politicians. Bad as the spoils system was, it was not bad enough to suit local Republicans. They condemned the higher officials of the Dawes Commission, the Inspector's office, the Agency, and the courts for their failure to fill all subordinate positions with "loyal, working Republicans." These administrative officials, they insisted, were overlooking their "solemn duty" to strengthen the party against the day of statehood; they were offering no encouragement to the untried voter to join the Republican ranks."

—**Angie Debo**

Buffalo graze near the Wichita Mountains in 1908, the early stages of growing back a portion of the magnificent herds decimated in the late 1870s.

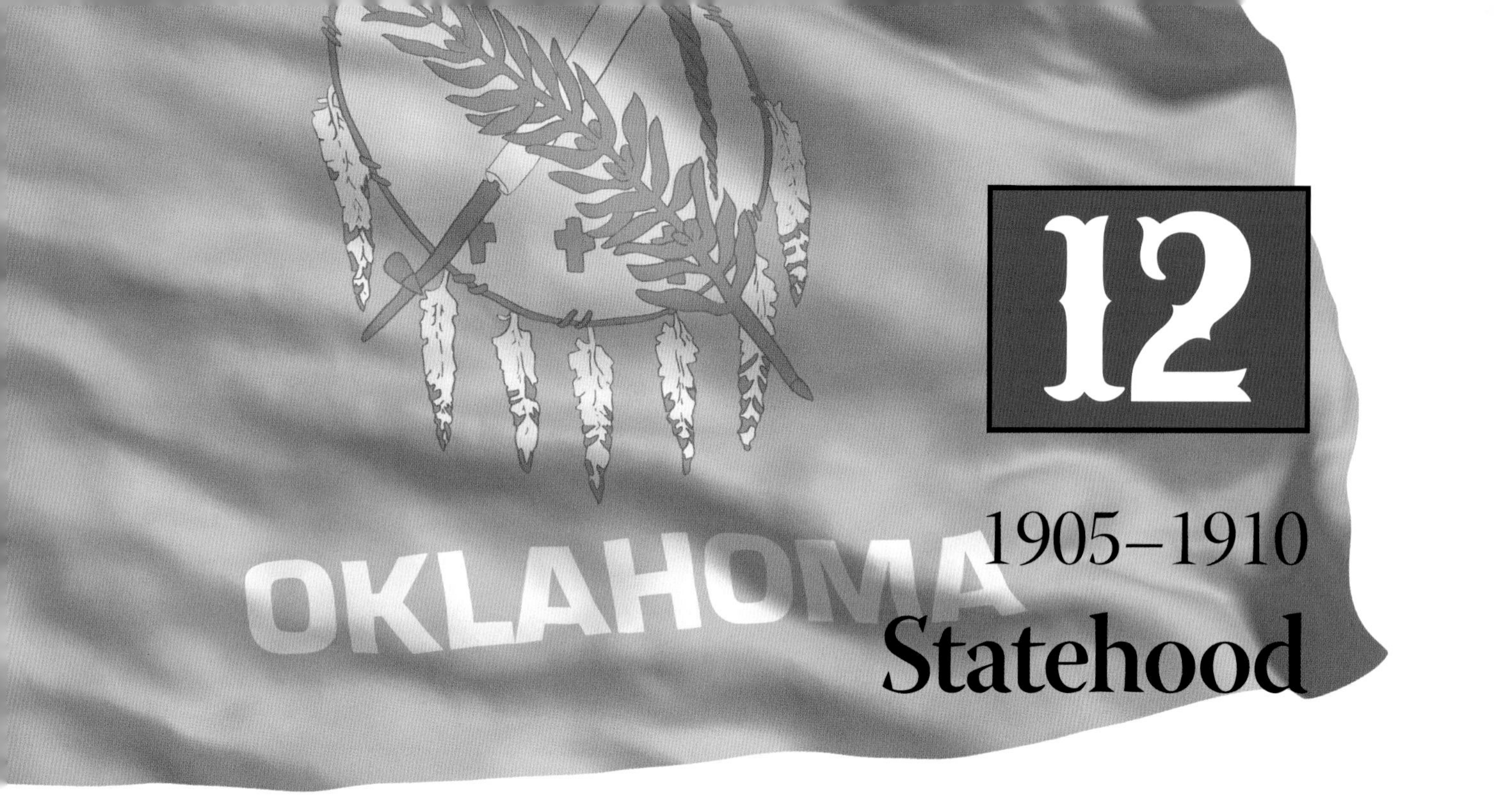

12

1905–1910
Statehood

Oklahoma, so long a maverick of the southwest, has finally received the coveted brand of statehood and been admitted to the corral

21,040
DAILY AVERAGE FOR OCT.

THE DAILY OKLAHOMAN

LARGEST DAILY NEWSPAPER
IN GREATER OKLAHOMA

OKLAHOMA CITY, OKLAHOMA, SUNDAY, NOVEMBER 17, 1907—THIRTY-SIX PAGES

PRICE 5 CENTS

OKLAHOMA BECOMES STATE

SALOON DUEL CAUSE OF DEATH

Theft of a Bottle of Whisky Responsible for Fight

ROBT. JOHNSON IS DEAD

His Assailant, Fred Morris, Surrenders to Under Sheriff Garrison

CHAUFFEUR IS FATALLY CUT DURING FIGHT

BELIEVED THAT VICTIM OF FIGHT AT THREADGILL WILL NOT LIVE.

SCRATCH OF QUILL PEN LETS THE NEW STATE INTO UNION

"That Makes Oklahoma a State," Says Roosevelt, When He Affixes Signature

Special to The Oklahoman.

Washington, Nov. 16.—"There, that makes Oklahoma a state," declared President Roosevelt this morning as he smiled at the spectators in the cabinet room after he had appended his signature to the document admitting Oklahoma and Indian Territory as the forty-sixth state.

INDIAN TERRITORY AND OKLAHOMA ARE SYMBOLICALLY WED

Thirty Thousand People Attend the Inaugural Ceremonies at State Capitol

Special to The Oklahoman.

ENID FIREBUG CAUGHT WHILE MAKING BLAZE

NIGHT WATCHMAN DETECTED FIRING OIL SOAKED SACKS NEAR BIG MILL.

Special to The Oklahoman.

BATTLE WITH GUNS; TWO DEAD

Marshal and Bootlegger Victims of Fatal Shooting

"BAD MAN" STARTS IT

Officers Attempts to Arrest, Bootlegger Kills and Is Slain

The November 17, 1907 edition of *The Daily Oklahoman* announces statehood.

c. 1900–1916	Progressive Era
1906	Oklahoma Enabling Act
1906	Oklahoma Constitutional Convention
1907	Oklahoma becomes 46th American state
1907	Charles Haskell elected first governor
1907	Kate Barnard wins statewide election before women allowed to vote
1907	First Jim Crow segregation laws passed
1908	State Bank Guaranty Law passed
1908	Indian allotment sales restrictions rolled back
1908	African-American state representative A. C. Hamlin elected
1909	Columbia Bank & Trust fails

First, then, if you are a statesman and true to your country, safeguard the child.
—Kate Barnard

With the statehood issue settled by the Republican-dominated national government as the single entity of Oklahoma—and thus no separate, Indian-dominated "Sequoyah"—the Democratic-dominated populace of that state now set about determining what kind of state it would be. They crafted a constitution whose enormity was matched only by its tediousness. Those characteristics, however, were driven by the delegates' desperation to throw off what they felt was the yoke of "carpetbagging" moneyed elites from afar seeking to impose the culture of a minority on the majority, whilst extracting wealth and power from them.

The conservative white majority was deadly serious about shifting the balance of social and economic power to the local and more economically modest population, at least its white and, to some degree, Indian portions. A bonanza of unprecedented opportunity had arisen for African-Americans in the Oklahoma country, but that was soon, at statehood, to be tempered by an armada of discriminatory laws.

Withal, history erupted faster than the booming population of America's newest state could digest it. Economic calamity loomed through a national banking crisis, but the Oklahomans—unlike others—rallied to vanquish it. Millions more acres of Native land were opened to settlement and a golden agricultural age blossomed, even as ominous signs appeared on the western horizon.

It was the bold, brash, and epic birth of a new kind of state, molded and built as only America could, by Americans and immigrants alike coming from Nebraska (Barnard), Ohio (Haskell), Kansas (McCabe and Hamlin), Texas (Colcord), Texas again (Murray), Texas yet again (Parker), Scotland (Hanraty), Germany (the Beckers), and many other places.

Enabling Act

Having quashed Indian Territory hopes for separate statehood, the U.S. Congress finally passed the Enabling Act. It commissioned a constitutional convention to craft the structure of a new American state. President Roosevelt—who scored headlines the previous year wolf hunting in the Big Pasture area of southern Oklahoma Territory with both Quanah Parker and celebrated Frederick cowboy Jack Abernathy—signed it on June 16, 1906. The Enabling Act laid down several mandates, left latitude to the state framers, and inferred a number of other items.

Historian Irwin Hurst recalls the key requirements:

- 55 delegates apiece from the Twin Territories
- Two delegates from the still semi-autonomous Osage Nation
- Republican stronghold Guthrie as convention site and capital till 1913
- Tax exemptions on some Indian lands
- Prohibition of alcohol for twenty-one years in Indian Territory and Osage Nation
- Republican (form of) government "without distinction" in civil or political rights

Chickasha, Indian Territory, a year before statehood. At the junction of the Old West and the new, with lots of wagons and one motor car.

Among other things, those requirements aimed toward such Republican (Party) progressive notions as helping folks facing social problems like alcohol abuse and racism, as well as locating the state capitol in a GOP stronghold. They reflected the (Northern-dominated) Republican-controlled federal government's efforts to level as much influence as possible on the (Southern-dominated) Democratic-heavy state. This occurred in an environment where politics in America generated about as much of the passion, partisanship, and raw emotion as twenty-first century big-time athletics.

Indeed, the spirit of progressivism that dominated America for most of the first two decades of the new century greatly influenced the delegates of both major parties at the convention. The Democrats who increasingly populated the Oklahoma country, though not the more consistently liberal party they would later become, shouldered their own progressive agenda, voicing different and sometimes conflicting emphases than the Republicans. This contributed to Democratic fury when the Roosevelt Administration placed the crucial county boundary and seat-selection process, soon to establish the foundation of the new state's political superstructure, in the hands of the President's friend and fellow Spanish–American War Rough Rider Frank Frantz—the administration-appointed territorial governor—and other Republican political appointees.

Shawnee Demands

The ground was rumbling beneath the Republicans, however. One ominous portent occurred that fall in Shawnee, where representatives of a powerful farm and labor alliance gathered. Representing the Oklahoma Farmers' Union, the Twin Territories Federation of Labor, the independent railroad brotherhoods, and even (in the person of Kate Barnard) the Women's International Union Label League, they crafted the famous Shawnee Demands.

> *Incensed by years of "carpetbag" governance engineered by faraway Republican politicians, the Democrats electrified the nation when they swept around a hundred of the 112 delegate spots to the convention that would write the constitution and birth the laws and government of Oklahoma.*

The alliance, whose membership included one-fifth of eligible Oklahoma voters, declared its support for Constitutional Convention delegate candidates who supported its demands, and its opposition to those who did not. The twenty-four planks spotlighted the interests of farmers, miners, factory workers, child laborers, school children, women, and the public itself through strong citizen participation in the coming state political process. African-American social, political, and economic rights soon to be dismantled were not addressed.

Subsequent crowds numbering in the thousands in Ardmore, Coalgate, and elsewhere, before whom Barnard spoke with her lilting, passionate Celtic sentiment, revealed the progressive momentum sweeping the Twin Territories. Also, according to historian Kenny Brown, the support the Shawnee Demands drew outside its immediate constituency included "many non-union workers, unaffiliated farmers, businessmen, and professionals [who] liked the Shawnee proposals to restrain the railroads, utilities, and other corporations." There was no love lost among most of the Republican delegate nominees for the Shawnee Demands, while most Democrats championed them.

Nothing the Republicans did, from President Roosevelt down to federally appointed judges, could thwart the will of the popular majority, and the vast sweep of the electorate stood Democratic. Incensed by years of "carpetbag" governance engineered by faraway Republican politicians, some of whom had come to the Twin Territories only long enough to rule as appointed officials before returning to their distant homes, the Democrats electrified the nation and left their GOP opponents reeling when they swept around a hundred of the 112 delegate spots to the convention that would write the constitution and birth the laws and government of the state of Oklahoma. Two-thirds of those Democrats had campaigned their support for the Shawnee Demands.

Kate Barnard, who thrilled crowds across the Twin Territories with her soaring vision for the common—and less than common—folk that would soon form the heart of an American state. (Courtesy Oklahoma Historical Society)

Democratic Dominance

Party affiliation and the regional and cultural loyalties that accompanied it contributed to this historic result, but so did other factors. By the turn of the twentieth century, American manufacturing had exploded from second-tier world status to outstrip the combined production of the three European industrial giants—Britain, Germany, and France. However, this dramatic industrialization process included negative elements. Some of these, most conspicuously embodied by the continent-crossing and mostly Republican-engineered government-subsidized railroads, exerted huge impact on the citizenry and fueled passionate opinions of all sorts.

Southerners from one end of Dixie to the other had lived through the bitter experience of the federal government-backed railroad giants. During Reconstruction, carpetbag railroad and government officials fleeced the suffering people of Georgia, North Carolina, and Florida while lining their own pockets. In southern Missouri, the Rock Island Railroad, backed by the federal army, virtually fought another civil war with the pro-South populace. Former Confederate guerrillas led by the legendary Jesse James spearheaded the latter. The people of this region loathed the increasing power held over their business, government, and even lives by Northern commercial giants like Rock Island and Santa Fe. These dominating industries were supported to the hilt by the same federal government that had lately devastated their towns and properties and continued the military occupation of them.

In Indian Territory, Reconstruction Era railroads whistled the death knell of independence for the five great Native republics who had largely sided with the South during the war. Decades later, from his entrance to the United States Senate at statehood till the end of his life more than forty years later, Thomas Gore fought for federal legislation to defend the coal rights of the Choctaws from the railroads.

Against this volatile backdrop, the Republicans nominated Henry Asp for the high profile delegate seat from capital city Guthrie. Even though Asp was able, honorable, and respected by leaders of both parties, Democrats utilized Asp's two decades of Guthrie-based legal work for the Santa Fe railroad as a symbol of everything that so many Oklahomans detested about carpetbagging railroad influence.

The centrist *Oklahoma State Register* newspaper wrote, "The Democratic landslide . . . is so terrific it has taken the breath of the Republicans. The defeat of the Republican party is due to prohibition, lack of organization, and the nomination of Henry Asp. . . . Other railroad attorneys were nominated, but none were so conspicuous. None had a reputation for ability, and none struck the popular prejudice against railroad domination as he did. He was the issue everywhere—in Indian territory and Oklahoma—and cost the party thousands of votes away from home for the loyalty for him at home."

> *[Single statehood] would make Oklahoma a southern state [and] fill her with southern people, a civilization many years behind our own.*
>
> **—Thompson Ferguson**

The sentiments of former Oklahoma Territory Governor Thompson Ferguson (1901-06) well illustrated the uphill battle the Republicans faced. Ferguson, a former Methodist minister, founder of the *Watonga Republican* newspaper, and champion of common (public) schools as governor, disagreed with his patron Roosevelt over the merits of single statehood status. A longtime Kansan, he wanted no marriage to an Indian Territory full of Confederate sympathizers. He feared this "would make Oklahoma a southern state" and "fill her with southern people, a civilization many years behind our own."

Unfortunately for Ferguson and his fellow Republicans, that benighted civilization furnished seventy-five delegates to the Oklahoma Constitutional Convention, as elected by the citizens of the Twin Territories. Seventeen came from Texas alone and twelve from Missouri (then considered a Southern state), nearly as many as the thirty-three delegates from the rest of the Union. Two were foreign born.

Constitutional Convention

On November 20, 1906, "Alfalfa Bill" Murray, voted the chairman by the majority Democrats, called the Oklahoma Constitutional Convention to order in Guthrie. Murray wielded enormous influence in both the deliberations of the convention and the writing of the constitution, as he had at the Sequoyah Convention. The delegates concluded their final session on March 15, 1907.

Other convention leaders included the coal miner, labor union chieftain, and vice chair Pete Hanraty; Democratic floor leader and Sequoyah luminary Charles Haskell; and a remarkable little daughter of Irish immigrants, the afore-mentioned Kate Barnard.

The budding state, with its sudden birth and lack of economic and political infrastructure, proved to be fertile ground for the general progressive agenda of using government to right perceived social, economic, and political wrongs, thus reining in the haves and supposedly protecting the have-nots. Indeed, it took a document that historians Danney Goble and David Baird called "the longest constitution yet written by human hand, in which their convention manifested their beliefs with agonizing detail" to codify these and other laws to the delegates' satisfaction.

The document ran nearly fifty thousand words, about ten times the length of the American constitution and equal to the length of a book running two hundred to two hundred and fifty pages. In fairness, the tedious and fractious business of determining counties, county seats, and county boundaries

The 1906–07 Constitutional Convention for the future state of Oklahoma. Chairman William B. Murray holds the

caused much of this. Nevertheless, the document seemed to at least attempt to address every conceivable issue, including the proper flash point and gravity for kerosene lamps!

Incorporating most of the major planks of both the Sequoyah Convention and the Shawnee Demands, the state constitution in cases such as child labor, mining safety, and certain railroad fees empowered the government to accomplish what the private sector had not done as well as it should have. In others, however, the constitution either replaced individual responsibility with government coercion or addressed valid problems with controversial or even ill-founded solutions. Elsewhere, it failed to address inequalities such as women's suffrage, African-American rights of many stripes, and the land rights of Indians.

The new constitution also established legislative, executive, and judicial branches of government, outlining its separation of powers and checks and balances—all similar to those of the federal government. Their frustrating and sometimes bitter experiences with Reconstruction and the carpetbagging territorial era, however, propelled the delegates to implement restrictions on each branch, particularly the executive (governor), which were not present on the national level.

Learning that the Oklahoma State Constitutional Convention was on the verge of referring to "The Supreme Ruler of the Universe" in the Constitution preamble but not mentioning God, Speaker William "Alfalfa Bill" Murray exploded. "Damn it, you can't leave God out of the Constitution!" he protested. He rallied delegates into inserting the words "invoking the guidance of Almighty God" into the preamble.

The Constitution

Among the many noteworthy facets of the Oklahoma Constitution, which declares it is "Invoking the guidance of Almighty God," and closes with the phrase "In the year of our Lord one thousand nine hundred and seven," are these:

Acknowledging God—Unlike the United States Constitution—much vaunted by some conservatives as the founding document of a "Christian" or "Judeo-Christian" nation, though it never even mentions the name of God—the Preamble invoked "the guidance of Almighty God" for liberty, just government, and the welfare and happiness of the people. It also affixed the date of the document "In the year of our Lord (Jesus Christ)."

Corporations—With railroads in particular view, but banks and others as well, delegates crafted

gavel, far left. The Guthrie City Hall hosted the assembly. (Courtesy Oklahoma Historical Society)

a web of constraints on businesses, especially large corporations based outside Oklahoma. This included the creation of a strong Corporation Commission to grant charters and regulate railroads and utilities in the state. They also outlawed monopolies.

Popular Political Rule—Fed up with long years of government run by appointed carpetbaggers and distant Washington politicos, the convention delivered a host of laws enabling direct democratic acts by the citizens of Oklahoma to circumvent the representative democratic actions of their elected officials.

With the "initiative," after gathering sufficient signatures, the public can author new laws and constitutional amendments to submit to the vote of the people. In the "referendum," the public, again with sufficient signatures, can vote its will on laws previously enacted by legislative bodies. A related provision mandated popular election, rather than political appointment, as the means for determining nearly every statewide office. Indeed, the people may "alter or reform the (state government) whenever the public good may require it." Some Oklahoma cities and towns also empower their citizens to vote whether to retain or remove elected officials through recall elections.

Farmers—Board of agriculture, liberal homestead exemption laws, and protection through the aforementioned restrictions on corporations and out-of-state entities.

Other laborers—Eight-hour work day in mines (and for government workers), plus labor, insurance, and corporation commissioners.

Oklahoma founding father William "Alfalfa Bill" Murray with his wife and children on their Tishomingo farm in 1905. This picture contains two future Oklahoma governors and the niece of Chickasaw Governor Douglas H. Johnston, Murray's wife, Mary Alice. (Courtesy Oklahoma Historical Society)

Guarding and sometimes expanding the rights of laborers comprised a significant portion of all these commissioners' duties.

Children—Despite not possessing delegate status, Kate Barnard, through force of intellect, passion, and moral authority, spearheaded the abolition of child labor (over vigorous opposition from convention president William Murray and others); the regulation of "sweat shop" factories where adults and children alike had suffered; the establishment of compulsory, state-financed school education for all children; and the birth of an elected statewide office, Commissioner of Charities and Corrections. The people of Oklahoma subsequently elected her to that post, even though she was unable to vote. (The constitution did not provide for women's suffrage.)

> *The Constitution failed to address women's suffrage, African-American rights of many stripes, and the land rights of Indians.*

Prohibition—The Enabling Act banned the sale of alcoholic beverages in Indian Territory for twenty-one years following statehood. Charles Haskell and other Democratic politicians, sensing the majority's support and perceiving the subsequent political opportunity, successfully championed a rider triggering a popular referendum that would soon extend this restriction to the entire new state.

African-Americans—Separation of the black and white races proved to be the guiding principle. President Roosevelt's threats to veto the Constitution forced the delegates to mute their Jim Crow sympathies till statehood was secured. Still, they managed to codify segregation of African-American children from whites, Natives, and others by restricting them to their own schools. Furthermore, they defined the "African" race in such a manner that made a mockery of U.S. constitutional law regarding the rights of black citizens.

Indians—Again, opinions diverged on the impact of the Constitution for the tribes. Many Natives, particularly among the mixed bloods, cheered it as a gateway to opportunity, prosperity, and legal rights and protection from the outlawry and myriad other legal conflicts that had plagued Indian Territory with the tribes in charge. Many others, especially among full bloods, supported Creek Chief Pleasant Porter's sentiments: "The white element and the element that it can control is in the saddle, and in the ordering of things the Indians has neither place nor part."

A pro-Republican cartoonist depicts President Roosevelt's anger toward a proponent of the new Oklahoma Constitution.

Statehood and Terror

Oklahoma's long-awaited entrance into the union of American states came on November 16, 1907. One newspaper headline declared "Oklahoma Passes from Carpetbag Rule Into Sisterhood of States." Over fifteen thousand people witnessed the official ceremony in the Republican-selected state capital of Guthrie. A symbolic act, the "marriage" of a white man to a Native woman, highlighted the event, representing the union of Indian and Oklahoma Territories as well as those two races.

Lost to history amidst that historic jubilee is the frightening national economic convulsion that exploded only a few days previously. "Widely interpreted as confirming and punishing the perfidy of Wall Street speculators," according to Oklahoma political scientist Loren C. Gatch, the Panic of 1907 involved bank runs in New York

City. Perhaps the worst financial upheaval to that point in American history, it led to the establishment of the controversial Federal Reserve System in 1913.

A *Tulsa (Daily) World* newspaper editorial revealed the common view of Oklahomans toward the Eastern financial colossus that had brought malaise on itself and the country at numerous junctures throughout the Gilded Age: "The legitimate business of the country is better off when it keeps out of Wall Street. One of the reasons why Wall Street is suffering such acute pangs just now, in fact, is the scarcity of suckers. When the outside crop runs short, the sharks must feed on themselves, and it is little wonder that there is an uproar."

No doubt those sentiments hardened when what began as a financial calamity in New York City on October 22—just twenty-five days before Oklahoma statehood—spread across the country. New York banks lost access to their cash holdings, depriving regional banks in Chicago, Kansas City, and other cities that depended on payments from them, which in turn stopped Indian and Oklahoma Territory banks from accessing funds they needed.

Oklahoma Constitutional "Reforms"

1. Child labor law
2. Eight-hour day for government workers
3. Safety code for mine workers
4. Factory inspection law
5. Favorable homestead exemption for farmers
6. State income tax
7. Graduated income tax
8. Prohibition of alcohol sales
9. Property tax
10. Vigorous taxes on business and industry
11. Increased regulation of business and industry
12. Prohibition of monopolies
13. Corporations must incorporate in Oklahoma

Muskogee native Mike Wimmer's vivid portrait of President Theodore Roosevelt signing the proclamation for Oklahoma statehood on the morning of November 16, 1907. Courtesy Oklahoma State Senate Historical Preservation Fund, Inc. and Mike Wimmer.

Charles Haskell's inauguration in Guthrie as first governor of Oklahoma on November 16, 1907. His actual swearing in took place three hours earlier. (Courtesy Oklahoma Historical Society)

This calamity descended on the heads of merchants, laborers, and farmers alike, whose bank deposits became inaccessible and vulnerable to total loss. Central and southern sections of the Twin Territories faced utter devastation because the Panic occurred just when cotton farmers needed abundant cash to finance their annual harvest.

It presented the Twin Territories with both challenge and opportunity on the largest scale. Could Oklahomans, divided by social, political, economic, racial, and geographical perspectives, lacking much of the most basic civil infrastructure and institutions, and not yet constituting one political entity, rally their efforts to prevent wholesale financial cataclysm in their country, even as they prepared for statehood?

Uniting Against Calamity

Banks like those in Pawhuska, Osage Nation, and elsewhere ignored pressure to temporarily close, so that Oklahomans could continue to access their money and accounts as desired. Lacking cash, banks across the Twin Territories, including those in Mangum, Cordell, Ardmore, Okmulgee, Muskogee, and the big cities, issued their customers various types of negotiable checks, certificates of deposit, and other instruments of worth, credit, and trade. The First National Bank of

Mrs. Anna Bennett, the part-Cherokee woman whose beauty stunned the gathered, mostly white host as she represented Indian Territory and Natives in the statehood "marriage" of the two territories and races. Historian Carolyn Foreman wrote of this remarkable woman who continued to devote herself to others despite being widowed *four* times, "A devoted wife and homemaker, (she) also possessed great executive ability. The orphan children she cared for and her (World War I) work testify to her humanitarian interests. In addition to her beauty she had unusual charm and she was never heard to make critical or unkind remarks of other people. She met life with a smile in spite of troubles that would have overcome most persons." (Courtesy Oklahoma Historical Society)

First Oklahoma Governor Charles Haskell at the colossal statehood barbecue he organized.

The West Jes' Smiled

Front page verse in the *Enid Daily Wave* newspaper revealed the Oklahomans' attitude regarding Wall Street's self-inflicted Panic of 1907 misfortunes and the West's avoidance of the same. The following is the final stanza of *The West Jes' Smiled*. The "red display," as of blood, referred to the panicked headlines of Eastern newspapers regarding the financial calamity.

The west looked over its fruitful fields,
Gazed proudly on their enormous yields,
Peeked into the banks and saw the stacks
Of gold piled up at the tellers' backs.
It swept its eyes o'er the great Westland,
O'er the signs of plenty on every hand.
And carelessly glanced at the red display
Spread over papers every day,
And smiled, an'smiled.

A Muskogee cotton gin. In the early 1900s the crop still drove the local economy, on the eve of the region's oil boom. (Courtesy Oklahoma Historical Society)

Chickasha promised "piles of greenbacks a foot high and gold by the sack" and backed the boast with cash on demand.

Kingfisher farmers declared that "no brother farmer would remove their money from the bank." Five hundred Shawnee citizens convened at City Hall to declare they would keep their funds in local banks. Oklahoma pioneer J. J. McAlester (Chapter 8) guaranteed his own property to cover anyone's loss in his McAlester bank, as did George and John Gerlach for their Woods County banks. Altus citizens allowed area farmers to pay for supplies to harvest their cotton with checks to be drawn from later, rather than cash.

Downtown Bartlesville in 1907, already a booming oil center and home to such present and future energy legends as Phillips Petroleum founders Frank Phillips and L. E. Phillips, their brother Waite Phillips, Harry Sinclair, and J. Paul Getty.

Still, the hardships multiplied. Some railroads and government agencies refused to accept locally generated scrip (certificates redeemable for goods or later for cash). Several bankers attempted suicide. Numerous farmers lost their savings after withdrawing them from their bank. Mice ate one family's nest egg that was tucked in a corn crib. A robber divested another farmer of forty thousand dollars (around a million dollars in 2010s value). At least two other farmers robbed their own banks to get their money.

In general, however, despite fear and suffering, Oklahomans combined their courage, creativity, and teamwork into a rally of historic proportions that helped confirm the readiness of the Twin Territories for statehood. Historian Irwin Hurst takes that theme a step further: "The contrast between the bank runs in New York and the dogged ingenuity of Oklahomans in finding ways around the national payment restrictions was undeniable and stark. Unlike the bank closures that occurred during the Panic of 1893, those of 1907 were confined largely to New York City."

> *The contrast between the bank runs in New York and the dogged ingenuity of Oklahomans in finding ways around the national payment restrictions was undeniable and stark.*
>
> **—Irwin Hurst**

Charles Haskell—First Governor (1860–1933)

This Ohio-born railroad, building, and law magnate proved to be a big enough man to lead a big and brawling new Western state through its baptism of fire. He was a man of action in a titanic era and land. Controversy and accolades alike festooned him, and he made close friends and bitter enemies of those who would be President and those who were. He led the infant state with a cocksure confidence that he backed up with deeds—and he might even have saved it a time or two. In a distant generation, he rises up as a preeminent founding father of Oklahoma and one of the great men in its history.

Clash of Titans: Governor vs. President

Demonstrating the significance of Oklahoma and the people who founded and led it, the new state's first governor and the sitting President of the United States—among the most famous in American history—tore into each other in one of the most vicious public feuds ever to take place in the high corridors of American power. President Theodore Roosevelt did his best not just to destroy Governor Charles Haskell's political career but his freedom—and even his life.

The Battle for Oklahoma City

When Boomers and Sooners raised Oklahoma City up along the north bank of the parched North Canadian River in 1889, an epic conflict commenced between the forces of spiritual light and darkness. The battle escalated as the future capital catapulted to the fastest growing city in the United States during the early years of the twentieth century. Nearly everything forming that singular historical setting seemed to be a magnified version of the American norm—heroes versus the villains, selfless sacrifice versus violence and vice, and Christianity versus corruption.

Oklahoma City City Manager Albert L. McRill's classic account of the early battle between the forces of law and order and those of vice and corruption.

Jim Crow Laws

Whatever the merits of the many progressive reforms encased in the Oklahoma Constitution, they did not address the prevailing white and Native racism against blacks. Now that Oklahoma had officially joined the Union, state lawmakers ceased fearing anti-Jim Crow reprisals from the Roosevelt administration. Over the protests of Oklahoma's African-American leaders, they hastened to craft state laws that, in tandem with various federal statues, determined to separate blacks and whites everywhere—from schools to toilets to marriages.

> *Jim Crow: Societal segregation or discrimination against African-Americans, such as in public places, public transportation, housing, and employment. The term originated from a nineteenth-century minstrel show that featured racist stereotypes.*

Only one month after statehood, Senate Bill One, also known as the Coach Bill, inaugurated Jim Crow into Oklahoma law. It declared:

> Every railway company, urban or suburban car company, street car or interurban car or railway company . . . shall provide separate coaches or compartments as hereinafter provided for the accommodation of the white and negro races, which separate coaches or cars shall be equal in all points of comfort and convenience.

The bill also required separate railroad station waiting rooms for African-Americans and whites/others. It established stiff fines for organizations failing to erect separate facilities as well as individuals failing to utilize them after warnings. Once again, blacks did not cower in submission because of such hurtful treatment. Their responses ran the gamut from foolish riots in African-American towns such as Taft and Red Bird, to devout Christian prayer, to an admirable though unsuccessful legal battle helmed by black pioneer E. P. McCabe.

This pulsating display of streetcar-laden twentieth-century urbanity looking north on Broadway in downtown Oklahoma City during a parade occurred less than two years after statehood. Courtesy Oklahoma Historical Society.

"They . . . dug in for another intense fight to prevent the new state from erecting a Jim Crow system to limit their rights," wrote historian Jimmie Lewis Franklin. "They would fail. Their children, and their children's children, would have to drink from the bitter cup of discrimination and segregation for many years to come."

Meanwhile, the state-sanctioned Jim Crow laws apparently emboldened many white citizens with a more aggressive, sometimes violent attitude toward African-Americans. Lynchings (in Oklahoma, typically the hanging till death without due process of law of a person suspected of criminal activity) of blacks increased after statehood to around one per year in Oklahoma till 1930. "Whipping parties," during which a white posse would beat or whip blacks suspected of law-breaking, also multiplied in number, as did "race riots."

According to historian Dianna Everett, the race riot usually involved an attempt by whites to run African-Americans out of a town. Nearly a dozen such episodes occurred across the state around the turn of the century, most notably in Lexington (1892), Berwyn (1895), Lawton (1902), Boynton (1904), and Henryetta (1907). These were mere foreshadowings, however, of the cataclysmic 1921 Tulsa Race Riot, which Volume 2 of this work will explore in depth.

Causes of Jim Crow

Many factors contributed to this heartbreaking trend. First and foremost stood the ancient Western civilization view of blacks as inherently inferior due to the violent, backward, and pagan cultures predominant in the African communities of their origin. Political scholar and presidential advisor Pat Buchanan illustrated this perceived contrast: "When the British arrived in Africa, they found primitive tribal societies. When they departed, they left behind roads, railways, telephone and telegraph

This 1908 *Daily Oklahoman* cartoon reminds its readers that Jim Crow laws are in effect. The clownish, animalistic depiction of the African-American passenger sitting in the white rather than "colored" railcar section, the smirking condescension toward him, and the fact the largest publication in the state featured the sketch, present a bracing window into the era's dramatic racism toward blacks. *Oklahoman* owner and publisher Roy E. Stafford was a Democratic state senator at the time.

"Jim Crow As I Saw It." (1908)

"Sitting in the waiting room at Ardmore, (I mean the Jim Crow waiting room.) I drew my first impression of the Jim Crow law. The room set apart for Negroes, joins the men's closet."

Samuel Robert Cassius (1853–1931)

This dauntless visionary, born a slave in Virginia, migrated to future Logan County before the age of forty. When he departed over thirty years later, he left a regional and national legacy as a leading African-American in the famed Restoration Christian movement. He dared to challenge white Christians on their racism and blacks on both their religious orthodoxy and orthopraxy. He stirred controversy aplenty from all quarters, sustained by the conviction that the very words that angered folks could stir them to greater faithfulness as Americans, followers of Christ, and human beings.

systems, farms, factories, fisheries, mines, trained police, and a civil service." African-Americans' stark external physiological differences from whites and other races strengthened the perception. So did the fact that European and Arabic slave traders, as well as slave owners in many countries, had been able to exercise such decisive control over them once they acquired them from their black African captors.

In 1896, the U.S. Supreme Court enshrined segregation as a legal and socially acceptable practice in the American states. It confirmed the constitutionality of separate but equal facilities, services, and opportunities for African-Americans and whites.

Other factors concerned the nature and character of Oklahoma itself. The state was birthed from a rough, rowdy frontier, one baptized in blood and war. Many who migrated to the Twin Territories and then Oklahoma faced difficult, even desperate economic circumstances in a hard land amidst a turbulent emerging industrial economy and the aforementioned series of withering financial recessions and depressions. For thousands of its pioneers, Oklahoma was a second, third, or even last chance for social and economic survival.

> *Factors contributing to Jim Crow laws included the ancient Western civilization view of blacks as inherently inferior, due to the violent, backward, and pagan cultures predominant in the African communities of their origin.*

Against this roiling tableau swarmed a whole series of circumstances—unwelcomed by many whites and Indians alike—related to the Oklahoma country's ambitious black pioneers, as recounted by Everett:

> (The) high visibility and relative prosperity of the freedmen's towns in Indian Territory, blacks' demands for political rights, a mass migration of blacks to Oklahoma Territory, and the suggestion that Oklahoma might become an All-Black state apparently posed a social, economic, and political threat, stimulating a time-honored method of social control mob violence.

Whites, particularly those poor and uneducated, recognized that African-Americans—free, numerous, and in many cases now landowners—posed a new source of competition for desperately needed, often scarce jobs. White Americans had won a continent and an incipient empire by handling the British, the French, the Spanish, the Mexicans, Confederate secession, and the Natives. Now, in Oklahoma, they would deal with ascendant free blacks.

Blacks and Ballots

Statehood and the Oklahoma constitution left one important area for African-Americans to exert their influence—the ballot box. They did so the following year in the 1908 elections. Blacks again mobilized the vote for candidates of the Republican

Party that had forsaken their interests during the crafting of that constitution. Their votes, coupled with the whites', swung some statewide offices to the Republicans, increased GOP congressional seats from one to three of Oklahoma's five, and even elected handsome, twenty-seven-year-old African-American A. C. Hamlin as a state representative from the largely black third legislative district of Logan County.

With the dawn of the new decade, the number of African-Americans elected to state office would plummet to zero, even as the number of lynchings rose.

Hamlin proved to be no shrinking violet in the state legislature. He attended, participated, and, as a Republican and the only black man in the Democrat-dominated House, even sponsored several successful pieces of legislation. One sought to ensure the supposed equal quality of separate railway facilities for African-Americans and whites. Another aimed at strengthening the sanctity of the Bible's fourth commandment, the honoring of the Sabbath, by prohibiting such secular public activities as theatrical performances and baseball games on Sundays. Still another appropriated thirty-five thousand dollars to fund the Taft School for deaf, blind, and orphaned black children.

This courageous African-American trail-blazer lost his re-election bid two years later, however, and more than fifty years would pass before another black would serve in the Oklahoma legislature. Volume 2 of this work will examine the historic vote responsible for this 1910 "grandfather clause."

The white Democratic preponderance of the new state's legislature did not rest during their second term. Led by Haskell in the governor's office and Murray in the speaker's chair of the state house of representatives, they continued their aggressive approach to state governance. Legislative actions ranged from outlawing monopolies to requiring separate accommodations for African-Americans and whites (a designation that included any race besides African-American) in all public transportation. The latter bill was the state's first and erected the scaffolding for the Jim Crow infrastructure that would plague Oklahoma for better than half-a-century.

Banking Suspense Continues

Financial turbulence in the new state did not pass away with 1907. Fortunately, Governor Haskell's ringing inaugural address had championed passage of the bitterly contested Bank Deposit Guaranty Law. This landmark bill established Oklahoma as the first state in America to require its state-chartered banks to insure their depositors' money against any loss with a Depositors' Guaranty Fund. He proposed that they contribute 1 percent of their respective assets to the fund.

Governor Haskell's ringing inaugural address championed passage of a landmark bill establishing Oklahoma as the first state to require its state-chartered banks to insure their depositors' money.

Haskell had tried to include such a law in the state constitution. He aimed to ensure that the working people of Oklahoma would not lose a dollar, particularly when the periodic national economic panics tended to roll downward onto them from the folly and greed of the

The Columbia Bank and Trust in Oklahoma City, the state's largest financial institution.

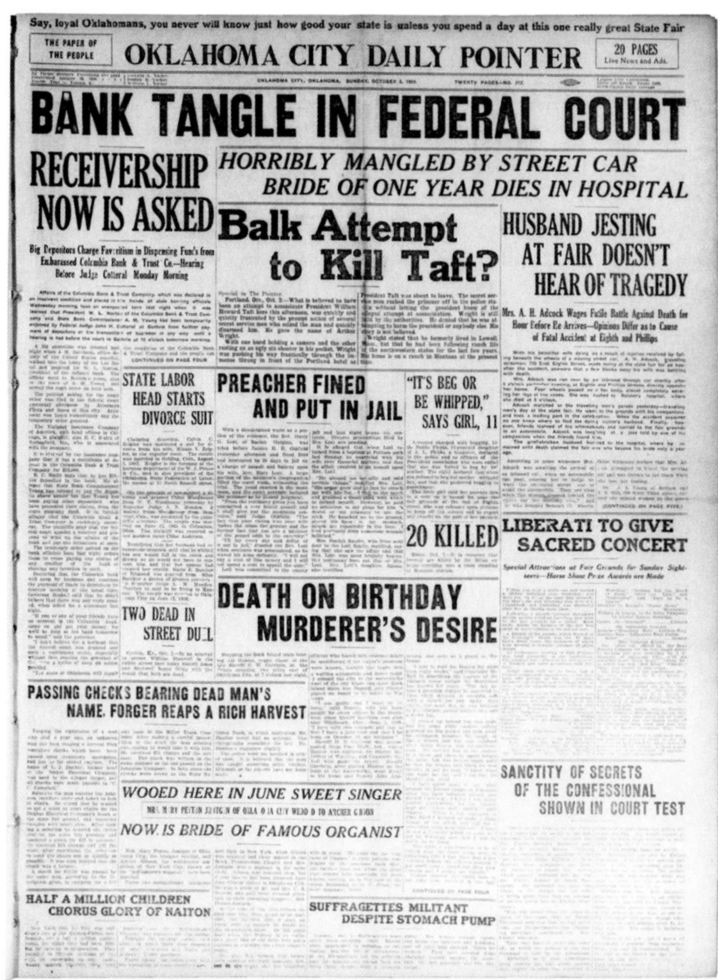

Say, loyal Oklahomans, you never will know just how good your state is unless you spend a day at this one really great State Fair

THE PAPER OF THE PEOPLE

OKLAHOMA CITY DAILY POINTER

20 PAGES Live News and Ads.

BANK TANGLE IN FEDERAL COURT

RECEIVERSHIP NOW IS ASKED

Big Depositors Charge Favoritism in Dispensing Funds from Embarrassed Columbia Bank & Trust Co.—Hearing Before Judge Cotteral Monday Morning

HORRIBLY MANGLED BY STREET CAR BRIDE OF ONE YEAR DIES IN HOSPITAL

Balk Attempt to Kill Taft?

HUSBAND JESTING AT FAIR DOESN'T HEAR OF TRAGEDY

Mrs. A. H. Adcock Wages Futile Battle Against Death for Hour Before He Arrives—Opinions Differ as to Cause of Fatal Accident at Eighth and Phillips

STATE LABOR HEAD STARTS DIVORCE SUIT

PREACHER FINED AND PUT IN JAIL

"IT'S BEG OR BE WHIPPED," SAYS GIRL, 11

20 KILLED

LIBERATI TO GIVE SACRED CONCERT

DEATH ON BIRTHDAY MURDERER'S DESIRE

TWO DEAD IN STREET DUEL

PASSING CHECKS BEARING DEAD MAN'S NAME, FORGER REAPS A RICH HARVEST

SANCTITY OF SECRETS OF THE CONFESSIONAL SHOWN IN COURT TEST

WOOED HERE IN JUNE SWEET SINGER NOW IS BRIDE OF FAMOUS ORGANIST

HALF A MILLION CHILDREN CHORUS GLORY OF NAITON

SUFFRAGETTES MILITANT DESPITE STOMACH PUMP

Newspaper headlines blared the story of Oklahoma's most frightening early financial crisis, the fall of Columbia Bank and Trust, the state's largest financial institution. (Courtesy Oklahoma Historical Society)

wealthy and powerful—"the avariciousness of man," as Haskell declared it. Oklahoma wanted "protection of its banks from the excesses of New York," according to historian Loren Gatch.

Some of the state's large banks opposed the law from its inception. They knew their assets would provide the bulk of the Guaranty's funds and that without those funds some small banks would fail. Then, the larger banks could replace them with branches.

The law received a dramatic early baptism of economic fire. Almost immediately following its February 15, 1908, passage, the Noble State Bank challenged its legality in court. The Coalgate State Bank—closed, then covered by the Guaranty Law—accused Haskell of orchestrating the shutdown to score political points during a presidential campaign with the success of "his pet scheme." The Coalgate imbroglio lumbered along with ugliness. A grand jury eventually censured the state banking commissioner, closed the bank, and recommended his removal.

The 1908 episodes paled in comparison with the challenge Haskell, the Deposit Guaranty Fund, and Oklahoma faced when the state's largest bank, Columbia Bank & Trust in Oklahoma City, failed in September of 1909. Columbia's dramatic crash resembled another spectacular demise three quarters of a century later in the same city—Penn Square Bank (Volume 2). The crashes of both banks had surprising similarities, including recklessly daring executives, foolhardy oil-related loans, and collateral damage to other banks.

Columbia presented Oklahoma with a frightening specter. Due to its size and influence, the individuals, other banks and organizations, and even towns and cities whose continued welfare hinged on a wise remedy to the bank's situation were legion. For starters, the Deposit Guaranty Fund had nowhere near enough cash on hand to cover the millions of exposed depositor dollars.

Oklahoma Conquers Crisis

Haskell exhibited the formidable stature that prompted Edward Everett Dale, the dean of Oklahoma historians, to write, "Oklahoma was fortunate in having as its first governor a man of rare ability and wide experience, both in government and business." With colossal stakes in the balance as he faced some big banks' continued opposition and negative media coverage inspired in part by his political enemies, Haskell rallied the state's political and banking establishments and even his friends among banking heavyweights in much larger cities like Kansas City and St. Louis. He scored enormous cash advances from both those cities to cover possible quick withdrawals by Columbia depositors.

Haskell's efforts, coupled with the Bank Guaranty Deposit Law and the people of Oklahoma, conquered the crisis. The doors to Columbia never closed until its liquidation. The expected "run" at the bank as in New York City during the Panic of 1907 never occurred, and all depositors were paid in full, though some experienced a delay.

Aware of the persistent opposition from some of the state's big-city banks and their business allies, Haskell triumphantly drew a bead on them. "The Oklahoma banking law is a complete success, even against the persistent opposition of a strong element of other classes of bankers," he declared. "We adjust the affairs of an embarrassed state bank with perfect ease in a very few days, and with no public clamor whatever. Everybody is in good humor and conditions are normal. Depositors' money was not tied up a single hour. Other state banks are quiet and gaining in deposits."

Accomplishing its mission, the legislature terminated the Bank Deposit Guaranty Law in 1923. The legacy it left included the first such protection of citizens' money by any state, numerous successful securings of that money in failed banks, and passage a quarter-century before its parallel on the national level, the Federal Deposit Insurance Corporation. Haskell perhaps pronounced the consummate valedictory in 1910:

> Theorizing may do when we consider untried things, but two years of actual experience has qualified our people to judge of the efficiency of the Oklahoma banking law. It has been subjected to the severest test possible to have occurred within our state. It has arisen from this test, supreme in its power, and blessed by the people for its beneficial effects.

Farming's Golden Age

The Twin Territories also spearheaded a two-decade American agricultural bonanza that stretched from around 1898 till about 1918. Historian Bob Blackburn called it the "Golden Age of Farming" in Oklahoma. Buoyed by strong annual rainfalls, farmers accomplished monumental feats during the seventeen territorial years between 1890 and 1907. Against formidable, even overwhelming, obstacles, they came from Texas, Arkansas, Missouri, Mississippi, Kansas, Nebraska, Illinois, and elsewhere. They toiled and innovated and helped one another transform empty vistas stretching far as the eye could discern, and then farther, into productive lands.

Buoyed by strong annual rainfalls, farmers accomplished monumental feats during the seventeen territorial years between 1890 and 1907.

In perhaps the greatest agricultural boom in American history, the number of farms in the Oklahoma country leaped from less than nine thousand in 1890 to over a hundred and ninety thousand in 1910—better than a 1,000 percent increase in just twenty years. African-American farmers ran more than thirteen thousand of these farms. Just one year

A Native wagon train hauling eleven hundred bushels of wheat they raised at the Seger Colony sixty miles to market in the early 1900s.

Early 1900s African-American sharecroppers. There were no pensions, retirement plans, nor Social Security for these folks at any age—only their own labor.

after statehood, farmers had planted nearly two-thirds of the state's entire land mass of 44,424,960 acres.

Cotton, grown primarily in the southwest, south central, and central regions of the state, helped cement Oklahoma's identity as a southern state as it rapidly became the leading cash crop. The people of the land produced over 923,000 bales in 1910 on 2.3 million acres of land, for nearly $62 million in revenue. The Sooner State ranked sixth in American cotton production after only a couple years of statehood.

Versatile in feeding people and stock alike, corn, a malleable vegetable that could be turned into grits, cornbread, and other foods with a cornmeal base, stood second in state crop rankings at nearly $48 million in revenue on more than five million Oklahoma acres, and wheat ranked third at over $22 million. Other successful Oklahoma crops included oats, milo, maize, potatoes, sweet potatoes, peanuts, and alfalfa. Lindsey, in Garvin County, gained acclaim as "The Broomcorn Capital of the World." The state's farmers also churned out enormous amounts of dairy products such as eggs, butter, and cheese, as well as vegetables and fruits from gardens and orchards, and poultry.

Despite the demise of the sprawling spreads that had formed the legendary range cattle industry in the Twin Territories, livestock ranked even more important than crops in Oklahoma by the end of the decade. Nearly two million cattle, almost a million horses and mules, 1.3 million hogs, and eighty-five thousand sheep comprised a 150 million-dollar industry.

Why It Happened

Historians Odie Faulk and William Welge cite several other keys to the agricultural boom besides hard work, good weather, and free land during the first couple of decades in the twentieth century. These include the paving of farm-to-market dirt roads, consolidation and thus improvement of rural public schools, increased affordability—often through credit indebtedness—of Ford Model T automobiles, marketing cooperatives that secured higher selling prices for husbandry groups, and scientific improvement of everything from dairy cattle to seed.

Also, farmers and ranchers could draw on the expertise and sometimes material assistance of numerous private and governmental organizations when they were confused, facing trouble, or just wanting to grow more profitable. These included the recently founded agricultural college

An Oklahoma family picking cherries in the early 1900s, complete with baby in a stroller.

of Oklahoma A&M in Stillwater; county agricultural experiment stations; growers' associations or unions for grain, poultry, dairy, cotton, livestock, and pecans; the State Board of Agriculture; district agricultural schools created by the new state legislature; county farm inspectors; the U.S. Department of Agriculture; various farm publications; and even the famed Future Farmers of America (FFA) and Future Homemakers of America (FHA) for youth.

As the Golden Age of Farming progressed and statehood loomed and then happened, many Oklahomans working their land grew better acquainted with it, and many adjusted their tactics in ways that enhanced profits. These methods included raising livestock, then selling it when they needed cash; compiling the necessary outbuildings to support their work; and especially, growing wiser regarding the best crops to plant.

Trouble on Horizon

Even during the booming early years of the twentieth century, however, dark clouds gathered on the state's agricultural horizon. Most Indian Territory/eastern Oklahoma farmers worked farms divided by a well-intentioned federal government through an allotment system for both commercial viability and manageability. The latter often proved true, but at the expense of the former. Moreover, although

Wilson Hurley's *A Storm Passing Northwest of Anadarko*, one of his four-painting *Visions of the Land: Centennial Suite*. The original set, hanging in the Oklahoma State Capitol, represents the diverse quadrants of the state's landscape.

By the 1900s, increasing numbers of Oklahoma farm families were losing ownership of their land, particularly in the rough western country. Even sharecropping—working other folks' land for a share of the revenue—usually required the labors of the entire family. Here, six-year-old Jewel Walker picks cotton in Comanche County.

better watered than western Oklahoma, hills and rocks encompassed much IT terrain, further reducing the number of arable acres.

And since many cash-poor farmers wound up with acreage in less productive higher elevations, they felt increasing pressure to overplant that land with soil nutrient-depleting cash crops like cotton and corn. Though producing banner crops through the 1900s, this combination set in motion a process that played a huge role in the mass migration of Oklahoma farmers to California and elsewhere a few decades later (Volume 2).

Another vulnerability most IT farmers shared with their Oklahoma Territory/western Oklahoma peers was meager capital (money, property, and other resources) to invest in their land and operations and sustain them through economic downturns. Free land, after all, drew hundreds of thousands of people to the Twin Territories, including a far higher percentage of cash-poor folks than those who previously migrated to land that required purchase, such as Nebraska and Kansas.

The state's growing emphasis on cotton farming proved to be a double-edged sword as well. Cotton's production cycle led farmers into debt even during flush times; when cotton prices dipped, many lost ownership of their land. The State Board of Agriculture and the other previously-cited farm support organizations urged planters toward several courses of action. These included diversifying their crops, adjusting production more toward self-sufficiency, and raising more livestock to improve their cash fluidity.

All this proved easier said than done for many cotton farmers, however, who continued to practice what they and their forefathers had done for generations. Tenant farming—working land owned by someone else and sharing crop proceeds with them—more than doubled over the first decade of the twentieth century. Already by 1910, over half (54 percent) of all Oklahoma farmers worked land they did not own. The percentage stood even higher for cotton farmers, and higher still for African-American farmers.

Western Oklahoma Struggles

Western farmers, meanwhile, took hold of plains and prairie land bereft of basic natural resources their counterparts possessed nearly anywhere else in America. These included water for people, stock, and crops; trees for materials for homes, outbuildings, and implements; and foliage of all sorts for wind, dust, and water breaks.

The importance of many of these factors was not at first widely recognized or at least conceded, especially with the great-hearted courage of the pioneers. By the end of the decade, however, nearly half the farmers in western Oklahoma who did still own their land—many of them striving to follow better agrarian practices—had mortgaged it. Then, only their ability to make those payments on time, while often possessing little or no cash savings, stood between the farmers and losing their land to the mortgage holder. For increasing numbers, even during the farm boom, the latter is what happened.

Many other factors conspired to ensnare early western Oklahoma farmers in a desperate struggle for financial and even physical survival. These included inadequate transportation for produce as well as expensive railroad freight rates and grain elevator storage charges when transportation was available. Southwest Oklahoma pioneer Edward Everett Dale cited numerous other challenges:

> Soil exhaustion was common, because of inadequate agricultural implements. . . . Settlers coming from states (with) greater rainfall did not know how to farm the Oklahoma soils in such fashion as to prevent erosion. . . . When western Oklahoma was opened to white settlement, the land had never been touched by a plow. Not only were the settlers unacquainted with the nature of the soil but they were eager to get the most money from their farms at the earliest possible time. This was conducive to poor farming methods. Within a few years thousands of acres were so wasted by erosion that entire farms were abandoned. Thousands of acres were plowed and cultivated when they should have been left for pasture lands . . . too few good horses, poor farm improvements."

Kate Barnard and "The Least of These" (1875–1930)

This ninety-pound bundle of heart and Irish grit shines through the generations as the single greatest defender of the weak, needy, and abused in Oklahoma history. Many prisoners; working mothers; suffering factory, construction, and coal mine laborers; orphans; and other children had only one advocate against the unsavory characteristics of American "progress." That person was "Our Kate." Alas, like so many of those before and after her who dared to call a self-righteous society to live by its own declared principles, she died rejected and unwanted.

Hard, tough, determined—the treeless early twentieth-century northwest Oklahoma frontier, as well as the pioneers who settled it. Their sod-walled house insulated them from the heat and cold but not snakes, rodents, and insects. However, windows, a wood-shingle roof, and some wood siding help. (Courtesy Oklahoma Historical Society)

Last Great Opening

Perhaps the greatest land opening of all unfolded in 1908, the year after statehood. Spearheaded by Oklahoma's brilliant and able U.S. Senator Owen of Muskogee, the state sought the removal of federal restrictions against the sale of allotted Indian lands larger than eighty acres, which most of them were. The government had implemented the restrictions as a shield to prevent the Natives—particularly the mass of full bloods unlearned in the ways of American society and commerce—from getting maneuvered out of their land by those well versed in such practices.

> *There were only two little shacks on the (Lawton) town-site when I located my tent on the Eastern Boundary which was then called 'Goo-goo' avenue. The blue grass was waist high on most of the town-site, particularly where there were 'hog-wallers.'"*
>
> **—Thomas Gore**

Proponents of removal again played the "us against them" card. Regarding naïve full-blood allottees, Owen asked, "Will it be the interior department (or) will it be the generous hearted sons of Oklahoma who will take care of their own defectives? They are our children and we want to take care of our own children and we don't want any stepmother."

Historian Debo chronicled how well the "generous hearted sons of Oklahoma" took care of their own defectives:

> The immediate effect of the law of 1908 was a new orgy of buying land from allottees too innocent or too thriftless to protect themselves against their new freedom. But the most significant result was the enormous increase in opportunities for exploitation through the courts . . . and a speculator who had obtained temporary control of large areas through legal or almost legal leases might now resort to forgery, kidnapping, or even murder to acquire permanent possession. An enormous inducement to crime arose from the increasing value of oil property. . . . More serious than the losses of adult allottees was the legalized robbery of the children through the probate courts.

Left to right, Post Oak Mennonite Missionary Abraham Becker, Mo-Wat (No Hand), the first Comanche baptized at Post Oak (west of Lawton), the first Mennonite foreign mission, and Fairview Mennonite Pastor M. M. Just. Courtesy Oklahoma Historical Society.

Standing Against Removals

Removal of restrictions against the sale of individual Natives' land did not prove strictly an effort of Oklahoma Democrats. The Republican-controlled federal government supported the effort, right up through the administration of President Teddy Roosevelt, who advocated that Congress abolish land sale restrictions on everything larger than forty-acre homesteads, rather than eighty.

The American public generally backed removal as well. Not everyone did, however. Besides many of the allottees themselves, that stalwart champion of the underdog, Kate Barnard, worked tirelessly on behalf of the Indians in her role as Commissioner of Charities and Corrections. The new state's Socialist Party, potent during the Progressive Era, defended them, too. So did many Oklahoma county judges, distraught over the armada of unfolding schemes they had attempted to thwart.

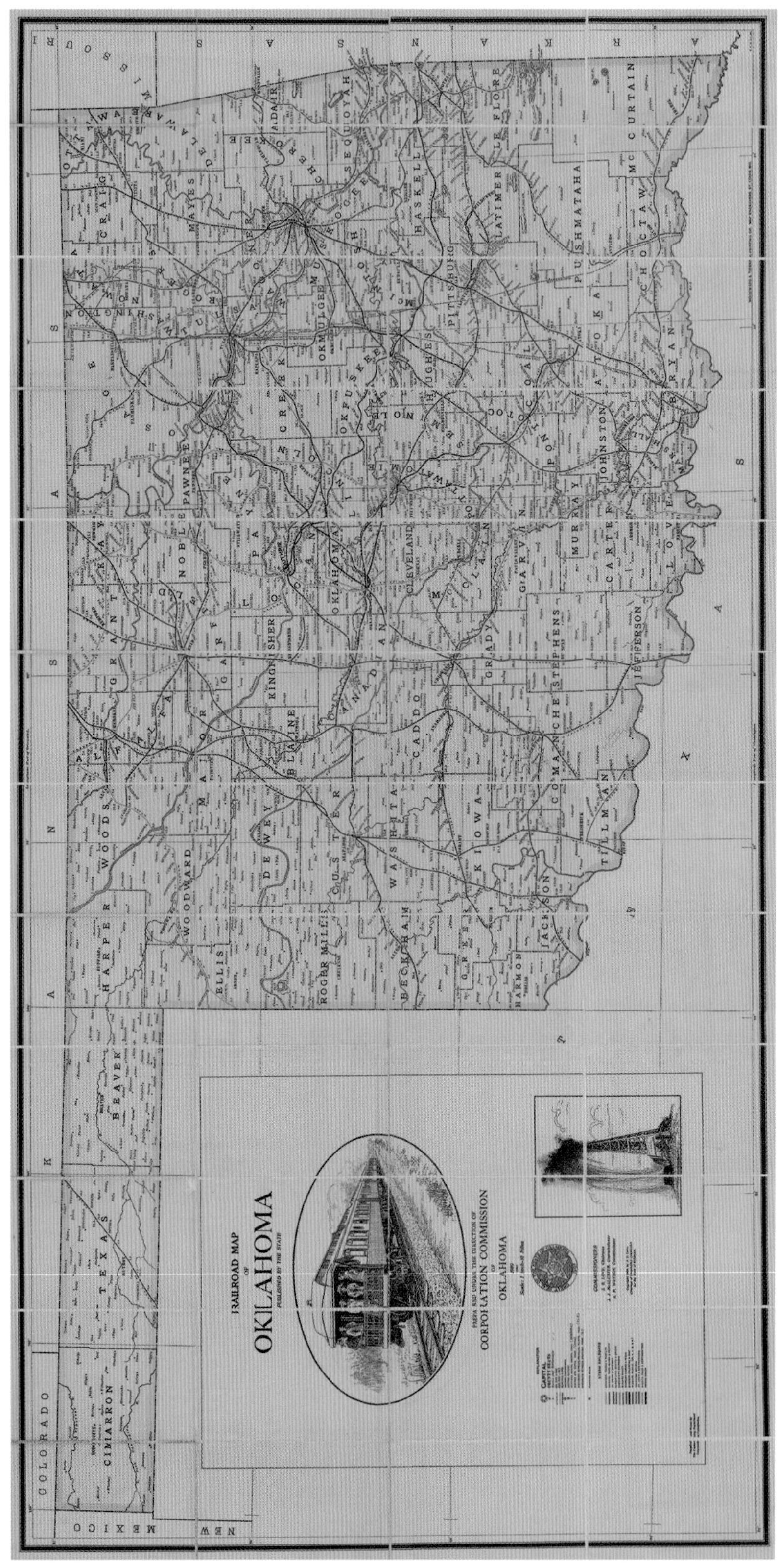

A 1909 map displaying the proliferation of early Oklahoma railroad lines in red. Courtesy Oklahoma Historical Society.

Oklahoma City's "first skyscraper," pioneer and visionary Charles Colcord's Colcord Building, around the time of its 1909 completion. Gleaming and refurbished, it prospers as one of OKC's most fashionable hotels—Colcord's original vision for it—more than a century later.

Perhaps no one spoke truth to power more memorably than Creek Chief Moty Tiger, who had just succeeded Pleasant Porter upon the latter's unexpected death. Speaking mere feet from the nationally acclaimed Owen, he unveiled words as piercing as they were prescient, with the handsome new senator his obvious—and furious—subject:

> *It is a fight between greed and conscience with this great government as arbiter, and upon the decision rests for generations, the fate of these untutored children of nature.*
>
> **—Moty Tiger**

> The polished and educated man with the Indian blood in his veins who advocates the removal of restrictions from the lands of my ignorant people . . . is only reaching for gold to ease his itching palms, and our posterity will remember him only for his avarice and his treachery. It is a fight between greed and conscience with this great government as arbiter, and upon the decision rests for generations, the fate of these untutored children of nature.

Epilogue

John Clymer's painting of Comanche Chief Quanah Parker greeting legendary Texas Ranger and cattle baron Charles Goodnight following the Plains Indian Wars near the tribal encampment on Goodnight's land. The two men had been mortal enemies, but would become lifelong friends. Courtesy John Clymer Estate and National Museum of Wildlife Art, Jackson, Wyoming (www.wildlifeart.org).

> *This was a man.*
>
> —S. C. Gwynne

And so the new American state of Oklahoma galloped toward the second decade of the twentieth century, Volume 2 of this work, and its destiny. Nearly two million people spread across its seventy-seven counties. A network of roads, some paved, and railroad lines crosshatched the state. Vibrant institutions of higher learning and commerce, towns, and cities with skyscrapers rose from erstwhile prairie. A muscular, often raucous, but friendly, increasingly Christian Western-Southern-Midwestern society emerged, determined, irresistible.

The Oklahomans had already overcome many challenges, but just as many now clamored for attention and innovative solutions. America's final frontier, after all, was not likely to be a quiescent haven of rest and gentility. A land full of forcibly migrated Natives and armed American citizenry, most of them drawn by free land and often their final shot at material prosperity and even survival, was not likely to be populated by the wealthy. And the agricultural golden age that thrust many toward prosperity would soon spiral into a welter of heat, dust, wind, drought, debt, foreclosure, and raw, ravaged vistas. An oil boom like none other in history would build family dynasties, cities, and a state—but would it last? War on an unprecedented worldwide scale loomed just around the corner.

What about the perpetual tension in a free market society between the dream-chasing, opportunity, and material prosperity that it enabled and encouraged, and the less gifted, less connected, and less fortunate who toiled alongside? Or those who struggled because their skin pigmentation was black, brown, or "red" and not white?

Finally, as this book and the next shall explore through the lens of their providential worldview, spiritual war in the seen and unseen realms alike raged in the lives of Oklahomans as they sought to build "a new kind of state."

Archetypal Oklahoman

One person arises as perhaps the quintessential archetype of the bridge between the old pre-statehood Oklahoma country and the new one spanning to the present and into the future. As a link between this volume and the one to come that will cover the time period of 1910 to the present. As a connection between the old and new cultures that have rendered Oklahoma unique and endlessly fascinating.

Quanah Parker (Chapter 8) was born in the Wichita Mountains near the present-day southwest Oklahoma town of Cache in 1848, nearly a generation before the War Between the States. He died in 1911, amidst a new world replete with Ford Model T automobiles, airplanes, telephones—of which he owned one of the first in western Oklahoma—and silent motion pictures, the first of which he appeared in.

Quanah well illustrates the vast transformation from old Oklahoma to new, even as both he and the state retained so much of their essential strength and so many of their distinctives. He was born into the most fearsome warrior tribe ever to rumble across the earth. The Comanches stopped the Spanish, the French, the Mexicans, the Apaches and numerous other tribes—and for a long time the Americans—from conquering the Southwest. His father was a legendary war chief and his mother an even more famous white woman. A member of one of the great Texas pioneer dynasties, she was captured by the tribe in a bloody raid, and then recaptured by Texas Rangers in a battle years later in which Quanah's father may have fallen.

His Quahadi band was the only North American tribal group never to sign a treaty. The loss or capture of parents, siblings, close friends, and at least one wife at the hand of the Texans and other Americans kindled a volcanic hatred within Quanah. Through his mid-twenties, he himself killed numerous white and possibly black Americans, other Natives, and Mexicans, and participated in or led countless raids and slaughters that involved robbery, rape, torture, and murder. The Comanches' victims included women, children, and even babies. These events stretched across vast tracts of land and many years. His Quahadis were the final Native group to surrender in the Southwest, and only when they were nearing starvation and relentlessly pursued by the greatest Indian fighter in American history, the dauntless Colonel Ranald Slidell Mackenzie (Chapter 8).

Leader in Peace

While U.S. Army commander at Fort Sill, Mackenzie dispatched Comanche peace emissaries to persuade Quanah and his few holdouts to come in to the fort, lay down their arms, and take up peaceable ways as American citizens. Surprisingly, those Native ambassadors found Quanah ready to surrender and urging his fellow remaining Quahadis to do so.

Upon getting to know Quanah, Mackenzie recognized in the fabled warrior a strength and integrity of character that spurred him to mentor the Comanche, teach him American social manners and customs, and guide him toward leadership opportunities among both Indian and white societies. Mackenzie also persuaded Quanah's socially and politically prominent white Texas relatives—his mother's Parker forefathers founded the first Protestant church in Texas—to look past his bloody deeds and accept him.

After shielding the final Quahadi resistors from imprisonment in Fort Leavenworth, Quanah capitalized on Mackenzie's trust and influence. He also recognized the peaceful path of American citizenship as the best hope for his decimated tribe. (No more than three thousands Comanches remained alive at the time of their final surrender to Mackenzie in 1875.) As chronicled by S. C. Gwynne in his landmark work *Empire of the Summer Moon*, Quanah embraced and led them toward farming and ranching, attending American schools, getting involved in business, participating in the civic arena, and learning the English language. Eventually, he founded an American-style school district for Comanche children that was owned and run by the tribe, and served as school board president. He also cultivated relationships with white leaders on the local, territorial, state, and national levels.

Quanah Parker—American

During the 1880s, Quanah parlayed his innate entrepreneurial and interpersonal skills and his burgeoning friendships with white cattlemen and business leaders, into a large ranch and a lucrative Comanche land-leasing business. He even charged his white colleagues fees for grazing and driving their cattle herds across the tribal reservation.

As his influence grew, some of those same friends sponsored him on trips to Washington, D.C. There, this former intrepid enemy of the United States advocated these and other enterprises that he believed were in the tribe's best interests before high federal officials, including President Theodore Roosevelt. He and Roosevelt developed a lasting friendship, as evinced by their famous 1905 wolf hunt near Frederick (Chapter 11) and Quanah's riding in Roosevelt's inaugural parade. According to Gwynne, Quanah also influenced his tribe to avoid the Ghost Dance cult that led the Sioux to disaster at Wounded Knee, South Dakota, in 1890.

He also defended his tribe as he verbally dueled with government commissioners leading the Dawes Act (Chapter 9) process of wresting Plains Indian lands away for individual allotments to tribal members and sale of the remainder to settlers. Quanah helped delay the process, particularly regarding the large Big Pasture region. This enabled the Comanches to lease that half-million-acre area for grazing for scores of thousands of dollars for years. By the time all the land was allotted, Quanah had personally secured better terms and more money for the tribe.

He accomplished all of this amidst continual opposition from other Comanche leaders who were often older and usually jealous of him, and amidst a white-dominated society that for generations had bitterly fought the Comanches and other Plains tribes and retained much prejudice against them.

In 1890 Quanah accomplished two of his greatest feats. The U.S. government named him the first and only principal chief in Comanche history, a high station to which the tribe would later re-elect him. He also built the Star House, a renowned two-story, ten-room mansion near the Wichitas. It was a dwelling of which the wealthiest Oklahoma or Texas cattle baron would have been proud.

White and Indian guests alike filled the Star House's dining room with the twelve-foot ceiling. Many of them were well-known figures in American history books, including General Nelson Miles, Geronimo, Lone Wolf the Yonger, Charles Goodnight, Burk Burnett, and President Theodore Roosevelt. White cooks and servants waited upon them and Quanah hired white teachers as well.

Quanah's generous nature had drawn the loyalty of others at least as far back as his successfully recruiting other Comanches for raiding parties he led. It grew more evident as he aged. He spent most of the small fortune he had accumulated feeding the hungry who streamed to him and the Star House, and helping other needy people, not all of them Natives. Gwynne poignantly wrote how tipis often clustered around the house—even though Quanah filled it with guests—and he and other family members slept outside in those tipis.

The legendary enemy and killer of Americans, Mexicans, and other tribes had two white sons-in-law and adopted and raised two white boys, not counting former white captive Herman Lehmann, who considered him his foster father and applied for Comanche membership.

Tragedy and Destiny

Quanah retained a durable streak of independence, as reflected in his multiple wives in which he sired twenty-four children, his leadership in the peyote-based Native American religion, and his long coldness toward the Christian faith. Yet after his pride and joy, gifted eldest son Harold, fell gravely ill with tuberculosis in the mid- to late-1890s, he witnessed young German-born Mennonite missionary Henry Kohfeld's evangelistic message to his son. When Harold professed belief in Jesus Christ to the Mennonite, the great chief declared, "I see, I see now what I never could understand or grasp before." Harold soon died, but according to Quanah, his son spoke frequently in his final days about the scriptural teachings that Kohfeld had shared with him, and died happy that he had found God's love.

Marvin E. Kroeker, professor emeritus of history at East Central University in Ada and a member of the Oklahoma Historians Hall of Fame, recounted what happened after Harold's burial:

> Quanah asked the people to go back into the chapel. He stepped behind the pulpit, took the Bible in his hand, and addressed his fellow Comanches. He had been to Washington many times, he stated, and had met presidents and senators, but never had he heard anything as comforting or inspiring as what he heard from the Bible and 'this dear missionary today.' He urged his people to come to the mission every Sunday and listen to God's word. Here was the way to the heavenly home. Harold had told him he loved Jesus and wanted to go home, and God had granted his wish . . . Then Quanah said a prayer and departed.

Quanah was now the one person with the power to keep Christian ministers from building churches on Comanche land or even preaching the Christian gospel to the tribe. But he was also the only individual with the power to give that permission, which he did in 1896 to the persistent Kohfeld (Chapter 10). And thus began the conversion of the greatest warrior tribe in history to Christianity through the denomination most committed to being peacemakers in the history of the American Church. And thus also was born Post Oak, the first Mennonite mission in history to a foreign land—the Comanche reservation. Post Oak Mennonite Church continues to serve the Comanche people to this day.

Whether or not Quanah Parker himself trusted in Christ for eternal salvation is known to God. Following the loss of his son Harold, he periodically attended Mennonite church services. One of his own wives, To-pay, was among the first Comanche converts to Christianity. Another of his sons, White Parker, served the Comanches in and around Lawton for decades as a stalwart Methodist minister.

Legacy of a Man

Quanah died nearly broke due to his ceaseless and selfless sharing of his possessions with others, usually those of various races who had nothing with which to pay him back. He could not bear to see anyone hungry. And according to white Cache storekeeper Robert Thomas, "He was always kind, never speaking ill of anyone."

Well-known historian J. Evatts Haley wrote that near the end of Quanah's life, recruiters wooed young Comanche men to join the U.S. Army. This would have led at least some of them into the World War I trench warfare, mustard gas, machine gun massacres, and other horrors that killed, maimed, and psychologically scarred hundreds of thousands of Americans. The old warrior stepped in and stopped the recruiters, declaring the inconsistency of recruiting young men to fight and kill when the white missionaries taught that it was wrong to go to war.

Gwynne recounted how in the final months of his life, accompanied by his twelve-year-old son Gussie, Quanah spoke to an enormous crowd at the Texas State Fair in Dallas. In memorably unpredictable Quanah Parker fashion, he sported a war bonnet, buckskins, and moccasins, yet what he said was this: "I used to be a bad man. Now I am a citizen of the United States. I pay taxes same as you people do. We are the same people."

Indeed we are, my fellow Oklahomans.

Oklahoma-born artist Michelle Noah drew on the influence of Kiowa Ledger Art (Chapter 8) for this original work, *Star House*, as she did for *Here, Build Jesus House!* (Chapter 10). Ironically, Quanah Parker lost nearly all the wealth that built his sensational palace on the plains by serving and giving to the many needy folks who came to stay in it. (www.michellebnoah.com)

County Names

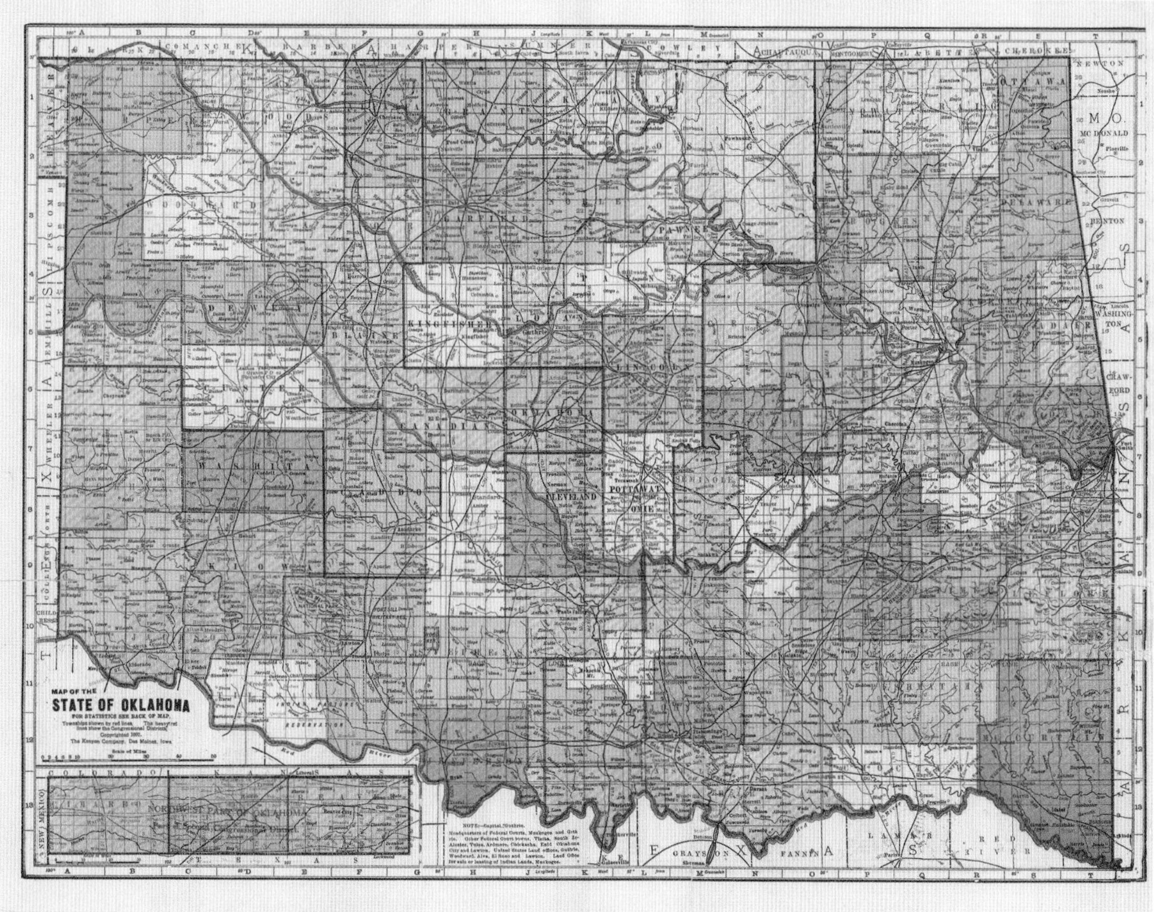

Adair William Penn Adair, Cherokee tribal leader and Confederate colonel in the War Between the States.

Alfalfa One of two counties named for William H. "Alfalfa Bill" Murray, Texas-born congressman, governor, and founding father of Oklahoma.

Atoka Captain Atoka, a Choctaw leader and signer of the Treaty of Dancing Rabbit Creek.

Beaver Beaver River, which flows through this Panhandle county.

Beckham Democratic governor and senator J. C. W. Beckham of Kentucky.

Blaine Republican congressman, senator, secretary of state, and 1884 presidential candidate James G. Blaine of Maine.

Bryan	U.S. Secretary of State, renowned orator, and three-time Democratic Presidential candidate William Jennings Bryan.
Caddo	The Caddo Indian tribe, from the Native word "kaadi," meaning "chief."
Canadian	The Canadian River, also referred to as the South Canadian, that begins at the Sangre de Cristo Mountains in Colorado and runs east-west the length of Oklahoma into the Arkansas River.
Carter	A prominent early family of the area, whose best-known member was twenty-year Chickasaw-Cherokee congressman Charles D. Carter.
Cherokee	The Cherokee Indian nation whose capital Tahlequah is the county seat.
Choctaw	The Choctaw Indian nation, whose country following Indian removal the county lies in.
Cimarron	The only county in America that borders five states, from the Cimarron River that runs through it and across northern Oklahoma, gathering salt and other mineral deposits before flowing into the Arkansas River.
Cleveland	Two-time Democratic President Grover Cleveland, a leader in opening the area to American settlement with the 1889 Unassigned Lands Run and whose name residents selected over Abraham Lincoln's.
Coal	The mineral that was then the major product of the region and which spurred its economic development.
Comanche	The Comanche Indian tribe long centered in the area.
Cotton	Its principal economic product.
Craig	Granville Craig, a generous mixed-blood Cherokee rancher of the area.
Creek	The Creek Nation, whose country following Indian removal included the county.
Custer	Famed Civil War and Plains Indian War General George Armstrong Custer, who led a successful military campaign against the Cheyenne and Arapaho tribes, culminating in the 1868 Battle of the Washita River a few miles west in Cheyenne.
Delaware	The Delaware Indian tribe, many of whom live in the region.
Dewey	George Dewey, victor of the Spanish–American War Battle of Manila Bay—still fresh in the public mind at the time of Oklahoma statehood—and the only person in history to have attained the rank of Admiral of the Navy.
Ellis	Albert H. Ellis, a pioneer who won land in the Cherokee Outlet Run of '93, then served as a territorial legislator, vice president of the Oklahoma Constitutional Convention, and speaker pro tempore of the state's first House of Representatives.
Garfield	U.S. President James A. Garfield, a Republican like the majority of settlers in the area, who was assassinated in 1881, just six months after taking office.
Garvin	Samuel J. Garvin, a prominent cattleman, merchant, and banker who settled in the area in 1870.
Grady	Georgian Henry W. Grady, editor of the *Atlanta Constitution* newspaper, who eloquently encouraged Northern financial investment in the ravaged South following the War Between the States.
Grant	Ulysses S. Grant, triumphant Federal Civil War military commander and two-time post-war President of the United States.
Greer	John Alexander Greer, Republic of Texas statesman and Lieutenant Governor of the state of Texas.
Harmon	Judson C. Harmon, governor of Ohio and U.S. secretary of state.
Harper	Oscar G. Harper, clerk of the Oklahoma Constitutional Convention
Haskell	Charles N. Haskell, Oklahoma business titan, Constitutional Convention leader, and first governor.
Hughes	W. C. Hughes, prominent member of the Oklahoma Constitutional Convention.

Jackson Presbyterian deacon and Confederate General Thomas J. "Stonewall" Jackson, whose historic battle victories had given the Confederacy the upper hand halfway through the Civil War at the time of his death.

Jefferson Thomas Jefferson, author of the Declaration of Independence and third president of the United States.

Johnston Douglas H. Johnston, governor of the Chickasaw Nation.

Kay Derived from "K," the previous designation of the area as an Oklahoma Territory county.

Kingfisher King David Fisher, legendary frontiersman, cattleman, and horseman.

Kiowa The Kiowa tribe of Natives, many of whom lived in the area before, during, and since their reservation period.

Latimer James S. Latimer, Wilburton (county seat)-area representative to the Oklahoma Constitutional Convention.

Le Flore Choctaw family of French descent, from whom Greenwood Le Flore served as chief and a leading force in the tribe's survival migration to present-day Oklahoma.

Lincoln Abraham Lincoln, sixteenth president of the United States, including during the War Between the States, and signer of the Emancipation Proclamation.

Logan John A. Logan, Federal general in the War Between the States, U.S. senator from Illinois.

Love A leading Chickasaw family, whose descendants have built the nationwide Love's Travel Stops & Country Stores chain.

Major John C. Major, member of the Oklahoma Constitutional Convention.

Marshall Maiden name of the mother of Oklahoma Constitutional Convention member George A. Henshaw of Madill, now the county seat.

Mayes Samuel Houston Mayes, teenaged Confederate cavalryman, cattleman, and mixed-blood Principal Chief of the Cherokee Nation.

McClain Charles M. McClain, member of the Oklahoma Constitutional Convention.

McCurtain The McCurtains, a prominent Choctaw Nation family, several of whom served as Principal Chiefs.

McIntosh The prominent Creek family that included controversial tribal martyr William McIntosh and other chiefs, Confederate commanders, Christian missionaries, and artists among McIntosh's Indian Territory and Oklahoma descendants.

Murray One of two counties named for William H. "Alfalfa Bill" Murray, Texas-born congressman, governor, and founding father of Oklahoma.

Muskogee The Muskogee, or Creek, confederation of tribes that inhabited lands after Indian removal that included the county.

Noble John W. Noble, Civil War Union general and later U.S. secretary of the interior during the period that land runs opened vast, barren areas of Oklahoma Territory to settlement.

Nowata The Delaware language word "no-we-ata," meaning welcome; some members of the tribe lived in the area.

Okfuskee Creek town of the same name in Alabama, in the area from which the Creeks were removed to Indian Territory, including this county, from a word denoting the origin of a clan of Muskogee, or Creek, Indians.

Oklahoma Derived from the principal community in the county, originally Oklahoma Station, then Oklahoma City, the word meaning "red people" in the Choctaw language.

Okmulgee Creek town of the same name in Alabama, in the area from which the Creek were removed to Indian Territory, including this county, from a word meaning "boiling waters."

Osage The Indian nation that figured prominently in the history of present-day Oklahoma beginning in the eighteenth-century, and whose reservation spanned the area.

Ottawa	The tribe who inhabited the area, and whose name originated from an Algonquin word meaning "to buy and sell."
Pawnee	The tribe whom the U.S. government settled in the area following the War Between the States.
Payne	David L. Payne, leader of the "Boomer" movement that spearheaded white settlement of Oklahoma Territory.
Pittsburg	Pittsburgh, Pennsylvania, which county leaders invoked as a similar bastion of coal production, the economic engine of this area at the time of statehood.
Pontotoc	A county in the earlier, post-Indian removal Chickasaw country of the same name, which emanated from a likewise-named settlement of the tribe in Mississippi, meaning "cat tails growing on the prairie."
Pottawatomie	The tribe which resided in the area, its name a Chippewa term meaning "people of the place of the fire."
Pushmataha	The district of the same name in the earlier Choctaw Nation of Indian Territory, which was the namesake of the legendary Choctaw chief Pushmataha, who faced down the Shawnee chief Tecumseh when he tried to lure the Choctaw into an alliance against the U.S., with whom the tribe sided with in the War of 1812.
Roger Mills	Roger Q. Mills, Confederate officer, congressman, and U.S. senator from Texas, and champion against protective tariffs.
Rogers	Mixed-blood Cherokee Clem Rogers, Confederate cavalry scout for Stand Watie, Oklahoma Constitutional Convention leader, and father of Will Rogers.
Seminole	The Seminole Nation, whose capital is also the county seat of Wewoka.
Sequoyah	The legendary Cherokee who created the tribe's alphabet-like syllabary, and whose home the last many years of his life was in the present-day county.
Stephens	Texas Congressman John H. Stephens, a champion of Oklahoma statehood.
Texas	The state bordering it to the south and from which many of its settlers came.
Tillman	U.S. Senator Benjamin Tillman of South Carolina.
Tulsa	The county seat and eventual second-largest city in Oklahoma, and the Creek village of Tulsey Town in Alabama from which the name derived.
Wagoner	The county seat of the same name, which derived from Henry "Big Foot" Parsons, a dispatcher for the Katy Railroad that ran through the town.
Washington	George Washington, a founding father of the United States, commander-in-chief of the victorious Continental Army in the American War of Independence, and first president of the United States.
Washita	The nearly-three hundred-mile-long river that runs through it and empties into Lake Texoma and Red River.
Woods	Samuel Newitt Woods, Kansas anti-slavery activist, territorial legislator, Union officer in the Civil War, and newspaper publisher.
Woodward	Probably Kansas territorial legislator, educator, and Santa Fe Railroad Director Brinton W. Woodward.

Selected Bibliography

Following is a partial bibliography of sources utilized in the writing of this book, together with topics. Numerous of these sources were utilized for multiple topics, though not cited in every case, just as not all topics are cited for which each of these and other sources were used. The author drew upon the following helpful sources throughout the work: Odie B. Faulk and William D. Welge, *Oklahoma: A Rich History*; Arrell M. Gibson, *Harlow's Oklahoma History*; Gaston Little, *History of Oklahoma*; W. David Baird and Danney Goble, *The Story of Oklahoma*; Edward Everett Dale, *History of Oklahoma*; Edwin C. McReynolds, *Oklahoma: A History of the Sooner State*; Paul F. Lambert and Bob L. Blackburn, *You Know We Belong to the Land*; *Encyclopedia of Oklahoma History & Culture*; and the *Chronicles of Oklahoma*.

Also, the author conducted many hours of interviews with Blackburn, Welge, and Bruce Fisher, all of the Oklahoma Historical Society, from which material throughout the book was drawn.

Chapter 1

Coronado, Quivira, Southwest Oklahoma: Tom Lewis and Sara Jane Richter, "Coronado Expedition," *Encyclopedia of Oklahoma History & Culture*; Charles M. Cooper, "The Big Pasture," *Chronicles of Oklahoma*, Volume 35, 1957; Herbert E. Belton, *The Spanish Borderlands*; Edwin C. McReynolds, *A History of the Sooner State*; Article, *The Temple Tribune*, August 22, 1907. Europe, mercantilism: Adam Smith, *The Wealth of Nations*; Thomas J. DiLorenzo, *How Capitalism Saved America*; Jackson J. Spielvogel, *Western Civilization*; *Exploring American History: From Colonial Times to 1877*, Tom Lansford and Thomas Woods, Jr., eds.

Chapter 2

Thomas Jefferson: *The Life and Selected Writings of Thomas Jefferson*, Adrienne Koch and William Peden, eds.; Mark Thornton, "Happy Birthday to Our Greatest American, Thomas Jefferson," *Dallas Morning News*, April 11, 1993; Mary Ann Hemphill, "Happy 250th, Mr. Jefferson," *Dallas Morning News*, April 11, 1993; William G. Hyland, *In Defense of Thomas Jefferson: The Sally Hemings Sex Scandal*; Thomas Woods, Jr., *The Politically Incorrect Guide to American History*; Steve Byas, *History's Greatest Libels*. Creek Wars: "Creek Chief Red Eagle Address to General Andrew Jackson," Great American Indian Speeches, Vol. 1

(Phonographic Disc); Sparks Expedition: Carl N. Tyson, "Freeman-Custis Expedition (1806)," *Encyclopedia of Oklahoma History & Culture*. Osages: Osage Treaty of 1808; Stan Hoig, *The Chouteaus*. The Chouteaus: Stan Hoig, *The Chouteaus*

Chapter 3

William Becknell: Larry M. Beachum, *Father of the Santa Fe Trade, Southwestern Studies, El Paso., Texas, Monograph No. 68*; "The Interactive Santa Fe Trail," Kansas Heritage Group. Nathaniel Pryor: Stan Hoig, *The Chouteaus*; Jon D. May, "Nathaniel Pryor," *Encyclopedia of Oklahoma History & Culture*; John H. Prior, "Nathaniel Pryor, c. 1775–1831, U.S. Explorer, Solider, Trader & Indian Agent, Part One"; Joseph Musselma, "Nathaniel Pryor," Discovering Lewis and Clark, the Lewis and Clark Fort Mandan Foundation; Grant Foreman, "Nathaniel Pryor," *Chronicles of Oklahoma*, Volume 7, No. 2, June 1929; Stan Hoig, *The Chouteaus*. Long and James on the Canadian River: *Cherokee Phoenix and Indians' Advocate*, March 3, 1830, Vol. II. Stephen Long: Roger L. Nichols, "Long-Bell Expedition," *Encyclopedia of Oklahoma History & Culture*; "Beyond Lewis and Clark, Timeline 1819–1820: The Army Explores the West, Captain William Clark (1770–1838)," Kansas State Historical Society. Mu-na-we (Menawa): Miriam R. Fowler, "Menawa, a Chief of the Upper Creeks," Shelby County (AL) Historical Society. Seminoles: William C. Sturdevant, "Creek Into Seminole," *North American Indians in Historical Perspective*, Eleanor Burke Leacok and Nacy Oestreich Lurie, eds. William McIntosh: George Chapman, *Chief William McIntosh: A Man of Two Worlds*. Pushmataha: Ruth Tenison West, "Pushmataha's Travels," *Chronicles of Oklahoma*, Volume 37, 1959; (Negotiations with Andrew Jackson) "Pushmataha, Choctaw Indian Chief," Access Genealogy Indian Tribal Records and *Handbook of American Indians North of Mexico*; (Speech to Tecumseh) "The Story of Pushmataha, Historic Choctaw Chief," *Meridian (MS) Star*, August 6, 2010; Mike Boucher's Web Page on Choctaw History; "Choctaw Chief Pushmataha's Response to Chief Tecumseh on War Against the Americans," American Rhetoric Online Speech Bank. John Jolly: *Encyclopedia of Arkansas History and Culture*. Dwight Mission: *Encyclopedia of Arkansas History and Culture*. Battle of Claremore Mound: Jon D. May, "Battle of Claremound Mound," *Encyclopedia of Oklahoma History & Culture*. Creeks: (As slaves of English) Gaston Litton, *History of Oklahoma*; Jack M. Schultz, *The Seminole Baptist Churches of Oklahoma*. Byingtons: Clyde A. Milner and Floyd A. O'Neil, *Churchmen and the Western Indians, 1820–1920*; Angie Debo, *The Rise and Fall of the Choctaw Republic*. Chickasaws: Horatio B. Cushman, *History of the Choctaw, Chickasaw, and Natchez Indians*.

Chapter 4

Washington Irving: Stan Hoig, "Irving, Ellsworth, Latrobe, and Pourtales Expedition," *Encyclopedia of Oklahoma History & Culture*. Samuel Worcester: Althea Bass, *Cherokee Messenger*; William G. McLoughlin, *Cherokees & Missionaries, 1789–1839*; Grant Foreman, *Indian Removal*; Thurman Wilkins, *Cherokee Tragedy*; Hope Holway, "The Cold Water Army," *Chronicles of Oklahoma*, Volume 37, Spring 1959; Muriel H. Wright, "Samuel Austin Worcester: A Dedication," *Chronicles of Oklahoma*, Volume 37, Spring 1959; A. J. Langguth, *Driven West: Andrew Jackson and the Trail of Tears to the Civil War*. Elias Boudinot: Ralph Gabriel, *Elias Boudinot, Cherokee, and His America*; Theda Perdue, *Cherokee Editor*; *Cherokee Cavaliers*, Edward Everett Dale, ed.; "Elias Boudinot," *About North Georgia*, Spring 2012; Thurman Wilkins, *Cherokee Tragedy*; House Documents, Otherwise Published as Executive Documents: 13th Congress, 2d–49th Congress, United States Congress; Theresa Strouth Gaul, *To Marry an Indian*; Elias

Boudinot, *Poor Sarah: Or Religion Exmplified in the Life and Death of An Indian Woman*; Leola Selman, "Homes of Distinguished Cherokee Indians," *Chronicles of Oklahoma*, Volume 11, No. 3 September 1933. Opothleyaholo: John Bartlett Meserve, "Chief Opothleyaholo," *Chronicles of Oklahoma*, Volume 9, No. 4 December 1931; Steve Cottrell, *The Civil War in Indian Territory*; W. David Baird *A Creek Warrior for the Confederacy: The Autobiography of Chief G. W. Grayson*; Anna Eddings, "Opothleyahola," *Encyclopedia of Oklahoma History & Culture*. Seminole Wars: Edwin McReynolds, *The Seminoles*. George Harkins quote: *Niles' Register*, February 25, 1832. Choctaws' later suffering in Mississippi: John H. Peterson, Jr., "Three Efforts at Development among the Choctaws of Mississippi," *Southeastern Indians: Since the Removal Era*, Walter Williams, ed.;. David Folsom: Rusty Lang, "Colonel David Folsom"; Czarina C. Conlan, "David Folsom," *Chronicles of Oklahoma*, Volume 4, No. 4, December 1926; Clyde A. Milner and Floyd A. O'Neil, *Churchmen and the Western Indians, 1820–1920*; Angie Debo, *The Rise and Fall of the Choctaw Republic*; "David Folsom Calls Missionaries West," *The Missionary Herald*, Volume 20, American Board of Commissioners for Foreign Missions; "Nathaniel Folsom Memoirs"; "Official Seals of Indian Nations, Territorial and State Governments of Oklahoma, *Chronicles of Oklahoma*, Winter 1955–56. Trails of Tears: Grant Foreman, *Indian Removal*; Angie Debo, *The Road to Disappearance*; Angie Debo, *The Rise and Fall of the Choctaw Republic*; Edwin C. McReynolds, *The Seminoles*; Grace Steele Woodward, *The Cherokees*; Thurman Wilkins, *Cherokee Tragedy*; Muriel H. Wright, "The Removal of the Choctaws to the Indian Territory 1830–33," *Chronicles of Oklahoma*, Volume 6, No. 2, June 1928. Liquor and Indians: Grant Foreman, "A Century of Prohibition," *Chronicles of Oklahoma*, Volume 12, No. 2 June 1934. Comparisons of blacks and Indians: Charles Hudson, "The Ante-Bellum Elite," Red, White, and Black: Symposium on Indians in the Old South. Five Civilized Tribes and Christianity: Angie Debo, *And Still the Waters Run*; W. David Baird and Danney Goble, *The Story of Oklahoma*. Persecution of Cherokees: Gary Moulton, *John Ross: Cherokee Chief*; *Cherokee General*, Tully Productions. Dodge and the Dragoons: J. G. Clift, "Notes on the Early History of Stephens County," *Chronicles of Oklahoma*, Volume 20, No. 1, March 1942. Comanche horsemanship: Texas Beyond History, The Passing of the Indian Era, University of Texas at Austin. George Catlin art: Donald W. Reynolds Center for American Art and Portraiture, Smithsonian American Art Museum; "George Catlin and His Indian Gallery," Autry Museum of the American West.

Chapter 5

Cyrus Kingsbury: Clyde A. Milner and Floyd A. O'Neil, *Churchmen and the Western Indians, 1820–1920*; Angie Debo, *The Rise and Fall of the Choctaw Republic*; W. B. Morrison, "Diary of Rev. Cyrus Kingsbury," *Chronicles of Oklahoma*, Volume 3, No. 2,June, 1925. Alice Eliza Worcester Robertson: Hope Holway, "Ann Eliza Worcester Robertson as a Linguist," *Chronicles of Oklahoma* 37 (Spring 1959); Dianna Everett, "Alice Eliza Worcester Robertson," *Encyclopedia of Oklahoma History & Culture*; Grant Foreman, "The Honorable Alice M. Robertson," *Chronicles of Oklahoma*, March, 1932; Paul F. Lambert and Bob L. Blackburn, "You Know We Belong to the Land"; Hope Holway, "The Cold Water Army," *Chronicles of Oklahoma*, Volume 37, Spring 1959; Althea Bass, "William Schenck Robertson," *Chronicles of Oklahoma*, Volume 37, Spring 1959; Althea Bass, *Cherokee Messenger*. Wildcat: "Coacoochee (Wild Cat)," The Handbook of Texas Online; Arrell Gibson, *The Kickapoos, Lords of the Middle Border*, Arrell Gibson; Susan A. Miller, *Coacoochee's Bones: A Seminole Saga*; Edwin C. McReynolds, *The Seminoles*; Kenneth W. Porter, "Wild Cat's Death and Burial." Creek prayer/whiskey quote: E. C. Routh, *The Story of Oklahoma Baptists*. Robert M. Jones: Paul F. Lambert and Bob L. Blackburn, *You Know We Belong to the Land: the Centennial History of Oklahoma*; W. B. Morrison, "The Tragedy of Rose Hill," *The Daily Oklahoman*; Grant Foreman, *Indian Removal*; Michael L. Bruce, "Robert M. Jones," *Encyclopedia of Oklahoma History & Culture*; Litton; W. B. Morrison, "Diary of Rev. Cyrus Kingsbury, *Chronicles of Oklahoma*,Volume 3, No. 2 June, 1925; "Old Choctaw Plantation

Part of Oklahoma Archaeology Site," The African-Native American Genealogy Blog; W. B. Morrison, "The Tragedy of Rose Hill," *The Daily Oklahoman*. Choctaw-Chickasaw sovereignty conflict: Gaston Litton, "The Establishment of Tribal Governments, *History of Oklahoma*. Steamboat travel: Gaston Litton, "River Traffic," *History of Oklahoma*. Jerusha Swain: Meg Devlin O'Sullivan, "Missionary and Mother: Jerusha Swain's Transformation in the Cherokee Nation, 1852–1861," *Chronicles of Oklahoma*, Vol. 83–4 2005–06; "Jerusha Swain, letters, 1851–1860," State Historical Society of Wisconsin, Archives Division. Church and slavery: John J. Dwyer, *The War Between the States: America's Uncivil War*. 1842 slave revolt: Art Burton, "Slave Revolt of 1842," *Encyclopedia of Oklahoma History & Culture*. Tribal slave codes, social restrictions: Arrell Gibson, *Harlow's Oklahoma History*; Gaston D. Litton, *History of Oklahoma*. Evan Jones: E. C. Routh, "Early Missionaries to the Cherokee," *Chronicles of Oklahoma*, Volume 15, No. 4 December, 1937; Jerry L. Faught II, "Evan Jones," *Encyclopedia of Oklahoma History & Culture*; Patrick Minges, "The Keetoowah Society and the Avocation of Religious Nationalism in the Cherokee Nation, 1855–1867"; William G. McLoughlin, *Champions of the Cherokees: Evan and John B. Jones*; Daniel Blake Smith, *An American Betrayal: Cherokee Patriots and the Trail of Tears*. Uncle Wallace Willis and Aunt Minerva Wallis: *Swing Low, Sweet Chariot*; Judith Michener, "Uncle Wallace and Aunt Minerva Wallis," *Encyclopedia of Oklahoma History & Culture*; Robert Flickinger, *The Choctaw Freedmen and the Story of the Oak Hill Industrial Academy*; Angie Debo, *Foot-Loose and Fancy-Free*;

Chapter 6

The Civil War/The War Between the States: Steve Cottrell, *The Civil War in Oklahoma*; James L. Huston, "Civil War Era," *Encyclopedia of Oklahoma History & Culture*; John J. Dwyer, *The War Between the States: America's Uncivil War*; Phillip W. Steele, *The Last Cherokee Warriors*; Albert Castel, *William Clarke Quantrill: His Life and Times*; Steven Warren, *The Second Battle of Cabin Creek: Brilliant Victory*. Stand Watie: Wilfred Knight, *Red Fox: Stand Watie's Civil War Years*; Frank Cunningham, *General Stand Watie's Confederate Indians*; Kenny Franks, *Stand Watie and the Agony of the Cherokee Nation*; (Quote) John J. Dwyer, "Stand Watie and the Confederate Indians"; Edward Everett Dale, *Cherokee Cavaliers*; Thurman Wilkins, *Cherokee Tragedy*. George Washington Grayson: W. David Baird, *A Creek Warrior for the Confederacy: The Autobiography of Chief G. W. Grayson*; Mary Jane Warde, "George Washington Grayson," *Encyclopedia of Oklahoma History & Culture*; Angie Debo, *The Road to Disappearance*. Confederates appeals to Indians, Camp Napoleon Council: Anna Lewis, "Camp Napoleon," *Chronicles of Oklahoma*, Volume 9, No. 4, December, 1931. Joseph Murrow: Alice Hurley Mackey, "Father Murrow: Civil War Period," *Chronicles of Oklahoma*, Volume 12, No. 1, March, 1934; Frank A. Balyeat, "Joseph Samuel Murrow, Apostle to the Indians," *Chronicles of Oklahoma*, Volume 35, 1957; Andrea M. Martin, "Joseph Samuel Murrow"; W. H. Underwood, "Rev. Dr. Joseph Samuel Morrow," *Chronicles of Oklahoma*, Volume 7, Number 4, December 1929. William A. Phillips Campaign, Middle Boggy: Steven Warren, "Battle of Middle Boggy," *Encyclopedia of Oklahoma History & Culture*; Whit Edwards interview, *The Oklahoman*. Indian Territory Slaves remembrances: *WPA Slave Narratives*. Opotholeyahola: Steve Cottrell, *The Civil War in Indian Territory*.

Chapter 7

James Lane, Kansas Indians: Gaston D. Litton, *History of Oklahoma*; John J. Dwyer, *The War Between the States: America's Uncivil War*. Lane-Pomeroy enmity: George Reynolds, *Kansas Historical Quarterly*, Volume XIX, 1951. Indian republics' suffering, 1865–66: Gaston D. Litton, *History of Oklahoma*. Chief

Joseph: S. R. A. Marshall, *Crimsoned Prairie*; Ingrid P. Westmoreland, "Nez Perce," *Encyclopedia of Oklahoma History & Culture.* Standing Bear: Mark R. Little, "Standing Bear," *Encyclopedia of Oklahoma History & Culture.* Skilled Choctaws and Chickasaws: Gaston D. Litton, *History of Oklahoma.* Black tribal membership: bell hooks, "Revolutionary Renegades," *Black Looks: Race and Representation.* Federal officers' Reconstruction attitude toward Indians: Gaston D. Litton, *History of Oklahoma.* Indians and Christianity: J. J. Methvin, "Reminiscences of Life Among the Indians," *Chronicles of Oklahoma*, Volume 5, No. 2, June, 1927. Kiowas' hunger: Jacki Thompason Rand, *Kiowa Humanity and the Invasion of the State.* Camp Supply: Bob Rea, "Fort Supply," *Encyclopedia of Oklahoma History & Culture.* Sand Creek: S. R. A. Marshall, *Crimsoned Prairie*; Bruce Cutler, *The Massacre at Sand Creek.* Battle of the Washita: Stephen Black, "Battle of the Washita," *Encyclopedia of Oklahoma History & Culture*; Gaston D. Litton, *History of Oklahoma*; S. R. A. Marshall, *Crimsoned Prairie.*

Chapter 8

Petroleum/Chickasaw Oil Company: Kenny A. Franks, *The Oklahoma Petroleum Industry*; Kenny A. Franks, Paul F. Lambert, and Carl N. Tyson, *Early Oklahoma Oil: A Photographic History, 1859–1936*; Carl Coke Rister, *Oil! Titan of the Southwest*; Muriel H. Wright, "First Oklahoma Oil Was Produced in 1859," *Chronicles of Oklahoma* 4, December 1962; Jon D. May, "Chickasaw Oil Company," *Encyclopedia of Oklahoma History & Culture.* Robber's Roost: Norma Gene Young, editor, *The Tracks We Followed.* Philip A. Sheridan: Robert Stackpole, *Sheridan in the Shenandoah*; John Heatwole, *The Burning: Sheridan's Devastation of the Shenandoah*; Dee Brown, *Bury My Heart at Wounded Knee*; S. R. A. Marshall, *Crimsoned Prairie*; John J. Dwyer, *The War Between the States: America's Uncivil War*; Thomas J. DiLorenzo, "The Culture of Violence in the American West: Myth versus Reality." The Comanches, Quanah Parker, Ranald Slidell MacKenzie: Daniel A. Becker, "Comanche Civilization with History of Quanah Parker," *Chronicles of Oklahoma*, Volume 1, No. 3, June, 1923; S. C. Gwynne, *Empire of the Summer Moon*; T. R. Fehrenbach, *Comanches: The History of a People*; T. R. Fehrenbach, *Lone Star*; Tom Crum and Paul H. Carlson, "Did Quanah Parker Lie?", *Chronicles of Oklahoma*, Volume 93, Number 3, Fall, 2015; Marvin D. Kroeker, *Comanches and Mennonites on the Oklahoma Plains.*

Chapter 9

John H. Seger: Dan W. Peery, "The Indians' Friend John H. Seger," *Chronicles of Oklahoma*, Vol. 10, No. 3, September 1932; Jack Rairdon, "John Homer Seger, The Practical Indian Educator," *Chronicles of Oklahoma*, 34, 1956; Karen K. McKellips, "Educational Practices In Two Nineteenth Century American Indian Mission Schools," *Journal of American Indian Education*, Volume 32, Number 1, October 1992. Cattle drives, white settlement: Edward Everett Dale, *Frontier Ways: Sketches of Life in the Old West*; J. L. Hefley, *Apache Prophet*; Handbook of Texas Online; Edward Everett Dale, *History of Oklahoma.* J. J. Methvin: Sidney H. Babcock, "John Jasper Methvin 1846–1941," *Chronicles of Oklahoma*, Volume 19, No. 2 June, 1941; J. J. Methvin, "Reminiscences of Life Among the Indians," *Chronicles of Oklahoma*, 5, No. 2, June 1927; Dianna Everett, "John Jasper Methvin," *Encyclopedia of Oklahoma History & Culture.* Charles Journeycake: E. C. Routh, *The Story of Oklahoma Baptists.* Railroad line locations: Odie B. Faulk and William D. Welge, *Oklahoma: A Rich History.* Scottish, English Cattlemen: Larry O'Dell, "English, Scottish, and Welsh," *Encyclopedia of Oklahoma History & Culture.* German immigrants: Richard Rohrs, *The Germans in Oklahoma*; Richard C. Rohrs, "Germans," *Encyclopedia of Oklahoma History & Culture.*

Coal mining towns: Eric Goostree, "Mining Towns," *Encyclopedia of Oklahoma History & Culture*; Gaston D. Litton, *History of Oklahoma*. Petroleum: Kenny Franks, "Petroleum Industry," *Encyclopedia of Oklahoma History & Culture*; Muriel H. Wright, "First Oklahoma Oil Was Produced in 1859," *Chronicles of Oklahoma* 4, No. 4, December 1926; (Byrd oil strike) David Craighead, "The Shallow Field," *Oklahoma Today*, Autumn 1965, Volume 15, No. 4; (H. W. Faucett) Jon D. May, "Choctaw Oil and Refining Company, *Encyclopedia of Oklahoma History & Culture*. Land Runs: Indian-Pioneer Papers Collection, Western History Collections, University of Oklahoma; "Land Run of 1889," Stan Hoig, *Encyclopedia of Oklahoma History & Culture*; Stan Hoig, *The Oklahoma Land Rush of 1889*; Brad Agnew, "Voices of the Land Run of 1889," *Chronicles of Oklahoma*, 67, Spring 1989. Marlow Brothers: William Rathmell, *Life of the Marlows*, Robert K. DeArment, ed. Mennonites: Marvin E. Kroeker, "In Death You Shall Not Wear It Either: The Persecution of Mennonite Pacifists in Oklahoma," *An Oklahoma I Had Never Seen Before*, Davis D. Joyce, ed.; Marvin E. Kroeker, *Comanches and Mennonites on the Oklahoma Plains*; Marvin E. Kroeker, "Mennonites," *Encyclopedia of Oklahoma History & Culture*; Sharon Hartin Iorio, *Faith's Harvest: Mennonite Identity in Northwest Oklahoma*; Guy Franklin Hershberger, *War, Peace, and Nonresistance.*

Chapter 10

Land Runs: Edna Ferber, *Cimarron*; Sac & Fox, Cheyenne/Arapaho Land Runs: Linda D. Wilson, *Encyclopedia of Oklahoma History & Culture*. Cheyenne & Arapaho Land Run: Michael Reggio, *Encyclopedia of Oklahoma History & Culture*. Big Tree: Jon D. May, *Encyclopedia of Oklahoma History & Culture*. Cherokee Outlet run: Alvin O. Turner, *Encyclopedia of Oklahoma History & Culture*. Republicans and African-Americans: Claude Bower, *The Tragic Era*. Evolution: Clarence Carson, "The Growth of America," Vol. 4, *A Basic History of the United States*. Coal mining: Fred W. Dunbar, "Coal Mining Strikes," *Encyclopedia of Oklahoma History & Culture*; Steven L. Sewell, "Coal Mining Disasters," *Encyclopedia of Oklahoma History & Culture*; Peter Hanraty and Coal Mining: Fred W. Dunbar, *Champion of The Working Man: The Life and Times of Peter Hanraty*; Patrick J. Blessing, *The British and Irish in Oklahoma*; Irvin Hurst, *The 46th Star*; Larry O'Dell, "Organized Labor," *Encyclopedia of Oklahoma History & Culture*. Petroleum: Kenny Franks, "Petroleum Industry," *Encyclopedia of Oklahoma History & Culture*; Linda D. Wilson, "Nellie Johnstone Number One," *Encyclopedia of Oklahoma History & Culture*. George L. Miller: Corb Sarchet, *Chronicles of Oklahoma*,Volume 7, No. 2, June, 1929. Bass Reeves: Art Burton, *Black, Red, and Deadly*. Billy McGinty: Billy McGinty, *Oklahoma Rough Rider: Billy McGinty's Own Story*; Leslie A. McRill, "The Story of an Oklahoma Cowboy, William McGinty, and His Wife," *Chronicles of Oklahoma*, 34, No. 4, Winter 1956.

Chapter 11

Oklahoma City growth: Bob Blackburn, lecture to Wordwrights, September 2009. Pleasant Porter options for Creeks: Angie Debo, *And Still the Waters Run*. Chitto Harjo, Crazy Snakes: Kenneth McIntosh, "Chitto Harjo," *Encyclopedia of Oklahoma History & Culture* ; Kenneth McIntosh, "Crazy Snake Uprising," *Encyclopedia of Oklahoma History & Culture*. Pleasant Porter: John Bartlett Meserve, "Chief Pleasant Porter," *Chronicles of Oklahoma*, Volume 9, No. 3 September 1931; Dianna Everett, "Pleasant Porter," *Encyclopedia of Oklahoma History & Culture*; W. David Baird, *A Creek Warrior for the Confederacy: The Autobiography of Chief G. W. Grayson*. Theodore Roosevelt and Oklahoma Constitution cartoon: C. D. Foster, *Foster's Comic History of Oklahoma*. Bill Pickett: Handbook of Texas Onine. Bass Reeves: Art

Burton, Black Gun, Silver Star: The Life and Legend of Frontier Marshall Bass Reeves. W. H. Twine: Jimmie L. White, Jr., William Henry Twine, *Encyclopedia of Oklahoma History & Culture*; African-American lawyers: Bruce Fisher and Jerome Holmes, "African-American Lawyers in Oklahoma," 75 *Oklahoma Bar Journal* 66, Sept. 11, 2007. Kate Barnard: Bob Burke, *Oklahoma's Good Angel*; Lynn R. Musslewhite, Suzanne J. Crawford, *One Woman's Political Journey: Kate Barnard and Social Reform 1875–1930*; Lynn R. Musslewhite, Suzanne J. Crawford, "Kate Barnard, Progressivism, and the West," *An Oklahoma I had Never Seen Before*, Davis D. Joyce, ed. Black Indian freedmen, allotment rights: Angie Debo, *And Still the Waters Run*. A. C. Hamlin election: Edward Everett Dale, *The History of Oklahoma*. African-American Jim Crow resistance, per Jimmie Franklin: Arnold Rampersad, *Ralph Ellison, A Biography*. All-black towns: William E. Bittle and Gilbert Geis, *The Longest Way Home*. Blacks in Oklahoma: Jimmie Franklin, *Journey Toward Hope: A History of Blacks in Oklahoma*; Bruce Fisher, Oklahoma Historical Society, interviews, 2009, 2010. Progressives re. Constitution, Christianity, etc.: Lyman Abbott, *The Outlook*, Sept. 21, 1912; William Weyl, *The New Democracy*. Lynchings: Dianna Everett, "Lynchings, *Encyclopedia of Oklahoma History & Culture*. Farm challenges: Sheila Manes, "Pioneers and Survivors: Oklahoma's Landless Farmers," *Oklahoma: New Views of the Forty-Sixth State*, ed. Anne Hodges Morgan and H. Wayne Morgan. Crop statistics: Gilbert C. Fite, "Farming," *Encyclopedia of Oklahoma History & Culture*. Livestock statistics: Odie B. Faulk and William D. Welge, *Oklahoma: A Rich History*; Edward Everett Dale, *History of Oklahoma*. Red Fork: Bobby D. Weaver, "Red Fork Field," *Encyclopedia of Oklahoma History & Culture*. Sequoyah Convention: Richard Mize, "Sequoyah Convention," *Encyclopedia of Oklahoma History & Culture*; Irwin Hurst, "The 46th State." Enabling Act: Dianna Everett, "Enabling Act (1906)," *Encyclopedia of Oklahoma History & Culture*. William Murray and Preamble; Irwin Hurst, "46th State." Robert Galbreath; "Robert Galbreath, Larry O'Dell, *Encyclopedia of Oklahoma History & Culture*; "Biography of Robert (Bob) Galbreath," Oklahoma Genealogy Trails; Gaston Litton, *History of Oklahoma*. Thomas P. Gore: Ralph Arden Wasson, "A Study of the Speaking Career and Speeches of Thomas Pryor Gore," Thomas P. Gore Collection, 1890–1940, Carl Albert Center Archives, University of Oklahoma; Thomas L. Bore, various speeches, correspondence, articles, Thomas P. Gore Collection, 1890–1940, Carl Albert Center Archives, University of Oklahoma; Monroe L. Billington, "Thomas P. Gore: The Blind Senator from Oklahoma"; Gore Vidal, author interview, 2009. Progressivism, Shawnee Demands: Kenny L. Brown, "Progressive Movement," *Encyclopedia of Oklahoma History & Culture*; Kenny L. Brown, "Progressivism in Oklahoma Politics, 1900–1913: A Reinterpretation," *An Oklahoma I had Never Seen Before*, Davis D. Joyce, ed.; Matthew Rex Fox, "Shawnee Demands," *Encyclopedia of Oklahoma History & Culture*; Lynn R. Musslewhite, Suzanne J. Crawford, *One Woman's Political Journey: Kate Barnard and Social Reform 1875–1930*. Kiowa-Comanche-Apache opening: Benjamin R. Kracht, "Kiowa-Comanche-Apache Opening," *Encyclopedia of Oklahoma History & Culture*. Indian land restrictions removal: Angie Debo, *And Still the Waters Run*. Glenn Pool: Charles F. Colcord, *The Autobiography of Charles Francis Colcord, 1859–1934*; Bobby D. Weaver, "Glenn Pool Field," *Encyclopedia of Oklahoma History & Culture*. Theodore Roosevelt, the Abernathys, the Great Wolf Hunt: Alta Abernathy, *Bud and Me: The True Adventures of the Abernathy Boys*; Foster Harris, "T. R. and the Great Wolf Hunt," *Oklahoma Today* 8, Fall 1958; Matthew Rex Cox, "Roosevelt's Wolf Hunt," *Encyclopedia of Oklahoma History & Culture*; Jack Meyers, "Roughriding Rover Boys," *Sports Illustrated*, May 17, 1976; Cova Williams, interview with author, Chisholm Trail Heritage Center, 2011.

Chapter 12

Oklahoma Constitution: Danny M. Adkison, *Encyclopedia of Oklahoma History & Culture*; "Oklahoma Consitution," Irwin Hurst, *The 46th Star*; Herbert W. Titus, "Oklahoma at 100: Thanks be to God"; Angie Debo, *And Still the Waters Run*; Bob Burke, *Oklahoma's Good Angel*; Lynn R. Musslewhite, Suzanne J.

Crawford, *One Woman's Political Journey: Kate Barnard and Social Reform 1875–1930.* William H. "Alfalfa Bill" Murray: Keith L. Bryant, "William Henry David Murray," *Encyclopedia of Oklahoma History & Culture.* Samuel Robert Cassius: Samuel Robert Cassius, *To Lift Up My Race: The Essential Writings of Samuel Robert Cassius,* Edward J. Robinson, ed.; Bob Chada, "Samuel Robert Cassius," Logan County Researchers Homepage, Oklahoma Genealogy & History. Panic of 1907, Bank Guarantee Law of 1908: Loren Gatch, "Oklahoma Bank Behavior and the Panic of 1907," *Essays in Business and Economic History* XXVIII; Loren Gatch, "An the west jes' smiled: Oklahoma Banking and the Panic of 1907," *Chronicles of Oklahoma* 87, No. 1, Spring 2009; Irwin Hurst, *The 46th Star.* Charles Haskell: James A. Howard, II, "Charles Nathaniel Haskell: Governor of Oklahoma, 1907–11," *Oklahoma's Governors, 1907–1929: Turbulent Politics,* LeRoy H. Fischer, ed. Black land ownership: Jimmie Franklin, *Journey Toward Hope,* ref. U.S. Bureau of the Census 1910 Census; Bruce Fisher, Oklahoma Historical Society, interviews, 2009, 2010. Agricultural "Golden Age": Bob Blackburn, lecture to Wordwrights, September 2009.

Index

A

B

C

D

E

F

G

H

M

N

O

P

Q

R

Y

Z